Machine Learning

3rd Edition

by Luca Massaron and John Paul Mueller

for **dummies**®

A Wiley Brand

Machine Learning For Dummies®, 3rd Edition

Published by: **John Wiley & Sons, Inc.**, 111 River Street, Hoboken, NJ 07030-5774, www.wiley.com

For general information on our other products and services, please contact our Customer Care Department within the U.S. at 877-762-2974, outside the U.S. at 317-572-3993, or fax 317-572-4002. For technical support, please visit https://hub.wiley.com/community/support/dummies.

Wiley publishes in a variety of print and electronic formats and by print-on-demand. Some material included with standard print versions of this book may not be included in e-books or in print-on-demand. If this book refers to media that is not included in the version you purchased, you may download this material at http://booksupport.wiley.com. For more information about Wiley products, visit www.wiley.com.

Library of Congress Control Number is available from the publisher.

ISBN 978-1-394-37322-2 (pbk); ISBN 978-1-394-37324-6 (ebk); ISBN 978-1-394-37323-9 (ebk)

Printed and bound by CPI Group (UK) Ltd, Croydon CR0 4YY

C9781394373222_141025

Contents at a Glance

Table of Contents

Introduction

The term *artificial intelligence* has all sorts of meanings attached to it today, especially after Hollywood (and other movie studios) have gotten into the picture. Films such as *Ex Machina* have tantalized the imaginations of moviegoers worldwide, portraying artificial intelligence in ways that misrepresent the technology. As a part of artificial intelligence, *machine learning* is also widely misunderstood. Of course, most of us have to live in the real world, where machine learning actually does perform an incredible array of tasks that have nothing to do with androids that can pass the Turing Test (fooling a human evaluator into believing they're human). This book gives you a view of machine learning in the real world and exposes you to the amazing feats you really can perform using this technology.

Even though the tasks that you perform using machine learning may seem a bit mundane when compared to the movie version, by the time you finish this book, you will realize that these mundane tasks have the power to impact nearly every aspect of daily life for people across the planet. In short, machine learning is an incredible technology, just not in the way that some people have imagined.

This third edition of the book features a significant number of changes, not the least of which is the use of Python code to run the examples on Google Colab, as requested by our readers. In addition, the book contains new materials that cover all the progress made since the previous edition.

About This Book

Machines and humans learn in entirely different ways, which is why the first part of this book is essential to your understanding of machine learning. Machines perform routine tasks at incredible speeds, but still require human oversight on many aspects, from how they learn to how they execute their tasks. This book will help you understand how to guide these machines to solve problems that traditionally required human thought.

The second part of this book focuses on utilizing the various Python coding examples on your computer by explaining how to access Google Colab and the example data encountered in the chapters, and using them to learn more from this book.

The third part of the book discusses basic math concepts in relation to machine learning requirements. It prepares you to perform math tasks associated with algorithms used in machine learning to make predictions from your data, such as forecasting a value (regression) or determining a category (classification).

The fourth part of the book helps you discover what to do about data that isn't quite up to par. This part is also where you start learning about similarity and working with linear models. The most advanced chapter tells you how to work with ensembles of learners to perform tasks that might not otherwise be reasonable to complete.

The fifth part of the book is about the practical application of machine learning techniques. You'll learn how to perform tasks such as classifying images, analyzing opinions and sentiments, and recommending products and movies, all using machine learning.

The last part of the book contains helpful information to enhance your machine learning experience. This part of the book also includes a chapter specifically focused on ethical data use.

To make absorbing the concepts easy, this book uses the following conventions:

>> Text that you're meant to type just as it appears in the book is in **bold**. The exception is when you're working through a step list: Because each step is bold, the text to type is not bold.

>> Web addresses and programming code appear in monofont. If you're reading a digital version of this book on a device connected to the Internet, you can click or tap the web address to visit that website.

>> When you need to type command sequences, you see them separated by a special arrow, like this: File ➪ New File. In this example, you go to the File menu first and then select the New File entry on that menu.

>> When you see words in *italics* as part of a typing sequence, you need to replace that value with something that works for you. For example, if you see "Type ***Your Name*** and press Enter," you need to replace *Your Name* with your actual name.

Foolish Assumptions

This book is designed for novices and professionals alike. You can either read this book from cover to cover or look up topics and treat the book as a reference guide. However, we've made some assumptions about your level of knowledge when we put the book together. You should already be familiar with using your device and working with the operating system that supports it. You also know how to perform tasks like downloading files and installing applications. You can interact with the Internet well enough to locate the resources you need. You know how to work with archives, such as the `.zip` file format. Finally, a basic knowledge of math is helpful.

Icons Used in This Book

As you read this book, you see icons in the margins that indicate material of interest. This section briefly describes each icon.

TIP

The tips in this book are time-saving techniques or pointers to resources that you should try so that you can get the maximum benefit from machine learning.

WARNING

You should avoid doing anything that's marked with a Warning icon. Otherwise, you might find that your application fails to work as expected, you get incorrect answers from seemingly bulletproof code, or (in the worst-case scenario) you lose data.

TECHNICAL STUFF

Whenever you see this icon, think advanced tip or technique. Skip these bits of information whenever you like.

REMEMBER

This text usually contains an essential process or a bit of information that you must know to perform machine learning tasks successfully.

Beyond the Book

Besides the contents you will find in the book, you can also access other cool materials:

>> **Cheat Sheet:** A cheat sheet provides you with some special notes on things you can do with machine learning that not every other expert knows. You can find the Cheat Sheet for this book at www.dummies.com. Type **Machine Learning For Dummies** in the Search box and click the Cheat Sheet option that appears.

>> **Errata:** You can find errata by entering this book's title in the Search box at `www.dummies.com`, which takes you to this book's page.

>> **Companion files:** The source code is available for download. All the book examples tell you precisely which example project to use. You can find these files on this book's page at `www.dummies.com/go/machinelearningfd3e`. Just enter the book title in the Search box, click Books on the page that appears, click the book's title, and scroll down the page to Downloads.

We've also had trouble with the datasets used in the previous edition of this book. Sometimes the datasets change or might become unavailable. Given that you likely don't want to download a large dataset unless you're interested in that example, we've made the datasets not included by default in a programming package available at `https://github.com/lmassaron/ml4dummies_3ed`. You don't actually need to download them, though; the example code will perform that task for you automatically when you run it.

Where to Go from Here

Most people will want to start this book from the beginning, because it contains a good deal of information about how the real-world view of machine learning differs from what movies might tell you. However, if you already have a first grounding in the reality of machine learning, you can always skip to the next part of the book. Chapters 4 and 5 are where you want to go to learn everything you need to run the code using Google Colab. You actually do not need to run the code in the book to learn about machine learning. However, testing some concepts hands-on could prove helpful, and we suggest giving it a try. If you decide to run the examples in the book, consider reviewing Chapter 6, unless you're already an expert Python coder.

If you're already an expert with Python and know how machine learning works, you could always skip to Chapter 7. Starting at Chapter 7 will help you get into the examples quickly so that you spend less time on basics and more time with intermediate machine learning tasks. You can always refer to and review the previous materials as needed.

1

Introducing How Machines Learn

Defining what machine learning is and how it relates to AI.

Recognizing the role of data in machine learning.

Understanding the role of statistics in machine learning.

Thinking about where machine learning will take society in the future.

Chapter **1**

Getting the Real Story About AI

A *rtificial intelligence (AI)*, the theory and development of computer systems capable of performing tasks that would otherwise require human intelligence, is a vast topic today, and it continues to grow larger all the time, thanks to the constant introduction of new technologies. Despite the complexity of these technologies, most people encounter AI through everyday applications, such as interacting with their digital assistants, receiving shopping recommendations, or creating text, images, and videos to post on social networks using generative AI tools. Talking to your smartphone is both fun and helpful for finding out things like the location of the best sushi restaurant in town or discovering how to get to the concert hall. As you interact with your smartphone, it learns more about the way you talk and makes fewer mistakes in understanding your requests. The capability of your smartphone to comprehend and interpret your unique way of speaking is an example of AI, and it is not the only application available. Part of the technology used to make everything happen is *machine learning*, which involves the use of various techniques to enable algorithms to make predictions based on historical data records.

You also likely encounter and make use of machine learning and AI all over the place today without really noticing. For example, when smart devices adapt to your preferences over time or when digital assistants improve their understanding of your commands, these are examples of machine learning in action. Likewise, recommender systems, such as those found on Amazon, help you decide what to buy based on criteria like previous purchases or products that complement your current choice. The use of both AI and machine learning is expected to keep increasing over time.

In this chapter, you are introduced to AI and machine learning and discover what it means from several perspectives, including how it affects you as a consumer and as a scientist or engineer. You also find that neither AI nor generative AI equals machine learning, even though the media often confuses all the terms. Machine learning is a crucial component of AI, focusing on predicting outcomes based on available information. Generative AI (genAI), which has recently gained importance in the news and our daily lives, is also part of the broader field of AI, but it serves purposes different from predictive machine learning because it aims to create new content, such as text, images, or videos, based on the instructions you provide.

Moving Beyond the Hype

As any technology becomes bigger, so does the hype, and AI certainly has a lot of hype surrounding it. For one thing, some people have chosen to engage in fear-mongering rather than science by equating AI with killer robots, such as those depicted in the film *The Terminator*. Actually, your first real experience with a robot is more likely to be in the form of a healthcare assistant or possibly as a coworker. The reality is that you interact with AI and machine learning in far more mundane ways than you might realize.

REMEMBER

You may have also heard more about AI than machine learning. AI is currently receiving the lion's share of attention, but in the form of genAI. As a discipline, AI includes both machine learning and genAI. This chapter helps you understand the relationship between machine learning and AI so that you can better understand how this book enables you to move into a technology that used to appear only within the confines of science fiction novels and films.

Machine learning and AI both have strong engineering components. That is, many aspects of these technologies, particularly the performance and behavior of systems and algorithms, can be measured and optimized through established practices and practical evaluation. In addition, both have strong scientific components, through which researchers test concepts and develop new approaches to simulating or approximating certain aspects of intelligence and decision-making. Finally, machine learning also has an artistic component where intuition, creativity, and experience can play a critical role. This is where a talented practitioner can excel, especially when the results from AI and machine learning may seem counterintuitive, and only the experience and creativity of a skilled practitioner can ensure that models or systems perform as expected.

Dreaming of Electric Sheep

Androids (a specialized kind of robot that looks and acts like a human, such as Data in *Star Trek: The Next Generation*) and some types of *humanoid robots* (a kind of robot that has human characteristics but is easily distinguished from a human, such as C-3PO in *Star Wars*) have become the poster children for AI. They present computers in a form that people can *anthropomorphize* (give human characteristics to, even though they aren't human). In fact, it's entirely possible that one day you won't be able to distinguish between human and artificial life with ease. Science fiction authors, such as Philip K. Dick, have long predicted such an occurrence, and it seems all too possible today. In his novel "Do Androids Dream of Electric Sheep?" Dick discusses the whole concept of more real than real. The idea appears as part of the plot in the movie *Blade Runner*. However, some uses of robots today are just plain fun, as seen with robots serving at restaurants. The sections that follow help you understand how close technology currently gets to the ideals presented by science fiction authors and the movies.

TECHNICAL STUFF

For physical androids, the current state of the art is impressive but still not even close to humans. In text-based interactions, some advanced AI can hold remarkable human-like conversations, but don't be fooled by their linguistic skills, as they lack genuine consciousness or understanding.

Understanding the history of AI and machine learning

There is a reason, other than anthropomorphism, that humans envision the ultimate AI as one that is embodied within some android. Ever since the ancient Greeks, humans have discussed the possibility of placing a mind inside a mechanical body. One such myth is that of a mechanical man called Talos. The fact that the ancient Greeks had complex mechanical devices, of which only one still exists (read about the Antikythera mechanism at www.ancient-wisdom.com/antikythera.htm), suggests that their dreams may have been inspired by more than just fantasy. Throughout the centuries, people have discussed mechanical persons capable of thought (such as Rabbi Judah Loew's Golem).

AI is built on the hypothesis that mechanizing thought is possible. During the first millennium, Greek, Indian, and Chinese philosophers all explored formal reasoning and logic, which are the building blocks of the idea of mechanizing thought. As early as the 17th century, Gottfried Leibniz, Thomas Hobbes, and René Descartes discussed the potential for rationalizing all thought as simply mathematical symbols. Of course, the complexity of the problem eluded them. The point is that the vision for AI has been around for an incredibly long time, but the implementation of some working AI is relatively new.

The actual birth of AI as we know it today began with Alan Turing's publication of "Computing Machinery and Intelligence" in 1950 (`https://courses.cs.umbc.edu/471/papers/turing.pdf`). In this paper, Turing explored the idea of how to determine whether machines can think. Of course, this paper led to the Imitation Game involving three players. Player A is a computer, and Player B is a human. Each must convince Player C (a human who can't see either Player A or Player B) that they are human. If Player C can't determine who is human and who isn't in a consistent way, the computer wins.

A persistent issue with AI is excessive optimism. The problem that scientists are trying to solve with AI is incredibly complex. However, the early optimism of the 1950s and 1960s led scientists to believe that the world would produce intelligent machines in as little as 20 years. After all, machines were doing all sorts of amazing things, such as playing complex games. AI currently has its greatest success in areas such as logistics, data mining, advanced natural language processing (conversational AI), advanced computer vision, medical diagnosis, drug discovery, scientific research (for example, protein folding with models like AlphaFold: `https://alphafold.com`), software development, and materials science.

Exploring what machine learning can do for AI

Machine learning relies on algorithms to analyze datasets. Currently, machine learning can't provide the sort of AI that the movies present. Even the best algorithms can't think, feel, present any form of self-awareness, or exercise free will. Machine learning can identify complex patterns, make predictions, and, with generative models, create new data, performing all these tasks far faster than any human can and at a scale that exceeds human capabilities. As a result, machine learning can help humans work more efficiently. A true AI might eventually emerge when computers can finally excel at the clever learning strategies used by nature:

>> **Evolution of models and architectures (akin to Genetics):** Slow learning over time, from one generation to the next

>> **Supervised Learning (akin to Teaching):** Fast learning from curated sources and explicit guidance

>> **Unsupervised Learning (akin to Exploration):** Discovering hidden patterns or intrinsic structures in data

>> **Reinforcement Learning (akin to Trial-and-Error):** Learning how to choose the best actions through interaction with an environment and receiving rewards or penalties

The current state of AI, then, is one of performing analysis and suggesting or automating actions, but humans must still consider the implications of that analysis and make the necessary moral and ethical decisions. This is because, as AI systems become more integrated into society and their impact and autonomy increase, it becomes crucial to consider how to use AI responsibly and in a manner that is fair, transparent, accountable, secure, and respectful of human rights. Key considerations include mitigating any bias derived from data or algorithms, ensuring data privacy, enabling human control and oversight, and assessing the societal impacts of any AI system used for automation and decision-making.

REMEMBER

The main point of confusion between learning and intelligence is that people assume that simply because a machine gets better at its job (learning), it's also aware (intelligence). Nothing supports this view of machine learning. The same phenomenon occurs when people assume that a computer is purposely causing problems for them. The computer can't assign emotions and therefore acts only upon the input provided and the instructions contained within an application to process that input.

Considering the goals of machine learning

Currently, AI is based on machine learning, which in turn builds on statistics. Yes, machine learning has a statistical basis, but it makes some different assumptions than statistics do because the goals and approaches are different. Table 1-1 lists some features to consider when comparing machine learning to statistics.

Defining machine learning limits based on hardware

Huge datasets require large amounts of memory. Unfortunately, the requirements don't end there. When you have vast amounts of data and memory, you must also have processors with multiple cores and high speeds. Modern hardware, such as powerful multi-core CPUs or specialized hardware like NVIDIA graphics processing units (GPUs) or Google's tensor processing units (TPUs), enables the massive computational demands of machine learning, especially of deep learning models. Such hardware has architectures that allow parallel computing (performing many calculations simultaneously), which is necessary for handling matrix operations in neural networks. Companies that develop specialized hardware have become central to the AI revolution, such as NVIDIA with its GPUs (including the A100 and H100 series) and software platforms (like CUDA). Other specialized hardware, such as Google's TPUs, which are power-efficient, custom-built chips optimized for speed in running machine learning models, as well as other AI accelerators (AMD, Intel Gaudi, Apple's M-series chips with Neural Engines, and many others), also play a significant role. Without such hardware advancements, the recent breakthroughs in large language models and generative AI would not have been feasible.

TABLE 1-1   ## Comparing Machine Learning to Statistics

Feature	Machine Learning	Statistics
Data handling	Works with large amounts of structured and unstructured data, aiming at achieving predictive accuracy on unseen data. Consequently, it is crucial to split data into training and test sets.	Methods are focused on hypothesis testing, inference from sample to population, and interpretability.
Data input	The data is sampled, randomized, and transformed to maximize accuracy scoring in the prediction of out-of-sample (or completely new) examples.	Aims to estimate parameters of a population based on an input sample and to quantify the uncertainty of these estimates.
Result	Outputs often include probabilities, scores, or direct predictions, which are used to make informed guesses or decisions.	The output typically includes estimates of parameters, along with measures of uncertainty such as confidence intervals and p-values.
Assumptions	The scientist learns from the patterns in data (data-driven model discovery).	The scientist often starts with a model based on some domain theory.
Distribution	Fewer assumptions are made about the data distribution, or it's learned directly from data.	The scientist tends to assume a well-defined distribution.
Fitting	The scientist creates a best fit, but generalizable, model, having prediction in mind.	The model is fit to the entire sample data to make inferences about the population or to explain relationships within the data.

TECHNICAL STUFF

You will hear more and more often about AI ASICs (Application-Specific Integrated Circuits for Artificial Intelligence). These are specially designed microchips with the type of operations in mind that you need when developing AI technologies, such as matrix multiplications and neural network computations. This specialized design allows them to execute these tasks with maximum efficiency, speed, and lower power consumption. Contrary to CPUs and even GPUs (which can be used for a range of activities), these microchips are not reprogrammable after manufacturing, but they outpace any other solution in the tasks they are designed for.

Apart from the necessary hardware, this book considers some of the following issues as part of making your machine learning experience better:

>> **Obtaining a useful result:** As you work through the book, you discover that you need to obtain a valid result first, before you can refine it. In addition, sometimes tuning an algorithm goes too far, and the result becomes quite fragile (and possibly useless outside a specific dataset).

>> **Asking the right question:** Many people get frustrated when trying to obtain an answer from machine learning because they keep tuning their algorithm without asking a different question. To use hardware efficiently, sometimes you must step back and review the question you're asking. The question might be wrong, which means that even the best hardware will never find the answer.

>> **Relying on intuition too heavily:** All machine learning questions begin as a hypothesis. A scientist uses intuition to create a starting point for discovering the answer to a question. Failure is more common than success when working through a machine learning experience. Your intuition adds the art to the machine learning experience, but sometimes, intuition is wrong, and you have to revisit your assumptions.

Overcoming AI Fantasies

As with many other technologies, AI and machine learning have both their practical and fantasy or fad uses. Of course, the problems with such uses are many. Even if image creation by generative AI has reached an extreme accuracy in generated details and scenery, for one thing, most people wouldn't really want a Picasso or another piece of art created in this manner, except as a fad item (because no one had done it before, or it is trendy to have one for a short time). The point of art isn't in creating an interesting interpretation of a particular real-world representation, but rather in seeing how the artist interpreted it. It was previously believed that computers could only replicate existing artistic styles. However, modern generative AI is increasingly capable of blending styles and producing outputs that can be perceived as novel, though the debate about the true artistic originality of such outputs remains. The following sections discuss AI and machine learning fantasies of various sorts.

Discovering the fad uses of AI and machine learning

AI is entering an era of innovation that you once only read about in science fiction. Given the hype surrounding the idea and possible applications of AI, it can be hard to determine whether a particular AI use is real or simply the dream child of a scientist. The fact is that AI and machine learning will both present potential opportunities to create something amazing, and that we're already at the stage of creating some of those technologies, but you still need to take what you hear with a huge grain of salt.

REMEMBER

To make the future uses of AI and machine learning match the concepts that science fiction has presented over the years, real-world programmers, data scientists, and other stakeholders need to create tools. Nothing happens by magic, even though it may look like magic when you don't know what's happening behind the scenes. In order for the fad uses for AI and machine learning to become real-world uses, developers, data scientists, and others need to continue building real-world tools that may be hard to imagine at this point.

Considering the true uses of AI and machine learning

You find AI and machine learning used in a great many applications today. The only problem is that the technology works so well that you don't know that it even exists. In fact, you might be surprised to find that many devices in your home already make use of both technologies. Both technologies definitely appear in your car, and most especially in the workplace. In fact, the uses for both AI and machine learning number in the millions, all safely out of sight, even when they're pretty dramatic in nature. Here are just a few of the ways in which you might see AI used:

>> **Fraud detection:** You get a call from your credit card company asking whether you made a particular purchase. The credit card company isn't being nosy; it's simply alerting you to the fact that someone else could be making a purchase using your card. The AI embedded within the credit card company's code detected an unfamiliar spending pattern and alerted someone to it.

- >> **Resource scheduling:** Many organizations need to schedule the use of resources efficiently. For example, a hospital may need to determine where to place a patient based on the patient's needs, availability of skilled experts, and the amount of time the doctor expects the patient to be in the hospital.

- >> **Complex analysis:** Humans often need help with complex analysis because there are literally too many factors to consider. For example, the same set of symptoms could indicate more than one problem. A doctor or other expert might need help making a diagnosis in a timely manner to save a patient's life.

- >> **Automation:** Any form of automation can benefit from the addition of AI to handle unexpected changes or events. A problem with some types of automation today is that an unforeseen event, such as an object in the wrong place, can actually cause the automation to stop. Adding AI to the automation can enable it to handle unexpected events and continue as if nothing had happened.

- >> **Customer service:** The customer service line you call today may not even have a human behind it. The automation is good enough to follow scripts and use various resources to handle the vast majority of your questions. With good voice inflection (provided by AI as well), you may not even be able to tell that you're talking with a computer.

- >> **Safety systems:** Many of the safety systems found in machines of various sorts today rely on AI to take over the vehicle in a time of crisis. For example, many automatic braking systems rely on AI to stop the car based on all the inputs that a vehicle can provide, such as the direction of a skid.

- >> **Machine efficiency:** AI can help control a machine in such a manner as to obtain maximum efficiency. The AI controls the use of resources so that the system doesn't overshoot speed or other goals. Every ounce of power is used precisely as needed to provide the desired services.

This list doesn't even begin to scratch the surface. You can find AI used in many other ways. However, beyond the widely publicized AI applications, machine learning powers many specific, often less visible, solutions that might not always be immediately associated with the usual concept of AI in popular discourse. Here are a few uses for machine learning that you might not commonly associate with an AI:

- >> **Access control:** In many cases, access control is a yes or no proposition. An employee smartcard grants access to a resource in much the same way that people have used keys for centuries. Some locks do offer the capability to set times and dates when access is allowed, but the coarse-grained control doesn't really answer every need. By using machine learning, you can determine whether an employee should gain access to a resource based on role and need. For example, an employee can gain access to a training room when the training reflects an employee's role.

>> **Animal protection:** The ocean might seem large enough to allow animals and ships to coexist without problem. Unfortunately, many animals get hit by boats each year. A machine learning algorithm could allow ships to avoid animals by learning the sounds and characteristics of both the animal and the ship.

>> **Predicting wait times:** Most people don't like waiting when they have no idea of how long the wait will be. Machine learning allows an application to determine waiting times based on staffing levels, staffing load, complexity of the problems the staff is trying to solve, availability of resources, and so on.

Being useful and being mundane

Even though the movies make it sound like AI is going to make a huge splash, and you do sometimes see some incredible uses for AI in real life, the fact of the matter is that most uses for AI are mundane, even boring. The act of performing this analysis using AI is dull when compared to other sorts of AI activities, but the benefits, such as cost savings and improved results from AI-driven analysis, are substantial.

First, Python developers (see Chapter 6 for an overview of the Python language) have developed a vast array of libraries available to make machine learning easy and effective. The Python open-source community is particularly active in creating libraries that make the development of complex machine learning applications accessible to everyone, as seen with the machine learning library Scikit-learn (`https://scikit-learn.org/stable`). In addition, numerous resources are available, such as Kaggle (`www.kaggle.com`), which offers competitions that enable machine learning developers and practitioners to refine their machine learning skills in creating practical applications. The results of these competitions often appear later as part of products that people actually use.

Considering the Relationship Between AI and Machine Learning

Machine learning is only part of what a system requires to become an AI. The machine learning portion of the picture enables an AI to perform these tasks:

>> Adapt to new circumstances that the original developer didn't envision

>> Detect patterns in all sorts of data sources

>> Create new behaviors based on the recognized patterns

>> Make decisions based on the success or failure of these behaviors

The use of algorithms to manipulate data is the centerpiece of machine learning. To be successful, a machine learning application must use an appropriate algorithm to achieve a desired result. In addition, the data must lend itself to analysis using the desired algorithm, or it requires careful preparation by scientists.

AI encompasses many other disciplines to simulate the thought process successfully. In addition to machine learning, AI usually includes

>> **Natural language processing:** The act of allowing language input and putting it into a form that a computer can use.

>> **Natural language understanding:** The act of deciphering the language in order to act upon the meaning it provides.

>> **Natural language generation:** The act of creating meaningful language outputs to communicate with humans.

>> **Knowledge representation:** The ability to store information in a form that makes fast access possible.

>> **Planning (in the form of goal seeking):** The ability to use stored information to draw conclusions in *near real time* (almost at the moment it happens, but with a slight delay, sometimes so short that a human won't notice, but the computer can).

>> **Perception and action (often employed in Robotics):** The ability to perceive the environment and act upon it, sometimes in a physical form.

In fact, you might be surprised to find that the number of disciplines required to create an AI is huge. Consequently, this book exposes you to only a portion of what an AI contains. However, even the machine learning portion of the picture can become complex because understanding the world through the data inputs that a computer receives is a complex task. Just think about all the decisions that you constantly make without thinking about them. For example, just the concept of seeing something and knowing whether you can interact successfully with it can become a complex task.

Considering AI and Machine Learning Specifications

As scientists continue to work with technology and turn hypotheses into theories, the technology becomes more related to *engineering* (where theories are implemented) than *science* (where theories are created). As the rules governing a technology become clearer, groups of experts work together to define these rules in written form. The result is a set of *specifications* (a group of rules that everyone agrees upon).

Eventually, implementations of the specifications become *standards* that a governing body, such as the IEEE (Institute of Electrical and Electronics Engineers) or a combination of the ISO/IEC (International Organization for Standardization/ International Electrotechnical Commission), manages. Although the field is still rapidly developing, AI and machine learning have both been around long enough to have established standards, such as methodologies, benchmarks, and frameworks, for development and risk management. Numerous domain-specific standards and influential frameworks have emerged, such as those from organizations like the National Institute of Standards and Technology (NIST) with its AI risk framework (`www.nist.gov/itl/ai-risk-management-framework`).

REMEMBER

The basis for machine learning is math. Algorithms determine how to interpret data in specific ways. The mathematical basics for machine learning are presented in Part 3 of this book. You discover that algorithms process input data in specific ways and create outputs by learning from data patterns, which are then used to make predictions or generate new content. What isn't predictable is the data itself. The reason you need AI and machine learning is to decipher the data in a way that allows you to identify patterns and make sense of them.

You can see the details of various algorithms in Part 4, which outlines the algorithms used to perform specific tasks. When you get to Part 5, you begin to see the best practices, common approaches, and established methods when using algorithms to perform tasks. The point is to use an algorithm that will best suit the data you have at hand to achieve the specific goals you've created. Professionals implement algorithms using programming languages that are best suited for the task. Machine learning relies on Python and R, as well as, to some extent, MATLAB, Java, Julia, and C++.

Defining the Divide Between Art, Science, and Engineering

AI and machine learning are considered to be, at the same time, scientific disciplines, engineering fields, and even art forms for good reasons. First, there are the scientific aspects that guide the research focused on machine learning. The scientific elements of AI involve hypothesis testing, experimentation, and the discovery of knowledge to be applied in solving practical problems. This brings us to the engineering aspect, as building machine learning systems that work effectively and solve problems requires software engineering, system design, and optimization of these systems.

The artistic element of machine learning, instead, takes many forms. Choosing the proper data, features, models, and hyperparameters often requires intuition and experience. There are no specific step-by-step instructions, like cooking recipes, to follow to obtain your result. Every problem presents different challenges and multiple acceptable solutions. You can only experiment creatively and iterate numerous times, looking for your way to solve the problem using machine learning algorithms, guided by intuition and sometimes ingenuity.

REMEMBER

Even trivial activities related to machine learning, such as data cleaning, can involve an element of judgment and experience that influences the outcome. How a scientist prepares the data for use is the key. Some tasks, such as removing duplicate records, occur regularly. However, a scientist may also choose to filter the data in some ways or look at only a subset of the data. As a result, the cleaned dataset used by one scientist for machine learning tasks may not precisely match the cleaned dataset used by another.

As a practitioner, you can also tune the algorithms in specific ways or, in this case, more as a researcher, refine how the algorithm works. Again, the goal is to generate output that reveals the desired patterns, allowing you to make sense of the data. For example, when analyzing a picture, a machine learning algorithm must determine which elements of the image reveal its contents and which elements are irrelevant. The answer to that question is crucial if the algorithm is to correctly classify the elements in the image and achieve specific goals.

When working in a machine learning environment, you also have the problem of input data to consider. For example, the microphone found in one smartphone won't produce precisely the same input data that a microphone in another smartphone will. The characteristics of the microphones differ, yet the result of interpreting the vocal commands provided by the user must remain the same. Likewise, environmental noise changes the input quality of the vocal command, and the smartphone can experience certain forms of electromagnetic interference. Clearly, the variables that a designer faces when creating a machine learning environment are both large and complex.

The art behind the engineering is an essential part of machine learning. The experience that a scientist gains in working through data problems is essential because it provides the means for the scientist to make informed choices that make the algorithm work better. A finely tuned algorithm can make the difference between a robot successfully threading a path through obstacles and hitting every one of them.

Predicting the Next AI Winter

The development of machine learning and AI has become increasingly relentless and unstoppable for several reasons, including the availability of more powerful hardware and vast amounts of data (much of it generated by the Internet) to feed algorithms. Businesses, however, don't care about the progress alone; they are looking for new ways to generate cash quickly based on these technologies. Obviously, that's not easy because new technologies like AI do not fit neatly into the existing framework since they are disruptive and so new that you lack guidance and experience on how to gain profit from them. Developer-entrepreneurs exacerbate the problem by overselling technologies. They suggest that the state of the art is more advanced than it actually is, often to secure funding, increase their influence, or advance their careers. In the past, because of the difference between timing and expectations, machine learning and AI have both experienced *AI winters*, a period of time when businesses show little to no interest in developing new processes, technologies, or strategies. At this very moment, the winds are in favor of AI development, as investments and resources are being poured in, and there is considerable excitement in every industry about the potential returns this technology promises. However, a sudden cool-off may always be around the corner, possibly caused by some unmet expectation that could throw investors into disillusionment. Other slowdowns may also contribute, driven by external factors such as climate change, economic downturns, or geopolitical risks.

The first AI winter occurred due to unfulfilled expectations stemming from the overselling of the technology and unexpected difficulties. During the summer of 1956, various scientists attended a workshop held on the campus of Dartmouth College to develop artificially intelligent machines. They predicted that machines that could reason as effectively as humans would require, at most, a generation to come about. They were wrong. Only recently, large language models, such as ChatGPT or Google Gemini, have shown surprising abilities in complex tasks, sometimes mimicking aspects of mathematical and logical reasoning. However, to achieve true human understanding, as Yann LeCun (he is Meta's chief AI scientist,

Turing Award winner, NYU data scientist, and one of the pioneers of artificial intelligence) has argued, an AI would also need to demonstrate intelligence in reasoning, as well as in the visual-spatial, bodily-kinesthetic, creative, interpersonal, intrapersonal, and linguistic realms. The stated problem with Dartmouth College and other endeavors of the time was often attributed to hardware — the processing capability to perform calculations quickly enough to create a simulation. However, that's not really the whole problem. Yes, hardware does figure into the picture, but you can't simulate processes that you don't understand, especially if you lack suitable data and algorithms. Even so, the reason that AI is somewhat effective today is that the hardware has finally become powerful enough to perform the required number of calculations and support improved algorithms and available data.

REMEMBER

While some argue that current AI paradigms might be approaching the limits of their existing architectures and that we shouldn't expect any further breakthroughs, the field is simultaneously experiencing an explosion of new applications and incremental improvements, particularly driven by large-scale models and generative AI. The debate continues as to whether this rapid expansion is sustainable or if inflated expectations in some areas could lead to disillusionment.

Some foresee an AI winter in the near future, partly because the terms *machine learning, deep learning,* and *AI* have become pervasively overused, sometimes in ill-defined ways that can inflate expectations. Undoubtedly, the recent GenAI deluge has accelerated the adoption of AI solutions and demonstrated how AI can power both background processes and customer interactions through sophisticated chatbots and personalized content creation. However, a hype correction may occur if businesses begin to critically scrutinize the return on investment (ROI) of AI solutions or realize that such solutions are only marginally better than simpler automations, albeit at a higher cost and complexity (which is often referred to as technical debt). In such a case, a broader disillusionment could set in, investment will decrease, and a new AI winter may ensue. In many cases, industry observers and scientists, who are concerned with an upcoming AI winter, advocate for a focus on the real, tangible, and demonstrable achievements of AI and machine learning today, rather than continuing to hype some nebulous, far-future capabilities that risk overpromising and underdelivering.

Before you get the idea that everyone is expecting another AI winter, you need to look at the other side of the argument. Some are saying that machine learning and AI have become so deeply embedded that an AI winter really isn't possible anymore. Typically, industry reports often highlight that machine learning and AI haven't met certain goals, such as creating autonomous vehicles or replacing workers in specific tasks. Even though these goals aren't feasible today, the potential exists for achieving them in the future when scientists have completed more research. Moreover, due to the research conducted and the applications created, both machine learning and AI have become profitable in certain fields, so businesses will continue to support them.

When considering the future of machine learning and AI, adopting a more moderate approach is likely the best course of action. At this point, data scientists and other researchers need to take a step back and consider the next level. The current technologies can only take us so far. They're profitable, but, for instance, they can't yet produce a fully autonomous self-driving car that can, without any human intervention, handle difficult weather conditions and unexpected driving scenarios. Also, the current technologies certainly can't produce a robot of the intelligence found in the film *Ex Machina.* There's so much more work to be done, yet. So, if there is an AI winter, it's likely to be a mild one because companies like Amazon.com and Google aren't going to throw their technologies out because a few reporters think that they should. In short, the concepts, ideas, and technologies that you discover in this book remain viable and allow you to move forward in a career of your choice.

Chapter **2**

Learning in the Age of Computers

This chapter provides you with the essential knowledge you need to perform machine learning tasks. This chapter doesn't go into detail on the topics that other chapters in the book will cover. Instead, it offers an overview to help you make sense of the information in future chapters. Of course, learning begins with data, so the first part of this chapter tells you about data — how data is categorized as structured or unstructured, and organized into datasets of varying size and complexity. Just as a human learns better with more input, so do machine learning applications.

In the previous chapter, we discussed the differences between *statistics* and *machine learning*. Both fields are about learning from data, but they have distinct goals (inference for statistics, prediction for machine learning) and approaches for achieving those goals (simple, interpretable models for statistics, more complex models for machine learning). However, machine learning would not exist without statistics because many ideas and techniques are shared. The second part of this chapter deals with statistics as it applies to machine learning.

After you have your data in hand and in an order that is useful and understandable, you can begin to feed it to machine learning algorithms that can learn parameters from the data in a particular way to enable them to produce a result. Besides driving machine learning systems, algorithms are fundamental to all of computer science. The third part of this chapter examines the relationship between algorithms and machine learning.

Machine learning algorithms are useful only when trained on data because training enables the computer to use patterns previously seen in data and apply them to new data that it hasn't seen before. The fourth part of this chapter gets you started with understanding algorithm training.

Understanding the Role of Data in Machine Learning

You see data everywhere every day: spreadsheets, sales reports, customer lists, but there are also images, videos, and texts of all kinds from the Internet. All of this is data. Everything that represents the world and its events is data, but not all of this data can be immediately used for machine learning. Most of this data is *unstructured*, meaning it lacks the necessary structure that machine learning algorithms require to process it effectively.

Machine learning is a mathematical form of learning, and mathematics loves order and tidy settings. When performing multiple operations in mathematics, you use matrices (more on this in Chapter 7), which are grids where numbers are arranged in rows and columns. Similarly, data for machine learning must be organized into rows and columns, where traditionally, rows represent individual cases and columns represent specific characteristics (also called *features*) of those particular cases, as shown in Figure 2-1. This format is called the *tabular data format*, and it may indeed seem dull because it confines everything in a row-by-column format. However, this is the format that already rules the digital world, since most computer programs read and process data in this way. It runs our banks, our stores, our governments, and our jobs.

Each column compares a specific characteristic across all the selected planets

FIGURE 2-1: An example of a structured tabular dataset using planetary data.

Each row represents a single planet and its key features

Planet	Diameter (km)	Avg. Temp (°C)	Day Length (Earth Hours)	Number of Moons
Mercury	4,879	167	1,408	0
Venus	12,104	464	5,832	0
Earth	12,742	15	24	1
Mars	6,779	−65	25	2

When data is organized in tabular format, it is called a *dataset,* and it describes events of the past that you can use to make evaluations and even make decisions. Machine learning provides a new perspective on this data by converting it into predictions for future events. That's the magic of Machine Learning.

It works simply: You take one column, one specific feature you need to predict in the future, and you call it a *target.* The algorithm will use all the other columns as predictive features. You also split the data by rows, using some rows as examples for the machine learning algorithm to learn from (the training examples), and reserving others for testing (the testing examples). By using the predictive features of the training examples, the machine learning algorithm will look for patterns in data that can be reused in situations where you don't have the target column information, thus effectively predicting the future or the hidden information in that situation. Machine learning algorithms have an undisputed ability to identify patterns that, due to their complexity, cannot be discerned by the human eye.

Considering the Sources of Data

Before you can use data for a machine learning application, you need a source of data. Of course, the first thing that most developers think about is the vast, corporate-owned database, which could contain interesting information, but it's just one source. The fact of the matter is that your corporate databases might not even contain particularly useful data for a specific need. The following sections describe locations you can use to obtain additional data.

Building a new data source

To create viable sources of data for specific needs, you may find you need to create a new data source. Data is the digital recording of something happening in the real world. Data can be input into digital systems directly by humans (for example, by typing on a keyboard) or in an automated manner, as the recording already occurs digitally (for instance, through sensors) or because there is a mechanism to read and write the information into a computer. Sometimes, data is already available, but it is scattered across different formats and locations. In such a case, all you have to do is assemble the data in the required form. As you become more adept at using machine learning, you find that you ask questions that standard corporate databases can't answer. With this in mind, the following sections describe some new interesting sources for data.

Obtaining data from public sources

Governments, universities, nonprofit organizations, and other entities often maintain publicly available databases that you can use alone or combined with other databases to create data for machine learning. For example, you can combine data from several geographic information systems (GIS) sources to help build the necessary data to inform decisions, such as where to locate new stores or factories. The machine learning algorithm can take all sorts of information into account — everything from the amount of taxes you have to pay to the elevation of the land (which can contribute to making your store easier to see).

The best part about using public data is that it's usually free, even for commercial use (or you pay a nominal fee for it). In addition, many of the organizations that created them maintain these sources in nearly perfect condition because the organization has a mandate, uses the data to attract income, or uses the data internally. When obtaining public source data, consider several key issues to ensure you obtain something useful. Here are some of the criteria you should think about when making a decision:

>> The cost, if any, of using the data source

>> The formatting of the data source

>> Access to the data source (which means having the proper infrastructure in place, such as an Internet connection when using Twitter data)

>> Potential issues in cleaning the data to make it useful for machine learning

>> Potential security issues in accessing the data, adding it to other data sources, and managing it locally

>> Ensuring that the data is the original data, rather than data that purports to be original but has been biased or modified in ways that would alter the results of its use

>> Considering whether the data will be maintained and accessible over time

>> Permission to use the data source (some data sources are copyrighted)

>> Determining that the data doesn't contain personally identifiable information that you may not have permission to use

Obtaining data from private sources

You can obtain data from private organizations, such as Amazon (see Open Data, https://aws.amazon.com/opendata) and Google (see Public Data Explorer, https://datacommons.org), both of which maintain extensive databases containing a wide range of information. In most cases, except for publicly shared data sources, you can expect to pay for access to the data, primarily when it is used in a commercial setting. You may not be allowed to download the data to your personal servers, which may affect how you use the data in a machine learning environment. For example, some algorithms work more slowly with data that they must access in small pieces.

The most significant advantage of using data from a private source is that you can expect consistency. The data is likely cleaner than that from a public source. In addition, you usually have access to larger datasets with a greater variety of data types. Of course, it all depends on where you get the data.

Creating new data from existing data

Your existing data may not work well for machine learning scenarios, but that doesn't keep you from creating a new data source using the old data as a starting point. For example, you may find that your customer database contains all the customer orders. Still, the data isn't helpful for machine learning because it lacks the tags required to group the data into specific types. The information about the orders needs to be organized in a numeric form. This process, often referred to as *feature engineering* or *encoding*, is a crucial component of the workflow for data scientists, data engineers, and machine learning engineers. In other cases, the data may require explicit *data labeling*, where a human annotator assigns a target outcome (such as "fraudulent" or "not fraudulent") to each transaction.

The point is that machine learning saves money by taking over repetitive tasks that humans don't really want to do in the first place (making them inefficient). However, machine learning doesn't eliminate the need for humans entirely, and it creates the need for new types of jobs that are somewhat more interesting than the ones that machine learning has taken over. Also important to consider is that you need more humans at the outset until the modifications they make train the algorithm to understand what sorts of changes to make to the data.

Using existing data sources

Your organization has data hidden in all sorts of places. The problem is in recognizing the data as data. For example, you may have sensors on an assembly line that track the movement of products through the assembly process, ensuring the assembly line remains efficient. Those same sensors can potentially feed information into a machine learning scenario, as they could provide insights into how product movement affects customer satisfaction or the price you pay for postage. The idea is to discover how to create mashups that present existing data in a new way, allowing you to do more to make your organization work effectively.

REMEMBER

Data can come from various sources, including your email, web browser history, and utility bills. Unstructured data, such as text and images, can now become a real treasure trove for data thanks to generative AI tools. You can use tools like ChatGPT or Google Gemini to perform information extraction, for example, by providing a block of text and asking the chatbot to pull out names, dates, and locations into a structured list.

Locating test data sources

As you progress through the book, you discover the need to teach whichever algorithm you're using (don't worry about specific algorithms; you see a number of them later in the book) how to recognize various kinds of data and then to do something interesting with it. This training process ensures that the algorithm responds correctly to the data it receives after training is complete. Of course, you also need to test the algorithm to determine whether the training was successful. In many cases, the book helps you discover ways to break down a data source into training and testing data components to achieve the desired result. Then, after training and testing, the algorithm can work with new data in real time to perform the tasks that you verified it can accomplish.

In some cases, you may not have sufficient data for both training (the initial essential test) and testing. When this happens, you may need to create a test setup to generate additional data, rely on real-time data, or artificially create the test data source. You can also use similar data from existing sources, such as a public or private database. The point is that you need both training and testing data that will produce a known result before you unleash your algorithm into the real world with uncertain data.

Specifying the Role of Statistics in Machine Learning

The relationship between statistics and machine learning is often debated. Obviously, they are not the same thing, but don't forget that they are profoundly connected. The fact is that statistics and machine learning share many similarities in the data they use and some methods they apply, but also have distinct objectives. The two fields grew from the same roots (probability theory and data analysis) but blossomed in different directions, driven by different goals and philosophies. Hence, you can find the same techniques, such as linear regression, in both statistics and machine learning, but used for different purposes and with distinct ideas in mind.

Leo Breiman, the creator of the Random Forest algorithm in machine learning, wrote about these differences in 2001, a time when statistics were predominant in the field. His paper "The Two Cultures: Statistical Modeling and Machine Learning" claimed a role for machine learning in the practical prediction of real-world problems. Today, we can confirm that Breiman was right, as the algorithmic culture is now dominant and machine learning is found running under the hood everywhere. However, driven by the incredible success of machine learning, machine learning and statistics are increasingly converging in fields like Explainable AI (XAI), as we need to use algorithms responsibly and transparently, achieving, at the same time, accurate predictions and a deeper understanding of how they are obtained.

Understanding the Role of Algorithms

Everything in machine learning revolves around algorithms. An *algorithm* is a procedure or formula used to solve a problem. Think of it as a recipe. An algorithm tells you how to solve a problem, with some ingredients, and obtain a specific result. In computing, typical examples of problems algorithms solve are sorting items or finding the shortest route in a network. The problem domain affects the kind of algorithm needed, but the basic premise is always the same: to solve some sort of problem, such as driving a car or playing dominoes.

TIP

If you are interested in knowing more about algorithms for general applications, have a look at *Algorithms For Dummies* by John Paul Mueller and Luca Massaron.

Defining what algorithms do

An algorithm is the set of rules or sequence of steps used to solve a particular type of problem. Algorithms process data through a series of well-defined states. The states need not be deterministic, but the states are defined nonetheless. Algorithms must express the transitions between states using a well-defined and formal language that the computer can understand. The goal is to create an output that solves a problem. In some cases, the algorithm receives inputs that help define the output, but the focus is always on producing the output.

While the concept of an algorithm is quite broad, in machine learning, we are referring to specific types of algorithms that can learn patterns from data to make predictions or take decisions. In processing the data and solving the problem, the algorithm finds or learns an optimal function, called the model, from the data. The optimal function is always specific to the kind of problem and data being addressed by the algorithm.

Considering the five main schools

In 2015, Pedro Domingos, professor emeritus of computer science and engineering at the University of Washington, wrote *The Master Algorithm*, which is still a reference for understanding the role that algorithms play in machine learning. Domingos described five tribes (schools of thought) that make machine learning feasible:

>> **Symbolists:** The origin of this tribe is in logic and philosophy. This group relies on induction to solve problems.

>> **Connectionists:** The origin of this tribe is in neuroscience. This group relies on backpropagation to solve problems.

>> **Evolutionaries:** The origin of this tribe is in evolutionary biology. This group relies on genetic programming to solve problems.

>> **Bayesians:** The origin of this tribe is in statistics. This group relies on probabilistic inference to solve problems.

>> **Analogizers:** The origin of this tribe is in psychology. This group relies on kernel machines to solve problems.

The ultimate goal of machine learning is to combine the technologies and strategies embraced by the five tribes to create a single algorithm (the master algorithm) that can learn anything. Of course, achieving that goal is a long way off. Even so, scientists are currently working toward that goal.

Each of the five tribes employs a distinct set of techniques and strategies for solving problems, resulting in unique algorithms. Combining these algorithms should lead to a master algorithm that can solve any problem.

Symbolic reasoning

Induction is the process of generalizing rules from specific examples. In symbolic reasoning, *deduction* expands the realm of human knowledge, while induction raises the level of human knowledge. Induction commonly opens new fields of exploration, while deduction explores those fields. However, the most crucial consideration is that deduction applies general rules to specific cases, whereas induction, conversely, creates general rules from particular observations. In machine learning, symbolic learners use induction to create a model (a set of rules) from data.

As an example of this strategy, deduction would say that if a tree is green and green trees are alive, the tree must be alive. When thinking about induction, you would say that the tree is green and the tree is also alive; therefore, green trees are alive. Induction provides the answer to what knowledge is missing, given a known input and output.

Connections modeled on the brain's neurons

The connectionists are perhaps the most famous of the five tribes. This tribe strives to reproduce the brain's functions using silicon instead of neurons. Essentially, each neuron (a mathematical function that models its real-world counterpart) solves a small part of the problem, and the use of many neurons in parallel solves the problem as a whole.

This tribe's key algorithm is *backpropagation,* also known as the backward propagation of errors. After the network makes a prediction, the algorithm computes an error value that measures how far off the prediction was from the correct answer. Backpropagation then works backward through the network, adjusting the *weights* (the degree to which a particular input contributes to the result) and *biases* (constants which help fit the data better) of the neurons in a way that reduces this error. This process is reiterated many times with different examples, gradually improving the network's accuracy in making new predictions.

Evolutionary algorithms that test variation

The evolutionaries rely on the principles of evolution to solve problems. In other words, this strategy is based on the survival of the fittest (removing any solutions that don't match the desired output). A fitness function determines the viability of each function in solving a problem.

Starting from a population of random candidate solutions, a fitness function searches for the best candidates based on their performance on the problem. The winners get to build the next-level functions by combination or random mutation. The idea is that the next level will bring us closer to solving the problem, but may not solve it completely, which means that additional levels will be needed. An interesting outcome of this strategy has been the development of algorithms that evolve: one generation of algorithms actually builds the next generation.

Bayesian inference

The Bayesians use various statistical methods to solve problems. Their idea is to start with general probability estimates, which are then refined into more precise ones by considering evidence. For example, when using these techniques, you can accept a set of symptoms as input and estimate the probability that a particular disease is causing the symptoms as output. Given that multiple diseases share the same symptoms, the algorithm assigns a probability to each based on the circumstances. This is crucial because while one disease might be generally the most probable, it's not always the correct one for a given circumstance.

Ultimately, this tribe supports the idea of building trust in a hypothesis by adding more and more evidence. Considering more evidence proves or disproves the hypothesis that it supports. Consequently, it is possible to make decisions under uncertainty without having all possible information, because at each stage, this tribe considers the hypothesis best supported by the evidence to be viable. One of the most recognizable outputs from this tribe is the spam filter.

Systems that learn by analogy

The analogyzers use kernel machines to recognize patterns in data. By recognizing the pattern of one set of inputs and comparing it to the pattern of a known output, you can create a problem solution. The goal is to use similarity to determine the best solution to a problem. It's the kind of reasoning that determines that using a particular solution worked in a given circumstance at some previous time; therefore, using that solution for a similar set of circumstances should also work. One of the most recognizable outputs from this tribe is recommender systems. For example, when you visit Amazon and buy a product, the recommender system suggests other related products that you might also want to buy.

Defining What Training Means

Many people are somewhat used to the idea that applications start with a function, accept data as input, and then provide a result. For example, a programmer might create a function called Add() that accepts two values as input, such as 1 and 2. The result of Add() is 3. The output of this process is a value. In traditional programming, writing a program meant understanding the functions used to manipulate data and create a given result with specific inputs.

Machine learning turns this process around. In this case, you know that you have inputs, such as 1 and 2. You also know that the desired result is 3. However, you don't know what function to apply to create the desired result. Training provides a learning algorithm with numerous examples of the desired inputs and the expected results from those inputs. The learner then uses these examples to learn the optimal parameters for a chosen model (a type of flexible function), making that general model specific to the problem. In other words, training is the process whereby the learning algorithm maps a flexible function to the data. For predictive models, the output is typically the probability of a specific class (for example, "spam" or "not spam") or a numeric value (for example, the price of a house). However, for generative models, the output is newly created data itself — such as a paragraph of text, a synthetic image, or a piece of music — that mimics the patterns in the training data.

A single learning algorithm can learn many different things, but not every algorithm is suited for certain tasks. Some complex models are general enough to handle recognizing objects or processing text, but no solution can handle all the problems, or even a wide variety of them, at once.

The secret to machine learning is generalization. The goal is to generalize the output function so that it works on data beyond the training set. For example, consider a spam filter. An English dictionary contains about 200,000 words. A limited training dataset of 4,000 or 5,000 sample emails, combined in very specific ways, must create a generalized function that can then find spam in new, unseen combinations and sequences of words, far exceeding what was in the training data. This is a real challenge.

When viewed from this perspective, training may seem impossible, and learning even more daunting. However, to create this generalized function, the learning algorithm relies on just three components:

» **Representation:** The learning algorithm creates a *model,* which is a function that will produce a given result for specific inputs. The representation defines the space of possible models (called the *hypothesis space*) from which a learning algorithm can select or construct a model. If the chosen representation (the space of possible models) can't capture the underlying patterns in the data, then no amount of training can produce an accurate model.

» **Evaluation:** The learning algorithm can create more than one model. However, it doesn't distinguish between better or worse models. An evaluation function (often called a *loss function* or *cost function*) determines which model works best in creating a desired result from a set of inputs. The evaluation function scores each potential model, allowing for the estimation of which one performs the best.

» **Optimization:** This is the engine that drives the learning. Once we have a way to evaluate models, optimization is the process of efficiently searching through the vast space of possible models (or parameter settings) to find the one that performs best according to our evaluation function. For many models, this involves an iterative process of refining the model's parameters to minimize error.

Much of this book focuses on representation. For example, in Chapter 10 you discover how to create a working spam detector using the Naïve Bayes algorithm, based on a probabilistic representation of the problem. However, the training process is more involved than simply choosing a representation. All three components come into play when performing the training process. Fortunately, you can start by focusing on selecting the right model representation for your problem and leave most of the other parts to the implementation of complex optimization and evaluation routines you find in the various libraries discussed in the book, like Scikit-learn, TensorFlow, and PyTorch.

Chapter **3**

Having a Glance at the Future

M achine learning technology is now available in many products, but it is still far from reaching its full potential, which remains huge for the future. Machine learning has made significant breakthroughs in various sectors, attracting increased attention from lawmakers for its potential pitfalls and becoming the predominant standard approach for solving complex tasks in computer science. In addition, thanks to the emergence of generative AI, recent years have marked a period of further advancements and widespread adoption for machine learning and AI, definitively leaving behind the initial pioneering times. This chapter looks at what may be possible in the future. It helps you understand the direction that machine learning is taking and how that direction could help integrate machine learning into every aspect of daily life.

Generally speaking, one of the concerns associated with new technology is the fear that it will take jobs away from people. This is precisely the fear that now surrounds AI and machine learning. However, although new technologies will impact existing jobs in one way or another, the reality is more nuanced: Machine learning will also open up new occupations that people will find more exciting than working on an assembly line or flipping burgers at a restaurant. One of the consequences will be more creative and engaging work for people to do. Of course, these new jobs will require more and new kinds of training before people can perform them well.

Every new technology also comes with pitfalls. It's a cliché, but true, that it's easier to destroy than to create. The potential pitfalls of machine learning need to be taken seriously. As this technology has become increasingly widespread, now is the time to consider the potential pitfalls and take action to mitigate them before they materialize. Instead of discussing inevitable problems, the last section focuses on potential difficulties that can be avoided through the correct use of the technology.

Creating Useful Technologies for the Future

To survive, a technology must prove useful. In fact, it must prove more than useful; it must meet perceived needs in a manner that existing technologies don't, as well as build a base of adherents who provide a monetary reason to continue investing in the technology. For example, looking back in the past at the history of computing, the Apple Lisa (https://computerhistory.org/blog/the-lisa-apples-most-influential-failure) was an interesting and valuable piece of technology that demonstrated the usefulness of the GUI to business users who had never seen one before. It solved the need to make computers more user-friendly. However, it failed because it didn't build a base of adherents. The computer simply failed to live up to the hype surrounding it. The next system that Apple built, the Macintosh, did live up to the hype somewhat better, yet it was built on the same technology that the Lisa used. The difference is that the Macintosh developed a considerable array of hardcore adherents.

Machine learning solves a considerable number of problems in a manner that other technologies would struggle to replicate. However, to become the must-have technology that everyone wants to invest in, machine learning needs a cadre of hardcore adherents. The bar chart at www.grandviewresearch.com/industry-analysis/machine-learning-market shows that machine learning is growing significantly, with services leading the way (you can download the associated free report). There are numerous reports like this that detail the significant growth of machine learning over the past few years and its continued expected expansion in the near future. The following sections discuss some of the ways in which machine learning is already affecting you personally and how this use will increase in the future, making machine learning a must-have technology.

Considering the role of machine learning in robots

Today, one goal of machine learning is to create functional, in-home robots. Now, you might be thinking of something along the lines of Rosey the robot found in *The Jetsons* (see `https://thejetsons.fandom.com/wiki/Rosey` for a quick description). However, real-world robots need to solve practical problems to attract attention. To become viable and attract funding, a technology must also amass a group of followers, and to do that, it must provide both interaction and ownership. According to research by MarketsAndMarkets, the market for home robots is projected to grow from $10.3 billion in 2023 to $24.5 billion by 2028, indicating a growing popularity of robots.

Examples of successful in-home robots that use machine learning to detect obstacles and navigate complex layouts include the iRobot Roomba series and the Roborock S8 MaxV Ultra. These popular robots can successfully navigate a home, which is a lot harder to accomplish than you might think. They can also spend more time on dirtier areas of the house. The idea has inspired other highly specialized robots, such as lawn mowing robots and even pool cleaning robots. However, it is the advanced prototypes that can handle generic household chores, such as Tesla's Optimus, Figure 01 (developed in collaboration with OpenAI, the creators of the generative AI chatbot ChatGPT), and Boston Dynamics' Robots (like Spot and the new Atlas) that show what inventors are actively trying to build and what we can expect in our houses.

REMEMBER

Before robots can enter a home and work as a generalized helper, machine learning needs to solve a wealth of problems, and the algorithms must become both more generalized and capable of more complex and exact reasoning. You can expect that robots will become a part of daily life, but it won't happen right away.

Using machine learning in health care

A significant issue receiving considerable attention is elder care. People are living longer, and a nursing home doesn't always seem like a good way to spend one's twilight years. Robots could enable people to live independently at home for longer while ensuring their safety and well-being. Ambient assisted living (AAL) systems, utilizing machine learning, can learn the daily patterns of individuals in the house, identify anomalies related to emerging health issues, and request immediate care.

Some countries are also facing a critical shortage of healthcare workers, and Japan is one, mainly due to its aging population. Given the popularity of robots among the Japanese people, thanks to long-term promotion by the state, media, and industry, the country is investing considerable resources to address the problems that robotics presents. The point is that most solutions still have limitations, such as the robot Paro, a therapeutic harp seal robot, or Pepper, a semi-humanoid robot. In truth, researchers found out they do not save work for caregivers but create more (the analysis by MIT Technology Review explains in detail the reasons for this issue: `www.technologyreview.com/2023/01/09/1065135/japan-automating-eldercare-robots`). Generative AI opens up the possibility for more sophisticated language to be generated, allowing users to engage in meaningful interactions and potentially reducing loneliness. Robots such as ElliQ and other advanced prototypes are paving the way for more personalized and proactive health monitoring and care.

Creating AI systems for various needs

Many of the solutions you can expect to see that employ machine learning will be assistants to humans. They can perform various tasks extremely well, but they are invaluable to humans when the tasks are mundane and repetitive. For example, you may need to find a restaurant that satisfies the needs of an out-of-town guest. You can waste time looking for an appropriate restaurant yourself, or you can access an AI to do it in far less time and with greater accuracy and efficiency. There are many AI-powered assistants available on mobile devices, with Apple's Siri and Amazon's Alexa being pioneers, and Google Gemini being the latest novelty at the time of writing this chapter.

What all these solutions have in common, and what we can expect to improve in the future thanks to machine learning, is their capability to generate natural conversations, understand the context from previous queries, and perform actions on your device and other connected devices. By learning your preferences and ways to interact, the AI-powered assistant can also offer more personalized suggestions and solutions.

Using machine learning in industrial settings

Machine learning is already playing a key role in industrial settings where the focus is on efficiency. Doing things faster, more accurately, and with fewer resources helps the bottom line and makes an organization more flexible, resulting in a higher profit margin. Fewer mistakes also benefit employees in an organization by reducing the frustration level. You can currently see machine learning at work in the following industries:

- >> Data mining and information retrieval
- >> Robotics and automation
- >> Supply chain optimization
- >> Generative AI in design and manufacturing
- >> Personalized medicine
- >> Predictive maintenance and quality control
- >> Cybersecurity

REMEMBER

Data mining is focused on discovering patterns in large datasets, whereas information retrieval is about finding relevant information from large amounts of data.

This list just scratches the surface. Machine learning is widely used in industry today, and its applications are expected to continue increasing as advanced algorithms enable higher levels of learning. Currently, machine learning performs tasks in several areas that include the following:

- >> **Descriptive and predictive analysis:** Descriptive analysis discovers the patterns (behaviors, associations, responses) in data to understand past events, whereas predictive analysis uses historical data to forecast what a user might want and why. Predictive analysis is also used on machinery to predict the quality of the productive output or possible malfunctions.

- >> **Enrichment:** Enrichment involves augmenting data or processes so that the user and organization can obtain additional benefits, such as increased productivity or improved sales.

- >> **Adaptation:** Adaptation refers to modifying a presentation so that it reflects the user's tastes and choice of enrichment. Each user ends up with a customized experience that reduces frustration and improves productivity.

- >> **Optimization:** Optimization refers to modifying the environment so that the presentation consumes fewer resources without diminishing the user experience. Examples are optimizing supply chain logistics or energy consumption in a manufacturing plant.

- >> **Control:** This area involves autonomous systems and process control, such as a self-driving vehicle navigating a route or a robotic arm adjusting its movements to specific production requirements.

A theoretical view of what machine learning does in industry is nice, but it's essential to see how some of this works in the real world. You can see machine learning used in relatively mundane but important ways. For example, machine learning has a role in automating employee access control, optimizing energy grids, enhancing agricultural yields, predicting emergency room wait times, identifying early signs of heart failure from wearable device data, and personalizing financial investment strategies.

Understanding the role of custom AI processors and other hardware

Chapter 2 tells you about the five schools of thought (tribes) popularized by *The Master Algorithm* by Pedro Domingos and related to machine learning. Each of these schools of thought suggests that while general-purpose CPUs are versatile, they have limitations, and specialized hardware can significantly improve the performance and efficiency of machine learning tasks. For example, you might talk to one tribe whose members tell you of the need for larger amounts of system memory and the use of GPUs to provide faster computations. The Connectionists tribe even champions the creation of new types of processors, the neuromorphic processors and neural processing units (NPUs), which are inspired by the structure and function of the human brain.

Based on these ideas, we now have a wide range of custom chips designed for specific AI operations. Examples of this specialized hardware include Google's tensor processing units (TPUs), the NVIDIA Jetson Orin family for robotics, NVIDIA's newer generation of GPUs for data centers and large-scale AI training and inference, the Blackwell architecture processors, and custom NPUs integrated into everything from smartphones to cars. The point is that everyone agrees that more tailored hardware will make AI and machine learning more feasible, and they are working to design new, custom hardware solutions for specific AI tasks.

Discovering New Job Opportunities with Machine Learning

In the past, you could easily find articles that described the complete loss of job opportunities for humans because of robots. Robots already perform a number of tasks that used to be performed by humans, and this usage will increase over time. You still hear claims that AI and machine learning may displace a significant portion of blue- and white-collar jobs. However, now that companies have more experience under their belts, you will more often hear opinions that discuss augmentation, which involves the robot or AI working side by side with humans to perform tasks.

Earlier sections of this chapter aided you in understanding some of the practical, real-world uses for machine learning today and helped you discover where those uses are likely to expand in the future. While reading this section, you must have also considered how those new uses could potentially cost you or a loved one a job. The World Economic Forum's Future of Jobs Report 2025 suggests that these new technologies will both eliminate and create jobs, resulting in a net positive outcome, with more new jobs being created in the long run. However, the situation is complex, as disruptions and opportunities seem to coexist. The fact of the matter is that figuring out how AI and machine learning will affect the work environment is challenging, just as it was for people to foresee the impact of the industrial revolution on mass-producing goods for the general consumer (see www.history. com/topics/industrial-revolution for details). Just as those workers needed to find new jobs, so people facing loss of occupation to machine learning today will need to find new employment or discover how to perform their tasks in new ways.

Working for a machine

It's entirely possible that you'll find yourself working for a machine now or in the near future. In fact, you may already work for a machine and not realize it. Many companies already utilize machine learning to analyze business processes and automatically enhance their efficiency. For example, Hitachi already employed this kind of setup affecting middle management in 2015 (see www.hitachi.com/ New/cnews/month/2015/09/150904.html). In this case, the AI actually issued the work orders based on its analysis of the workflow — just as a human middle manager might do. The difference is that the AI was actually more efficient than the humans it replaced.

However, the situation in 2025 is more nuanced. Rather than just replacing middle managers and workers, AI is augmenting their capabilities. Tedious activities, such as compiling reports, monitoring performance metrics, and analyzing vast amounts of data to identify trends and inefficiencies, are now easily done by generative AI tools organized as agents. Agents are AI-powered systems that, when addressed with a task, are capable of creating a plan and utilizing available software tools to reach their target. The idea is to free human managers from menial tasks and let them operate on functions they excel at as humans, such as strategic thinking, team development, and fostering innovation.

Machine learning and AI are bringing about a revolution in the workplace, and what brings more value, again, is not replacing humans (which is still possible, happening, and working in certain situations), but transforming them into *human-AI orchestrator*s, mixing autonomous AI conducted planning and activity, human supervision, and human intervention in critical functions. For instance, having humans in the loop allows for improvement and innovation that

AI systems, which tend to be very similar and standardized in their outputs, cannot effectively replace.

Unfortunately, the potential for AI-driven automation to replace jobs can create stress, depression, and burnout among employees. Another downside to this increase in productivity is that the nonhuman manager may create a stressful and unsafe job environment. To achieve a smooth integration, machine learning algorithms must also consider worker safety and well-being in the future, a task where human managers often excel.

Working with machines

People already work with machines on a regular basis — they may just not realize it. For example, when you speak a command to your digital assistant on your smartphone, it recognizes not just what you say, but also your intentions. Basically, you're interacting with a machine to achieve a desired goal. Most people realize that the voice interaction provided by a smartphone improves with time — the more you use it, the better it gets at recognizing your voice. As the machine learning algorithm is updated with more data, it becomes more efficient at recognizing your voice, your specific accent and phrasing, and understanding your desired result. This trend will continue.

However, machine learning is used in various ways beyond voice commands that may not be immediately apparent. When you point a camera at a subject and the camera can put a box around the face (to help target the picture), you're seeing the result of machine learning. However, there is even more to it, as AI is now the engine powering *computational photography*. *Portrait Mode* helps distinguish a subject from the background in a professional manner, while *Night Sight* produces a bright and clear image even in challenging dark lighting conditions. There are many other options, such as enhancing image quality, removing shaking and blurring, removing undesirable objects from an image, opening eyes when someone blinks, or even modifying the appearance of the subject of the photo through smart filtering. All these options incorporate specific AI and machine learning algorithms, enabling the camera to perform the task of taking a picture with far greater efficiency.

Generative AI and large language models (LLMs) are also changing the way we interact with machines, from imperative commands to declarative goals. Historically, to have a computer perform a complex task, you had to provide explicit step-by-step instructions (the programming), a task traditionally reserved for programmers. Nowadays, AI is advancing the way we interact with computers, allowing us to state our desired outcome, view the results, and make adjustments if the result is not entirely satisfactory. Vibe coding is an example. Popularized by

AI researcher Andrej Karpathy, *vibe coding* is a software development approach where a developer uses natural language to describe the desired outcome to an AI assistant, which then generates the working code. Eventually, in a not-so-distant future, someone trained to perform a particular task well will simply instruct a robot assistant or an AI-powered system on what to do, and the machine will devise the means to accomplish it. Humans will use creativity to find out *what* to do, whereas the details (the *how*) will become the domain of machines.

Avoiding the Potential Pitfalls of Future Technologies

Any new technology comes with potential pitfalls. The higher the expectations for that technology, the more severe the pitfalls become. Unrealistic expectations cause numerous problems with technologies such as machine learning, as people often believe that what they see in movies and other popular culture sources, or hear from commercial tech hype, is what they can realistically expect in the real world. It's essential to remember the basic concepts presented in Chapter 1 — that machine learning algorithms currently can't feel or think independently. They can create novel content, including text, images, music, and software code, but this is based on the contents of the training data. Unlike the omniscient *artificial general intelligence (AGI)* often depicted in movies, a machine learning algorithm does nothing more than what it has been designed to do, and sometimes it also fails at it (for instance, we have prediction errors). Of course, some of the results are amazing, but keeping expectations in line with what the actual technology can do is important. Otherwise, you'll promise something that the technology can never deliver, and those adherents whom you were expecting will go looking for the next big thing.

In fact, the uses for machine learning today are forms of *narrow AI*, also known as *weak AI*. A *narrow AI* can perform well on specific tasks, such as facial recognition, language translation, or analyzing large datasets for business insights. Think of machine learning as a highly specialized tool, which limits the use of the machine to the task for which the developer or data scientist designed it. In fact, a good analogy for today's algorithms is that they're like a tailored shirt. You need specialized data to create an algorithm tailored to meet specific needs today, but the future may see algorithms that can tackle nearly any task. Companies that rely on narrow AI must exercise caution in how they develop their products or services. Unfamiliar or unusual inputs may place the model used in the machine learning environment outside of the learned domain, reducing the usefulness of the machine learning algorithm's output to gibberish (or at least making it unreliable).

Using machine learning in an organization also requires that you hire people with the right set of skills and create a team. Machine learning in the corporate environment, where results mean an improvement in the bottom line, is relatively new. Companies face challenges in getting the right team together, developing a reasonable set of goals, and then actually accomplishing those goals with the available technology that actually keeps on improving and varying. To attract a world-class team, your company has to offer a problem that's exciting enough to entice the people needed from other organizations or from schools. It isn't an easy task, and you need to think about it as part of defining the goals for creating a machine learning environment.

2

Learning Machine Learning by Coding

Understanding the Google Colab environment.

Executing basic and advanced tasks on Colab.

Programming in Python for machine learning.

Chapter **4**

Working with Google Colab

olaboratory (`https://colab.research.google.com`), or Colab for short, is a Google cloud-based service that allows you to run notebooks in the cloud. Notebooks are interactive environments for coding, experimentation, and data storytelling, which are very popular in data science. Even if you have never used a notebook before, this chapter guides you, first by helping you access Google Colab, then by showing you how to use its features and how to work with code cells and text. You don't have to install anything on your system to use Google Colab because you can access it from any web browser.

REMEMBER

Because you may not be using the identical version of Colab tested in this book, the book's example source code may or may not work precisely as described in the text when you run it. Also, you may not see the same results presented in this book because of some differences in Colab or the hardware accelerator you decide to use. The early sections of this chapter go into more detail about Colab and help you understand what you can expect from it.

To use Colab, you must have a Google account and then access Colab using your account. Otherwise, most of the Colab features won't be available. The next section of the chapter gets you started with Google and helps you access Colab. Finally, this chapter can't address every aspect of Colab, so the final section of the chapter serves as a handy resource for locating the most reliable information about Colab.

Defining Google Colab

Notebooks are based on the concept of literate programming, initially defined by American computer scientist and mathematician Donald Knuth. The idea behind literate programming is to make learning and experimenting as easy as possible and provide a means of presenting code that can include graphics and explanatory text. To give you an idea, a notebook consists of cells, usually visualized in a web browser. Each cell can be operated on or run independently, though their execution order often matters for the overall results of the notebook. Each cell may contain:

>> Executable code (usually Python, but R or Julia can also be used) or bash scripts.

>> Explanatory and narrative text, using a simple formatting language called Markdown. This allows for the description of the code, methods, and findings to be directly in the notebook.

>> Charts, graphs, or images that the code has produced in the cells.

>> Mathematical equations written in LaTeX.

>> Embedded images, videos, and other multimedia from a local disk or the Internet.

TIP

You can learn everything about Markdown and how it formats text and images in a document by consulting the free Markdown Guide at www.markdownguide.org.

Notebooks arrived in the Python ecosystem in 2001, when Fernando Pérez, a Colombian-American physicist and software developer, launched the IPython project (https://ipython.org) as an improved interactive Python shell. The project aimed to make working with Python more productive and fun. The ideas blossomed in 2011 when the project transformed into the IPython Notebook, a web-based interface that allowed users to combine executable Python code, rich text, and visualizations. The IPython Notebook gained immense popularity and was immediately adopted for data science and modeling. That led to further development, extending the concept to other languages like R (a statistical programming language) and Julia, eventually evolving into the Project Jupyter and the Jupyter Notebook.

Google Colab is essentially a cloud version of Jupyter Notebooks. The Welcome page makes this fact apparent. It uses the ipynb (originally IPython Notebook) file format, the standard for Jupyter Notebooks. Google Colab started as a project by Google Research and was made public in 2017. The launch of Colab was motivated by the idea of providing free computing resources and tools for researchers, students, and developers so they could experiment with coding and machine learning without having specialized hardware or complicated software setups. In essence, the core characteristics of Google Colab are:

» **Zero setup:** You can immediately start coding, at no cost, without installing anything because the most popular Python packages, especially those for data handling and machine learning, come preinstalled.

» **Free computing resources:** The no-cost advantage is reinforced by the fact that Colab runs on various computing resources, including CPUs, GPUs, and later, TPUs (tensor processing units, which are custom chips created by Google to accelerate machine learning, especially matrix computations). However, Colab has some necessary limitations to keep it accessible to everyone. Nevertheless, it is an incredible free service that gives access to specialized resources.

» **Integration with the Google Ecosystem:** Colab is closely integrated with Google Drive to store and maintain your projects. Recently, it has been enhanced by access to Gemini, Google's most powerful AI that can help you code more efficiently by suggesting code snippets and corrections.

» **Rich document support:** Colab combines executable code, rich text, equations, images, and visualizations in a single interface, making it the ideal tool for scientific research and education.

Understanding what Google Colab does

You can use Colab to perform many tasks, but for this book, you will use it to write and run code, create documentation where necessary, and display graphics. You are not limited to Colab, though. If you prefer to use a local Jupyter notebook installation on your computer, the downloadable source for this book should run without much effort on your part.

However, compared to a Jupyter notebook that runs locally, Colab has a few advantages. If you use code repositories like GitHub (https://github.com), Colab allows complete interaction with your notebooks stored in GitHub repositories. In fact, Colab supports a number of online storage options, like Google Drive and GitHub, so you can regard Colab as your online partner in creating Python code. Another key reason to learn about Colab is that you can use it with an alternative device. Some of the example code was tested on an Android-based tablet (an ASUS ZenPad 3S 10, which is only about 4 inches wide and 9 inches tall) during the writing process. The target tablet has Chrome installed and executes the code well enough to follow the examples. However, you likely won't want to try to write code using a tablet of that size — the text was incredibly small, for one thing, and the lack of a keyboard could be a problem, too. Finally, consider that you don't necessarily need a specific Windows, Linux, Android, or macOS system to try the code: Colab works on a web browser, independently of the system you use.

Google Colab should generally work with most browsers, although it is tested thoroughly only with the latest Chrome, Firefox, or Safari versions. If you try to start Colab in a browser that isn't supported, you see an error message such as "This site may not work in your browser. Please use a supported browser."

Considering the differences between Colab and Jupyter

For the most part, you use Colab just as you would a Jupyter Notebook. However, some features work differently. For example, each cell starts with "Start coding or generate with AI," allowing you to write your code into the cell or, by clicking on the word "generate," access an input box where you can instruct an AI (Google Gemini) using natural language to generate some code to put into the cell itself. Then, to execute the code within a cell, you can still use the key combination Shift + Enter. This executes the cell, and a new cell appears below for you to work with.

Specific to Colab, you can select that cell and click the play button (right-facing arrow) for that cell. The current cell remains selected, so you must initiate the next cell's selection as a separate action. An icon (often an "X" or similar) next to the output lets you hide the output, make it full screen, or clear just that output without affecting any other cell. On the right side of the cell, you see a horizontal ellipsis containing another menu of options for that cell, such as moving the cell up or down, copying it, placing a comment, requesting AI assistance (from Google's Gemini), deleting the cell, and more. Some options are the same as when using a Jupyter Notebook. Still, other options are unique, and some advantages and limitations in what Google Colab offers are certainly dictated by the fact that Colab is mainly a cloud-based service. In contrast, Jupyter Notebooks are designed primarily to run on your local computer.

Jupyter Notebook offers more downloadable formats (like HTML, LaTeX, and PDF). While Colab primarily offers downloads as .ipynb and .py files, you can typically use your browser's Print to PDF function for PDF output.

A specific characteristic of Colab, determined by its being a cloud-based product, is that the notebooks running on it can operate for at most 12 hours, sometimes less, depending on the current demand for its computing resources. Peak requests from many users may lead to further limitations. Moreover, being a free service,

Colab prioritizes interactivity. If your notebooks go idle for too long because of an error or because they have completed their calculations, Colab will disconnect. In addition, you cannot run Colab in the background (unless you decide to pay for it, which we will discuss later). Hence, you must always have your Colab browser tab open as you run computations. If you close the tab using Colab, your computations will stop, and you won't be able to recover any of them.

TIP

Colab also offers more ways for you to manage the code. You can upload code from your local drive as desired and then save it to Google Drive or GitHub. At this point, the code becomes accessible from any device by accessing those same sources. All you need to do is load Colab to access it.

Another thing to consider when using Jupyter and Colab is that the two products use most of the same terminology and many of the same features, but they're not entirely the same. The methods used to perform tasks differ, and some of the terminology does as well. For example, a Markdown cell in a Jupyter Notebook is called a Text cell in Colab. Another important point in Colab is that the term *runtime* refers to the specific programming language and hardware configuration (like CPU, GPU, or TPU) your notebook uses for computations. Thus, if you choose Python 3 and a CPU or a particular GPU, you have selected the runtime for that session. "Performing Common Tasks" later in this chapter tells you about other differences you need to consider.

Finally, both Google Colab and Jupyter Notebook are free products. However, Google Colab has a few paid options that allow you to access more resources and be more integrated with Google Cloud services like BigQuery and Vertex AI, such as in the case of enterprise use. You can explore these paid options at `https://colab.research.google.com/signup`. For typical uses such as those of a student, a hobbyist, or even an ML researcher, the free version of Google Colab is powerful enough, so you don't need to apply for the paid version unless you have special needs.

Using local runtime support

Google Colab is not limited to running on the cloud, because it can also run on your computer (referred to as "local runtime"). You only need local runtime support when you want to work within a team environment or you need access to the speed or special resources offered by a local computer. Using a local runtime usually will let you access different types of resources than you obtain when relying on the cloud. In addition, a local runtime enables you to access files on your machine more easily. You can read more about Colab local runtime support at `https://research.google.com/colaboratory/local-runtimes.html`.

WARNING

You must consider several issues when determining the need for local runtime support. The most obvious is that you need a local runtime, which means that this option won't work with your computer unless your system has Windows, Linux, or macOS and the appropriate version of Jupyter Notebook (and Python/kernels) installed. Your computer will also need a proper browser.

The most important consideration when using a local runtime, however, is that your machine is now open to possible infection from malicious code within a notebook. You need to trust the party supplying the code. The local runtime option connects your Colab session to your local machine. It doesn't automatically grant access to others with whom you share the Colab notebook link. However, they would either use their own local runtimes (if configured) or rely on the default Colab cloud runtime to execute code.

Working with Google Colab features

Google Colab provides access to a number of features through the menu system. One of these features, hardware acceleration, appears in "Using Hardware Acceleration" later in this chapter. The features in this section all appear on the Tools menu.

The Tools ⇨ Command Palette displays a list of commands you can execute, as shown in Figure 4-1. Notice that some of these commands also have shortcut keys, such as Ctrl+Alt+M for adding a comment to a cell. All these commands help you to perform tasks associated with Notebook content, such as adding forms.

Type to search commands...	
Show table of contents	
Global find/replace	⌘/Ctrl+H
Show variable inspector	
Show file browser	
Show code snippets pane	⌘/Ctrl+Alt+P
View resources	
Add a comment	⌘/Ctrl+Alt+M
Add a form	
Add a form field	
Add code cell	
Add section header cell	
Add table of contents cell	
Add text cell	
Ask a question on Stack Overflow	

FIGURE 4-1: Using Colab commands makes configuring your notebook easy.

The Tools ⇨ Settings option displays the Settings dialog box. The six settings tabs perform these tasks:

>> **Site:** Configures how the site works. The most interesting setting is the Theme setting. Selecting Adaptive lets Colab choose the interface colors based on your operating system's theme (light or dark mode). You can also configure display and access settings on this tab.

>> **Editor:** Determines how text appears onscreen and how the interface works. You also select font size, spaces for each level of indentation, and a plethora of other settings.

>> **AI Assistance:** Sets what kind of features you use based on AI contributions. You can decide whether to enable or disable AI-powered inline completions, which help you complete your code as you write, or consent to use more sophisticated generative AI features, allowing you to write code created by natural language commands. There is also a flag to hide all the generative AI features.

>> **Colab Pro:** This is an advertisement for Colab Pro, which offers significant benefits like faster GPUs, longer runtimes, and more memory — all of which let you get more work done in a shorter time.

>> **GitHub:** Allows you to connect your GitHub account to your Google Drive account and permits access to private repositories and organizations (https://docs.github.com/en/apps/oauth-apps/using-oauth-apps/authorizing-oauth-apps).

>> **Miscellaneous:** Contains fun settings, such as enabling a "Power level" combo counter while typing or having an animated Corgi or kitten appear on screen. You can choose any mix of these visual effects.

You may not like the default keyboard shortcuts. When you choose Tools ⇨ Keyboard Shortcuts, you see the Keyboard Preferences dialog box, shown in Figure 4-2, where you can customize the keyboard shortcuts to match your needs. If you see Set Shortcut in the box next to a command, the command doesn't currently have a shortcut, so you can add one if desired. Here's how you work with shortcuts:

>> To add or change a shortcut, click the box next to the command and press the shortcut key you want to use for that command.

>> To remove a shortcut, press the Delete or Backspace key.

Keyboard preferences

Editor key bindings
default

☑ Enter key accepts suggestions

Shortcuts   Restore defaults

To add or change a shortcut, click the key combination and then type the new keys. Note that ⌘/Ctrl+M can be used as a prefix for multi-key-event shortcuts.

⌘/Ctrl+Alt+M	Add a comment	Set shortcut	Open in playground mode
Set shortcut	Add a form	⌘/Ctrl+O	Open notebook
Set shortcut	Add a form field	Set shortcut	Open notebook settings
Set shortcut	Add code cell	⌘/Ctrl+Alt+N	Open scratch code cell
Set shortcut	Add section header cell	Set shortcut	Open settings
Set shortcut	Add text cell	Set shortcut	Open user secrets tab
Ctrl+Space, Option+Esc or Tab Autocomplete ⓘ		⌘/Ctrl+M P	Previous cell
Set shortcut	Clear all outputs	⌘/Ctrl+P	Print notebook
Set shortcut	Clear selected outputs	Set shortcut	Reconnect
⌘/Ctrl+]	Collapse all/selected sections	⌘/Ctrl+Shift+Y	Redo cell action
⌘/Ctrl+/	Comment current line	Shift+⌘/Ctrl+H	Replace all in current cell
Set shortcut	Connect to a custom GCE VM	⌘/Ctrl+M .	Restart session

Cancel   Save

FIGURE 4-2:
Customize shortcut keys for faster access to commands.

Sometimes you need to compare two files to see how they differ. When you select Tools ⇨ Diff Notebooks, Colab opens a new browser tab. You will then be prompted to choose the two notebooks you wish to compare (from your Google Drive, by providing URLs, or by uploading them). Once selected, the two notebooks will be shown side by side and their differences highlighted, as shown in Figure 4-3.

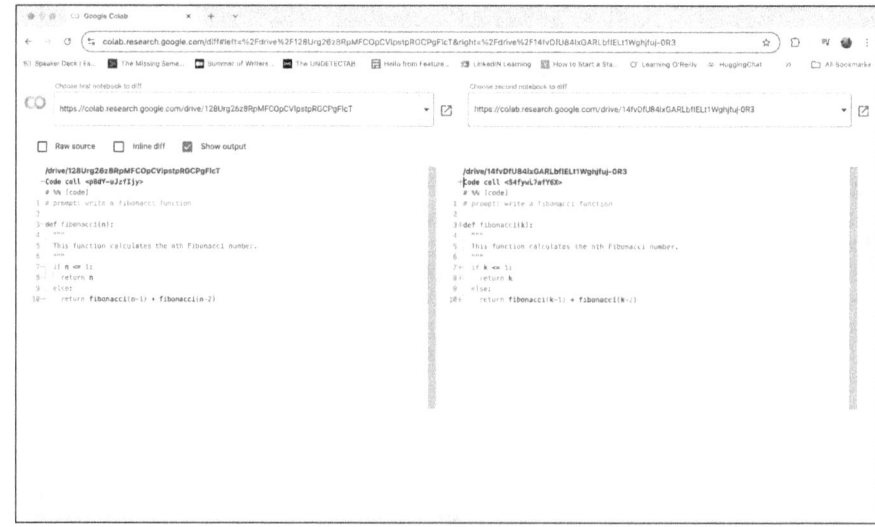

FIGURE 4-3:
Colab lets you compare two files to see how they differ.

Getting a Google Account

Before performing any significant tasks using Colab, you must have a Google account. You can use the same account for all sorts of purposes, not just development. For example, a Google account gives you access to Google Docs (`www.google.com/docs/about`), an online document management system similar to Office 365.

Creating the account

To create a Google account, simply navigate to `https://account.google.com` and click Create Account. This page also contains a wealth of information about what a Google account can provide. When you click Create Your Google Account, you start the account creation process, which spans several pages. You just provide the required information on each page and click Next.

Signing in

After you create and verify your account, you can sign in to it. Before you can use Colab effectively, you must sign in to your account. That's because Colab relies on your Google Drive for certain tasks. You can also store notebooks in other places, such as GitHub, but having your Google account ensures that everything works as planned. To sign into your account, navigate to `https://accounts.google.com`, provide your email address and password, and then click Next to access your Google Drive.

Working with Notebooks

Colab is built on notebooks, as previously mentioned. When you hover the mouse at the end of the contents of the Welcome page at `https://colab.research.google.com/notebooks/welcome.ipynb`, you see two buttons, labeled "+Code" and "+Text" for interacting with the page by adding either code or text cells (which you can use for notes as needed). These entries are active so that you can interact with them. You can also move cells around and copy the resulting material to your Google Drive. Of course, although interacting with the Welcome page is both unexpected and fun, the real purpose of this chapter is to demonstrate how to interact with Colab notebooks. The following sections describe how to perform basic notebook-related tasks with Colab.

Creating a new notebook

To create a new notebook, choose File ⇨ New Notebook in Drive. You see a new Python 3 notebook like the one shown in Figure 4-4. (The latest version of Colab doesn't support Python 2, which is good, since Python 2 has reached end-of-life and is no longer maintained.) The notebook shown in Figure 4-4 lets you change the filename by clicking it.

FIGURE 4-4:
Create a new Python 3 notebook.

Opening existing notebooks

You can open existing notebooks in local storage, Google Drive, or GitHub. You can also open any Colab examples or upload files from sources you can access, such as a network drive on your system. In all cases, you begin by choosing File ⇨ Open Notebook. You see the dialog box shown in Figure 4-5.

The default view shows all the files you opened recently, regardless of location. The files appear in order by the last opened date. You can filter the items displayed by typing a string into the Filter Notebooks field. Across the top are other options for opening notebooks.

TIP

Even if you're not logged in, you can still access the Colab example notebooks. These examples help you understand Colab but won't allow you to save changes or work on your own notebooks without logging in. Even so, you can still experiment with Colab without logging into Google first. The following sections discuss these options in more detail.

Using Google Drive for existing notebooks

Google Drive is the default location for many operations in Colab, and you can always choose it as a destination. When working with Drive, you see a list of files similar to those shown in Figure 4-5. To open a particular file, click its link in the dialog box. The file opens in your browser's current tab.

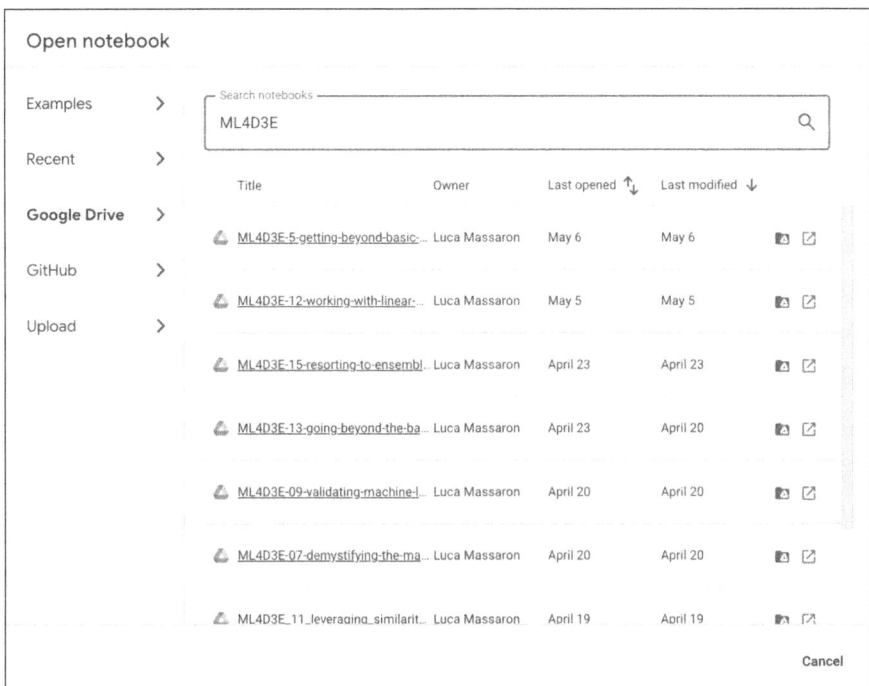

FIGURE 4-5:
Use this dialog
box to open
existing
notebooks.

Using GitHub for existing notebooks

When working with GitHub, you initially need to provide the location of the source code online, as shown in Figure 4-6. Colab can easily open notebooks from public GitHub repositories. You can also authorize Colab to access notebooks from your private GitHub repositories.

After you make the connection to GitHub, you will see two lists: repositories, which are containers for code related to a particular project, and branches, which are particular implementations of the code. Selecting a repository and branch displays a list of notebook files you can load into Colab. Simply click the required link, and it loads as if using Google Drive.

Using local storage for existing notebooks

If you want to use the downloadable source for this book that you have downloaded on your computer, or any local source for that matter, you first need to upload it to Google Colab. From the File menu at the top of the screen, select the option "Upload Notebook". A dialog box will appear with a single button, Browse, in the center. Clicking this button opens the File Open dialog box for your browser. You locate the file you want to upload, just as you normally would when opening any file.

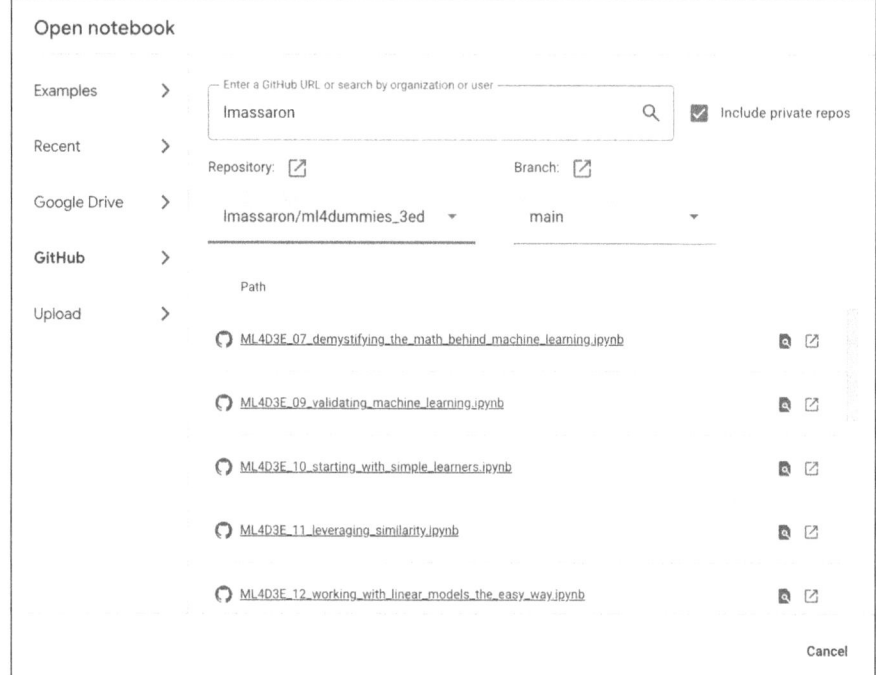

REMEMBER

TIP

FIGURE 4-6:
When using
GitHub, you must
provide the URL
of the GitHub
repository or
a specific
notebook file.

Selecting a file and clicking Open uploads a copy of that file to your Google Drive. If you change the file, those changes appear on Google Drive, not your local drive. The uploaded notebook opens in a new tab, in the same browser window. If not, you can find it in your Google Drive (often in the Colab Notebooks folder or Recents) and open it from there. Sometimes, your browser asks whether you want to leave the current page. You should tell the browser to do so.

The File ⇨ Upload Notebook command also uploads a notebook file to Google Drive. In fact, uploading a notebook works like uploading any other kind of file, and you see the same dialog box. If you want to upload other kinds of files (such as CSV data files or images), users typically use the Files pane on the left sidebar in Colab (the folder icon) and click the Upload To Session Storage button, or mount Google Drive.

Uploading a notebook

You use the technique described in "Using local storage for existing notebooks" to upload a notebook. The main reason you perform this task for this book is to upload the downloadable source to your Google Drive. (The book's Introduction tells you where to find the downloadable source, and the authors highly recommend that you use the downloadable source when working through the examples.)

Some examples will work differently in Colab because of the support it provides. For example, if you upload `ML4D3E-04-Sample.ipynb`, the results differ from what you get on a desktop using a Jupyter Notebook installation, as shown in Figure 4-7.

FIGURE 4-7: Your output may differ from the book's output when using Colab.

WARNING

In addition, be aware that frequent updates to Python and package versions in the Google Colab environment could affect the outcome of some code in this book.

Saving notebooks

Colab provides a significant number of options for saving your notebook. However, these options save to cloud storage. Download the notebook to save a copy to your local drive. After you upload content from your local drive to Google Drive or GitHub, Colab manages the content in the cloud, not on your local drive. To save updates to your local drive, you must download the file using the techniques found in the "Downloading notebooks" section, later in this chapter.

Using Drive to save notebooks

The default location for storing your data is Google Drive. When you choose File ⇨ Save, the content you create typically goes to a Colab Notebooks folder in your Google Drive or to the root if that folder doesn't exist. If you opened a notebook from a specific Drive folder, Save updates it in that location. If you want to save the content to a different folder, you first need to place your notebook in that folder in Google Drive (`https://drive.google.com`).

REMEMBER

Colab tracks the versions of your project as you perform saves. However, as these revisions age, Colab may prune the older, unpinned versions. To save a version that won't age, you use the File ⇨ Save and Pin Revision command. To see the revisions for your project, choose File ⇨ Revision History. You see the output shown in Figure 4-8. Notice that the entries are pinned. You can also pin specific revisions by clicking the vertical ellipsis (three dots) next to an entry in the Revision history list and selecting Pin revision. The revision history also shows you the modification date, who made the revision, and the resulting file size. You can use this list to restore a previous revision or download the revision to your local drive.

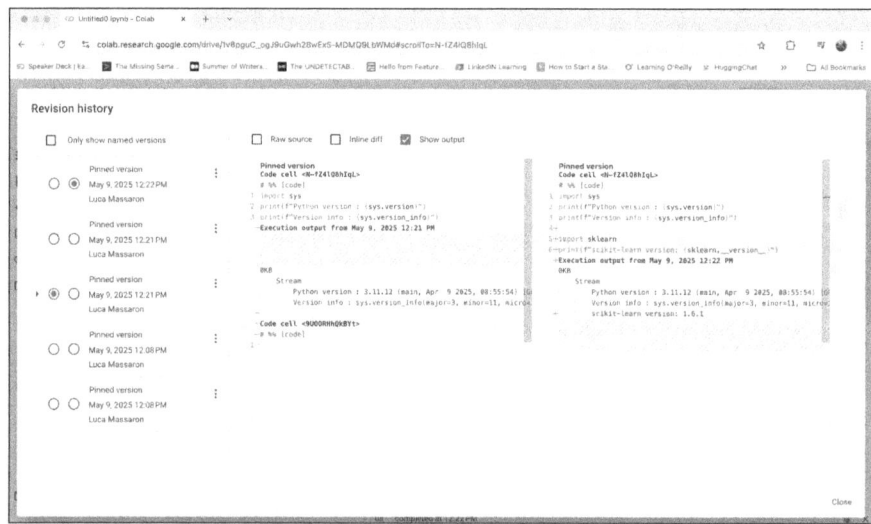

FIGURE 4-8:
Colab maintains a history of the revisions for your project.

You can also save a copy of your project by choosing File ⇨ Save a Copy In Drive. The copy gets the word *Copy* as part of its name, but you can rename it later. Colab stores the copy in the current Google Drive folder.

Using GitHub to save notebooks

GitHub provides an alternative to Google Drive for saving content. It offers an organized method of sharing code for discussion, review, and distribution. You can find GitHub at `https://github.com`.

REMEMBER

You can save a copy of your notebook to a public GitHub repository. If you've authorized Colab, you can also save to your private repositories. When saving to GitHub, you'll typically be prompted to select the repository and branch and provide a commit message. To save a file to GitHub, choose File ⇨ Save a Copy in GitHub. If you aren't already signed into GitHub, Colab displays a window that requests your sign-in information. After you sign in, you see a dialog box similar to the one shown in Figure 4-9.

FIGURE 4-9:
Using GitHub
means storing
your data in a
repository.

If your account doesn't currently have a repository, you must either create a new one or choose an existing one to store your data. After you save the file, it will appear in the GitHub repository of your choice. The commit can include a badge or link to open the notebook in Colab by default, unless you choose not to opt for this feature.

Using GitHub Gist to save notebooks

You use GitHub Gists as a means of sharing single files or other resources with other people. Some people use them for complete projects as well, but the idea is that you have a concept that you want to share — something that isn't quite fully formed and doesn't represent a usable application. You can read more about Gists at https://docs.github.com/en/get-started/writing-on-github/editing-and-sharing-content-with-gists/creating-gists.

While GitHub repositories offer public and private visibility options, Gists have a similar function and come in public or secret forms. You can access both public and secret Gists from Colab, but when you choose to save your notebook as a GitHub Gist, Colab creates a secret Gist by default. You can change its visibility to public later on the GitHub Gist website if needed. To save your current project as a Gist, you choose File ➪ Save a Copy as a GitHub Gist. Unlike GitHub, you don't need to create a repository or do anything fancy in this case. The file saves as a Gist without any extra effort. The resulting entry always contains an Open in Colab button.

Downloading notebooks

Colab allows you to download your notebook to your local drive in two formats: .ipynb files (using File ⇨ Download .ipynb) and .py files (using File ⇨ Download .py). In both cases, the file appears in the default download directory for your browser; Colab doesn't offer a method for downloading the file to a specific directory.

Performing Common Tasks

Most tasks in Colab work similarly to their Jupyter Notebook counterparts. For example, you can create code cells just as you do in a Jupyter Notebook by using the options on the Insert menu. Colab primarily uses two types of cells: code cells and text cells. Text cells use Markdown for formatting. Colab also offers features such as:

>> Scratch code cell, which allows you to experiment with code in real time

>> Code snippets, which are canned code for performing specific tasks (you just insert them where needed)

>> Form fields, which are elements added to code cells to create interactive UIs for your code that come in these types:

- Dropdown

- Input

- Slider

You can also edit and move cells, and you can convert cells between types, for instance, from a Text cell to a Code cell, or vice-versa. You can convert using menu options or keyboard shortcuts, like pressing Ctrl+M and then Y for text to code conversion, or pressing Ctrl+M and then M for text to code. Of course, content may need some adjustment after a conversion.

Creating code cells

The first cell that Colab creates for you is a code cell. Off the side of the cell, you see a menu of extras that you can use with Colab, as shown in Figure 4-10.

FIGURE 4-10:
Colab code cells contain a few extras.

You use the icons in Figure 4-10 to augment your Colab code experience. The following list provides a short description of these features (in order of appearance, left to right, in the figure):

>> **Move cell up:** Moves the cell up one position in the cell order.

>> **Move cell down:** Moves the cell down one position in the cell order.

>> **Link to cell:** Displays a dialog box containing a link you can use to access a specific cell within the notebook. You can embed this link anywhere on a web page or within a notebook to allow someone to access that specific cell. The person still sees the entire notebook but doesn't have to search for the cell you want to discuss.

>> **Add comment:** Creates a comment balloon to the right of the cell, assuming that you have the right to comment. This is not the same as a code comment, which exists within the code and is part of the code itself, not a separate cell annotation. You can edit, delete, or resolve comments. A resolved comment receives attention and is no longer applicable.

>> **Open editor settings:** Opens the same dialog box shown in Figure 4-2 and discussed in "Working with Google Colab features" earlier in this chapter.

>> **Mirror cell in tab:** Mirrors the currently selected cell in a Cell pane that appears on the right side of the window, as shown in Figure 4-11. You can scroll wherever you want within the code in the left pane and keep this code accessible. The right-pointing arrow lets you execute the cell any time after making changes in the left pane code. With a single click, a pair of double-pointing arrows lets you move the focus back to the selected code in the left pane. You can also move the cell code to a scratch cell, where you can play with it without modifying your original code. It's possible to have more than one Cell pane. You select and switch between them as needed, which lets you move easily from place to place in your code. Close a Cell pane by clicking the X next to the word Cell.

>> **Delete cell:** Removes the cell from the notebook.

>> **Three vertical dots:** Contains a number of additional features in a menu:

- **Select Cell:** Selects all the content (code, text, images, generated output) of the cell you are editing.

- **Copy Cell:** Copies the content of the currently selected cell to the Clipboard.

- **Cut Cell:** Deletes the content of the currently selected cell and places it on the Clipboard.

- **Explain Code:** Opens a window where Gemini explains the selected code cell.

FIGURE 4-11:
Use Cell panes to
keep key cells
easily available
as needed.

- **Clear Output:** Removes the output from the cell. It is present only if you have run the cell and it generated output. After using it, you must rerun the code to regenerate the output.

- **View Output Fullscreen:** Displays the output (not the entire cell or any other part of the notebook) in full-screen mode on the host device. This option is present only if you have run the cell and it generated output. It is useful when displaying a significant amount of content or when a detailed view of a graphic helps explain a topic. Press Esc to exit full-screen mode.

- **Add Form:** This option helps add interactive form fields (like sliders or input boxes) to the code cell. These form elements appear above your code within the cell, allowing you to change parameter values easily. Note that these interactive forms are a Colab-specific feature. You can read more about forms at https://colab.research.google.com/notebooks/forms.ipynb.

Code cells also tell you about the code and its execution. The run icon next to the output displays information about the execution when you hover your mouse over it, as shown in Figure 4-12.

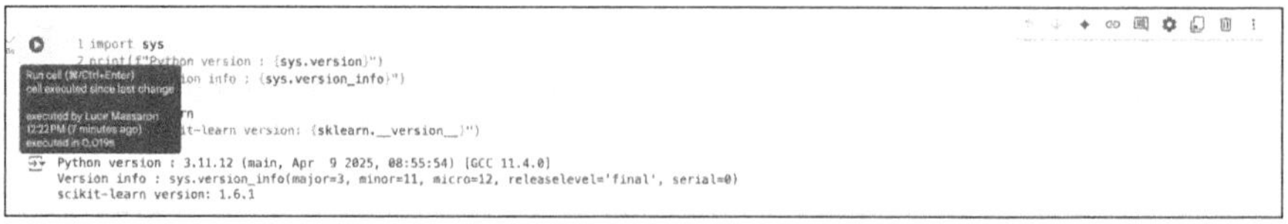

FIGURE 4-12:
Colab code
cells contain a
few extras.

Creating text cells

Text cells work using Markdown. Figure 4-13 shows that you receive additional help formatting the text using a graphical interface. The markup is the same, but you can allow the GUI to help you create the markup. For example, in this case, to make the # sign for a heading, you click the double T icon that appears first in the list. Clicking the double T icon typically cycles through heading levels (for example, H1, H2, H3) or toggles heading formatting. To the right, you see how the text will appear in the notebook.

FIGURE 4-13:
Use the GUI to make formatting your text easier.

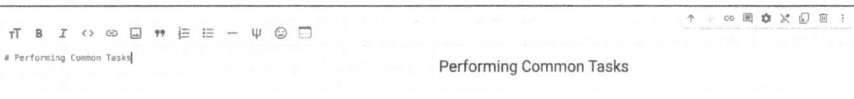

Notice the menu to the right of the text cell. This menu contains many of the same options that a code cell does. For example, you can create a numbered or bulleted list, insert an image, or an Internet link. Text cells are rendered to display formatted Markdown when you "run" them (for example, using Shift + Enter) or when the cell loses focus after editing.

Creating special cells

The special cells that Colab provides are variations of the text cell. These special cells, which you access using the Insert menu option, make creating the required cells faster. The following sections describe each of these special cell types.

Working with headings

When you choose Insert ⇨ Section Header Cell, a new cell is created below the currently selected cell with the appropriate header level 1 entry. You can change the heading level by adding or removing # symbols at the beginning of the line in the Markdown source or using the double T icon on the toolbar. The GUI looks the same as the one in Figure 4-13, so you have all the standard formatting features for your text.

Working with a table of contents

An interesting addition to Colab is automatically generating a table of contents for your notebook. To use this feature, click the Table of Contents icon on the left side of the window.

The table of contents contains one heading for each heading you provide in your code. The headings are automatically organized according to level, so you see the hierarchy of your code. Clicking a header automatically takes you to that location in your code.

Editing cells

Colab has an Edit menu containing the options you expect, such as cutting, copying, and pasting cells. Colab includes an option to show or hide the code as a toggle.

Moving cells

For moving cells around, Colab offers toolbar buttons (up/down arrows that appear when a cell is selected), Edit menu options (for example, Move cell up/down), and keyboard shortcuts.

Using Hardware Acceleration

Your Colab code executes on a Google server while your browser displays the code and its results. Consequently, any special hardware on your computing device is ignored unless you execute code locally.

TIP

Fortunately, you do have another option when working with Colab. Choose Runtime ⇨ Change Runtime Type to display the Notebook Settings dialog box, shown in Figure 4-14. This dialog box lets you choose the level of hardware acceleration for your code by adding a graphics processing unit (GPU) or tensor processing unit (TPU). The article at `https://medium.com/deep-learning-turkey/google-colab-free-gpu-tutorial-e113627b9f5d` provides additional details on how this works.

WARNING

The availability of a GPU or TPU isn't an invitation to run large computations using Colab. The content at `https://research.google.com/colaboratory/faq.html#gpu-availability` tells you about the limitations of the Colab hardware acceleration (including that it may not be available when needed).

The Notebook Settings dialog box also lets you choose whether to include cell output when saving the notebook. Since you store your notebook in the cloud in most cases, and loading large files into your browser can be time-consuming, removing the cell output when saving can make the notebook file smaller, allowing it to load more quickly in your browser. Of course, the trade-off is that you must now regenerate all the necessary outputs.

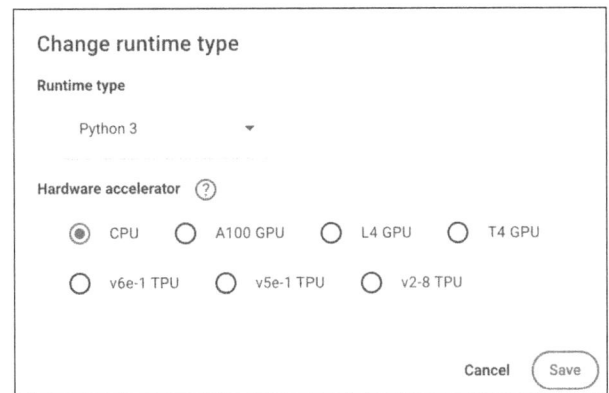

FIGURE 4-14:
Hardware
acceleration can
significantly
speed up code
execution for
compatible tasks.

Viewing Your Notebook

A notebook has a series of six icons in its left sidebar, like those shown earlier in Figure 4-4. Clicking any of these icons displays a pane containing tabs showing various information about your notebook. For example, clicking the first icon displays a Table of Contents pane. You can also choose specific pieces of information to see from the View menu. To close this pane, click the X in the upper-right corner. The following sections describe each of these pieces of information.

Displaying the table of contents

Choose View ⇨ Table of Contents to see a table of contents for your notebook. Clicking any of the entries takes you to that section of the notebook. At the bottom of the pane is a + Section button. Click this button to create a new header cell below the currently selected cell.

Getting notebook information

When you choose View ⇨ Notebook Info, a dialog box opens in the browser, as shown in Figure 4-15. This dialog box contains the notebook size, settings, and owner. Notice that the display also tells you the maximum notebook size.

The Notebook Info dialog box also includes an Open Notebook Settings link that displays the Notebook Settings dialog box, in which you can choose the runtime type and whether the notebook relies on hardware acceleration, as described in "Using Hardware Acceleration" earlier in this chapter.

FIGURE 4-15:
The notebook
information
includes details
like its size on
Drive and
runtime settings.

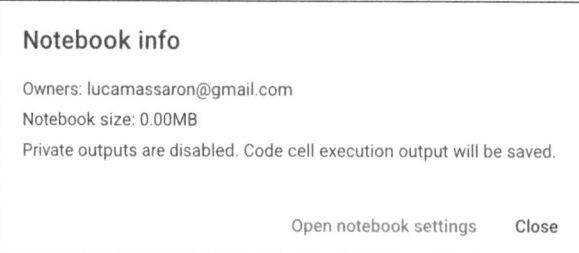

Notebook info

Owners: lucamassaron@gmail.com

Notebook size: 0.00MB

Private outputs are disabled. Code cell execution output will be saved.

Open notebook settings   Close

Checking code execution

Colab keeps track of your code as you execute it. Choose View ➪ Executed Code History to display the Execution History tab in the pane, typically in the right sidebar, as shown in Figure 4-16. Note that the number associated with the entries in the Executed Code tab may not match those associated with the related cells. In addition, each unique execution of code receives a separate number.

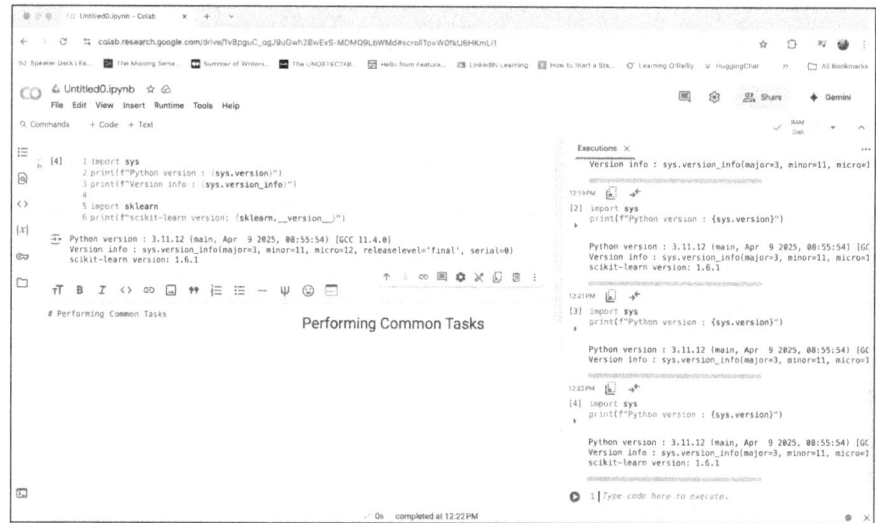

FIGURE 4-16:
Colab tracks
which code cells
you execute and
in what order in
the Executed
Code History tab.

Executing the Code

For your code to be useful, you must run it at some point. Previous sections have mentioned the right-pointing arrow that appears in the current cell. Clicking it runs just the current cell. Of course, you have other options than clicking the right-pointing arrow, and all these options appear on the Runtime menu. The following list summarizes these options:

- ≫ **Running the current cell:** Besides clicking the right-pointing arrow, you can also choose Runtime ⇨ Run the Focused Cell to execute the code in the current cell.

- ≫ **Running other cells:** Colab provides options on the Runtime menu for executing code, such as Run Selection, Run the Focused Cell, Run Before, and Run Cell and Below. Simply choose the option that matches the cell or set of cells you want to execute.

- ≫ **Running all the cells:** In some cases, you want to execute all the code in a notebook. In this case, choose Runtime ⇨ Run All. Execution starts at the top of the notebook, in the first cell containing code, and continues to the last cell that contains code in the notebook. You can stop execution at any time by choosing Runtime ⇨ Interrupt Execution.

TIP

Choosing Runtime ⇨ Manage Sessions displays a dialog box containing a list of all the sessions that are currently executing for your account on Colab. You can use this dialog box to determine when the code in that notebook last executed and how much memory the notebook consumes. Click the trash can icon to end execution for a particular notebook.

Sharing Your Notebook

You can share your Colab notebooks in a number of ways. For example, you can save it to GitHub or GitHub Gists. However, the two most direct methods are to

- ≫ Create a share message and send it to the recipient.

- ≫ Obtain a link to the code and send the link to the recipient.

In both cases, you click the Share button in the upper right of the Colab window. A dialog box opens, as shown in Figure 4-17, typically with sections for adding people/groups and getting a shareable link.

When you enter one or more names in the Add people, groups, and calendar events field, an additional field opens to add a sharing message. You can type a message and click Send to send the link immediately. If you click the gear icon instead, you see another dialog box, where you can define how to share the notebook.

Click Copy Link in the Get Link dialog box to place the URL on your device's clipboard. You can then paste it into messages or other forms of communication with others.

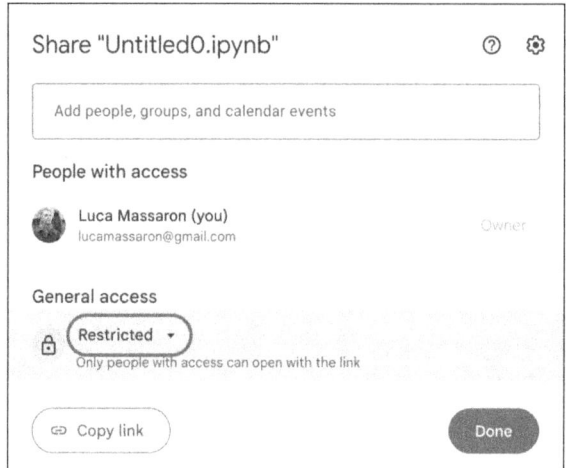

FIGURE 4-17:
Send a message
or obtain a
link to share
your notebook.

Getting Help

The most obvious place to obtain help with Colab is from the Colab Help menu. The Help menu provides several resources. The Welcome to Colaboratory link (often under Help) takes you to an introductory notebook `https://colab.research.google.com/notebooks/welcome.ipynb`, which is viewable without login. The Help menu also contains more entries:

>> **Frequently Asked Questions (FAQs):** Takes you to a page containing other people's questions.

>> **Search Code Snippets:** Opens a pane showing everyday tasks, such as working with a camera, in which you can search for example code that could meet your needs with a bit of modification. Clicking the Insert button inserts the code at the current cursor location in the cell that has focus. Each of the entries also shows an example of the code.

>> **Report a Bug:** Takes you to a page where you can report Colab errors.

>> **Send Feedback:** Displays a dialog box with links for locations where you can obtain additional information.

Chapter **5**

Understanding the Tools of the Trade

The previous chapter helped you get up and running with a Google Colab session. In this chapter, we continue exploring the features offered by the Colaboratory notebook environment and discover the different types of hardware you can use, how to store and retrieve secrets (API keys for online machine learning services), how to use useful macro-like functionalities (called magic commands in notebooks), and how to integrate colorful graphics and other multimedia into your notebooks. Finally, we look at the datasets used as examples in this book and provide you with more context about how data for machine learning is structured.

Understanding Hardware Options

Google Colab offers various hardware options for running your code in the cloud. These options may change over time, so the available hardware might differ from what is described here. Nevertheless, some options should always be available in some form to help you train machine learning models or analyze large datasets.

The CPU option is the default hardware for Colab notebooks. It is the workhorse for data manipulation of small and medium-sized datasets, statistical analysis, and machine learning. Running these commands will report to you the CPU being used in the Google Colab cloud environment and its characteristics:

```
!lscpu | grep 'Model name'
!lscpu | grep 'Socket(s)'
!lscpu | grep 'Core(s) per socket'
!lscpu | grep 'Thread(s) per core'
!lscpu | grep "MHz"
!free -h
```

You can determine the total number of logical cores available for multitasking by multiplying the number of sockets by the cores per socket, and then multiplying that result by the threads per core. At the time of writing this chapter, we were offered by Google Colab an Intel Xeon CPU running at 2.20GHz with two cores and 12GB of RAM.

If you opt for running an NVIDIA GPU because you need to run a neural network or some package that leverages GPUs for speed, such as NVIDIA RAPIDS, your choices from most to least performing include the following:

>> The NVIDIA A100 is a high-end GPU based on the Ampere architecture, featuring up to 40GB of VRAM. It is a powerful solution, suitable for natural language processing, generative models, and heavy computer vision workloads.

>> The NVIDIA L4 is a newer, more energy-efficient GPU built on the Ada Lovelace architecture with 24GB VRAM. It can assist with advanced image or video tasks, fine-tuning large models, and the most recent neural network architectures and solutions.

>> The NVIDIA T4, based on the Turing architecture, offers 16GB of VRAM and is an older model that remains popular and accessible for various tasks. It works perfectly with less demanding computer vision models and transformer-based NLP models.

If you selected a specific GPU as the runtime, you can check its characteristics by running the following command on Google Colab:

```
!nvidia-smi
```

Finally, if you really need the most power for large-scale machine learning operations, TPUs could be your answer. TPUs (with versions of increasing power: v2, v5e, v6e) are application-specific integrated circuits (ASICs), that is, special chips created by Google to accelerate machine learning. To utilize these specialized solutions, you must program your application using frameworks such as TensorFlow, PyTorch, and JAX, all of which provide support for TPU usage.

REMEMBER

You cannot run a Google Colab session forever. You must be connected to it through a browser, and a session can run for a maximum of 12 hours in the free tier and 24 hours for Colab Pro and Pro+.

Putting Secrets in a Safe Place

Many online services require API keys, which are sequences of letters and numbers connected to your billing account. You need API keys to access data repositories, monitoring services, chatbot services, and other similar services. A dangerous practice is to write down your API key directly into your code. It works, but anyone can take note of your API key and use it to their advantage. A solution to this security concern is to keep API keys in environment variables for temporary storage. Google Colab has its way of handling environment variables by using a built-in module within the google.colab library, *userdata*, which can be imported and used to access any key stored in its *Secrets* section, as shown in Figure 5-1.

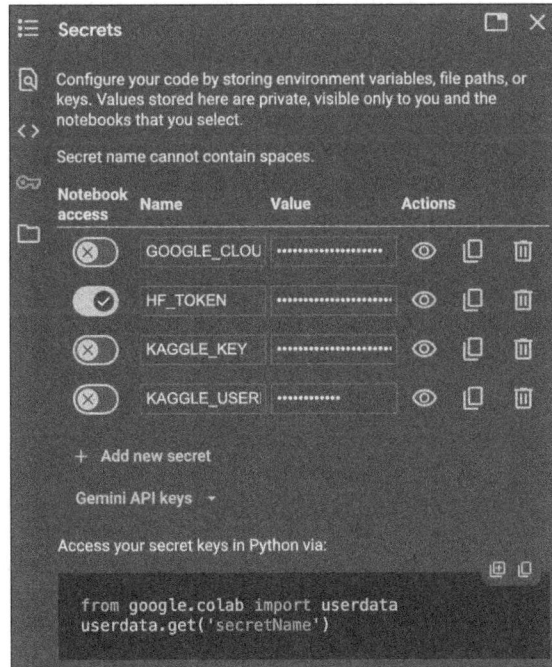

FIGURE 5-1:
The secrets section on Google Colab.

The Secrets section is accessible via the key icon on the left panel. There, interactively, you can add all the keys you need (called the *value*) and assign names to them. For instance, you can add a key named CLOUD_PROJECT and give it the key of your cloud project as a value. When you need to activate that project by using its key, all you need to do is import the userdata module and obtain the key you need by utilizing the .get method and the name of the key:

```
from google.colab import userdata
key = userdata.get("CLOUD_PROJECT")
```

TIP

You can control each secret's availability in the notebook using the toggle switch. The Secrets panel also allows you to view, copy, or delete secrets.

Using Magic Functions

Amazingly, you really can get magic on your Google Colab! Jupyter provides a special feature called magic functions, and these are also available on Google Colab. These so-called "magics" are special commands prefixed with one (%) or two (%%) percent signs, designed to make common tasks easier and more efficient within your notebook environment. The functions enable you to perform a wide range of amazing tasks with your notebook. The following sections provide an overview of the magic functions. You will also see some of them used later in the book. However, it pays to spend some time checking out these functions for yourself.

Obtaining the magic functions list

The best way to start working with magic functions is to obtain a list of them by typing **%quickref** and pressing Shift + Enter. What you see is a help (pager) window similar to the one shown in Figure 5-2.

Working with magic functions

Most magic functions start with either a single percent sign (%) or two percent signs (%%). Those with a single percent sign work at the command-line level, while those that have two percent signs work at the cell level. The Jupyter Notebook discussion later in the chapter provides further information about cells. For now, all you need to know is that you generally use magic functions with a single percent sign.

FIGURE 5-2:
Take your time going through the magic function help; it has a lot of information.

REMEMBER

Most of the magic functions display status information when you use them by themselves. For example, when you type **%cd** and click Run, the current directory is displayed. To change directories, type **%cd** followed by the new directory location on your system.

Getting object help

You can request information about specific objects using the object name and a question mark (?). For example, to learn more about a list object named mylist, type **mylist?** and click Run. You see a pager window displaying the mylist type, content in string form, length, and a document string (docstring) that provides a quick overview of the mylist.

When you need detailed help with mylist, type **help(mylist)** and click Run instead. You see the same help provided as when requesting information about the Python list. However, you receive the information that's appropriate to the particular object you need help with, rather than having to first discover the object type and then request information for that object. Additionally, this information is displayed as part of the cell output, rather than in a separate window, which makes referencing the help information easier later.

Obtaining object specifics

The dir() function is often overlooked, but it's an essential way to learn about the specifics of an object. To see a list of properties and methods associated with any object, use dir(<object name>). For example, if you create a list called mylist and want to know what sorts of things you can do with it, type **dir(mylist)** and click Run. The cell displays a list of methods and properties that are specific to mylist.

Using extended Python object help

Using a single question mark accesses an object's docstring and other general help information. To display the source code of an object, provided it is written in Python and the source code is accessible, use the double question mark (??). For example, type **mylist??** and click Run to view any clipped details (although there may not be any additional details).

You can use magic functions with objects as well. You type the magic function followed by the object, such as in %pdoc object. These functions simplify the help output and provide only the information you need, as shown here:

» %pdoc: Displays the docstring for the object

» %pdef: Shows how to call the object (assuming that the object is callable)

» %pfile: Prints the file that contains the source code for the object (assuming that the source is available)

» %pinfo: Displays detailed information about the object (often more than provided by help alone)

» %pinfo2: Displays extra detailed information about the object (when available)

Performing Multimedia Integration

Pictures say a lot of things that words can't say (or at least they do it with far less effort). A Colab notebook is both a coding platform and a presentation platform. You may be surprised at just what you can do with it. The following sections provide a brief overview of some of the more interesting features.

Embedding plots and other images

At some point, you might have spotted a notebook with multimedia or graphics embedded into it and wondered why you didn't see the same effects in your files. All the graphics examples in the book appear as part of the code. Fortunately, you can perform some more magic by using the %matplotlib magic function. When you run %matplotlib inline, any plots you create appear as part of the document.

Loading examples from online sites

Because some examples you see online can be complex to understand unless you have them loaded on your system, you should also keep the `%load` magic function in mind. All you need is the URL of an example you want to see on your system. For instance, try `%load https://matplotlib.org/_downloads/pyplot_text.py`. When you click Run Cell, Notebook loads the example directly in the cell and comments out the `%load` call. You can then run the example and view the output.

Obtaining online graphics and multimedia

Many of the functionalities required for special multimedia and graphics processing are available within `IPython.display`. By importing a required class, you can perform tasks such as embedding images into your notebook. Here's an example of embedding one of the pictures from the author's blog into the notebook for this chapter:

```
from urllib.request import Request, urlopen
from IPython import display

req = Request("https://upload.wikimedia.org/wikipedia" +
              "/commons/1/1a/Picography-shiba-inu-dog" +
              "-forest-walk-sm-1.jpg",
              headers={'User-Agent': 'XYZ/3.0'})
image = urlopen(req, timeout=10).read()

display.Image(image)
```

The code begins by importing the required resources. It then requests the file from the website. Notice the inclusion of the `headers` property. If you don't include this property, the call will fail with an error message. The call to `urlopen()` retrieves the image, which is then displayed using `display.Image()`. The output from this example appears in Figure 5-3.

When working with embedded images regularly, you might want to set the format in which the images are embedded. For example, you may prefer to embed them as PDFs. To perform this task, you use code similar to this:

```
from matplotlib_inline.backend_inline import (
                set_matplotlib_formats)
set_matplotlib_formats('pdf', 'svg')
```

You have access to several formats when working with a notebook. The supported formats are `'png'`, `'retina'`, `'jpeg'`, `'svg'`, and `'pdf'`.

Picography/Wikimedia Commons/CC0 1.0

FIGURE 5-3:
Embedding images can dress up your notebook presentation.

Downloading the Datasets and Code

This book explores the use of Python for machine learning tasks. Of course, it is an excellent learning exercise if you can spend all your time creating the example code from scratch, debugging it, and only then discovering how it relates to machine learning, or you can take the easy way and download the prewritten code at `www.dummies.com` so that you can get right to work. (Refer to the Introduction for information on downloading the book's source code.) Likewise, creating datasets large enough for machine learning purposes would take considerable time. Fortunately, you can access standardized, pre-created datasets quite easily using features provided in some data science libraries (which also work well for machine learning), or you can get your data from data repositories freely available on the Web. The following sections guide you through downloading and using the example code and datasets, allowing you to save time and focus on data science–specific tasks.

TIP

You can also find the book's source code at `https://github.com/lmassaron/ml4dummies_3ed`.

In addition to the datasets provided by Scikit-learn (`https://scikit-learn.org/stable/datasets`), this book utilizes numerous datasets that can be accessed at `https://github.com/lmassaron/ml4dummies_3ed/releases/tag/v1.0`. All these datasets are tabular, meaning they can be represented in the form of a table. Data is organized into rows, which represent the observations, and columns, which represent the characteristics of the observations, commonly referred to as features or variables.

These datasets demonstrate various ways in which you can interact with data, and you use them in the examples to perform a variety of tasks. All these datasets are in the CSV format. The CSV format is a text file format used to store data in a tabular format, including numbers and text, in a simple yet structured manner. Each line in a CSV file represents a single record (or row). Within that record, each field (or column), separated by a comma, represents a feature. The following list provides a quick overview of the datasets used in this book:

- **Air Passengers** (`https://pkg.robjhyndman.com/fma/reference/airpass.html`): This file contains the number of passengers on an example airline per month for 12 years starting in 1949. Originally, this data comes from the work by Box and Jenkins (1976) as part of their book *Time Series Analysis, Forecasting and Control*.

- **IMDB 50K** (`https://paperswithcode.com/dataset/imdb-movie-reviews`): A dataset for binary sentiment classification containing a set of 25,000 popular movie reviews for training and 25,000 for testing. The IMDB 50K dataset (often called the IMDB Movie Reviews Dataset) is widely used as a benchmark for sentiment analysis in natural language processing.

- **Fashion MNIST** (`https://github.com/zalandoresearch/fashion-mnist`): A dataset of article images from the fashion retailer Zalando. It consists of a training set of 60,000 examples and a test set of 10,000 examples, each labeled with one of ten categories.

- **Palmer Penguins** (`https://github.com/allisonhorst/palmerpenguins`): A package containing two datasets collected and made available by Dr. Kristen Gorman and the Palmer Station, Antarctica LTER, a member of the Long Term Ecological Research Network.

- **Shakespeare** (`https://www.kaggle.com/kingburrito666/shakespeare-plays`): A listing of all Shakespeare's plays, lines from these plays, and who is speaking the line.

- **SMS Spam Collection** (`www.kaggle.com/uciml/sms-spam-collection-dataset`): A set of SMS tagged messages collected for SMS Spam research. It contains one set of 5,574 English SMS messages, tagged according to whether the message is ham (legitimate) or spam.

- **Tennis** (`https://data.mendeley.com/datasets/3ch7s5tdzp/1`): The Play Tennis dataset is a classic and widely used dataset in machine learning, illustrating how weather conditions affect the decision to play tennis. It is a highly accessible dataset for beginners and educators.

>> **Titanic** (`https://www.openml.org/d/40945`): A dataset describing the survival status of individual passengers on the Titanic. The Titanic data does not contain information from the crew, but it does contain the actual ages of half the passengers.

>> **Wine** (`https://archive.ics.uci.edu/dataset/186/wine+quality`): Contains statistics related to the quality of wine.

Chapter **6**

Getting Beyond Basic Coding in Python

This chapter provides an overview of Python, emphasizing features commonly used when solving machine learning problems. It starts with data types and operators and then moves to functions and data structures, such as sets, lists, tuples, and dictionaries. If you already know Python, skip this chapter and move on to the next one. You may also be interested in reading *Python for Data Science For Dummies*, which contains many advanced Python examples and applications to machine learning problems.

If you're new to Python, you can't use this book to learn Python from scratch — for that, you need a book such as *Beginning Programming with Python For Dummies*, or you need a tutorial such as the one at https://docs.python. org/3/tutorial. This chapter assumes that you've worked with other programming languages and have at least an idea of how Python works. This limitation aside, you can use this chapter for a refresher on how things work in Python. You learn the basics of working with Python data types, coding structures, and data manipulation strategies.

REMEMBER

You can find the source code for this chapter in the ML4D3E folder of the downloadable code file. The example files for this chapter will begin with ML4D3E-06-. See the Introduction for details on how to find these source files.

Defining the Basics You Should Know

Any language possesses basic characteristics, and Python is no different. For example, languages provide various data types, operators, methods of interacting with data, and so on. In addition, Python supports both functions and modules. You use this knowledge when working through the examples in this book. Python is a rich language that provides a great deal of flexibility in an easy-to-use language.

Considering Python basics

In all programming languages, data types are a core concept because they determine the values a variable can store and the operations that can be done with them. For instance, you can perform arithmetic operations on numeric data types, but the same operations applied to a string of text would result in an error or an entirely different output.

Python is a dynamically typed and interpreted language. This means the code is run line by line by a special program called an *interpreter* (python or python3, which you call when running any .py file containing the code), and the data type of the variable that you use is determined and checked while running the code, whereas in other programming languages, you are required first to declare the type. Python possesses a variety of built-in data types to handle the most common and practical kinds of data. Table 6-1 provides an overview of the common numeric Python data types.

TABLE 6-1   **Python Numeric Data Types**

Type	Range	Example
int	Arbitrary precision, meaning Python can support integers of any size, only limited by available memory.	1
float	$\pm 2.2250738585072014 \times 10^{-308}$ and $\pm 1.7976931348623157 \times 10^{308}$ (defined by sys.float_info.max and sys.float_info.min for a particular platform).	1.0
complex	A complex number in Python consists of two floating-point numbers (a real part and an imaginary part). Each one has the same range as a float.	$3 + 4j$
bool	True or False.	True

Binary (requiring two values or variables to operate), unary (operating on a single value or variable), and bitwise (operating on integers at the bit level) operators provide the means for manipulating data in various ways. Table 6-2 shows these operators.

TABLE 6-2 **Python Binary, Unary, and Bitwise Operators**

Operator	Description	Example
+	Adds two values together.	5 + 2 = 7
–	Subtracts the right operand from the left operand.	5 – 2 = 3
*	Multiplies the right operand by the left operand.	5 * 2 = 10
/	Divides the left operand by the right operand.	5 / 2 = 2.5
%	Divides the left operand by the right operand and returns the remainder.	5 % 2 = 1
**	Calculates the exponential value of the right operand by the left operand.	5 ** 2 = 25
//	Performs integer division, in which the left operand is divided by the right operand and only the whole number is returned (also called floor division).	5 // 2 = 2
~	Inverts the bits in a number so that all of the 0 bits become 1 bits and vice versa.	~4 results in a value of –5
–(unary)	Negates the original value so that positive becomes negative and vice versa.	–(–4) results in 4 and –4 results in –4
+(unary)	Is provided purely for the sake of completeness. This operator returns the same value that you provide as input.	+4 results in a value of 4
& (And)	Determines whether both individual bits within two operators are true and sets the resulting bit to True when they are.	0b1100 & 0b0110 = 0b0100
| (Or)	Determines whether either of the individual bits within two operators is true and sets the resulting bit to True when they are.	0b1100 | 0b0110 = 0b1110
^ (Exclusive or)	Determines whether just one of the individual bits within two operators is true and sets the resulting bit to True when one is. When both bits are true or both bits are false, the result is False.	0b1100 ^ 0b0110 = 0b1010
<< (Left shift)	Shifts the bits in the left operand left by the value of the right operand. Bits shifted off the left end are lost; new bits added on the right end are always 0.	0b00110011 << 2 = 0b11001100
>> (Right shift)	Shifts the bits in the left operand right by the value of the right operand. Bits shifted off the right end are lost. The behavior of the new bits added on the left end depends on the type of the left operand. Arithmetic Shift (signed types): New bits are copies of the sign bit. Logical Shift (unsigned types): New bits are always 0.	0b00110011 >> 2 = 0b00001100

CHAPTER 6 **Getting Beyond Basic Coding in Python**   83

To create variables used to hold data, you make assignments. Table 6-3 contains a list of Python assignment operators (assume that myvar begins by containing the value 5 in each case).

TABLE 6-3
Python Assignment Operators

Operator	Description	Example
=	Assigns the value found in the right operand to the left operand	myvar = 5 results in myvar containing 5
+=	Adds the value found in the right operand to the value found in the left operand and places the result in the left operand	myvar += 2 results in myvar containing 7
−=	Subtracts the value found in the right operand from the value found in the left operand and places the result in the left operand	myvar −= 2 results in myvar containing 3
*=	Multiplies the value found in the right operand by the value found in the left operand and places the result in the left operand	myvar *= 2 results in myvar containing 10
/=	Divides the value found in the left operand by the value found in the right operand and places the result in the left operand	myvar /= 2 results in myvar containing 2.5
%=	Divides the value found in the left operand by the value found in the right operand and places the remainder in the left operand	myvar %= 2 results in myvar containing 1
**=	Determines the exponential value found in the left operand when raised to the power of the value found in the right operand and places the result in the left operand	myvar **= 2 results in myvar containing 25
//=	Divides the value found in the left operand by the value found in the right operand and places the integer (whole number) result in the left operand	myvar //= 2 results in myvar containing 2

Sometimes, you need to check the relationship between two variables or compare them in some way. Table 6-4 provides a listing of Python relational and logical operators.

You can use some special operators with objects, such as strings. The *member operators* let you determine when a string contains specific content. You use the *identity operators* to assess the kind of data that variables contain. Table 6-5 shows these operators.

Computers provide order to comparisons by making some operators more significant than others. The ordering of operators is *operator precedence*. Table 6-6 shows the operator precedence of all the standard Python operators, including a few you haven't seen as part of a discussion yet. When making comparisons, always consider operator precedence.

TABLE 6-4
Python Relational and Logical Operators

Operator	Description	Example
==	Determines whether two values are equal. Notice that the relational operator uses two equals signs. A mistake that many developers make is to use just one equals sign, which results in one value being assigned to another.	1 == 2 is False
!=	Determines whether two values are not equal. Some older versions of Python allowed you to use the <> operator in place of the != operator. Using the <> operator results in an error in current versions of Python.	1 != 2 is True
>	Verifies that the left operand value is greater than the right operand value.	1 > 2 is False
<	Verifies that the left operand value is less than the right operand value.	1 < 2 is True
>=	Verifies that the left operand value is greater than or equal to the right operand value.	1 >= 2 is False
<=	Verifies that the left operand value is less than or equal to the right operand value.	1 <= 2 is True
and	Determines whether both operands are true.	True and True is True True and False is False False and True is False False and False is False
or	Determines when one of two operands is true.	True or True is True True or False is True False or True is True False or False is False
not	Negates the truth value of a single operand. A true value becomes false, and a false value becomes true.	not True is False not False is True

TABLE 6-5
Python Membership and Identity Operators

Operator	Description	Example
in	Determines whether the value in the left operand appears in the right operand	"Hello" in "Hello Goodbye" is True
not in	Determines whether the value in the left operand is missing from the right operand	"Hello" not in "Hello Goodbye" is False
is	Evaluates to true when both operands point to the exact same object	type(2) is int is True
is not	Evaluates to true when both operands point to different objects	type(2) is not int is False

TABLE 6-6 **Python Operator Precedence**

Operator	Description
()	You use parentheses to group expressions and to override the default precedence so that you can force an operation of lower precedence (such as addition) to take precedence over an operation of higher precedence (such as multiplication).
**	Exponentiation raises the value of the left operand to the power of the right operand.
+x, −x, ~x	Unary plus, unary minus, and bitwise NOT.
*, /, //, %	Multiplication, division, floor division, and modulo.
+ −	Addition and subtraction.
<<, >>	Right and left bitwise shift.
&	Bitwise AND.
^	Bitwise XOR (exclusive OR).
in, not in, is, is not, <, <=, >, >=, !=, ==	Comparison operators, including membership and identity tests.
not x	Logical NOT.
and	Logical AND.
or	Logical OR.
if-else	Conditional expression.
=, %=, /=, //=, −=, +=, *=, **=	Assignment operators.

Working with functions

To manage information correctly, you need to organize the tools used to perform the required tasks. Each line of code you create performs a specific task, and you combine these lines to achieve a desired result. Sometimes you need to repeat the instructions with different data, and in some cases, your code becomes so long that keeping track of what each part does is hard. Functions serve as organizational tools that keep your code neat and tidy. In addition, functions let you easily reuse the instructions you've created as needed with different data. This section of the chapter tells you all about functions, and you start defining how to make your first serious applications like professional developers do.

Creating reusable functions

You go to your closet, take out pants and a shirt, remove the labels, and put them on. At the end of the day, you take everything off and throw it in the trash. Hmmm . . . that really isn't what most people do. Most people take the clothes off, wash them, and then return them to the closet for reuse. Functions are reusable, too. No one wants to keep repeating the same task; it becomes monotonous and boring. When you create a function, you define a package of code that you can use over and over to perform the same task. All you need to do is tell the computer to perform a specific task by telling it which function to use. The computer faithfully executes each instruction in the function absolutely every time you ask it to do so.

REMEMBER

When you work with functions, the code that needs services from the function is named the *caller,* and it calls upon the function to perform tasks for it. Much of the information you see about functions refers to the caller. The caller must supply information to the function, which returns information to the caller.

At one time, computer programs didn't include the concept of code reusability. As a result, developers had to keep reinventing the same code. Before long, someone came up with the idea of functions, and the concept has evolved over the years until functions have become quite flexible. You can make functions do anything you want. Code reusability is a necessary part of applications to

- » Reduce development time

- » Reduce programmer error

- » Increase application reliability

- » Allow entire groups to benefit from the work of one programmer

- » Make code easier to understand

- » Improve application efficiency

In fact, functions do a whole list of things for applications in the form of reusability. As you work through the examples in this book, you see how reusability makes your life significantly easier. If not for reusability, you'd still be programming by plugging 0s and 1s manually into the computer.

Creating a function doesn't require much work. To see how functions work, open Google Colab, and type the following code in a cell (pressing Enter at the end of each line):

```
def say_hello():
    return "Hello There!"
```

To execute the cell, press Shift + Enter after the last line. A function begins with the keyword def (for define). You provide a function name, parentheses that can contain function *parameters* (data used in the function), and a colon. The editor automatically indents the following line for you. Python relies on indentation to define *code blocks* (statements associated with each other in a function).

You can now use the function. Type **say_hello()** in a new cell and press Shift + Enter. The parentheses after the function name are important because they tell Python to execute the function, rather than tell you that you are accessing a function as an object (to determine what it is). You see Hello There! as the output from this function.

Calling functions

Functions can accept arguments (additional bits of data) and return values. The ability to exchange data makes functions far more helpful than they otherwise might be. The following sections describe how to call functions in a variety of ways to both send and receive data.

SENDING REQUIRED ARGUMENTS

A function can require the caller to provide arguments to it. A required argument is a value or a variable that contains data for the function to work. Open Google Colab, and type the following code in a cell:

```
def do_sum(value_1, value_2):
    return value_1 + value_2
```

You have a new function, do_sum(). This function requires that you provide two arguments for its use. To see how this works, after having run the cell containing the function, type **do_sum(1, 2)** in a new cell and press Shift + Enter. You see an output of 3. Notice that do_sum() always provides an output value of 3 when you supply 1 and 2 as inputs. The return statement provides the output value. Whenever you see return in a function, you know that the function provides an output value.

SENDING ARGUMENTS BY KEYWORD

As your functions become more complex and the methods to use them do as well, you should provide more control over precisely what you call the function and provide arguments for it. Until now, you have used *positional arguments,* which means that you have supplied values in the order in which they appear in the parameter list for the function definition. However, Python also has a method for sending arguments by keyword. In this case, you supply the name of the argument followed by an equals sign (=) and the argument value. To see how this works, open Google Colab, and type the following code in a cell and then execute it by pressing Shift + Enter:

```
def display_sum(value_1, value_2):
    print(str(value_1) + ' ' + ' ' + str(value_2) + ' = ' +
        str((value_1 + value_2)))
```

Notice that the `print()` function argument includes a list of items to print and that those items are separated by plus signs (+). In addition, the arguments are of different types, so you must convert them using the `str()` function. Python lets you easily mix and match arguments in this manner. This function also introduces the concept of automatic line continuation. The `print()` function appears on two lines, and Python automatically continues the function from the first line to the second.

When you are writing code in Python, you will often need to break up a line because the line will be too long and will not be readable. Python will allow you to break up a line of code automatically if it is inside an opening and closing pair of parentheses, brackets, or braces. If your code is not inside one of those pairs of characters, you must use the line continuation character, a backslash (\), to tell Python that the code on the next line is a continuation of the present line.

Next, it's time to test `display_sum()`. Of course, you want to try the function using positional arguments first, so get a new cell and type **display_sum(2, 3)** and press Shift + Enter. You see the expected output of 2 + 3 = 5. Now type **display_sum(value_2=3, value_1=2)** in a new cell and press Shift + Enter. Again, you receive the output 2 + 3 = 5 even though the position of the arguments has been reversed.

GIVING FUNCTION ARGUMENTS A DEFAULT VALUE

Whether you make the call using positional or keyword arguments, the functions to this point have required that you supply a value. Sometimes a function can use default values when a common value is available. To create a default value, you follow the parameter name with an equals sign and the default value. To see how this works, open Google Colab, type the following code in a cell, and then press Shift + Enter:

```
def say_hello(Greeting = "No Value Supplied"):
    print(Greeting)
```

The `say_hello()` function provides an automatic value for `Greeting` when a caller doesn't provide one. When someone tries to call `say_hello()` without an argument, Python doesn't raise an error; instead, it outputs `No Value Supplied`. Type **say_hello()** in a new cell and press Shift + Enter to see for yourself. You see the default message. Type **say_hello("Howdy!")** to see a normal response.

CREATING FUNCTIONS WITH A VARIABLE NUMBER OF ARGUMENTS

In most cases, you know precisely how many arguments to provide to your function. However, there are situations where you need to handle a variable number of inputs. Fortunately, Python provides a technique for sending various arguments to a function. You simply create an argument that has an asterisk in front of it, such as `*args`. To see how this works, open Google Colab, type the following code in a cell, then press Shift + Enter:

```
def display_multi(*args):
    print('You passed ' + str(len(args)) +
        ' arguments.', args)
```

Notice that the `print()` function displays a string and the list of arguments. Because of the way this function is designed, you can type **display_multi()** in a cell and press Shift + Enter to see that it's possible to pass zero arguments. To see multiple arguments at work, type **display_multi(3, "Hello ", 1, True)** and press Shift + Enter. The output `You passed 3 arguments. ('Hello', 1, True)` shows that you need not pass values of any particular type.

Working with modules and packages

A Python *module* is simply a file of Python code, typically with the extension `.py`. A module can contain function, class, and variable definitions that you can reuse elsewhere in your program. Modules are similar to toolboxes. Instead of having all your tools in one giant, messy pile (one single, large code file), you can have similar tools in specific toolboxes (modules). For example, you may have one module for numerical operations and another for handling text. Instead, a Python *package* is a way of organizing related modules in a directory structure. A package is just a directory that contains one or more modules. In this book, we will often resort to various packages specialized in specific operations related to data and machine learning.

To obtain the code of a module (or of a package, it works the same), you must first import it within your current script. The import statement asks Python to find the chosen module, execute its code, and import its content.

You have two ways to import modules. Each technique is used in specific circumstances:

>> **import:** You use this statement when you want to import an entire module. This is the most common method developers use to import modules because it saves time and requires only one line of code. However, this approach also uses more memory resources than does the approach of selectively importing the attributes you need, which the following paragraph describes.

>> **from. . .import:** You use this statement to import individual module attributes selectively. This method saves resources, but at the cost of complexity. In addition, if you try to use an attribute you didn't import, Python registers an error. Yes, the module still contains the attribute, but Python can't see it because you didn't import it.

Python must be able to locate the module and load it into memory to use its code. The location information is stored as paths within Python. Whenever you request that Python import a module, Python looks at all the files in its list of paths to find it. The path information comes from three sources:

>> **Environment variables:** An environment variable provides a platform-specific operating system-level variable you can use to store information about an application. You use various means to set environment variables depending on the platform. For example, when working with Windows, you can set environment variables at the command prompt or use the Environment Variables dialog. One of the most important environment variables for Python developers is PYTHONPATH, which shows the default location for searching for files on your drive.

>> **Current directory:** Python uses the current directory to look for files it needs. The following code helps discover the current Python directory:

```
import os
os.getcwd()
```

If you want to change the current directory so that Python looks in another location, you use the following code:

```
import os
os.chdir('new_path')
```

where new_path is the location you want to use.

>> **Default directories:** Even when you don't define any environment variables and the current directory doesn't yield any usable modules, Python can still find its own libraries in the set of default directories included as part of its own path information.

It's important to know where Python is looking for modules. Sometimes you might encounter an error when Python can't find a module, even though you know the module exists on disk. The following code shows how to determine where Python is looking for modules on disk:

```
import os
os.environ['PYTHONPATH']
```

If you receive a `KeyError:  'PYTHONPATH'` error message, it means that the PYTHONPATH environment variable isn't defined. Python can still find files; it just doesn't have PYTHONPATH as a resource.

Storing Data Using Sets, Lists, and Tuples

Python provides a host of methods for storing data in memory. Each method has advantages and disadvantages, so choosing the most appropriate method for your needs is important.

Using lists

The Python specification defines a list as a kind of sequence. *Sequences* provide some means of allowing multiple data items to exist together in a single storage unit, but as separate entities. Think about one of those large mail holders you see in apartment buildings. A single mail holder contains a number of small mailboxes, each of which can contain mail. Python supports other kinds of sequences as well:

>> **Tuples:** A *tuple* is a collection that creates complex list-like sequences. As with lists, you can nest the content of a tuple. This feature lets you create structures that can hold employee records or x-y coordinate pairs.

>> **Dictionaries:** As with the real dictionaries, you create key/value pairs when using the dictionary collection (think of a word and its associated definition). A dictionary provides swift search and retrieval times.

>> **Stacks:** Most programming languages support stacks directly. A stack is a last-in/first-out (LIFO) sequence. Think of a pile of pancakes: You can add new ones to the top and take them off. In Python, a stack is most easily implemented using a standard list. The append( ) method adds an item to the top of the stack, and the pop( ) method removes the most recently added item from the top. If you need performance, collections.deque is an even more efficient choice for implementing a stack.

>> **Queues:** A queue is a first-in/first-out (FIFO) collection. You use it to track items that need to be processed. Think of a queue as a line at the bank where you wait your turn, and eventually are called to talk with a teller. While a list can be used to create a queue, it is inefficient, and it is better to use `collections.deque` (it has fast appends and pops on either end).

TIP

A double-ended queue (deque, pronounced *deck*) is a queue-like structure that lets you add or remove items from either end, but not from the middle. You can use a deque as a queue, a stack, or any other kind of collection to which you're adding and from which you're removing items in an orderly manner. For performance reasons, deque from the collections library (`https://docs.python.org/3/library/collections.html#collections.deque`) is generally preferred to lists when implementing stacks and queues.

Of all the sequences, lists are the easiest to understand and are the most directly related to a real-world object. Working with lists helps you become better able to work with other kinds of sequences that provide greater functionality and improved flexibility. The point is that the data is stored in a list much as you would write it on a piece of paper — one item comes after another. The following sections help you understand lists better.

Defining a list

The list has a beginning, a middle, and an end. The items are numbered. (Even if you might not normally number them in real life, Python always numbers the items for you.) To see how you can work with lists, open Google Colab, and type the following code in a cell:

```
list_a = [0, 1, 2, 3]
list_b = [4, 5, 6, 7]
list_a.extend(list_b)
list_a
```

When you type the last line of code, you see the output of [0, 1, 2, 3, 4, 5, 6, 7]. The `extend()` function adds the members of `list_b` to `list_a`. Besides extending lists, you can also add to them using the `append()` function. Type **list_a.append(-5)** and press Shift + Enter. When you type **list_a** in a new cell and press Shift + Enter, you see that Python has added −5 to the end of the list. You may find that you need to remove items again, and you do that using the `remove()` function. For example, type **list_a.remove(-5)** in a cell and press Shift + Enter. When you list `list_a` again, you see that the added entry is gone.

Combining lists using concatenation

Lists support concatenation using the plus (+) sign. For example, if you type **list_x = list_a + list_b** and press Shift + Enter, the newly created `list_x` contains both `list_a` and `list_b`, with the elements of `list_a` coming first.

Constructing lists using loops and comprehensions

A for loop is a Python instruction used to loop through a sequence, which can be a list, a tuple, a dictionary, a set, or a string. This is useful when you have to repeat a block of code a specified number of times. You can use the for command and indentation to iterate over a sequence such as a string, as in the following example:

```
my_list = []
for letter in "Hello":
  my_list.append(letter)

print(my_list)
```

The printed output will contain `['H', 'e', 'l', 'l', 'o']`. For loops are useful for executing repeated commands and creating lists, but there are other ways to achieve the same results. List comprehensions provide an elegant and straightforward method of creating lists with specific content. A comprehension appears in square brackets after the list name assignment. It includes three elements: an expression, an individual item upon which to act, and a list of items to work with. For example, the following list comprehension would place the individual letters of the string `"Hello"` into the list `Letters` after converting them to uppercase:

```
letters = [letter.upper() for letter in "Hello"]
print(letters)
```

The output would contain `['H', 'E', 'L', 'L', 'O']`. Normally, to create a list like this, you'd need a `for` loop and several lines of code, as shown earlier. The list comprehension does it in just one line and is easy to read.

Accessing list methods

You can access a broad range of list methods and techniques for acting on the list or only part of a list. The following list provides some of the most common strategies for interacting with lists. You see several other methods in the book examples.

- **»** `mylist.append(x)`: Adds an element to the end of the list.

- **»** `mylist.insert(index, value)`: Adds an element, `value`, to the location specified by `index` in the list.

TIP

  The first item in a list is numbered 0, rather than 1, as you might think. So, when adding the number 4 to the front of `mylist`, you use `mylist.insert(0, 4)`.

- **»** `mylist.remove(x)`: Removes the first occurrence of x from the list.

- **»** `mylist.extend(list_b)`: Appends the elements in `list_b` to the end of `mylist`.

- **»** `mylist[a:b]`: Returns just the part of the list expressed by the beginning point, a, and the ending point, b (which is not included because the values stop just before index b). You may optionally add a third element, a step, that tells how many elements to skip between outputs.

- **»** `mylist.index(value)`: Returns the index of the first occurrence of value in the list.

- **»** `mylist.sort()`: Sorts the list in order. You may specify `reverse=True` to sort the list in reverse order. In addition, you can provide a special function to define the sort order.

- **»** `len(mylist)`: Returns the list length.

- **»** `max(mylist)`: Returns the maximum value in the list.

- **»** `min(mylist)`: Returns the minimum value in the list.

Slicing and dicing lists

To access individual values across multiple data structures, you can use a technique called *slicing*. With slicing, you create a sub-list by extracting a specific portion from an existing list. *Dicing* is a practical application of slicing, where you combine small slices from a list, such as when you have a list of sales data for a year, and you extract four separate lists, one for each quarter, and place them into a new list (a list of lists).

In our examples here, you use two simple lists, defined as follows:

```
list_a = ['Orange', 'Yellow', 'Green', 'Brown']
list_b = [1, 2, 3, 4]
```

An index is used to access a particular value in a specific position. For example, if you type **list_a[1]** and press Shift + Enter, you see `'Yellow'`. All indices in Python are zero-based, meaning the first entry is 0, not 1.

Slices provide another simple method of accessing values. For example, if you type **list_b[1:3]** in a cell and press Shift + Enter, the output is [2, 3] (because the index where the slice ends is always excluded). Instead of the entire list, you see just 2 and 3 as outputs. In this case, the slice has two values separated by a colon. However, the values are optional. For example, list_b[:3] would output [1, 2, 3]. When you leave out a value, the range starts at the beginning or the end of the list, as appropriate.

Python also supports negative indices, which can be used in slices and are extremely useful in referring to elements from the end of a list without knowing its length. -1 refers to the last one, -2 to the second-to-last, and so on. For instance, list_b[-2:] returns the output [3, 4].

Iterating multiple lists using zip

Sometimes you need to process two lists in parallel. The simplest method of doing this is to use the zip() function. Here's an example of the zip() function in action:

```
for value_1, value_2 in zip(list_a, list_b):
    print(value_1, '\t', value_2)
```

This code processes both list_a and list_b at the same time. The processing ends when the for loop reaches the end of the shortest of the two lists. In this case, you see the following:

```
Orange  1
Yellow  2
Green   3
Brown   4
```

Creating and using tuples

A *tuple* is a collection used to create complex lists, in which you can embed one tuple within another. This embedding lets you create hierarchies with tuples. A hierarchy could be something as simple as the directory listing of your hard drive or an organizational chart for your company. The idea is that you can create complex data structures using a tuple.

REMEMBER

Tuples are *immutable,* which means that you can't change them. You can create a new tuple with the same name and modify it in some way, but you can't modify an existing tuple. Lists are mutable, which means that you can change them. So, a tuple can initially seem to be at a disadvantage, but immutability has all sorts of advantages, such as being more secure and faster. In addition, immutable objects are easier to use with multiple processors. To see how you can work with tuples, open Google Colab, and type the following code in a cell:

```
mytuple = (1, 2, 3, (4, 5, 6, (7, 8, 9)))
```

`mytuple` is nested three levels deep. The first level consists of the values 1, 2, 3, and a tuple. The second level consists of the values 4, 5, 6, and yet another tuple. The third level consists of the values 7, 8, and 9. To see how nesting works, type the following code into a new cell:

```
for value_1 in mytuple:
    if isinstance(value_1, int):
        print(value_1)
    else:
        for value_2 in value_1:
            if type(value_2) == int:
                print("\t", value_2)
            else:
                for value_3 in value_2:
                    print("\t\t", value_3)
```

When you run this code, you find that the values really are at three different levels. You can see the indentations showing the level:

```
1
2
3
        4
        5
        6
                7
                8
                9
```

TIP

You can perform tasks such as adding new values, but you must do it by adding the original entries and the new values to a new tuple. In addition, you can add tuples to an existing tuple only. To see how to add tuples, type **mynewtuple = mytuple + ((10, 11, 12, (13, 14, 15)))** and press Shift + Enter. `mynewtuple` contains new entries at both the first and second levels, like this: (1, 2, 3, (4, 5, 6, (7, 8, 9)), 10, 11, 12, (13, 14, 15)).

Creating sets

Most people have used sets in school to create lists of items that belong together. These lists then became the topic of manipulation using math operations such as intersection, union, difference, and symmetric difference. Sets are the best option when performing membership testing and removing duplicates from a list. You can't perform sequence-related tasks using sets, such as indexing or slicing. To see how you can work with sets, open Google Colab, and type the following code in a cell:

```
set_a = set(['Red', 'Blue', 'Green', 'Black'])
set_b = set(['Black', 'Green', 'Yellow', 'Orange'])
```

Performing operations on sets

Assuming that you created the sets found in the previous section, you may have noticed that each of them has some common elements. To see how these sets are similar, create some new sets that rely on math operations for comparison purposes, as shown in the following code:

```
set_x = set_a.union(set_b)
set_y = set_a.intersection(set_b)
set_z = set_a.difference(set_b)
```

To see the results of each math operation, type **print(f"{set_x}\n{set_y}\n{set_z}")** in a new cell and press Shift + Enter. You see one set printed on each line, like this:

```
{'Red', 'Black', 'Yellow', 'Green', 'Blue', 'Orange'}
{'Green', 'Black'}
{'Blue', 'Red'}
```

TIP

The outputs show the results of the math operations: union(), intersection(), and difference(). Python's fancier print formatting can be helpful in working with collections such as sets. The format() function tells Python which objects to place within each placeholder in the string. A *placeholder* is a set of curly brackets ({}) with an optional number. The *escape character* (essentially a kind of control or special character), \n, provides a newline character between entries. You can read more about fancy formatting at https://docs.python.org/3/tutorial/inputoutput.html.

You can also test relationships between the various sets. For example, type **set_a.issuperset(set_y)** in a cell and press Shift + Enter. The output value of True tells you that set_a is a superset of set_y. Likewise, if you type **set_a.issubset(set_x)** and press Shift + Enter, you find that set_a is a subset of set_x.

It's important to understand that sets are either mutable (changeable) or immutable (once you define them, you cannot change them). Standard Python set objects are mutable. For an immutable version, you can use frozenset. All the sets in our example are mutable, meaning you can add or remove elements from them. For example, if you type **set_a.add('Purple')** and press Shift + Enter, set_a receives a new element. If you type **set_a.issubset(set_x)** and press Shift + Enter now, you find that set_a is no longer a subset of set_x because set_a has the 'Purple' element.

Indexing Data Using Dictionaries

A *dictionary* is a special sequence that uses a key and a value pair. Using a key lets you easily access particular values with a non-numeric index.

Creating dictionaries

To create a dictionary, you enclose key and value pairs in curly brackets. Create a test dictionary by typing **my_dict = {'Orange':1, 'Blue':2, 'Pink':3}** and pressing Shift + Enter.

Storing and retrieving data

To access a particular value, you use the key as an index. For example, type **my_dict['Pink']** and press Shift + Enter to see the output value 3. Using dictionaries as data structures lets you easily access incredibly complex data sets using terms everyone can understand. In many other respects, working with a dictionary is the same as working with any other sequence.

Dictionaries do have some special features. For example, type **my_dict.keys()** and press Shift + Enter to see a view of the keys. You can use the values() function to view the values in the dictionary.

Dictionary keys are case-sensitive. Consequently, 'Pink', 'PINK', and 'pink' are different keys.

Understanding the Basics of Classes

Classes group together related attributes and methods. Attributes are variables belonging to the class. For instance, if we create a Student class to represent students enrolled in a school, you can imagine it would have attributes such as name, age, courses, and scores. Methods, on the other hand, are functions defined within the class. They can access, process, and modify the attributes of an object created from that class. For example, a method for our Student class could access the scores attribute and calculate the average score.

REMEMBER

Classes are relevant in machine learning because many key specialized packages, such as Scikit-learn (https://scikit-learn.org/stable), which is also used throughout this book for many examples, use classes to define models. Within a model's class, you pass the necessary arguments into methods and use methods for learning from data or performing predictions.

Building your first class

For example, we can create a class representing students and their scores. We set the student's name and her or his scores as attributes and a method for calculating the average score. We also define a method __init__, a set of instructions to be executed when you first instantiate the class.

```
class Student:
  def __init__(self, name, scores):
    self.name = name
    self.scores = list(scores)
    print(f"Student object created for: {self.name}")
  def calculate_average_score(self):
    return sum(self.scores) / len(self.scores)
```

Putting your first class into action

To use a class, you first instantiate it by assigning it to a variable and providing all the necessary arguments for the __init__ method:

```
alfred = Student(name="Alfred", scores=[80, 91, 78])
```

You can then run the method to calculate its average by:

```
alfred.calculate_average_score()
```

The output average score will be 83. Once instantiated, you can modify the attributes of a class by referring to the single attribute as a variable and re-assign its values. In this case, we can assign a list of four scores:

```
alfred.scores = [80, 91, 78, 95]
alfred.calculate_average_score()
```

Now the output average score is 86. Classes are powerful tools because they allow you to combine data and algorithms in a self-contained unit. As we will discover in the next chapter, machine learning libraries like Scikit-learn exclusively rely on classes to represent models. Understanding instantiation, attribute setting (parameter tuning), and method calling (fit, predict) are essential skills for practical machine learning.

3

Building the Foundations

Understanding the math used in machine learning.

Considering how machine learning processes data.

Ensuring that you get valid results from machine learning.

Avoiding common problems and pitfalls with data and models.

Chapter **7**

Demystifying the Math Behind Machine Learning

I f you want to implement existing machine learning algorithms from scratch or devise new ones, you need a good knowledge of probability, linear algebra, linear programming, and multivariable calculus. You also need to learn how to translate math into working code, which means acquiring sophisticated computing skills. If words like multivariable calculus urge you to scream and rush for the hills, take a deep breath! You don't need to be a math whiz to use machine learning effectively, but knowing the basics helps you understand what the computer is actually doing (and why it sometimes gets things wrong). This chapter begins by helping you understand the mechanics of the math behind machine learning and describes how to translate math basics into usable code.

If you want to apply machine learning for practical purposes instead, you can leverage existing Python software libraries using a basic knowledge of math and statistics. In the end, you can't avoid having some of the math skills described in this chapter because machine learning has strong roots in both math and statistics, but you don't need to overdo it. After you get some math basics, the chapter shows how even simple Bayesian principles can help you perform interesting machine learning tasks.

TIP

Even though this introductory book focuses on machine learning experiments using Python, you still find many references to vectors, matrices, variables, probabilities, and their distributions in the text. The book sometimes uses descriptive statistics as well. Consequently, it helps to know what a mean, a median, and a standard deviation are to understand what happens under the hood of the software you use. This knowledge makes it easier to learn how to use the software better. The last part of the chapter demonstrates how machine learning can help you make better predictions, even when you don't have all the information you need.

REMEMBER

You don't have to type the source code for this chapter manually. In fact, using the downloadable source code is a lot easier. You can find the source code for this chapter in the ML4D3E folder of the downloadable code file. The example files for this chapter will begin with ML4D3E-07-. See the Introduction for details on how to find these source files.

Working with Data

Machine learning is so appealing because it allows machines to learn from real-world examples (such as sales records, signals from sensors, and textual data streaming from the Internet) and determine what such data implies. Typical outputs from a machine learning algorithm are predictions of the future, prescriptions to act on now, or new knowledge in terms of examples categorized by groups. Many applications that can produce such results have already become a reality:

>> Diagnosing rare diseases

>> Discovering criminal behavior and detecting criminals in action

>> Recommending the right product to the right person

>> Filtering and classifying data from the Internet at an enormous scale

>> Driving a car autonomously

The mathematical and statistical basis of machine learning makes outputting such useful results possible. Using math and statistics in this way enables the algorithms to understand anything with a numerical basis. The following sections help you understand basic data manipulation using scalars, vectors, and matrices:

>> **Scalar:** A single base data item. For example, the number 2 shown by itself is a scalar.

- » **Vector:** A one-dimensional array (essentially a list) of data items. For example, an array containing the numbers 2, 3, 4, and 5 is a vector. You access items in a vector using a zero-based *index,* a pointer to the item you want. The item at index 0 is the first item in the vector, which is 2 in this case.

- » **Matrix:** A two-dimensional *array* (essentially a table) of data items. For example, an array containing the numbers 2, 3, 4, and 5 in the first row and 6, 7, 8, and 9 in the second row is a matrix. You access items in a matrix using a zero-based row-and-column index. The item at row 0, column 0, is the first item in the matrix, which is 2 in this case.

Other data structures you'll encounter include multidimensional arrays (three or more dimensions) and tensors (a generalized matrix with any number of dimensions). This chapter doesn't cover these specialized data structures. You use these more complicated data structures in complex data processing tasks and deep learning, which heavily rely on tensors for data representation of images and sequences of text. Instead, when using more classical machine learning, most such algorithms will expect to work just with a numeric data matrix.

Learning the terminology

To begin the process, you represent the solution to the problem as a number. For example, if you want to diagnose a disease using a machine learning algorithm, you can make the response a 1 or a 0 (a binary response) to indicate whether the person is ill, with a 1 stating simply that the person is ill. Alternatively, you can use a number between 0 and 1 to convey a less definite answer. The value can represent the probability that the person is ill, with 0 indicating that the person isn't ill and 1 indicating that the person definitely has the disease.

A machine learning algorithm can provide an answer (*predictions*) when supported by the required information (*sample data*) and an associated response (examples of the predictions that you want to be able to guess). Information can include facts, events, observations, counts, measurements, and so on. Any information used as input is a *feature* or *variable* (a term taken from statistics). This book uses the term *feature* to make reading the material more manageable and to keep code variables separate from data features. Effective features describe the values related to the response and help the algorithm guess a response using the function it creates, given similar information in other circumstances.

There are two types of features: quantitative and qualitative. *Quantitative features* are perfect for machine learning because they define values as numbers (integers, floats, counts, rankings, or other measures). *Qualitative features* are usually labels or symbols that convey useful information in a non-numeric way, a way that you can define as more human-like (words, descriptions, or concepts).

You can find a classic example of qualitative features in the paper "Induction of Decision Trees" by John Ross Quinlan (https://dl.acm.org/doi/10.1023/A:1022643204877). Quinlan was a computer scientist who contributed to the foundations of the development of decision trees. Decision trees are one of the most popular machine learning algorithms to date. In his paper, he describes a set of helpful information for deciding whether to play tennis outside, something that a machine can learn using proper techniques. The set of features described by Quinlan is as follows:

>> **Outlook:** Sunny, overcast, or rainy

>> **Temperature:** Cool, mild, hot

>> **Humidity:** High or normal

>> **Windy:** True or false

A machine learning algorithm cannot really digest such information. You must first transform the information into numbers. Many ways are available to do so, and the most common is *one-hot encoding,* which turns every feature into a new set of binary (values 0 or 1) features for all its symbolic values. It's called "one-hot" because only one feature in the group is "hot" (set to 1) at a time, while the others are "cold" (set to 0). For instance, consider using one-hot encoding on the outlook variable, which then becomes three new features: *outlook:sunny*, *outlook:overcast*, and *outlook:rainy.* Each one will have a numeric value of 1 or 0 depending on whether the implied condition is present. So when the day is sunny, outlook:sunny has a value of 1, whereas outlook:overcast and outlook:rainy both have a value of 0.

In addition to one-hot encoding, you can use a few other techniques to turn qualitative features into numbers, especially when a feature is made of words, such as a social-media post, a chunk of text from an online review, or a news feed. In the latter part of the book, you have occasion to discuss other ways to effectively transform words and concepts into meaningful numbers that are understandable by a machine learning algorithm when dealing with textual analysis.

REMEMBER

No matter what kind of information is presented, a machine learning algorithm must transform it into a number to process it correctly.

Understanding scalar and vector operations

The NumPy package provides essential functionality for Python scientific computing. To use numpy, you import it using a command such as import numpy as np. Now you can access numpy using the common two-letter abbreviation np.

REMEMBER

The NumPy library provides access to multiple specific data types for various categories of data. For example, you can choose from several integer types for numbers without decimals or various floating-point types for numbers with decimals. NumPy offers a wide assortment of types overall. Using these specific data types is crucial for scientific computing because it allows you to control for the numerical precision, the computer memory usage, and the calculation speed most suitable for your needs.

Use the array() function from NumPy to create a vector. For example, myvect = np.array([1, 2, 3, 4]) creates a vector with four elements. In this case, the vector contains standard Python integers. You can also use the arange function to produce vectors, such as myvect = np.arange(1, 10, 2), which fills myvect with array([1, 3, 5, 7, 9]). The first input tells the starting point, the second the stopping point, and the third the step between each number. As happens with slicing, the vector's values stop just before the stopping value, as is expected in Python. A fourth argument lets you define the data type for the vector. You can also create a vector with a specific data type. All you need to do is specify the data type like this: myvect = np.array([1, 2, 3, 4], dtype = np.int16) to fill myvect with the values.

In some cases, you need special numpy functions to create a vector (or a matrix) of a specific type. For example, some math tasks require that you fill the vector with ones. In this case, you use the ones() function like this: myvect = np.ones(4, dtype = np.int16) to fill myvect with ones of a specific data type like this: array([1, 1, 1, 1], dtype = int16). You can also use a zeros() function to fill a vector with zeros.

TIP

You can perform basic math functions on vectors as a whole, which makes numpy incredibly useful and less prone to errors that can occur when using programming constructs such as loops to perform the same task. For the following examples, let's have myvect to hold values from 1 to 4 by typing **myvect = np.array([1, 2, 3, 4])** and then pressing Shift + Enter. Now, you can perform some math with it. For example, entering **myvect + 1** and then pressing Shift + Enter produces an output of array([2, 3, 4, 5]). As you might expect, typing **myvect - 1** and then pressing Shift + Enter produces an output array([0, 1, 2, 3]). You can even use vectors in more complex math scenarios, such as typing

2 ** myvect and then pressing Shift + Enter, where the output is array([2, 4, 8, 16]).

As a final thought on scalar and vector operations, you can also perform both logical and comparison tasks. For example, the following code performs comparison operations on two arrays:

```
a = np.array([1, 2, 3, 4])
b = np.array([2, 2, 4, 4])

print(a == b)
print(a < b)
```

Starting with two vectors, a and b, the code checks whether the individual elements in a equal those in b. In this case, a[0] doesn't equal b[0]. However, a[1] does equal b[1]. The output is a vector of type bool that contains true or false values based on the individual comparisons. Likewise, you can check for instances when a < b and produce another vector containing the truth values in this instance. Here is the output from this example:

```
[False True False True]
[ True False True False]
```

Logical operations rely on special functions. You check the logical output of the Boolean operators AND, OR, XOR, and NOT. Here is an example of the logical functions:

```
a = np.array([True, False, True, False])
b = np.array([True, True, False, False])

print(np.logical_or(a, b))
print(np.logical_and(a, b))
print(np.logical_not(a))
print(np.logical_xor(a, b))
```

Here is the output from this example:

```
[ True True True False]
[ True False False False]
[False True False True]
[False True True False]
```

You can also use numeric input for these functions. When using numeric input, a zero is false and any non-zero value is true. As with comparisons, the functions work on an element-by-element basis even though you make just one call.

Performing vector multiplication

Adding, subtracting, or dividing vectors occurs on an element-by-element basis, as described in the previous section. However, when it comes to multiplication, things get a little odd. In fact, depending on what you really want to do, there are two types of operations. First is element-wise multiplication, where you multiply the corresponding elements of two vectors or two matrices. In NumPy, this is done using the * operator or the np.multiply() function.

However, mathematical formulas and algorithms involving linear algebra, for instance, do not work with element-wise multiplication but instead need the dot product, which is the sum of the products of two number sequences. To obtain a dot product in NumPy, you use the .dot() method of a NumPy array, the @ operator, or the np.dot() function.

WARNING

Confusing these two types of multiplication is a common error. Using element-wise multiplication when the underlying algorithm requires a dot product will lead to incorrect results.

REMEMBER

When working with vectors, the dot product is always the sum of the individual element-by-element multiplications, and it results in a single number. For example, if you define myvect = np.array([1, 2, 3, 4]) by typing it in a cell and then pressing Shift + Enter, then myvect.dot(myvect) results in an output of 30. If you perform element-wise multiplication and then sum the results, you will find that they do indeed add up to 30.

Creating a matrix

After you make all the data numeric, the machine learning algorithm requires that you turn the individual features into a matrix of features and the individual responses into a vector or a matrix (when there are multiple responses). A *matrix* is a collection of numbers arranged in rows and columns, much like the squares in a chessboard. However, unlike a chessboard, which is always square, matrices can have a different number of rows and columns.

By convention, a matrix used for machine learning relies on rows to represent examples and columns to represent features. So, as in the example for learning the best weather conditions to play tennis, you would construct a matrix that uses a new row for each day and columns containing the different values for outlook, temperature, humidity, and wind. Typically, you represent a matrix as a series of numbers enclosed by square brackets, as shown here:

$$X = \begin{bmatrix} 1.1 & 1 & 545 & 1 \\ 4.6 & 0 & 345 & 2 \\ 7.2 & 1 & 754 & 3 \end{bmatrix}$$

In this example, the matrix called X contains three rows and four columns, so you can say that the matrix has dimensions of 3 by 4 (also written as 3 x 4). To quote the number of the rows in a formula, you commonly use the letter n. Instead, you use the letter m for the number of columns. Knowing the size of a matrix is fundamental for correctly operating on it.

Operating on a matrix also requires being able to retrieve a number or a portion of a matrix for specific calculations. You use *indexes,* numbers that tell the position of an element in a matrix to perform this task. Indexes point out the row and column number that correspond to the location of a value of interest. Usually, you use i for the row index and j for the column index. Depending on the programming language you use, both i and j indexes start counting rows and columns may begin with the number 0 (*0-indexed*) or 1(*1-indexed*). Python matrices are usually 0-indexed. The use of different index starting points can prove confusing, so you need to know how the language you use operates.

When viewing the example matrix, the element 1,2 is the element located in the second row intersecting with the third column; that is, 345. Therefore, if you need to express three different elements of matrix X, you can use the following notation:

```
X[0,0] = 1.1, X[1,2] = 345, X[2,3] = 3
```

Sometimes multiple matrices are stacked in slices of a more complex data structure called an *array.* In this context, an array is a collection of numeric data having more than two dimensions, although developers may use the term *array* in various ways, such as when referring to a vector and matrix earlier in the chapter. As an example of this use, you can have three-dimensional arrays where each matrix represents a different time frame, and the matrices are then stacked together as the slices of a cake. A case for such an array happens when you continuously record medical data, perhaps from a scanner recording body functions such as brain activity. In this case, rows are still examples and columns are features — with the third dimension representing time.

A matrix that has a single feature is a special case called a vector, as discussed in "Understanding scalar and vector operations" earlier in this chapter. You mostly use vectors when talking about response values (*response vector*) or when dealing with the internal coefficients of some algorithms. In this case, you call them a *vector of coefficients.*

In machine learning, the matrix of features usually appears as X and the corresponding vector of responses as y. More generally, matrices usually use a capital letter, and vectors use a lowercase letter for identification. In addition, you use lowercase letters for constants, so you need to exercise care when determining whether a letter is a vector or a constant because the set of possible operations is quite different.

You use matrices in machine learning quite often because they allow you to rapidly organize, index, and retrieve large amounts of data in a uniform and meaningful way. For every example i in the X feature matrix, you can then determine the i-th row of the matrix expressing its features and the i-th element on the response vector telling you the results that a specific set of features implies. This strategy allows the algorithm to look up data and make product predictions quickly.

Matrix notation also allows you to perform systematic operations on the entire matrix or portions of it quickly. Matrices are also useful for writing and executing programs in a speedy way because you can use computer commands to execute matrix operations.

Understanding basic operations

The basic matrix operations are addition, subtraction, and scalar multiplication. Addition and subtraction are possible only when you have two matrices of the same size, and the result is a new matrix of the same dimensions. In fact, you apply the operation to each corresponding position in the two matrices. Therefore, to perform addition, you start summing the values in the first row and first column of the two source matrices and place the resulting value in the same position in the resulting matrix. You continue the process for each paired element in the two matrices until you complete all the operations. The same process holds true for subtraction, as shown in the following example:

```
a = np.array([[1, 1], [1, 0]])
b = np.array([[1, 0], [0, 1]])
c = a - b

print(c)
```

The output, in this case, is:

```
[[ 0  1]
 [ 1 -1]]
```

In scalar multiplication, you instead take a single numeric value (the *scalar*) and multiply it by each element in the matrix. If your value is fractional, such as ½ or ¼, your multiplication becomes equivalent to a division. In the previous example, you can multiply the resulting matrix by −2 using `print(c * -2)` with a result of:

```
[[ 0 -2]
 [-2  2]]
```

You can also perform scalar addition and subtraction. In this case, you add or subtract a single value from all the elements of a matrix.

Performing matrix multiplication

Using indexes and basic matrix operations, you can express quite a few operations in a compact way. The combination of indexes and operations allows you to

» Slice a part of a matrix

» Mask a part of the matrix, reducing it to zero

» Center the values of a matrix by removing a value from all elements

» Rescale the values of a matrix, changing its range of values

However, you can achieve the largest number of operations at one time only when you multiply a matrix against a vector or against another matrix. You perform these tasks often in machine learning, and multiplying a matrix by a vector occurs frequently. Many machine learning algorithms rely on finding a vector of coefficients that, multiplied by the matrix of features, can result in an approximation of the vector of response values. In such models, you have formulations like this:

```
y = Xb
```

where y is the response vector, X is the feature matrix, and b is a vector of coefficients. Often, the algorithm also includes a scalar named a to add to the result. In this example, you can imagine it as being zero, so it isn't present. As a result, y is a vector constituted by three elements:

```
[ 2 -2 3]
```

With this in mind, you can express the multiplication between X and b as

```
X = np.array([[4, 5], [2, 4], [3, 3]])
b = [3, -2]

print(X @ b)
```

Next, you need to know how X multiplied by b can result in y. As a check of being able to perform the multiplication, the matrix and the vector involved in the multiplication should have compatible sizes. In fact, the number of columns of the matrix should equal the number of rows in the vector. In this case, there is a match because X is 3 by 2 and b is 2 by 1. Knowing the shapes of the terms, you can figure out in advance the shape of the resulting matrix, which is given by the rows of the matrix and the columns of the vector, or 3 by 1.

Matrix vector multiplication works as a series of summed vector-vector multiplications. Multiplication treats each row of the X matrix as a vector and multiplies it by the b vector. The result becomes the corresponding row element of the resulting vector. For instance, the dot product of the first row [4, 5] and the vector [3, −2] is (4 * 3) + (5 * −2), resulting in the sum 12-10 whose final result is the value of 2. This first summed multiplication corresponds to the first row of the resulting vector, and then all the other calculations follow:

```
sum([4*3, 5*-2]) = 2
sum([2*3, 4*-2]) = -2
sum([3*3, 3*-2]) = 3
```

The resulting vector is [2, −2, 3]. Things get a little bit trickier when multiplying two matrices, but you can perform the operation as a series of matrix-vector multiplications, just as in the previous example, by viewing the second matrix as a series of feature vectors. By multiplying the first matrix by the m vectors, you obtain a single column of the resulting matrix for each multiplication.

An example can clarify the steps in a matrix-by-matrix multiplication. The following example multiplies X by B, which is a square matrix 2 x 2:

```
B = np.array([[3, -2], [-2, 5]])

print(X @ B)
```

You can divide the operation into two distinct matrix/vector multiplications by splitting the matrix B into column vectors.

$$\begin{bmatrix} 4 & 5 \\ 2 & 4 \\ 3 & 3 \end{bmatrix} \begin{bmatrix} 3 \\ -2 \end{bmatrix} = \begin{bmatrix} 2 \\ -2 \\ 3 \end{bmatrix}$$

$$\begin{bmatrix} 4 & 5 \\ 2 & 4 \\ 3 & 3 \end{bmatrix} \begin{bmatrix} -2 \\ 5 \end{bmatrix} = \begin{bmatrix} 17 \\ 16 \\ 9 \end{bmatrix}$$

Now all you have to do is take the resulting column vectors and use them to rebuild the output matrix using the multiplication of the first column vector as the first column in the new matrix, and so on.

$$XB = \begin{bmatrix} 4 & 5 \\ 2 & 4 \\ 3 & 3 \end{bmatrix} \begin{bmatrix} 3 & -2 \\ -2 & 5 \end{bmatrix} = \begin{bmatrix} 2 & 17 \\ -2 & 16 \\ 3 & 9 \end{bmatrix}$$

REMEMBER

In matrix multiplication, because of matrix shapes, order matters. Consequently, you cannot commute terms as you would in a multiplication of scalar numbers. Multiplying 5*2 or 2*5 is the same thing because of the commutative property of scalar multiplication, but XB is not the same as BX because sometimes the multiplication isn't possible (because the shapes of the matrices are incompatible) or, worse, it produces a different result. When you have a series of matrix multiplications, such as ABC, the order of the operations doesn't matter; whether you go with AB first or BC first, you get the same result because, like scalars, matrix multiplication is associative.

Glancing at advanced matrix operations

You may encounter two important matrix operations in some algorithm formulations. They are the transpose and inverse of a matrix. *Transposition* occurs when a matrix of shape n x m is transformed into a matrix m x n by exchanging the rows with the columns. Most texts indicate this operation using the superscript T, as in A^T. You see this operation used most often for multiplication in order to obtain the right dimensions. When working with Python, you use code like this to perform a transposition:

```
a = np.array([[1, 2, 3], [2, 3, 5], [7, 11, 13]])
print(a.transpose())
```

The output shows the transposition:

```
[[ 1  2  7]
 [ 2  3 11]
 [ 3  5 13]]
```

You apply *matrix inversion* to matrices of shape m x m, which are square matrices that have the same number of rows and columns. This operation is quite important because it allows the immediate resolution of equations involving matrix multiplication, such as y = Xb, where you have to discover the values in the vector b. As most scalar numbers (exceptions include zero) have a number whose multiplication results in a value of 1 (called a reciprocal), many square matrices have an inverse matrix whose multiplication will result in a special matrix called the identity matrix. An identity matrix is a matrix whose elements are zero, except for the diagonal elements (the elements in positions where the index i is equal to the index j), which are ones. Finding the inverse of a scalar is quite easy (the scalar number n has an inverse of n^{-1} that is 1/n). It's a different story for a matrix. Matrix inversion involves quite a large number of computations, so special math functions perform the calculations in Python. The inverse of matrix A is indicated as A^{-1}. You use the following code to invert a matrix:

```
print(np.linalg.inv(a))
```

The output shows the inverted matrix:

```
[[-3.2  1.4  0.2]
 [ 1.8 -1.6  0.2]
 [ 0.2  0.6 -0.2]]
```

REMEMBER

Sometimes, finding the inverse of a matrix is impossible. When a matrix cannot be inverted, it is referred to as a *singular matrix* or a *degenerate matrix*. Singular matrices aren't the norm. However, when they occur, they cause problems.

Using vectorization effectively

If performing matrix operations, such as matrix by vector multiplication, seems a bit hard, consider that your computer does all the work. In Python, the NumPy package has all the functionality needed to create and manipulate matrices. The ndarray objects allow fast creation of an array, such as a multidimensional matrix, by starting with data queued into lists.

TIP

The term *ndarray* means "n-dimensional array," implying that you can create arrays of multiple dimensions, not just row-by-column matrices. Using a simple list, ndarray can quickly create a 1D array, as shown in the Python example here:

```
y = np.array([44, 21, 37])
print(y)
print(y.shape)
```

```
[44 21 37]
(3,)
```

The method `shape` can promptly inform you about the shape of a matrix. In this case, it reports only three rows and no columns, which means that the object is a 1D array.

To create matrices made of rows and columns, you can use a list of lists. The contents of the lists inside the main list are the rows of your matrix. Here's an example:

```
X = np.array([[1.1, 1, 545, 1],[4.6, 0, 345, 2],
              [7.2, 1, 754, 3]])
print(X)

[[   1.1    1.    545.     1. ]
 [   4.6    0.    345.     2. ]
 [   7.2    1.    754.     3. ]]
```

You can also obtain the same result by using a single list, which creates a 1D array that you can reshape into the desired number of rows and columns. Numbers are filled into the new matrix row by row, starting from the element (0,0) down to the last one, like this:

```
X = np.array([1.1, 1, 545, 1, 4.6, 0, 345, 2,
              7.2, 1, 754, 3]).reshape(3, 4)
```

Once your data is structured into NumPy arrays, you can finally unlock the power of vectorization. This means you can apply mathematical operations, such as addition, subtraction, multiplication, division, or even more complex functions, directly to these entire arrays. NumPy handles all the sequences of operations at once using low-level optimized code much faster than you could achieve using standard Python loops and operations. This vectorization is crucial to achieve the highest possible performance in the numerical tasks required by machine learning algorithms.

Exploring the World of Probabilities

Probability tells you the likelihood of an event, and you express it as a number. It is your mathematical tool for dealing with "maybe." It ranges from 0 (nope, not happening) to 1 (absolutely, definitely happening), with lots of "might happen" in between. Intermediate values, such as 0.25, 0.5, and 0.75, say that the event will tendentially happen with a specific frequency. The following sections describe probability in more detail.

Getting an overview of probability

If you multiply the probability by an integer number representing the number of trials you're going to try, you'll get an estimate of how many times an event should happen on average if all the trials are tried. For instance, if you have an event occurring with probability p = 0.25 and you try 100 times, you're likely to witness that event happen 0.25 * 100 = 25 times. This is, for example, the probability of picking a certain suit when choosing a card randomly from a deck of cards. French playing cards make a classic example of explaining probabilities. The deck contains 52 cards equally divided into four suits: clubs and spades, which are black, and diamonds and hearts, which are red. Hence, if you want to determine the probability of picking an ace, you must consider that there are four aces of different suits. The answer in terms of probability is p = 4/52 = 0.077.

REMEMBER

Probabilities are between 0 and 1; no probability can exceed such boundaries. You define probabilities empirically from observations. Simply count the number of times a specific event happens with respect to all the events that interest you. For example, say that you want to calculate the probability of how many times fraud happens when doing banking transactions or how many times people get a certain disease in a particular country. After witnessing the event, you can estimate the probability associated with it by counting the number of times the event occurs and dividing by the total number of events.

You can count the number of times the fraud or the disease happens using recorded data (mostly taken from databases) and then divide that figure by the total number of generic events or observations available. Therefore, you divide the number of frauds by the number of transactions in a year, or you count the number of people who fell ill during the year with respect to the population of a certain area. The result is a number ranging from 0 to 1, which you can use as your baseline probability for a certain event given certain circumstances.

REMEMBER

Counting all the occurrences of an event is not always possible, so you need to know about sampling. By *sampling,* which is an act based on certain probability expectations, you can observe a small part of a larger set of events or objects, yet be able to infer correct probabilities for an event, as well as exact measures such as quantitative measurements or qualitative classes related to a set of objects.

For instance, if you want to track the sales of cars in the United States for the last month, you don't need to track every sale in the country. Using a sample comprising the sales from a few car sellers around the country, you can determine quantitative measures, such as the average price of a car sold, or qualitative measures, such as the car model sold most often.

Operating on probabilities

Operations on probabilities are indeed a bit different from numeric operations. Because they always have to be in the range of 0 to 1, you must rely on particular rules in order for the operation to make sense. For example, summations between probabilities are possible if the events are *mutually exclusive* (they can't happen together). Say that you want to know the probability of drawing a spade or a diamond from a deck of cards. You can sum the probability of drawing a spade and the probability of drawing a diamond this way: p = 0.25 + 0.25 = 0.5.

You use subtraction (difference) to determine the probability of events that are different from the probability of an event that you have already computed. For instance, to determine the probability of drawing a card that isn't a diamond from the deck, you just subtract from the probability of drawing any kind of card, which is p = 1, the probability of drawing a diamond, like so: p = 1 – 0.25 = 0.75. You get the *complement* of a probability when you subtract a probability from 1.

Multiplication helps you compute the intersection of independent events. *Independent events* are events that do not influence each other. For instance, if you play a game of dice and you throw two dice, the probability of getting two sixes is 1/6 (the probability of getting six from the first die) multiplied by 1/6 (the probability of getting six from the second die), which is p = 1/6 * 1/6 = 0.028. This means that if you throw the dice one hundred times, you can expect two sixes to come up only two or three times. Note that you can use simple math in Python to perform these sorts of calculations (just make sure you use parentheses to ensure order of calculation as needed): `Sixes = (1/6) * (1/6)`.

Using summation, difference, and multiplication, you can get the probability of most complex situations dealing with events. For instance, you can now compute the probability of getting at least one six from two thrown dice, which is a summation of mutually exclusive events:

>> The probability of having two sixes: `(1/6) * (1/6) = 1/36`

>> The probability of having a six on the first die and something other than a six on the second one: `(1/6) * (1 - (1/6)) = 5/36`

>> The probability of having a six on the second die and something other than a six on the first one: `(1 - (1/6)) * (1/6) = 5/36`

Your probability of getting at least one six from two thrown dice is 1/36 + 5/36 + 5/36 = 11/36. In this case, the chance of getting a six from the first die is 1/6, and the chance of getting a six from the second die is 1/6, but the likelihood of at least one of the two being a six is the summation of the likelihood of different possible outcomes, which results in 11/36.

Conditioning chance by Bayes' theorem

Probability makes sense in terms of time and space, but some other conditions also influence the probability you measure. The context is important. When you estimate the probability of an event, you may (sometimes wrongly) tend to believe that you can apply the probability you calculated to each possible situation. The term to express this belief is *a priori probability,* meaning the general probability of an event.

For example, when you toss a coin, if the coin is fair, the *a priori* probability of a head is 50 percent. No matter how many times you toss the coin, when faced with a new toss, the probability for heads is still 50 percent.

WARNING

The coin toss is an example of a situation in which the true probability isn't calculated. If the toss is truly fair, there is a chance, albeit an incredibly small one, that the coin will land on its edge — neither heads nor tails. When performing a probability calculation, you must consider whether to include conditions of this sort to obtain a more precise answer.

However, there are other situations in which, if you change the context, the *a priori* probability is not valid anymore because something subtle happened and changed it. In this case, you can express this belief as an *a posteriori* probability, which is the *a priori* probability after something happened to modify the count. For instance, the *a priori* probability of a person being female is roughly 50 percent.

For instance, the *a priori* probability of rain on any given day in a particular city may be calculated as 10 percent based on historical observations. However, this probability changes significantly if we introduce new information, such as that on days when a significant drop in barometric pressure is recorded, the *a posteriori* probability of rain occurring within the next few hours may jump to 70 percent (or some other elevated value). As another example, consider a factory producing components. The *a priori* probability of any single component being defective may be 0.5 percent. But, if we examine only the components produced by a specific machine that is known to require more frequent calibration, the *a posteriori* probability of a defect for a component from that machine may be 2 percent. Therefore, given these specific contexts (a falling barometer reading, isolating output from a specific machine), the *a posteriori* probability differs from the general *a priori* one.

Natural atmospheric conditions or specific operational factors can both create a different *a posteriori* probability.

You can view such a case as a *conditional probability* and express it as p(y|x), which is read as *the probability of event y happening given that x has happened.* Conditional probabilities are a very powerful tool for machine learning. In fact, if the *a priori* probability can change so much because of certain circumstances, knowing the possible circumstances can boost your chances of correctly predicting an event by observing examples — exactly what machine learning is intended to do. For instance, one possible example to demonstrate the importance of previous circumstances (a priori probabilities) could be related to the probability of a person being a student based on whether they carry a backpack. Assume that in the general population, 30 percent of people use a backpack, while among students, who amount to 20 percent of the population, 90 percent carry a backpack. If you encounter a person who is carrying a backpack, based on a priori probabilities, a machine learning algorithm can benefit from that information in determining the a posteriori probability that the encountered person is a student.

In fact, the Naïve Bayes' algorithm can boost the chance of making a correct prediction by knowing the circumstances surrounding the prediction, as explained in Chapter 10, which covers the first, simplest learners. Everything starts with Reverend Bayes and his revolutionary theorem of probabilities. Reverend Thomas Bayes was a statistician and philosopher who formulated his theorem during the first half of the 18th century. The theorem was never published while he was alive. When published, it revolutionized the theory of probability by introducing the idea of conditional probability. The foundations of the theorem aren't all that complicated, although they may look a bit counterintuitive. The idea is that you can update your initial beliefs regarding the likelihood of an event, the so-called prior probability, by using some evidence and arrive at more refined estimates, the posterior probability.

While the theorem dates back to the mid-18th century and had some first applications in the 19th century, its popularity is indeed recent. This is highlighted by the fact that one of the machine learning tribes (see Chapter 2) is named after Reverend Bayes. There also remains considerable interest and research focused on developing learning algorithms using Bayesian probability. Although much recent attention and research have focused on deep neural networks, particularly in computer vision and natural language processing, Bayesian methods are still used and studied for their interpretability and effectiveness in uncertainty estimation, even when working with smaller datasets.

Thanks to Bayes' theorem, estimations nowadays, such as predicting the probability of a person being a student, become easier thanks to additional information, such as the simple fact that a person carries a backpack. The formula used by Thomas Bayes proves quite useful in doing so:

```
P(B|E) = P(E|B) * P(B) / P(E)
```

Reading the formula using the previous example as input can provide a better understanding of an otherwise counterintuitive formula:

- » **P(B|E):** The probability of a belief (B) given a set of evidence (E) is known as the posterior probability. *Belief* is an alternative way to express a *hypothesis.* In this case, the hypothesis is that a person is a student, and the evidence is the backpack. Given the evidence, knowing the probability of such a belief can help predict with some confidence.

- » **P(E|B):** The probability of carrying a backpack if you are a student. That's the likelihood of the evidence in the subgroup, which is itself a conditional probability. In this case, the figure is 90 percent, which translates to a value of 0.9 in the formula.

- » **P(B):** The general probability of being a student; that is, the *a priori* probability of the belief. In this case, the probability is 20 percent or a value of 0.2.

- » **P(E):** The general probability of carrying a backpack. Here, it is another *a priori* probability related to the observed evidence. In these calculations, it is a 30 percent probability, which is a value of 0.30. This is known as the probability of the evidence.

If you solve the previous problem of determining if the seen person is a student using the Bayes' formula and the values you have singled out, the result is `0.9 * 0.2 / 0.3 = 0.6`. This represents an increase in probability from the initial prior probability of 20 percent. A machine learning algorithm, given this evidence, may classify the person as a student, as it has a higher probability (60 percent) of being correct than incorrect (40 percent).

Get ready for a classic example that often tricks people's brains a little and is routinely found in textbooks and scientific magazines — the positive medical test example. It perfectly demonstrates why Bayesian methods are powerful, even if they initially feel weird and make you raise some eyebrows. The example will better explain how prior and posterior probabilities may change a lot under different circumstances.

Say that you're worried that you have a rare disease experienced by 1 percent of the population. You take the test, and the results are positive. Medical tests are never perfectly accurate, and the laboratory tells you that when you are ill, the test is positive in 99 percent of cases. In contrast, when you are healthy, the test will be negative in 99 percent of the cases. Now, using these figures, you immediately believe that you're undoubtedly ill, given the high percentage of positive tests when a person is ill (99 percent). However, the reality is quite different. In this case, the figures to plug into the Bayes' theorem are as follows:

>> 0.99 as P(E|B), the probability of a positive test when ill

>> 0.01 as P(B), the probability of being ill

We would also need the total probability of getting a positive test P(E) to complete the Bayes' formula. However, because these are the only two ways a positive test can occur, P(E) can be found as the sum of the probabilities of two mutually exclusive situations:

>> The person is ill and tests positive, which can be found by multiplying the probability of someone being ill with the probability of a positive test when ill: $0.01 * 0.99 = 0.0099$.

>> The person is not ill (probability P(Not B) = 1 – P(B) = 0.99) and tests positive (probability P(E|Not B) = 1 – P(Negative|Not B) = 1 – 0.99 = 0.01). This occurs with probability P(Not B) * P(E|Not B) = 0.99 * 0.01 = 0.0099.

By summing these probabilities, you get the probability of testing positive, P(E), no matter whether the person is ill or not: $0.0099 + 0.0099 = 0.0198$.

The calculations of the formula are then $0.99 * 0.01 / 0.0198 = 0.5$, which corresponds to just a 50 percent probability that you're ill. In the end, your chances of being healthy, despite the positive test, are higher than you might have initially expected. You may wonder how this is possible. The fact is that the number of people seeing a positive response from the test is as follows:

>> **Who is ill and gets the correct answer from the test:** This group is the *true positives,* and it amounts to 99 percent of the 1 percent of the population who gets the illness.

>> **Who isn't ill and gets the wrong answer from the test:** This group is the 1 percent false positive rate applied to the 99 percent of the population who are healthy. Again, this is a multiplication of 99 percent and 1 percent. This group corresponds to the *false positives.*

If you look at the problem using this perspective, it becomes evident why, when limiting the context to people who get a positive response to the test, the probability of being in the group of the true positives is the same as that of being in the group of false positives.

Describing the Use of Statistics

As a concluding topic related to probability, it's important to skim through some basic statistical concepts related to probability and statistics and understand how they can better help you describe the information used by machine learning algorithms. Previous sections discuss probability in ways that come in handy because sampling, statistical distributions, and statistical descriptive measures are all, in one way or another, based on concepts of probability.

Here, the matter is not simply about how to describe an event by counting its occurrences; it's about describing an event without counting all the times it occurs in a reliable way. For example, if you want an algorithm to learn how to detect a disease or criminal intent, you have to face the fact that you can't create a matrix comprising all the occurrences of the disease or the crime so the information that you'll elaborate will be necessarily partial. Moreover, if you measure something in the real world, you often don't get the exact measurements because of some error in the procedure, imprecision in the instrument you use, or simply because of a random nuisance disturbing the process of recording the measure. A simple measure such as your weight, for example, will differ every time you get on the scale, slightly oscillating around what you believe to be your true weight. If you were to take this measurement on a larger scale, such as by weighing all the people who live in your city on one huge scale, you could get a picture of how difficult it is to measure accurately (because error occurs) and completely (because it is difficult to measure everything).

Having partial information, especially if what you want to describe is quite complex and variegated, isn't an entirely negative condition because you can use smaller matrices and run fewer computations. Sometimes, you can't even get a sample of what you want to describe and learn for specific problems because the event is complex and has a great variety of features. As another example, consider learning how to determine sentiment from a text taken from the Internet, such as from social media posts. Apart from reposts, you're unlikely to see an identical post (expressing the same sentiment using precisely the same words for precisely the same topic) by another person in a lifetime. You may happen to see something similar but never identical. Therefore, it's impossible to know all the possible posts that associate certain words with sentiments in advance. In short, you have to use a sample and derive general rules from a partial set.

Even given such practical restrictions and the impossibility of getting all the possible data, you can still grasp what you want to describe and learn from it. Sampling is a part of the statistical practice. When using samples, you choose your examples according to specific criteria, granting a certain probability that your partial view resembles the global view well.

In statistics, *population* refers to everything you want to measure, and a *sample* is a part of it chosen by certain criteria. Using random sampling, which is picking the events or objects to represent randomly, helps create a set of examples for machine learning to learn, as it would learn from all the possible examples. The sample works because the value distributions in the sample are similar to those in the population, and that's enough.

TIP
Random sampling isn't the only possible approach. You can also apply *stratified sampling,* through which you can control some aspects of the random sample in order to avoid picking too many or too few events of a certain kind. After all, random is random, and you have no absolute assurance of always replicating the exact distribution of the population.

A *distribution* is a statistical formulation describing how to observe an event or a measure by telling you the probability of witnessing a certain value. Distributions are described in mathematical formulas and can be graphically described using charts such as histograms or distribution plots. The information you put into your matrix has different distributions on rows and columns. And some distributions may be related to each other. A distribution naturally implies a variation, and it is important to figure out the center of variation, which is often the statistical mean.

The *mean* is calculated by summing all your values and dividing the sum by the number of values you considered. It is a descriptive measure, telling you the value to expect the most, considering all the possible cases. It is also best suited for a symmetrical and bell-shaped distribution so that when values are above the mean, the distribution is similarly shaped as for the values below it. A famous distribution, the normal or Gaussian distribution, is shaped just like that, but in the real world, you can also find many skewed distributions that have extreme values only on one side of the distribution, thereby influencing the mean too much.

The *median* is a measure that takes the value in the middle after you order all your observations from the smallest to the largest. Because it is based on the value order, the median is insensitive to values in the distribution and can represent a fairer descriptor than the mean in certain cases. For instance, the median doesn't care if one billionaire walks into a room full of people with average incomes; it still points to the middle person. The mean, however, would suddenly think everyone in the room is rich!

The significance of the mean and median descriptors is that they describe a value in the distribution around which there is a variation, and machine learning algorithms do care about such variation. Most people refer to such variation as *variance.* There is also a root equivalent to variance, termed the *standard deviation.* Machine learning considers the variance in every single variable (*univariate distributions*) and in all features together (*multivariate distributions*) to determine how much variation impacts the response. In other words, statistics matter in machine learning because they convey that features have a distribution, which implies variation. Variation is like a measure of information — the more variance in your features. This information can be matched to the response to draw a rule from certain types of information to specific responses. You can then use statistics to assess the quality of your feature matrix and even leverage statistical measures to build machine learning algorithms, as discussed later in the book, where matrix operations, statistics, and probability all contribute to solutions and enable computers to effectively learn from data.

Chapter **8**

Descending the Gradient

achine learning may appear as some kind of magic to any newcomer to the discipline. That's something to be expected from any application of advanced scientific discovery. Arthur C. Clarke, the futurist and author of popular sci-fi stories (one of which became the landmark movie *2001: A Space Odyssey)*, stated when he wrote his third law of future prediction: "*Any sufficiently advanced technology is indistinguishable from magic.*" However, machine learning isn't magic at all. The design and development of mathematical formulations and algorithms allow computers to learn.

Assuming the world can be represented by mathematical and statistical formulations, machine learning algorithms strive to learn about such formulations by inferring them from a limited number of observations. Just as you don't need to see all the trees in the world to learn to recognize one (because humans can understand the distinguishing characteristics of trees), so machine learning algorithms can use the computational power of computers and the wide availability of data about everything to learn how to solve a large number of essential and impactful problems.

Although machine learning is inherently complex, humans devised it, and in its initial inception, it simply mimicked how we learn from the world. We can express simple data problems and basic learning algorithms based on how a child perceives and understands the world, or solve a challenging optimization problem by using, in a mathematical form, the analogy of descending from the top of a mountain by taking the proper slope. This chapter helps you understand machine learning as a technology rather than as magic. To that end, the following sections offer some basic theories and then discuss some demonstrative examples.

Acknowledging Different Kinds of Learning

Learning comes in many different flavors, depending on the algorithm and its objectives. You can divide machine learning algorithms into three main groups based on their purpose:

» Supervised learning

» Unsupervised learning

» Reinforcement learning

Supervised learning

Supervised learning occurs when an algorithm learns from example data and an associated target response made of numeric values or string labels, such as classes or tags. The data consists of *features,* which are informative variables or attributes of numeric and non-numeric data, each one representing a characteristic of the problem. Associated with the features is a *response* (or outcome), which is the solution to be learned.

After seeing enough of the data, the algorithm learns to predict the correct response when later presented with new examples. The supervised approach is indeed similar to human learning under the supervision of a teacher. The teacher provides good examples for the student to memorize, and the student then derives general rules from these specific examples.

REMEMBER

In machine learning, you're the teacher who sets up the data for solving a problem. You can imagine that you are preparing some flashcards or notes (the examples) for your student. Your student is the algorithm, usually referred to as a *predictor* or a *model.* Actually, your student is eager to learn (hopefully, it pays more attention than we did in high school geometry lessons!); however, it is a bit clueless at the beginning. It takes time and many examples before it can finally get the lesson learned (how to classify or predict) and be ready for the test examination (predicting new data).

The learning process is commonly indicated using the term *training*. Moreover, you must distinguish between regression problems, whose target is a numeric value, and classification problems, whose target is a qualitative variable, such as a class or a tag. Referring to the examples used in the book, a regression task determines the average prices of houses in an area, and a classification task distinguishes between types of animal or vegetable species based on their physical measures.

Unsupervised learning

Unsupervised learning occurs when an algorithm learns from plain examples without any associated response, leaving it to the algorithm to determine the data patterns on its own. It's like dumping a giant box of colorful toy bricks on the floor without any instructions and seeing the algorithm start sorting them by color and size because it thinks this is a reasonable thing to do. Unsupervised learning can find a structure even if you didn't explicitly point it out. This type of algorithm tends to restructure the data into something else, such as new data features that may represent a class or some new values helpful for additional analysis or for training a predictive model.

Unsupervised learning is useful in providing humans with insights into the meaning of data and new useful inputs to supervised machine learning algorithms. As a kind of learning, it resembles the methods humans use to figure out that particular objects or events are from the same class, such as by observing the degree of similarity between objects. A common example of an unsupervised learning algorithm is segmentation or cluster analysis, a technique that helps you partition a set of examples into similar groups.

Reinforcement learning

Reinforcement learning occurs when the algorithm interacts with an environment, receiving observations that lack explicit labels. However, the algorithm receives positive (a reward) or negative (a penalty) feedback based on the answers in response to those observations. Reinforcement learning is connected to applications for which the algorithm must make decisions (so the product is prescriptive, not just descriptive, as in unsupervised learning), and the decisions bear consequences. On the positive side, the approach is experiencing growing popularity because it helps complex models, such as large language models, to align with our rules and expectations. On the negative side, it is really difficult to apply reinforcement learning properly, much more difficult than using supervised learning. In fact, algorithms under reinforcement learning will often try to hack their way to rewards in unexpected ways and fool your attempts to tame them (this is called *reward hacking*).

Think of reinforcement learning like training a puppy. Predicting correctly gets a "Good dog!" and a pat on the head and maybe a biscuit (reward). Messing up gets a "No! Bad algorithm, no biscuit!" (penalty) — metaphorically speaking, of course — but pay attention, the puppy may prove smarter than you and trick you along the way.

An interesting example of reinforcement learning occurs when computers learn to play video games by themselves. In this case, an application presents the algorithm with examples of specific situations, such as having the gamer stuck in a maze while avoiding an enemy. The application lets the algorithm know the outcome of actions it takes, and learning occurs while trying to avoid what it discovers to be dangerous and to pursue survival. You can have a look at how the company DeepMind has created a reinforcement learning program that plays old Atari video games at `https://www.youtube.com/watch?v=V1eYniJ0Rnk`. When watching the video, notice how the program is initially clumsy and unskilled but steadily improves with training until it becomes a champion.

The Learning Process

Even though supervised, unsupervised, and reinforcement learning present different learning approaches, all machine learning algorithms share the same underlying idea. The central idea is that you can represent reality using a mathematical function that the algorithm doesn't know in advance but can guess after seeing some data. You can express reality and all its challenging complexity in terms of unknown mathematical functions that machine learning algorithms aim to discover and utilize. This concept is the core idea for all kinds of machine learning algorithms. This chapter focuses on supervised classification as the most emblematic of all the learning types and provides explanations of its inner functioning that you can extend later to other types of learning approaches.

The objective of a supervised classifier is to assign a class (also called a *label*) to an example after having examined some characteristics of the example itself. Such characteristics are called *features* and can be either *quantitative* (numeric values) or *qualitative* (non-numeric values such as string labels). To assign classes correctly, the classifier must first closely examine a certain number of known examples (examples that already have a class assigned to them), each one accompanied by the same features. This learning procedure, also called the *training phase,* involves the observation of many examples and their labels by the classifier that helps it learn so that it can provide an answer in terms of a class when it sees an example without a class later at prediction time.

Both the data you use for the training phase and the data you use to make new predictions using your trained model, the phase called *testing,* should share the exact same features you used during training. Otherwise, the predictions will not work correctly.

Mapping an unknown function

To give an idea of what happens in the training process, imagine a child learning to distinguish trees from other objects. Before the child can do so independently, a teacher presents the child with a certain number of tree images, complete with all the facts that make a tree distinguishable from other objects in the world. Such facts could be features such as its material (wood), its parts (trunk, branches, leaves or needles, roots), and location (planted into the soil). The child produces an idea of what a tree looks like by contrasting the display of tree features with the images of other different objects, such as pieces of furniture that are made of wood but do not share other characteristics with a tree.

A machine learning classifier works the same. It builds its cognitive capabilities by creating a mathematical formulation, incorporating the given features, that defines a function capable of distinguishing one class from another. Assume that a specific mathematical formulation, also called a *target function,* exists to express the characteristics of a tree. In such a case, a machine learning classifier could devise a function as a replica or as an approximation (something that works alike) of the target function. Being capable of expressing such a mathematical formulation is the *representation capability* of the classifier.

The underlying actual function we are trying to model by the representation process in machine learning is typically called the *target function.* In addition, from a mathematical perspective, you can express the representation process in machine learning using the equivalent term *mapping.* Mapping happens when you discover the function that fully (or best) matches given inputs with expected outputs. A successful mapping means the algorithm has learned such a relationship.

Such a representation (abstract rules derived from real-world facts) is possible because the learning algorithm has many internal parameters (constituted of vectors and matrices of values), which store the learned patterns necessary for the mapping activity that connects features to response classes. The dimensions and type of internal parameters delimit the kind of target functions that an algorithm can learn. An optimization engine in the algorithm changes parameters from their initial values during learning to represent the target's hidden function.

During optimization, the algorithm searches among possible variants of its parameter combinations to find the best combination that allows correct mapping between features and classes during training. This process evaluates many candidate functions, defined by different parameter combinations, from the set the learning algorithm can represent. The set of all the potential functions the learning algorithm can evaluate is the *hypothesis space*.

TECHNICAL
STUFF

You may also hear of *inductive bias,* a concept related to the hypothesis space. Because data is limited, you can fit many target functions on that data (potentially infinite). Inductive bias refers to the assumptions that the learning algorithm makes to restrict the hypothesis space and generalize to new, unseen data. For instance, many simpler models, such as linear regression, have the bias that variables are linearly related to the target (in other words, changes in features lead to proportional changes in the target). This type of inductive bias enables these models to handle new data effectively.

You can call the resulting classifier with all its set parameters a *hypothesis,* a way in machine learning to say that the algorithm has set parameters to replicate the target function and is now ready to work out correct classifications (a fact demonstrated later).

REMEMBER

The hypothesis space must contain all the parameter variants of all the machine learning algorithms that you want to try to map to an unknown function when solving a classification problem. Different algorithms can have different hypothesis spaces. What really matters is that the hypothesis space contains the target function (or its approximation, which is a different but similar function).

You can imagine this phase as the time when a child, in an effort to figure out the idea of a tree, experiments with many different creative ideas by assembling knowledge and experiences (an analogy for the given features). Naturally, the parents are involved in this phase, and they provide relevant environmental inputs. In machine learning, someone has to provide the right learning algorithms, supply some unlearnable parameters (called *hyper-parameters*), choose a set of examples to learn from, and select the features that accompany the examples. Just as a child can't always learn to distinguish between right and wrong if left alone in the world, machine learning algorithms need human guidance to learn successfully.

After completing the learning process, the learned hypothesis might not perfectly match the actual target function due to noise, insufficient data, or the target function being outside the hypothesis space. As shown in Figure 8-1, inexact mappings occur because the algorithm lacks enough data to discover the right function. *Noise,* erroneous or distorted examples, mixed with correct data, can also cause problems, as shown in Figure 8-2.

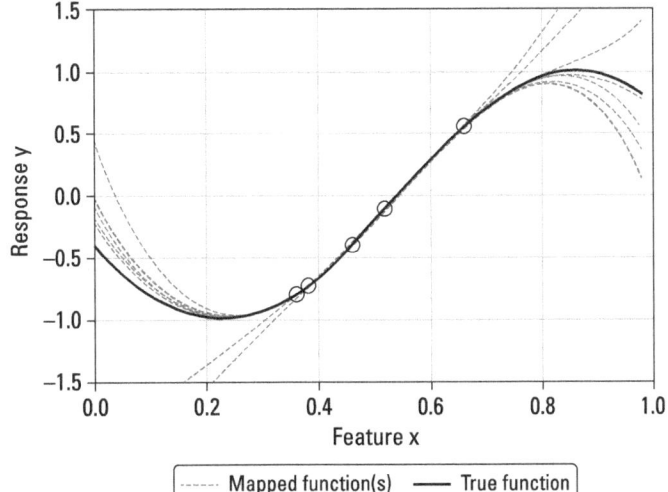

FIGURE 8-1:
Insufficient data
makes it hard to
map back to the
target function.

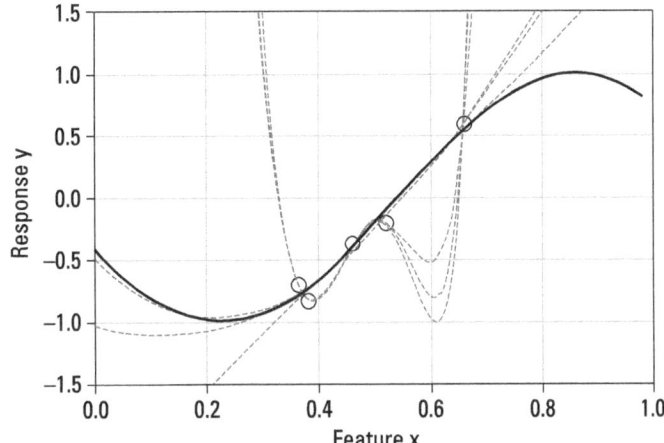

FIGURE 8-2:
Noise can cause
mismatches in
the data points.

REMEMBER

Noise in real-world data is the norm. Many extraneous factors and errors that occur when recording data distort the values of the features. A good machine learning algorithm should distinguish the signals that can map back to the target function and ignore extraneous noise. You can imagine the situation as walking into a messy room. A good algorithm learns to see the way to go through the scattered socks and pizza boxes!

Exploring cost functions

The driving force behind optimization in machine learning is the response from a function internal to the algorithm, called the *cost function*. In some contexts, you may see other terms used, such as *loss function* or *objective function*. The cost function measures the discrepancy between the algorithm's predictions and the actual target outcomes that it's striving to guess. In addition, a cost function determines how well a machine learning algorithm performs in a supervised prediction or an unsupervised optimization problem. In this latter case, the cost function is not related to the target outcome but to something else. For instance, in clustering, a typical unsupervised problem where you group similar data points, the cost function is the sum of the distances of all data points from the center of their assigned group.

The cost function compares the algorithm's predictions against the actual outcome recorded from the real world. Comparing a prediction against its real value using a cost function determines the algorithm's error level. Because it's a mathematical formulation, the cost function expresses the error level in a numerical form, a cost value that has to be minimized. The cost function transmits what is actually important and meaningful for your purposes to the learning algorithm. As a result, you must choose or accurately define the cost function based on an understanding of the problem you want to solve or the level of achievement you want to reach.

For example, when considering stock market forecasting, the cost function expresses the importance of avoiding incorrect predictions. In this case, you want to make money by avoiding significant losses. In forecasting sales, the concern is different because you need to reduce the error in common and frequent situations, not in the rare and exceptional ones, so you use a different cost function.

When the problem is to predict who will likely become ill from a disease, you prioritize algorithms that effectively identify a high proportion of individuals who will become ill later. Based on the severity of the illness, you may also prefer that the algorithm wrongly chooses some people who don't get ill, rather than miss the people who actually do get ill.

The cost function is what truly drives the success of a machine learning application. It's as critical to the learning process as *representation* (the capability to approximate certain mathematical functions) and *optimization* (how the machine learning algorithms set their internal parameters). Most algorithms optimize their own cost function, and you have little choice but to apply them as they are. Some algorithms allow you to choose among a certain number of possible functions, providing more flexibility. When an algorithm uses a cost function directly in the optimization process, the cost function is used internally. Given that algorithms are set to work with certain cost functions, the optimization objective may differ from your desired objective. In such a case, you measure the results using an external cost function that, for clarity of terminology, you call an *error function* or *loss function* (if it has to be minimized) or a *scoring function* (if it has instead to be maximized).

TIP

With respect to your target, a good practice is to define the cost function that works the best in solving your problem and then figure out which algorithms work best in optimizing for that cost function. When you work with algorithms that don't allow the cost function you want, you can still indirectly influence their optimization process and fit your preferred cost function by fixing their hyperparameters (the parameters that you have to provide for the algorithm to work) and selecting the input features that work the best with your cost function. Everything boils down to deciding what mix of algorithms, hyperparameters, and features best solves your problem in the way you want.

When an algorithm learns from data, the cost function guides the optimization process by pointing out the changes in the internal parameters that are the most beneficial for making better predictions. The optimization continues as the cost function response improves iteration by iteration. When the response stalls or worsens, it's time to stop tweaking the algorithm's parameters because the algorithm isn't likely to achieve better prediction results from there on. When the algorithm works on new data and makes predictions, the cost function helps you evaluate whether it's working properly and is indeed effective.

REMEMBER

Deciding on the cost function is an underrated activity in machine learning. It's a fundamental task because it determines how the algorithm behaves during the learning phase and how it handles the problem you want to solve. Never rely on default options, but always ask yourself what you want to achieve using machine learning and check what cost function can best represent the achievement.

TIP

In Part 4, you discover some machine learning algorithms, and in Part 5, you see how to apply theory to real problems, introducing classification problems for scoring text and sentiments. If you need to pick a cost function, machine learning explanations and examples introduce a range of error functions for regression and classification. These include root mean squared errors, log loss, accuracy, precision, recall, and area under the curve (AUC). (Don't worry if these terms aren't clear now; they're explained in detail in Parts 4 and 5.)

Descending the optimization curve

The gradient descent algorithm offers a perfect example of how machine learning works. It sums up the concepts expressed up to this point in the chapter because you can figure it out using intuitive visual examples, not just a mathematical formulation. Moreover, though it is just one of many possible methods, gradient descent is a widely used approach that's applied to a series of machine learning algorithms presented in the book, such as linear models, neural networks, and gradient boosting machines.

Given a set of inputs, such as a data matrix made of features and a response vector, gradient descent finds a solution by starting from an initial set of parameters chosen randomly. It then proceeds in various iterations using the feedback from the cost function, thus changing its parameters with values that gradually improve the initial random solution and lower the error. Even though the optimization may take a large number of iterations before reaching a good mapping, it relies on moving parameters in the opposite direction to the gradient of the cost function, which is the direction of the steepest descent after each iteration. Figure 8-3 shows an example of a complex optimization process with some local minima (the minimum points at the middle of the valleys) and a place where the process can get stuck (because of the flat surface at the saddle point) and cannot continue its descent.

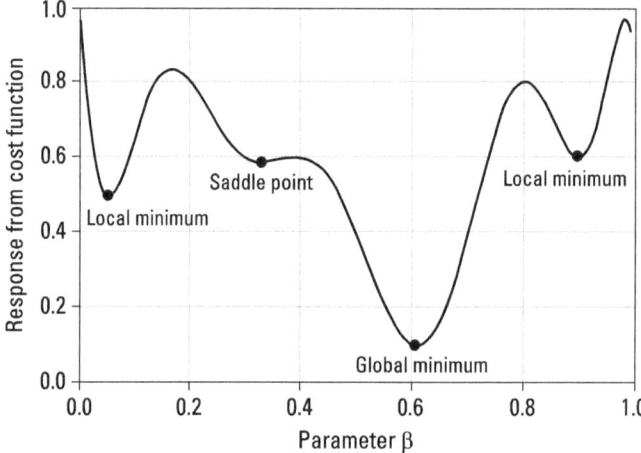

FIGURE 8-3: A plotting of parameter data against the output of the cost function.

Based on Figure 8-3, you can visualize the optimization process as a walk in high mountains during a misty day or while being blindfolded (because the algorithm doesn't see the whole picture at once), with the parameters being the different paths to descend to the valley. A gradient descent optimization occurs at each step. Basically, you can only feel the slope right under your feet and decide to follow that direction for the way down. In the same way, the algorithm chooses the path that reduces errors the most at each iteration and heads in that direction. The idea is that if steps aren't too large (causing the algorithm to overshoot the target), following the most downward direction will result in arriving at the lowest place.

Unfortunately, finding the lowest place doesn't always occur because the algorithm can arrive at intermediate valleys, creating the illusion that it has reached the target. You might see the situation as having found a comfortable ledge halfway down the mountain and declaring you have finally arrived at the base camp, even though it is still way further down!

However, in most cases, gradient descent leads the machine learning algorithm to discover the correct hypothesis for successfully mapping the problem. Figure 8-4 shows how a different starting point can make a difference. Starting point A ends toward a local minimum, whereas not far away, point B manages to reach the global minimum.

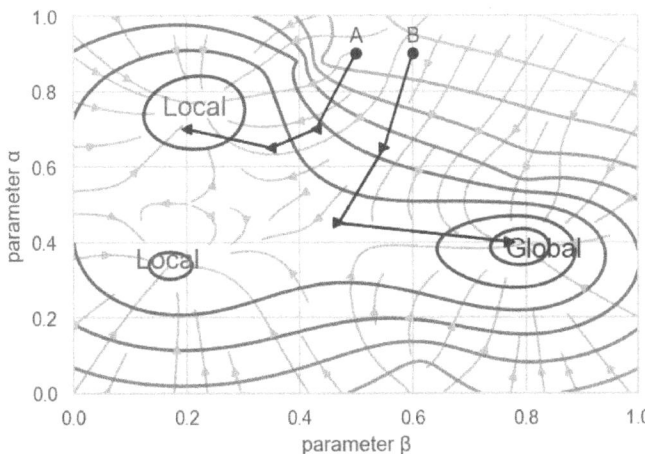

FIGURE 8-4:
Visualizing the effect of starting point on outcome.

TIP

In an optimization process, you distinguish between different optimization outcomes. You can have a global minimum that's truly the minimum error from the cost function, and you can have many local minima — solutions that *seem* to produce the minimum error but actually don't (the intermediate valleys where the algorithm gets stuck). As a remedy, given the optimization process's random initialization, running the optimization many times is good practice. This means trying different descending path sequences and not getting stuck in the same local minimum.

Optimizing with Big Data

Machine learning boils down to an optimization problem in which you look for a global minimum given a specific cost function. Consequently, working out an optimization using all the data available is clearly an advantage because, at each iteration, it allows you to find the best learning parameters correction with respect to all the data. That's why most machine learning algorithms prefer to use all data available, and they want it accessible inside the computer memory.

Furthermore, you also have to distinguish between statistical algorithms and other optimizations. Some learning techniques, based on solutions derived from matrix algebra, require the entire dataset in memory for computation. Iterative algorithms, such as gradient descent, can compute a solution in the most accurate way when using the entire dataset, but can also be adapted to work with subsets of data as small as a single data row. In fact, iterative algorithms can perform a step-by-step search for the next best solution by proceeding through partial solutions.

Given the advantage of using all the data available, you have to consider that your available hardware could be a bottleneck. When operating with data within the limits of the computer's memory (assuming typical desktop/laptop memory limits), you're working in *core memory*. You can solve most machine learning problems using this approach. Algorithms that work with core memory are called *batch algorithms* because, as in a factory where machines process single batches of materials, such algorithms learn to handle and predict a single data batch at a time, arranged in a data matrix.

However, sometimes data can't fit into core memory because it's too big. Data derived from the web is a typical example of information that can't fit easily into memory. In addition, data generated from sensors, tracking devices, satellites, and video monitoring are often problematic because of their dimensions when compared to computer RAM; however, they can be stored easily on local disk storage, given the availability of cheap and large storage devices that easily hold terabytes of data.

Leveraging sampling

A few strategies can save the day when data is too big to fit into the memory of a single computer:

>> **Subsampling:** Data is reshaped by a selection of cases (and sometimes even features) based on statistical sampling into a more manageable yet reduced data matrix. Clearly, reducing the amount of data can't always provide exactly the same results as when globally analyzing it. Working on less than the available data can even produce less powerful models. Yet, if subsampling is executed properly, the approach can generate almost equivalent and still reliable results. A successful subsampling must correctly use statistical sampling by employing random or stratified sample drawings.

>> **Random sampling:** You create a sample by randomly choosing the examples that appear as part of the sample. The larger the sample, the more likely the sample will resemble the original structure and variety of data, but even with few drawn examples, the results are often acceptable, both in terms of representation of the original data and for machine learning purposes.

>> **Stratified sampling:** You control the final distribution of the target variable or of certain features in data that you deem critical for successfully replicating the characteristics of your complete data. A classic example is to draw a sample in a classroom made up of different proportions of males and females to guess the average height. If females are, on average, shorter and in a smaller proportion than males, you want to draw a sample that replicates the same proportion to obtain a reliable estimate of the average height. Stratifying based on your knowledge of the data (such as knowing that gender can matter in height guessing) helps a lot in obtaining a good working sample.

After you choose a sampling strategy, you have to draw a subsample of enough examples, given your memory limitations, to represent the variety of data. Data with high dimensionality, characterized by many cases and many features, is more difficult to subsample because it is necessary to draw a much larger sample, which may not even fit into your core memory.

Using parallelism

Beyond subsampling, another possible solution to fitting data in memory is to leverage *network parallelism,* which splits data across multiple computers that are connected to a network. Each computer handles part of the data for optimization. A solution is achieved after each computer has done its own computations and all the parallel optimization jobs have been reduced to a single result or solution.

To understand how this solution works, compare the process of building a car piece by piece using a single worker to having many workers working separately on car part aggregates — leaving a single worker to perform the final assembly. Apart from having a faster assembly execution, you don't have to keep all the parts in the factory simultaneously. Similarly, you don't have to keep all the data parts in a single computer, but you can take advantage of processing them separately on different computers, thus overcoming core memory limitations.

This approach is the basis of map-reduce technology and cluster-computer frameworks, such as Apache Hadoop and Apache Spark, which are focused on mapping a problem onto multiple machines and finally reducing their output into the desired solution.

Unfortunately, you can't easily split all machine learning algorithms into separable processes, which limits the usability of such an approach. More importantly, you encounter significant cost and time overhead in setup and maintenance when you keep a network of computers ready for such data processing, something only large organizations can manage.

Learning out-of-core

Another memory use solution is to rely on out-of-core algorithms, which work by keeping data on the storage device and feeding it in chunks into computer memory for processing. The feeding process is called *streaming*. Because the chunks are smaller than the available memory, the algorithm can process them and properly update the algorithm optimization. After the update, the system discards them in favor of new chunks, which the algorithm uses for learning. This process goes on repetitively until there are no more chunks. Chunks can be small (depending on core memory), and the process is called *mini-batch learning*, or they can even be constituted by just a single data point, called *online learning*.

Out-of-core learning resembles "eating the elephant one bite at a time," but here the elephant is data. Since the whole dataset won't fit on the plate (computer memory), the algorithm takes bites it can handle (chunks or mini-batches), chews on them (processes them), updates its understanding, and then takes on the next bite. Online learning is taking really tiny bites — one data point at a time.

The previously described gradient descent can, like other iterative algorithms, work fine with such an approach; however, reaching an optimization takes longer because the gradient's path is more erratic and nonlinear with respect to a batch approach. The online algorithm can even reach an unsatisfactory solution, with respect to its in-memory batch version, when not run for a sufficient number of passes through the data.

When working with repeated updates of its parameters based on mini-batches and single examples, the gradient descent takes the name *stochastic gradient descent*. Stochastic is just a fancy statistical word for being random. Because the algorithm only looks at random chunks of data at each step, its path down the optimization mountain is less than smooth. Think of it as a slightly tipsy walk downhill instead of a determined straight march. It still gets to its destination, usually, but it might wobble around a bit on the way.

The algorithm will converge toward a proper minimum under these conditions:

>> The examples streamed are randomly decided.

>> A proper learning rate is defined as fixed or flexible according to the number of observations or other criteria.

If examples are not randomly streamed and carry some implicit ordering, the gradient estimates can be biased, leading the optimization path astray and potentially resulting in slower or poorer convergence. The learning rate makes the algorithm more or less open to updates, allowing flexibility in dealing with novelty in the data, which may appear later in the stream.

A learning rate that is too high, though faster in the optimization, can constrain the parameters to the effects of noisy or erroneous examples seen at the beginning or during the stream. Because of such effects, a high learning rate may more easily lead to sub-optimal solutions. On the other hand, a high learning rate renders the algorithm reactive to the more recent streamed observations. A reactive algorithm can prove to be an advantage when the algorithm is learning from rapidly evolving and dynamic sources, such as data from the digital advertising sector, where new advertising campaigns often start mutating the level of attention and response of targeted individuals. If this is not the case, choosing a lower learning rate implies a slower convergence on a solution, but it is often a safer choice.

TIP

The learning parameter can affect the quality of an out-of-core optimization. Finding the best value for this parameter is often a matter of experimentation and trial and error.

Chapter **9**

Validating Machine Learning

This chapter helps you understand how machine learning works with data. It begins by looking at the data itself and helps you consider how machine learning systems sample and use it to create a solution. The next section of the chapter helps you understand some basic algorithm concepts using standard algorithms like linear regression and K-Nearest Neighbors. After you have data and an algorithm to explore it with, you need to validate and test the solutions you create. The human element in all this is ensuring that the solution provides more than just an output; it provides output that is accurate and reflects the real world.

REMEMBER

You don't have to type the source code for this chapter manually. In fact, using the downloadable source code is a lot easier. You can find the source code for this chapter in the ML4D3E folder of the downloadable code file. The example files for this chapter will begin with ML4D3E-09-. See the Introduction for details on how to find these source files.

Considering the Use of Example Data

Having examples (in the form of datasets) and a machine learning algorithm at hand doesn't assure that solving a learning problem is possible or that the results will provide the desired solution. For example, if you want your computer to distinguish a photo of a dog from a picture of a cat, you can give it good examples of images of dogs and cats. You then train a dog versus cat classifier based on some machine learning algorithm that could output the probability that a given photo is a dog or a cat. Of course, the output is a probability — not an absolute assurance that the image is a dog or cat.

Based on the probability that the classifier reports, you can decide the class (dog or cat) of a photo based on the estimated probability calculated by the algorithm. When the probability is higher for a dog, you can minimize the risk of a wrong assessment by selecting the class (dog) with the higher probability. The greater the probability difference between the likelihood of a dog and that of a cat, the higher the confidence you can have in your choice. A close choice likely occurs because of some ambiguity in the photo (the photo is unclear or the dog is actually a bit cattish). For that matter, it might not even be a dog — and the algorithm doesn't know anything about the raccoon, which is what the picture shows.

Such is the power of training a classifier: You pose the problem and offer examples, each carefully marked with the label or class that the algorithm should learn. (Labeling is a challenging activity, as you discover in the following chapters.) Your computer trains the algorithm for a while, and finally, you get a resulting model, which provides you with an answer or probability. In the end, probability represents just an opportunity — or a risk, from another perspective — to propose a solution and get a correct answer. At this point, you may seem to have addressed every issue and believe the work is finished, but you must still validate the results. This chapter helps you discover why machine learning isn't just a push-the-button-and-forget-it activity but most often requires deep reflection, careful planning, and controlled experimentation, above all.

REMEMBER

This chapter and those that follow help you understand machine learning concepts using small datasets that help you understand techniques without added complexity. Examples often rely on a *toy dataset,* that is, a dataset with few examples and features, but a toy dataset offers limited insights into real-world complexity. Yes, some real-world problems are relatively simple, but the majority that you tackle using the techniques you learn in this chapter will require far more complex datasets.

Checking Out-of-Sample Errors

The following sections help you consider the basis for errors when using a trained algorithm to analyze data that the algorithm hasn't seen yet, which is *out-of-sample* data. The purpose of training an algorithm is so that you can keep using it to understand new or unseen data. Consequently, errors in that analysis can cause serious problems, making it likely that whatever you want the algorithm to do will fail. For example, you might use machine learning to analyze market trends. If the algorithm used for the purpose fails, you might find yourself buying stock in a company that has no chance whatsoever of succeeding. The following sections consider errors at these levels:

» Sampling the data

» Ensuring that a data source isn't biased or problematic in other ways

» Understanding the role of bias and variance

» Keeping model complexity in check

» Creating a balanced solution

» Visualizing the solution

Understanding the concept of samples

When you first receive the data used to train an algorithm, the data is just *sample data*. Generally, except for rare circumstances, the data you receive isn't all the data that you could possibly get. For instance, if you receive sales data from your marketing department, the data you receive is not all the possible sales data because, unless sales are stopped, there will always be new data representing new sales in the future.

If your data is not all the data possible, you must call it a sample. A sample is a selection, and as with all selections, the data could reflect different motivations as to why someone selected it in such a way. Therefore, when you receive data, the first question you have to consider is how someone has selected it. Suppose someone selected it arbitrarily, without any specific criteria. Then, you should have a *random sample*, and you can reasonably expect that future data won't differ too much from the data you have at hand if things do not change from the past.

REMEMBER

Statistics assume that the future won't differ too much from the past. If past distribution also persists in the future, learning from the past will enlighten your model about the future.

By employing random sampling theory, you can base future expectations on past data. If you select examples randomly without a criterion, you have a good chance of choosing a selection of examples that

» Don't differ too much from your actual examples

» Won't differ much from future examples

In statistical terms, you can expect your random sample to be *representative* of the actual distribution of your examples. In Chapter 8, we discussed different sampling strategies, besides random sampling, that can help you obtain representative samples in different situations.

However, when the sample you receive is somehow specific, it could present a problem when training the algorithm. In fact, the particular data could force your algorithm to learn a different mapping to the response than the mapping it might have created by using random data. As an example, if you receive sales data from just one shop or only the shops in a single region (which is actually a specific sample), the algorithm may not learn how to forecast the future sales of all the shops in all the areas. The particular sample causes problems because other shops may be different and follow different rules from the ones you're observing.

REMEMBER

Ensuring that your algorithm is learning correctly from data is why you should always check what the algorithm has learned from *in-sample* data (the data used for training) by testing your hypothesis on some out-of-sample data. *Out-of-sample* data is data you didn't have at learning time, and it's indispensable for testing your model when you want to create a *forecasting model*.

Looking for the holy grail of generalization

Generalization is the model's ability to adapt to and perform well on new, previously unseen data drawn from the same distribution as the data used for training. Therefore, out-of-sample data becomes essential to determining whether and to what extent learning from data is possible.

No matter how big your in-sample dataset is, it may produce highly unlikely predictions when your sampling process doesn't produce representative samples. In statistics, when a sampling process isn't producing representative samples for some reason, the process is *biased,* the result of which is *bias.* There is an anecdote about inferring from biased samples. It involves the 1936 U.S. presidential election between Alfred Landon and Franklin D. Roosevelt, in which the *Literary Digest* used biased poll information to predict the winner.

At that time, the *Literary Digest,* a respectable and popular magazine, polled its readers to determine the next president of the United States, a practice it had successfully performed since 1916. The poll response was strikingly in favor of Landon, with more than a 57 percent consensus on the candidate. The magazine also used such a huge sample — more than 10 million people (with only 2.4 million responding) — that the result seemed unassailable: A large sample coupled with a large difference between the winner and the loser tends not to raise many doubts. Yet the poll was completely unsuccessful. In the end, the margin of error was 19 percent, with Landon getting only 38 percent of the vote and Roosevelt getting 62 percent. This margin is the largest error ever for a public opinion poll.

The problem was that the magazine questioned people with names pulled from every telephone directory in the United States, as well as from the magazine's subscription list and rosters of clubs and associations, gathering more than ten million names. Impressive, but at the end of the Great Depression, having a telephone, subscribing to a magazine, or being part of a club meant that you were rich, so the sample consisted of only affluent voters and completely ignored lower-income voters, who happened to represent the majority (thereby resulting in a *selection bias*). In addition, the poll suffered from a *non-responsive bias* because only 2.4 million people responded, and people who respond to polls tend to differ from those who don't. The magnitude of error for this particular incident ushered in the beginning of a more scientific approach to sampling.

REMEMBER

Such classical examples of selection bias point out that if the selection process biases a sample, the learning process will have the same bias. However, sometimes bias is unavoidable and difficult to spot. As an example, when you go fishing with a net, you can see only the fish you catch, and that didn't pass through the net itself.

Another example comes from World War II. At that time, designers constantly improved U.S. warplanes by adding extra armor plating to the parts that took the most hits upon returning from bombing runs. It took the reasoning of the mathematician Abraham Wald to point out that designers actually needed to reinforce the places that *didn't* have bullet holes on returning planes. These locations were likely so critical that a plane hit there didn't return home, and consequently, no one could observe its damage (a kind of *survivorship bias* where the survivors skew the data). Survivorship bias is still a problem today. In fact, it may significantly affect both clinical research (if you study only survivors of pathologies or accidents) and studies on financial investments (when you try to back-trace the reasons for economic success).

Preliminary reasoning on your data and testing results with out-of-sample examples can help you spot or at least have an intuition of possible sampling problems. However, receiving new out-of-sample data is often difficult, costly, and requires investment in terms of timing. In the sales example discussed earlier, you have to wait for a long time to test your sales forecasting model — maybe an entire year — to determine if your hypothesis works. In addition, making the data ready for use can consume a great deal of time. For example, when you label photos of dogs and cats, you need to spend time examining a larger number of photos taken from the web or from a database.

A possible shortcut to expending additional effort is getting out-of-sample examples from your available data sample. You reserve a part of the data sample based on a separation between training and testing data dictated by time or random sampling. If time is an important component in your problem (as it is in forecasting sales), you look for a time label to use as a separator. Data before a certain date appears as in-sample data; data after that date appears as out-of-sample data. The same happens when you choose data randomly: What you extracted as in-sample data is just for training; what is left is devoted to testing purposes and serves as your out-of-sample data.

Experimenting how bias and variance work

Now that you know more about the in-sample and out-of-sample portions of your data, you also know that learning depends a lot on the in-sample data. This portion of your data is important because you want to discover a particular view of the world, and as with all points of view, it can be wrong, distorted, or partial. You also know you need out-of-sample data to check whether the learning process is working. However, these aspects form only part of the picture. When you make a machine learning algorithm work on data to guess a particular response, you're effectively taking a gamble, and that gamble is not just because of the sample you use for learning. There's more. For the moment, imagine that you have access to suitable, unbiased, in-sample data, so data isn't the problem. Instead, you need to concentrate on the method for learning and predicting.

First, consider that you're betting the algorithm can reasonably guess the response. You can't always make this assumption because figuring out certain answers isn't possible, no matter what you know in advance. For instance, you can't fully determine the behavior of human beings by knowing their previous history and behavior because of

>> A random effect in the generative process of behavior (the irrational part of us, for instance).

>> Free will (the problem is also a philosophical and religious one, and there are many discordant opinions).

Consequently, you can guess only some types of responses, and for many others, such as when you try to predict people's behavior, you have to accept a certain degree of uncertainty (which, hopefully, is acceptable for your purposes).

Second, you must consider that you're betting that the relationship between the information you have and the response you want to predict can be expressed as a mathematical formula of some kind, and that your machine learning algorithm is actually capable of guessing that formula. The capacity of your algorithm to guess the mathematical formula behind a response is intrinsically embedded in the nuts and bolts of the algorithm. Some algorithms can guess almost everything; others have a limited set of options. The set of all the possible functions an algorithm could learn is its hypothesis space. Consequently, the specific function learned from the training data is the resulting *hypothesis* or *model*.

Mathematics is fantastic. It can describe much of the real world by using some simple notation, and it's the core of machine learning because any learning algorithm has some capability to represent a mathematical formulation. Some algorithms, such as linear regression, explicitly use a specific mathematical formulation to describe how a response (such as the price of a house) relates to a set of predictive information (such as market information, house location, the surface of the estate, and so on).

REMEMBER

Linear regression offers an understandable formulation, but it won't fit all your problems because not all problems can be represented like linear regression. We discuss linear regression in more detail in Chapter 12. Some other sophisticated algorithms, such as decision trees (a topic of Chapter 10), are quite complicated to render using mathematical formulation. However, they can approximate a large range of formulations easily and thus solve a wider range of problems.

Some formulations are so complex and intricate that even though representing them on paper is possible, doing so is too difficult in practical terms. Nevertheless, complex formulations may have some important advantages over simple ones, based on the problem they should solve. As an example, consider a simple and easily explained formulation based on linear regression. The linear regression is just the formulation of a separator (which could be a simple line as well as a multidimensional plane) in a space of coordinates given by the response and all the predictors. In the easiest example, when a line represents the model, you have a response, y, and a single predictor, x, with a formulation of

$$y = \beta_1 x_1 + \beta_0$$

In a simple situation of a response predicted by a single feature, such a model is perfect when your data arranges itself as a line. However, what happens if it doesn't and instead shapes itself like a curve? To represent the situation, just observe the following bidimensional representations, as shown in Figure 9-1.

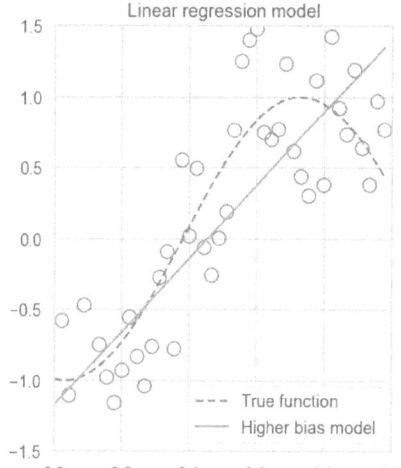

FIGURE 9-1:
Example of a
linear model
underfitting a
nonlinear
relationship
in the data.

Underfitting occurs when your algorithm is too simple, exhibiting what is called high *bias*, and it cannot capture underlying structures and nuances in the data. Failing to learn enough results in poor performance both during training and when encountering new data.

If the true relationship between a target variable and a predictor resembles a linear relationship (or it is close to it), the errors produced by the mappings of a linear regression model appear rather randomly in a scatterplot, because chance will dictate if some errors will be found above the mapped regression line or below it. However, when mapping a nonlinear relationship like a curve, the situation is different, because at times, the regression line may appear somewhat exact, but at other times it will be systematically wrong. In such cases, you frequently notice that projected points will at times be above the mapped line (underestimation), at times below it (overestimation).

REMEMBER

Given the simplicity of its mapping of the response, an algorithm could tend to systematically overestimate or underestimate the real rules behind complex data. In such a case, the algorithm is affected by the bias error. The bias error is characteristic of simpler algorithms that can't express complex mathematical formulations and in certain situations are therefore unable to map correctly the relationship between the features and the target variable.

Keeping model complexity in mind

Just as simplicity of formulations is a problem, automatically resorting to mapping very intricate formulations doesn't always provide a solution. In fact, you don't know the true complexity of the required response mapping (such as whether it fits in a straight line or in a curved one). Therefore, just as simplicity may create an unsuitable response (refer to Figure 9-1), it's also possible to represent the complexity in data with an overly complex mapping.

The problem with a complex mapping is that it has many terms and parameters — and in some extreme cases, your algorithm may have more parameters than your data has examples. Because you must specify all the parameters, the algorithm then starts memorizing everything in the data — not just the signals (the data that matters) but also

» Random noise

» Errors

» Specific sample characteristics

In some cases, the algorithm can even memorize the examples. However, unless you're working on a problem with a limited number of simple features with few distinct values, you're highly unlikely to encounter the same example twice, given the enormous number of possible combinations of all the available features in the dataset.

When memorization happens, you may have the illusion that everything is working well because your machine learning algorithm seems to have fitted the in-sample data so well. Instead, problems can quickly become evident when you start using the algorithm on out-of-sample data and notice that it produces errors in its predictions as well as errors that actually change a lot when you relearn from the same data with a slightly different approach. *Overfitting* occurs when your algorithm has learned too much from your data, up to the point of mapping curve shapes and rules that do not exist, as shown in Figure 9-2. Any slight change in the procedure or the training data produces erratic predictions, which is a condition we call *variance* of the estimates.

Keeping solutions balanced

To create better solutions with machine learning, you make a trade-off between simplicity (implying a higher bias) and complexity (which tends toward a higher variance of estimates). Statistical learning theory has mathematically demonstrated that in machine learning models:

$$Expected\ Error \approx Bias^2 + Variance + Irreducible\ Error$$

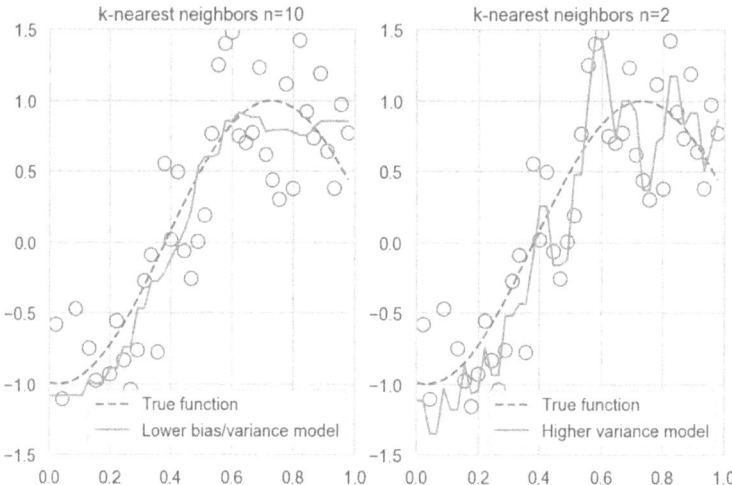

FIGURE 9-2:
A K-Nearest
Neighbor model
appropriately fits
the problem on
the left panel.
On the right
panel, the model
becomes too
complex
(overfits),
capturing noise
rather than the
underlying
nonlinear
relationship.

Since nothing can be done with irreducible error, if you intend to achieve the best predictive performance, you do need to find a solution balancing bias and variance. You can only achieve an optimal model complexity by trial and error on your specific problem. Data is what dictates the most suitable solution for a prediction problem. There doesn't exist either a panacea or a standard solution for all your machine learning dilemmas.

REMEMBER

A commonly referred theorem in the mathematical folklore is the no-free-lunch theorem by David Wolpert and William Macready, which states that "any two optimization algorithms are equivalent when their performance is averaged across all possible problems." If the algorithms are equivalent in the abstract, no one is superior to the other unless proven in a specific, practical problem. (See the discussion at http://www.no-free-lunch.org for more details about no-free-lunch theorems; two of them are used for machine learning.)

In particular, in his article "The Lack of A Priori Distinctions between Learning Algorithms," Wolpert declares there is no previous way, by reasoning or deduction, to distinguish in terms of performance between algorithms, no matter how simple or complex they are. Only the observation of an algorithm tackling specific problems will reveal if the algorithm is capable of solving a class of problems. In other words, data dictates what works and how well. Hence, you can't rely on a single machine learning algorithm to solve all the problems; you have to test many to find the best for your problem.

Besides being led into machine learning experimentation by the try-everything principle of the no-free-lunch theorem, you have another rule of thumb to consider: Occam's razor, attributed to William of Occam, a 14th-century philosopher and theologian. Occam's razor states that theories should be cut down to the minimum in order to plausibly represent the truth (hence the razor). The principle doesn't state that simpler solutions are better, but that, between a simple solution and a more complex solution offering the same result, the simpler solution is always preferred. The principle is at the very foundations of our modern scientific methodology, and even Albert Einstein seems to have often referred to it, stating that "everything should be as simple as it can be, but not simpler." Summarizing the evidence so far:

>> To get the best machine learning solution, try everything you can on your data and represent your data's performance with learning curves.

>> Start with simpler models, such as linear models, and always prefer a simpler solution when it performs nearly as well as a complex solution. You benefit from the choice when working on out-of-sample data from the real world.

>> Always check the performance of your solution using out-of-sample examples, as discussed in the preceding sections.

Depicting learning curves

To visualize the degree to which a machine learning algorithm is suffering from bias or variance with respect to a data problem, you can take advantage of a chart type named a learning curve. *Learning curves* are displays in which you plot the performance of one or more machine learning algorithms with respect to the quantity of data they use for training. The plotted values are the prediction error measurements, and the metric is measured both as in-sample and cross-validated or out-of-sample performance.

REMEMBER

If the chart depicts performance with respect to the quantity of data, it's a learning curve chart. When it depicts performance with respect to different hyperparameters or a set of learned features picked by the model, it's a validation curve chart instead. To create a learning curve chart, you must do the following:

>> Divide your data into in-sample and out-of-sample sets (split your data using a 70/30 ratio or use a sampling technique called cross-validation, explained later in this section).

>> Create portions of your training data of growing size. Depending on the size of the data available for training, increase the portions by 10 percent or, if you have a lot of data, grow the number of examples on a power scale, such as 10^3, 10^4, 10^5, and so on.

>> Train models on the different subsets of the training data. For each model, test and record its performance on the specific training subset it was trained on (for in-sample error) and on the entire out-of-sample set (for out-of-sample error).

>> Plot the recorded results on two curves, one for the in-sample results and the other for the out-of-sample results (see Figure 9-3). If instead of a train/test split, you used the cross-validation technique, you can also draw boundaries expressing the stability of the result across multiple validations (confidence intervals) based on the standard deviation of the results themselves.

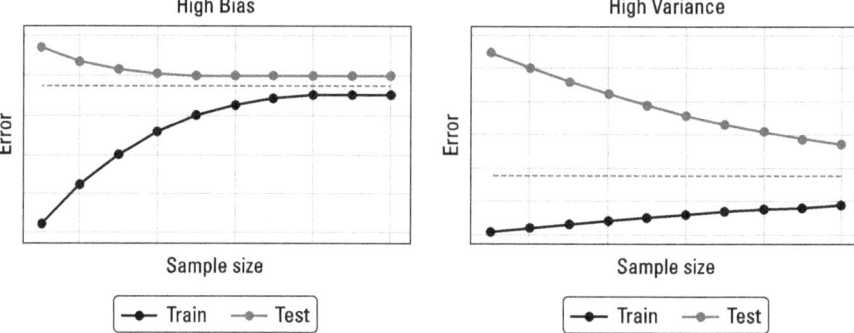

FIGURE 9-3: Learning curves affected by high bias (left) and high variance (right).

Ideally (but such doesn't always happen, as explained in the upcoming tip), you should obtain two curves with different starting error points: higher for the out-of-sample and lower for the in-sample. As the size of the training set increases, the difference in space between the two should reduce until, at a certain number of observations, they become close to a standard error value. Examining your chart, problems arise when:

>> **There is a gap between the two curves.** If the training error stays low but the out-of-sample error remains high with a significant gap between them, it indicates high variance. Adding more training data may help reduce the gap and lower the out-of-sample error.

>> **The final convergence point between the two curves has a high error, pointing to your algorithm as having too much bias.** Adding more examples here does not help because you have a convergence with the amount of data you have. You should increase the number of features or use a more complex learning algorithm as a solution.

>> **The two curves do not tend to converge because the out-of-sample curve starts to behave erratically.** Such a situation is clearly a sign of high variance of the estimates, which you can reduce by increasing the number of examples (at a certain number, the out-of-sample error will start to decrease again), reducing the number of features, or, sometimes, just fixing some key parameters of the learning algorithm.

Learning curves are provided as part of the Scikit-learn package using the `learning_curve` function that prepares all the computations for you (see the details at `https://scikit-learn.org/stable/modules/generated/sklearn.model_selection.learning_curve.html`). The book examples conveniently wrap the function to perform the plot of the results as well because the function outputs just a sequence of vectors of results.

TIP

Though it is expected that an algorithm better fits in-sample data than out-of-sample data, you can still find out-of-sample error that is better than in-sample error. A few reasons can explain that situation, all mainly related to the fact that out-of-sample data is, for some reason, simpler than in-sample data because of the way you divided out-of-sample from in-sample and processed it.

Training, Validating, and Testing

The sections that follow consider the methods employed to ensure that a model works as expected. In these sections, you encounter three splits of the data for use in these tasks:

» **Training:** Using part of the dataset to define the model's algorithm.

» **Validation:** Performing an unbiased evaluation of model fit to ensure that the model works with out-of-sample data.

» **Testing:** Providing a final, unbiased evaluation of the chosen model's performance on data held back from training and validation, giving an estimate of real-world performance and revealing any potential overfitting to the validation set.

Considering the split

In a perfect world, you should perform a test on data that your machine learning algorithm has never learned from before. However, waiting for fresh data isn't always feasible in terms of time and costs. As a first, simple remedy, you can randomly split your data into training (in-sample) and test (out-of-sample) sets. The common split is from 25 to 30 percent for testing and the remaining 75 to 70 percent for training. You split your data consisting of your response and features at the same time, keeping correspondence between each response and its features.

The second remedy occurs when you need to tune your learning algorithm. In this case, referring to the test split data to check whether your tuning works isn't a good practice because it causes another kind of overfitting called *snooping,* where you end up adapting your solution to the test set (we discuss more on this topic at the end of the chapter). To overcome snooping, you need a third split, called a validation *set*, which is a part of the data used to evaluate the model and fine-tune the model hyperparameters. A suggested split is to have your examples partitioned into three parts: 70 percent for training, 20 percent for validation, and 10 percent for testing.

You should perform the split randomly, that is, regardless of the initial ordering of the data. Otherwise, your test won't be reliable, because ordering could cause *overestimation* when there is some meaningful ordering to be learned by the algorithm, or underestimation if the train and test distributions differ by too much. As a solution, you must ensure that the test set distribution isn't very different from the training distribution and that no particular ordering occurs in the split data. Sometimes, even if you strictly abide by random sampling, you can't always obtain similar distributions among sets, especially when your sample size is small.

TIP

When your sample size n is high, such as exceeding 10,000 examples, you can quite confidently create a randomly split dataset. When the dataset is smaller, comparing the similarity among basic statistics such as mean, mode, median, and variance across the response and features in the training and test sets will help you understand whether the test set is suitable or unsuitable. When you aren't sure that the split is right because the statistics are too different, just recreate a new one.

Resorting to cross-validation

A noticeable problem with the train/test set split is that, if your sample is small, you can introduce bias into the testing by reducing the in-sample training data size. Moreover, when you split the data, you may keep some useful examples out of the training. Sometimes the data is so complex that a test set, though apparently similar to the training set, is not really similar because combinations of values are different (which is typical of highly dimensional datasets). These issues add to the instability of sampling results when you don't have many examples. The risk of splitting your data in an unfavorable way also explains why the train/test split isn't the favored solution by machine learning practitioners when you have to evaluate and tune a machine learning solution.

Cross-validation based on k-folds is the answer. It relies on random splitting, but this time it splits your data into a number k of *folds* (each one a separate partition of your data) of equal size. Then, each fold is used in turn as a test set and the others are used for training. Each iteration uses a different fold as a test, which produces an error estimate. After completing the test on one fold against the others used for training, a successive fold, different from the previous, is used and the procedure repeats to produce another error estimate. The process continues until all the k-folds are used once as a test set and you have a k number of error estimates that you can compute into a mean error estimate (the cross-validation score) and a standard error of the estimates. Figure 9-4 shows how this process works.

	Fold 1	Fold 2	Fold 3	Fold 4	Fold 5
Iteration 1	TRAIN	TRAIN	TRAIN	TRAIN	TEST
Iteration 2	TRAIN	TRAIN	TRAIN	TEST	TRAIN
Iteration 3	TRAIN	TRAIN	TEST	TRAIN	TRAIN
Iteration 4	TRAIN	TEST	TRAIN	TRAIN	TRAIN
Iteration 5	TEST	TRAIN	TRAIN	TRAIN	TRAIN

Dataset Partitioned Into Folds

FIGURE 9-4: A graphical representation of how cross-validation works.

This procedure provides the following advantages:

>> It works well regardless of the number of examples. By increasing the number of folds, you increase the size of your training set (larger k, larger training set, reduced bias) and decrease the size of the test set. However, very large k values can increase the variance of the cross-validation estimate because the training sets for each fold become too similar.

>> Differences in distribution for individual folds don't matter as much. When a fold has a different distribution compared to the others, it's used just once as a test set and is blended with others as part of the training set during the remaining tests.

>> You actually test all the observations, so you are fully testing your machine learning hypothesis using all the data you have.

>> By taking the mean of the results, you can expect a probabilistic estimate of predictive performance. In addition, the standard deviation of the results can tell you how much variation to expect in real out-of-sample data. A higher variation in the cross-validated performances hints at data whose variations the algorithm is incapable of adequately catching.

REMEMBER

Using k-fold cross-validation is always the optimal choice unless the data you're using has some kind of order that matters. For instance, it could involve a time series, such as sales. In that case, you shouldn't use a random sampling method but instead rely on a train/test split based on the original order of the data so that the time sequence is preserved and you can test on the last examples of that ordered series.

Looking for alternatives in validation

You have a few alternatives to cross-validation, all of which are derived from statistics. The first one to consider, if you have an in-sample made of a few examples, is the leave-one-out cross-validation (LOOCV). It is analogous to k-fold cross-validation, with the only difference being that k, the number of folds, is exactly n, the number of examples. Therefore, in LOOCV, you build n models (which may turn into a large number when you have many observations) and test each one on a single out-of-sample observation. Apart from being computationally intensive and requiring that you build many models to test your hypothesis, the problem with LOOCV is that the estimates from each fold are highly correlated (since the training sets differ by only one sample). The consequence is that LOOCV estimates have a higher variance than you would get with cross-validation ones. Understandably, if you are working with a small set of data, LOOCV is your only feasible choice for validation.

Another alternative from statistics is bootstrapping, a method long used to estimate the sampling distribution of statistics, which are presumed not to follow a previously assumed distribution. Bootstrapping works by building a number (the more, the better) of samples of size n (the original in-sample size) drawn with repetition. To *draw with repetition* means that the process could draw an example multiple times to use it as part of the bootstrapping resampling. Bootstrapping has the advantage of offering a simple and effective way to estimate a more accurate error measure. In fact, bootstrapped error measurements is a standard practice in statistics. On the other hand, validation becomes more complicated due to the sampling with replacement because your validation sample must come from the out-of-bootstrap examples. Moreover, using some training samples repeatedly can inject bias into the models you build.

REMEMBER

If you're using out-of-bootstrapping examples for your test, you'll notice that the test sample can be of various sizes, depending on the number of unique examples in the in-sample, likely accounting for about a third of your original in-sample size. This simple Python code snippet demonstrates randomly simulating a certain number of bootstraps:

```
import numpy as np

size = 1000
iters = 10000
results = list()
```

```
for i in range(iters):
    chosen = np.random.randint(0, size, size=size)
    results.append(len(np.unique(chosen)) / size)

avg_oob = 1 - np.mean(results)
print(f"Avg out-of-bootstrap: {avg_oob*100:.1f}%")
```

The code creates a large number of trials, each one sampling with repetition (meaning that a case can be reused multiple times). Each time, it computes the number of unique examples and the portion of cases left out as out-of-sample. Finally, the portion of the left-out samples is averaged across all the trials. Running the experiment may require some time, and your results may be different because of the random nature of the sampling. Here is some representative output: Out-of-bootstrap: 36.8 %.

Optimizing by Cross-Validation

Being able to validate a machine learning hypothesis effectively allows further optimization of your chosen algorithm. The following sections help you understand how to optimize a cross-validation solution.

Sources of predictive performance

As discussed in the previous sections, the algorithm provides most of the predictive performance on your data, given its ability to detect signals from data and fit the true functional form of the predictive function without overfitting and generating much estimate variance. Not every machine learning algorithm is a best fit for your data, and no single algorithm can suit every problem. It's up to you to find the right one for a specific problem.

A second source of predictive performance is the data itself when appropriately transformed and selected to enhance the learning capabilities of the chosen algorithm. Chapter 11 discusses the issue of transforming and selecting data.

The final source of predictive performance derives from fine-tuning the algorithm's *hyperparameters*, which are the parameters that you set (configure) before learning happens and that aren't learned from data. Their role is to delimit a set of *a priori* a hypotheses. In contrast, other parameters are specified *a posteriori*, that is, after the algorithm interacts with the data and, by using an optimization process, finds that certain parameter values work better in obtaining good predictions. Not all machine learning algorithms require much hyperparameter tuning, but some of the most complex ones do, and though such algorithms still work out of the box, pulling the right levers may make a large difference in the correctness of the predictions. Even when the hyperparameters aren't learned from data, you should consider the data you're working on when deciding hyperparameters, and make a choice based on cross-validation and careful evaluation of possibilities.

REMEMBER

Complex machine learning algorithms, the ones most exposed to variance of estimates, present many choices expressed in a large number of parameters. Twiddling with them makes them adapt more or less to the data they are learning from. Sometimes, too much hyperparameter twiddling may even cause the algorithm to detect false signals from the data. That makes hyperparameters themselves an undetected source of variance if you start manipulating them too much based on some fixed reference like a test set or a repeated cross-validation schema.

Exploring the hyperparameter space

The possible combinations of values that hyperparameters may form make deciding where to look for optimizations hard. As described when discussing gradient descent, an optimization space may contain value combinations that perform better or worse. Even after finding a good combination, you're not assured that it's the best option. (This is the problem of getting stuck in local minima, an issue described in Chapter 8 when talking about problems with gradient descent.)

As a practical way of solving this problem, the best way to verify hyperparameters for an algorithm applied to specific data is to test them all by cross-validation and to pick the best combination. This approach, called *grid search*, offers indisputable advantages by allowing you to sample the range of possible values to input into the algorithm systematically and to spot when the general minimum happens (for more about the Scikit-learn implementation: `https://scikit-learn.org/ stable/modules/grid_search.html#grid-search`). On the other hand, grid search also has serious drawbacks because it's computationally intensive (you can easily perform this task in parallel on modern multicore computers) and quite time-consuming. Moreover, systematic and intensive tests enhance the possibility of overfitting the validation process, where seemingly good validation results are actually due to matching with noise by chance in the specific validation folds or set, rather than true generalization ability. Some alternatives to grid search are available. Instead of testing everything, you can try the following:

>> Using a Bayesian approach (where the number of tests is minimized by taking advantage of knowing previous results).

>> Using random search (the I'm "Feeling Lucky" approach).

TIP

Bayesian optimization, though conceptually complex, has been made accessible thanks to several Python packages, such as Scikit-Optimize (`https://scikit-optimize.github.io/stable`), Optuna (`https://optuna.org`), and Hyperopt (`https://github.com/hyperopt/hyperopt`). All these libraries simplify the process of applying Bayesian optimization by providing pre-built tools and APIs. Refer to their online documentation to learn more about how each package works.

Surprisingly, random search works incredibly well, is simple to understand, and isn't just based on blind luck, though it may initially appear to be. In fact, the main point of the technique is that if you pick enough random tests, you have enough possibilities to spot the proper parameters without wasting energy on testing slightly different combinations of similarly performing combinations.

The graphical representation shown in Figure 9-5 explains why random search works fine. A systematic exploration, though practical, tends to test every combination, which turns into a waste of energy if some parameters don't influence the result. A random search tests fewer combinations but more in the range of each hyperparameter, a strategy that proves winning if, as often happens, certain parameters are more critical than others.

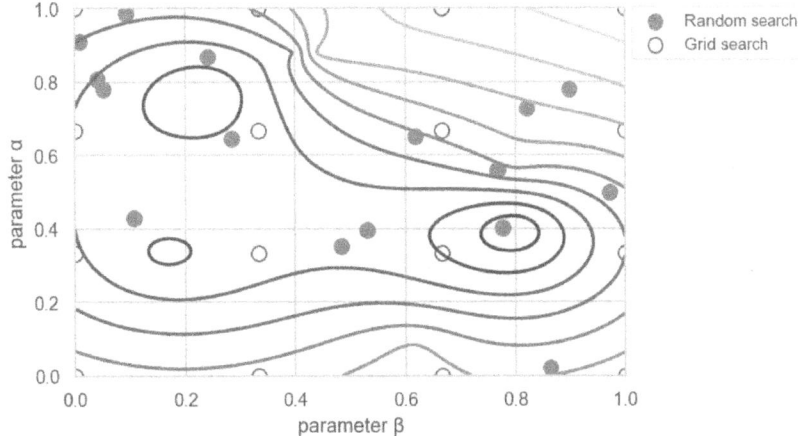

FIGURE 9-5:
Comparing grid search to random search.

TIP

For a randomized search to perform well, you should take at least 30 tests. It makes sense to resort to random search or to Bayesian optimization if a grid search really requires a more significant number of experiments.

Selecting relevant features

Hyperparameters are not the only aspect of a model that you question by cross-validation and grid search. All transformations that you apply to data can be evaluated in the same way to determine whether they improve the machine learning algorithm's efficacy in the problem you're working on.

In particular, one important transformation that you can apply to data to achieve better results is *feature selection.* With feature selection, you provide only a subset of the dataset features that you expect to work best. In fact, not all features are helpful, and some may even damage the learning process. Errors, noise, and high similarity with other features (high correlation among a set of features) can confuse the algorithm and increase estimate variance.

Selecting features is, therefore, another part of your data validation work. It could significantly change the results you get from machine learning. In this case, validation is always necessary because the effects of data characteristics are even more unpredictable than tuning hyperparameters. You can skip validation only when you know for sure that certain features work on your problem. However, that approach is more typical of statistics, in which many models are theory-driven, meaning that they are founded more on preliminary studies, reasoning, and experiments than on data itself.

TIP

The paper "Two Cultures," by Leo Breiman (available at `https://project euclid.org/euclid.ss/1009213726`), discusses the different approaches of machine learning and statistics to problems. It provides additional points of view on how and why we have a machine learning approach and a statistical one, and how they differ.

If you take the approach of checking data directly to determine which features are most useful — what you should keep and what to discard — you have three distinct options:

>> **Univariate statistics:** You use some simple statistics, such as the Pearson correlation or the Chi-square test, to rule out the less useful features. In Scikit-learn, you can use `SelectKBest` together with scoring functions `chi2`, `f_classif`, or `f_regression` (`https://scikit-learn.org/stable/modules/feature_selection.html#univariate-feature-selection`) to retain only the features that are more related to the prediction. Because you analyze each feature alone, you can't determine whether there are any synergies between them that could help the prediction.

>> **Model-based selection:** Some machine learning algorithms select the most useful features by themselves. In the following chapters, you will find out that tree-based models can provide you with importance rankings for features.

You also discover that linear models have their own ways of figuring out what features should be weighted less or even excluded. The great advantage of such methods is that they are holistic. That is, they evaluate the contribution of each feature in the overall set of features, so they always propose one of the best possible sets of features. On the other hand, the selection is strongly related to the functional form of the machine learning algorithm that made the selection. Hence, the selection could be less effective if you try applying it to another algorithm.

>> **Iterative feature selection:** This approach is a middle ground between testing features singularly and as a whole. You test an algorithm by progressively adding the most useful features, removing the less useful ones, or both. This approach can significantly reduce the number of features used (applied to any model), but it's also expensive from a computational point of view. Scikit-learn implements the Recursive Feature Elimination (RFE) iterative strategy (implemented with validation: `https://scikit-learn.org/stable/modules/feature_selection.html#rfe`), which starts by using all features and removing a portion of the less useful ones after each iteration.

Avoiding Variance of Estimates and Leakage Traps

One final aspect to include in this chapter's overview of the validation approach to machine learning is an examination of a possible remedy to high variance in your predicted estimates. High variance means your model is overly sensitive to the specific training data it has been presented. The reason may be that you used too complex models for the problem, had too little data, had too many features, optimized your algorithm too much, or simply a combination of all of these. In addition, this section warns about leakage traps that occur when some information from the out-of-sample passes to in-sample data. You can become aware of this issue too late when your machine learning model is already at work.

As for variance of estimates, besides going to the root of the problem (such as solving for model complexity and data problems), there is a practical remedy, which is called *ensembling of predictors,* which works perfectly when your training sample is reasonably representative of the underlying data distribution. In such cases, you can possibly stabilize your predictions by averaging together multiple predictions obtained in one of several ways: for example, by training models on different resamples of your data (like in bootstrapping) or on different subsamples (random subsets without replacement) of your training data.

To understand why ensembling works so effectively, visualize predictions as shots at a bullseye. If your model is sensitive to the training data, its predictions will be like scattered shots: some will land near the target, while others will be inaccurate, scattering randomly in different directions around the bullseye. When you switch to a different training sample, the locations of all shots might change due to the model's sensitivity. Predictions that were previously near the target might move, and the inaccurate ones will certainly land in different spots, wobbling around the target area. Repeating this procedure multiple times and combining the predictions by averaging reinforces the tendency for shots to cluster around the target. The random shots missing widely in different directions tend to cancel each other out, pulling the combined prediction closer to the bullseye more reliably than the majority of individual shots.

By comparing the results, you can guess that what is recurring is the right answer. You can also average the answers and guess that the right answer is in the middle of the values. With the bull's-eye game, you can visualize superimposing photos of different games: If the problem is variance, ultimately, you will guess that the target is in the most frequently hit area or at least at the center of all the shots.

In most cases, such an approach proves to be correct and improves your machine learning predictions a lot. When your problem is bias, and not variance, using ensembling doesn't cause harm unless you subsample too few samples. A good rule of thumb for subsampling is to take a sample from 70 to 90 percent compared to the original in-sample data. If you want to make ensembling work, you should do the following:

1. Iterate a large number of times through your data and models (from a minimum of three iterations to hundreds of times).

2. Every time you iterate, subsample (or else bootstrap) your in-sample data.

3. Use machine learning to build a model on the resampled data, and predict the out-of-sample results. Store those results away for later use.

4. At the end of the iterations, for every out-of-sample case you want to predict, take all its predictions and average them if you are doing a regression. Take the most frequent class if you are doing a classification.

Data leakage is a common pitfall when information from outside the training set, such as from the validation or the test set, influences the model training process, leading to overly optimistic performance estimates that don't hold up in practice. Often the leakage problem boils down to *snooping*, or otherwise observing the out-of-sample data too much and adapting to it too often. This can easily happen if you often verify your work on the test set and then keep on selecting or tuning your algorithm so that it performs better on the test set. In short, snooping is a kind of overfitting — and not just on the training data but also on the test data. That's because the way you arrange your experimenting and testing makes the overfitting problem itself harder to detect until you get a reality check using fresh data you never tested. Usually, you realize that the problem is snooping when you already have applied the machine learning algorithm to your business or to a service for the public, making the problem an issue that everyone can notice.

You can avoid snooping in two ways. First, when operating on the data, take care to neatly separate training, validation, and test data. Also, when processing, never take any information from validation or test, even the simplest and innocent-looking examples. Worse still is to apply a complex transformation using all the data. In finance, for instance, it is well known that calculating the mean and the standard deviation (which can actually tell you a lot about market conditions and risk) from all training and testing data can leak precious information about your models. When leakage happens, machine learning algorithms perform predictions based on the data you used rather than the out-of-sample data from the markets, which means that they don't work at all, thereby causing a loss of money.

Second, you seldom check the performance of your out-of-sample examples. In fact, you may bring back some information from your snooping on the test results. For instance, you may get the idea that specific parameters are better than others, or it may lead you to favor one modeling strategy or machine learning algorithm over another. For every model or parameter, apply your choice based only on cross-validation results or from the validation sample.

4

Learning from Smart Algorithms

Chapter **10**

Starting with Simple Learners

B eginning with this chapter, the book starts illustrating the basics of how to learn from data. The plan is to touch on some of the simplest learning strategies first — providing some essential formulas, intuition about how they function, and examples using Python with Scikit-learn to experiment and discover their most typical characteristics. The chapter begins by reviewing the use of the perceptron to separate classes.

At the root of many machine learning techniques presented in the book, you will find an algorithm that falls into one of three broad categories treated in this chapter: those based on linear combinations, like the perceptron, those using recursive partitioning, like decision trees, or those employing Bayesian probabilistic reasoning. A further category to add to the list is the algorithms based on analogical reasoning. We will present an example of such algorithms, the K-Nearest Neighbors (KNN) algorithm, in the following chapter devoted to the techniques for detecting similarity in data (Chapter 11).

Grasping these basic techniques will make it easier to understand and use more complex learning techniques later. If you master some of the basic methods now, you can later create even more effective algorithms using ensembles of the simpler ones — those often viewed as weak learners when used individually but powerful when combined. In this chapter, you discover how to predict when to play tennis based on weather conditions using these simpler algorithms. We also demonstrate how to use Bayesian probability to analyze text samples.

At the end of the chapter, none of these algorithms will appear to you as an opaque crystal ball. Generally speaking, most machine learning techniques have a strong intuitive and human vibe because they are a human creation (at least for the moment, unless a singularity appears), and are based on analogies with how we learn from the world or on the imitation of nature, for instance, drawing inspiration from how we believe the brain works. If you can grasp these core ideas, no algorithm will be too complex to understand.

REMEMBER

You don't have to type the source code for this chapter manually. In fact, using the downloadable source code is a lot easier. You can find the source code for this chapter in the ML4D3E folder of the downloadable code file. The example files for this chapter will begin with ML4D3E-10-. See the Introduction for details on how to find these source files.

Discovering the Incredible Perceptron

You can start the journey toward discovering how machine learning algorithms work by looking at models that determine their predictions using lines and surface formulations to divide examples into classes or to estimate numeric values. These are *linear models,* and this chapter presents one of the earliest linear algorithms used in machine learning: the perceptron. Later chapters will complete the overview of linear models. Chapter 12 introduces linear regression and its family of statistically derived algorithms. Chapter 13 discusses support vector machines. Finally, Chapter 14 helps you discover neural networks. However, before you can advance to these other advanced topics, you should understand the fascinating history of the perceptron.

Falling short of a miracle

Frank Rosenblatt, a psychologist and pioneer in artificial intelligence at the Cornell Aeronautical Laboratory, devised the perceptron in 1957 under the sponsorship of the U.S. Office of Naval Research. Rosenblatt was proficient in cognitive sciences and had the idea to create a computer that could learn by trial and error, just as humans do.

The idea was successfully developed as software running on dedicated hardware. The combination of special software and hardware allowed faster and more precise recognition of complex images than any other computer could do at the time. The new technology raised great expectations and caused a huge controversy when Rosenblatt affirmed that the perceptron was the embryo of a new computer that could walk, talk, see, write, and even reproduce itself and be conscious of its existence. If true, it would have been a powerful tool, and it introduced the world to the concept of strong AI, an artificial intelligence with capabilities and functions similar to those of a human brain.

Needless to say, the perceptron didn't live up to its creator's expectations. It soon displayed a limited capacity, even in its image-recognition specialization. The general disappointment ignited the first AI winter and the temporary abandonment of connectionism until the 1980s.

REMEMBER

Connectionism is the approach to machine learning that is based on neuroscience, as well as the example of biologically interconnected networks. You can retrace the root of connectionism to the perceptron. (See Chapter 2 for a discussion of the five tribes of machine learning.)

The perceptron is an iterative algorithm that strives to determine, by successive approximations, the best set of values for a vector, w, which is also called the *weight vector.* Vector w can help predict the class of an example when its dot product is taken with the vector of features, x (containing the information expressed in numeric values). Then a constant term, called the bias (b), is added. The output is a prediction in the sense that the previously described operations output a number whose sign should be able to predict the class of each example in a binary classification problem.

REMEMBER

So far, the book has discussed three different meanings of bias: the sampling bias, the error bias in a machine learning algorithm's predictions, and, now, the bias as the constant term in some machine learning formulations, such as the perceptron, based on the summation of weighted values.

The natural specialty of the perceptron is binary classification. However, you can use it to predict multiple classes using multiple models (one for each class, a training strategy called one-versus-all or OvA). Apart from classification, the perceptron can't provide much more information. For instance, you can't use it to estimate the probability of its predictions being correct. In mathematical terms, the perceptron tries to minimize the following loss function, but it does so only for the examples that are misclassified (in other words, whose sign doesn't correspond to the right class):

$$Error = -\Sigma_{ieM}\, y_i \left(x_i^T w + b \right)$$

The formula, which is an example of a cost function as defined in Chapter 8, involves only the examples of the matrix X, that are misclassified by the current weight vector w and bias b. To understand the function of the formula, you have to consider that there are only two classes. The examples from the first class are expressed as a +1 value in response to vector y, whereas the examples from the other class are consequently coded as −1. The formula picks up each of the misclassified examples and, in turn, computes the dot product of their feature vector and the weight vector w, and then adds the bias. You have to transpose the feature vector x, so that its multiplication with the weight vector, w, will result in a scalar result, a single number that represents the prediction. Transposing matrices and vectors is indispensable in matrix multiplication, as we discussed in Chapter 7.

REMEMBER

Multiplying two vectors is the same as creating a weighted sum of the values of the first vector using the values in the second vector as the weights. Therefore, if x_i has five features and the vector w has five coefficients, the result of their multiplication is the sum of all five features, each one first multiplied by its respective coefficient. Matrix multiplication makes the procedure compact to express in formulas, but in the end, the operation doesn't differ from a weighted average.

After calculating the dot product, you add the values to the bias and multiply everything by the value that you should have predicted (which is +1 for the first class and −1 for the second one). Because you're working only with misclassified examples, the result of the operation is always negative because the multiplication of two sign-mismatched values is negative.

Finally, after running the same computation for all the misclassified examples, you sum these negative results for all misclassified examples. The result is a negative number that becomes positive because of the negative sign at the head of the error formula shown earlier (which is like multiplying everything by 1). The size of the result increases as the number of perceptron errors becomes larger.

By observing the results, you realize that the formula is devised in a smart way, although far from being miraculous, as expected by Rosenblatt. The output is smaller when the number of errors is smaller. When you have no misclassification, the summation result turns to zero. Putting the formula in this form tells the computer to try to achieve perfect classification and never give up. The idea is that when it finds the right values for the vector w because there aren't prediction errors anymore, all that's left to do is to apply the following formula:

$$\hat{y} = sign(Xw + q)$$

Running the formula outputs a vector of predictions (y-hat) containing a sequence of +1 and −1 values that correspond to the expected classes.

Hitting the nonseparability limit

The secret to perceptron calculations is in how the algorithm updates the weight w. Such updates happen by randomly picking one of the misclassified examples (call it x_t) and changing the w vector using a simple weighted addition:

$$w = w + \eta * (x_t * y_t)$$

The Greek letter eta (η) is the *learning rate*. It's a positive floating number between 0 and 1. Setting this value near zero can reduce the magnitude of the update to the vector w, whereas setting the value near one will allow the update process to have a more considerable impact on the w vector values. Setting different learning rates can speed up or slow down the learning process. Many other algorithms use this strategy, and a lower eta often leads to smoother convergence, although it may require more iterations and a longer waiting time before getting the results.

The update strategy provides intuition about what happens when using a perceptron to learn the classes. If you imagine the examples projected on a Cartesian plane, the decision boundary created by a perceptron is nothing more than a straight line trying to separate the positive class from the negative one. As you may recall from linear algebra, everything expressed in the form of $y = x * b + a$ is actually a line in a plane.

Initially, when w is set to zero or to random values, the separating line is just one of the infinite possible lines found on a plane, as shown in Figure 10-1. The updating phase defines it by forcing it to become closer to the misclassified point. Using multiple iterations to determine the errors places the line at the exact border between the two classes.

FIGURE 10-1:
The separating line of a perceptron across two classes.

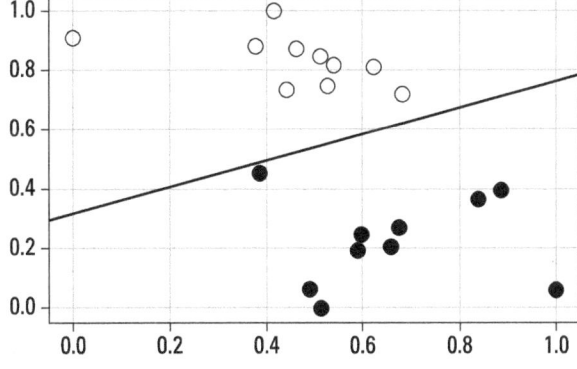

In spite of being such a smart algorithm, the perceptron showed its limits quite soon. Apart from being only capable of classifying two classes using exclusively numerical features, it had an important limit: If two classes cannot be clearly separated by a straight-line decision boundary due to mixing, the algorithm won't find a solution and will keep updating itself indefinitely. In this case, we deem the two classes *nonlinearly separable.*

Nonlinear separability happens when you can't divide two classes spread on two or more dimensions by any line or plane. Overcoming nonlinear separability is one of the challenges that machine learning has to accomplish to become effective against complex problems based on real data, not just on artificial data created for academic purposes.

When the nonlinear separability matter came under scrutiny and practitioners started losing interest in the perceptron, experts quickly theorized that they could fix the problem by creating a new feature space (by recombining original features into new ones) in which previously inseparable classes are tuned to become separable. Thus, the perceptron would be as fine as before. Unfortunately, creating new feature spaces is challenging because it requires computational power, although these techniques are now standard in many analyses. Creating a new feature space is an advanced topic discussed later in the book when studying the learning strategies of more complex algorithms, such as neural networks and support vector machines. The solution to the problem has been to develop new algorithms that inherently handle nonlinearity, like multilayer neural networks, or SVMs with kernels, which will be discussed in the following chapters.

In recent years, the algorithm has had a revival thanks to big data: A perceptron doesn't need to work with all the data in memory, but it can update its weights based on single examples (by updating its weight vector only when a misclassified case makes it necessary). It's therefore a perfect algorithm for online learning, such as learning from big data using small batches or even just by one example at a time.

Growing Greedy Classification Trees

Decision trees have a long history. The first algorithm of their kind dates back to the 1970s, but if you consider experiments and first original research, the use of decision trees goes back even earlier as they are roughly as old as the perceptron concept. As core algorithms of the symbolist tribe, decision trees have enjoyed long popularity because of their intuitive approach. Their output is easily translated into rules and is therefore quite understandable by humans. They're also extremely easy to use and versatile. All these characteristics make them an effective and appealing no-brainer with respect to models that require complex mathematical transformations of the input data matrix or extremely accurate tuning of their hyperparameters.

Predicting outcomes by splitting data

Using a sample of observations as a starting point, the algorithm attempts to discover rules that predict the output classes (or the numeric values when working through a regression problem) by dividing the input matrix into smaller and smaller partitions until the process triggers a rule for stopping. This process of inferring general rules from specific examples is a form of *inductive reasoning,* as treated by logic and philosophy. In a machine learning context, such an inductive process is achieved by applying a search among all the possible ways to split the training data and deciding, in a greedy way, to use the split that optimizes a chosen statistical measure on the resulting partitions.

REMEMBER

An algorithm is *greedy* when it always chooses its move to maximize the result in each step along the optimization process, regardless of what could happen in the following steps. In other words, the algorithm looks to maximize the current step without looking forward to achieving a global optimization. Think of this approach like someone at a buffet grabbing the biggest lobster right now, without checking if there's prime rib coming out later. Making the apparently best choice at the right time is easy and may work out great, sometimes. But other times it may leave you disappointed (and with no prime rib!).

The division occurs to enforce a simple principle: Each partition of the initial data must make it easier to predict the target outcome, which is characterized by a different and more homogeneous distribution of classes (or values) than the original sample. The algorithm creates partitions by splitting the data. It determines the data splits by first evaluating the features and then the values in the features that could bring the maximum improvement of a special statistical measure that plays the role of the cost function in a decision tree.

Several statistical measures determine how to make the splits in a decision tree. All abide by the idea that a split must improve on the original sample and any other possible split when it results in more homogeneous nodes with respect to the target variable. Among the most used measures are:

>> Gini impurity

>> Information gain

>> Variance reduction (for regression problems)

These measurements operate similarly, so this chapter focuses on information gain because it's the most intuitive measurement and conveys how a decision tree can detect an increased predictive ability (or a reduced risk) in the easiest way for a certain split. Ross Quinlan created a decision tree algorithm based on information gain (ID3) in the 1970s, and it's still quite popular thanks to its influential successor, C4.5. Information gain relies on the formula for *information entropy*, a generalized formulation that describes the expected value from the information contained in a message:

$$Entropy = \Sigma - p_i \log_2 p_i$$

In the formula, p_i is the proportion of examples belonging to class i within a given node (expressed in the range of 0 to 1) and $\log_2$ is the base two logarithm. Starting with a sample in which you want to classify two classes having the same probability (a 50/50 distribution), the maximum possible entropy is

```
Entropy = -0.5*log₂(0.5) -0.5*log₂(0.5) = 1.0
```

However, when the decision tree algorithm detects a feature that can split the dataset into two partitions, where the distribution of the two classes is 40/60, the average informative entropy diminishes:

```
Entropy = -0.4*log₂(0.4) -0.6*log₂(0.6) = 0.97
```

Note that the entropy calculations sum terms for all the classes. Using the 40/60 split, the sum is less than the theoretical maximum of 1 (diminishing the entropy). Think of the entropy as a measure of the mess in data: The less mess, the more order, and the easier it is to guess the right class. Think of high entropy like that nightmare sock drawer — a chaotic jumble of blacks, whites, blues, and that one weird pair that you impulsively bought once. Reaching in is a gamble! But if you carefully create new, less chaotic piles, thus lowering the entropy, maybe you can have one pile with mostly blacks and another with mostly whites, and finally pick the right pair of socks for going to the office in the mornings.

After a first split, the algorithm tries to split the obtained partitions further using the same logic of reducing entropy. It progressively splits any successive data partition until no more splits are possible because the subsample is a single example or because it has met a stopping rule.

REMEMBER

Stopping rules limit the expansion of a tree. These rules work by considering three aspects of a partition: initial partition size, resulting partition size, and information gain achievable by the split. Stopping rules are important because decision tree algorithms approximate many functions; however, noise and data errors can easily influence this algorithm. Consequently, depending on the sample, the instability and variance of the resulting estimates affect decision tree predictions.

As an example, look at what a decision tree can achieve using one of the original Ross Quinlan datasets that presents and describes the ID3 algorithm in *Induction of Decision Trees* (1986) (https://dl.acm.org/doi/10.1023/A%3A1022643204877). The dataset is quite simple, consisting of only 14 observations of weather conditions, with results that say whether it's appropriate to play tennis. The example contains four features: outlook, temperature, humidity, and wind, all expressed using qualitative classes instead of measurements (you could express temperature, humidity, and wind strength numerically) to convey a more intuitive understanding of how the features relate to the outcome. The following example uses pandas to load a dataset containing the play tennis data.

```
import pandas as pd

repository = \
    "https://github.com/lmassaron/ml4dummies_3ed/"
release = "releases/download/v1.0/"
filename = repository + release + "tennis.csv"
tennis = pd.read_csv(filename)
```

Before the algorithm can learn from this data, it needs to separate the predictors from the target and to transform the categorical predictor variables, represented by string labels, into another variable type. Decision trees can work with categorical data in two ways:

» **By one-hot encoding:** Converting each categorical feature into multiple binary features (dummy variables), one for each possible category

» **By label encoding:** Converting each category within a feature into a unique integer using functions such as Scikit-learn's LabelEncoder()

Label encoding imposes arbitrary values on the features, which might not be suitable for all situations, although often the decision tree will find a way to partition the label-encoded data and predict correctly. This approach also risks generating a complex tree. Given such problems, when faced with categorical variables, it's preferable to use the first option and create binary features for each feature combination and its values:

```
X = tennis[["outlook", "temperature",
            "humidity", "wind"]]
X = pd.get_dummies(X)
y = tennis.play
```

The algorithm can now fit all the available data and extract its rules.

```
from sklearn.tree import DecisionTreeClassifier

dt = DecisionTreeClassifier(random_state=0)
dt.fit(X, y)
```

After creating the tree, you can inspect it using dtreeviz, a library that specializes in representing decision trees. Prof. Terence Parr from San Francisco University and Prince Grover (who is an alumnus of the same faculty) developed the dtreeviz library. You can get the package and installation guidance at `https://github.com/parrt/dtreeviz`, and you can read about the development and the package functioning in Prof. Parr's blog entry "How to visualize decision trees" at `https://explained.ai/decision-tree-viz`.

After installing the package with the command `pip install dtreeviz`, you run it and plot the representation of the tree, as shown in Figure 10-2:

```
import dtreeviz

viz = dtreeviz.model(dt, X, y,
                     target_name="play_tennis",
                     feature_names=X.columns,
                     class_names=["No", "Yes"])
viz.view(fontname="monospace", scale=2.0)
```

To read the nodes of the tree represented in Figure 10-2, start with the topmost node, which begins by reporting the rule used to split that node into all the following nodes. Because each split is a binary one, you can see two bars, each representing the distribution of the target after the data is split into two.

The first split from the decision tree is made based on whether the outlook is overcast. On the right, you find the first *terminal leaf*: If the weather outlook is overcast (the condition has a greater than 0.50 probability), you can always play. On the left split, the partitioning continues based on high humidity, and then it goes on with further splits, sometimes ending in a leaf.

In the end, you get seven terminal leaves. Some of them comprise a single case, but notice that each terminal leaf contains only one target type, implying that the decision tree has created a set of deterministic rules for classifying when it's possible to play tennis.

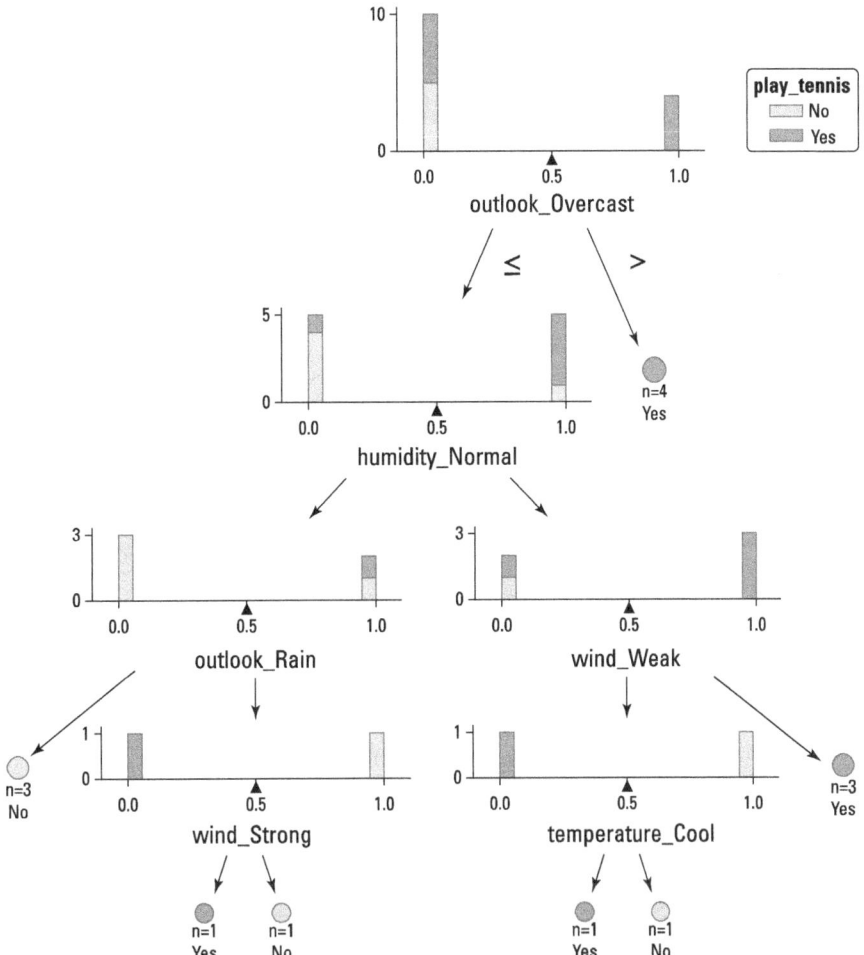

FIGURE 10-2:
A visualization of
the decision tree
built from the
play tennis
dataset.

Pruning overgrown trees

Even though the play tennis dataset in the previous section illustrates the nuts and bolts of a decision tree, it has little probabilistic appeal because it proposes a set of *deterministic actions* (there are no conflicting instructions). Training with real data usually doesn't feature such sharp rules, thereby providing room for ambiguity and probabilistic outcomes.

Another, more realistic, example is a dataset describing the survival rates of passengers from the *RMS Titanic,* the British passenger liner that sank in the North Atlantic Ocean in April 1912 after colliding with an iceberg. Various versions of the dataset exist — the version used in the example consists of a few key features such as gender, age, number of siblings or spouses aboard (sibsp), number of parents or children aboard (parch), passenger class (pclass), and survival, expressed as a binary variable where one means the individual has survived. As previously done with the play tennis dataset, you load the data directly from the Internet. This example also splits the data into a training and a validation set (25 percent of the initial available data).

```
import pandas as pd
from sklearn.model_selection import train_test_split

repository = \
    "https://github.com/lmassaron/ml4dummies_3ed/"
release = "releases/download/v1.0/"
filename = repository + release + "titanic.csv"
titanic = pd.read_csv(filename)

X = titanic.iloc[:,:-1]
y = titanic.iloc[:,-1]

(X_train, X_test, y_train, y_test) = train_test_split(
    X, y, test_size=0.25,random_state=0, shuffle=True)
```

Decision trees have more variance than bias in their estimations. To overfit the data less, the example specifies that the minimum split has to involve at least five examples.

```
from sklearn.tree import DecisionTreeClassifier
dt = DecisionTreeClassifier(min_samples_split=5,
                            random_state=0)
dt.fit(X_train, y_train)
accuracy = dt.score(X_test, y_test)

print(f"test accuracy: {accuracy:0.3f}")
```

The test accuracy of 0.774 is a good result. However, you can improve it because the code allowed the decision tree to grow its branches without restraint. Using a more controlled approach usually brings better solutions, which usually means pruning the tree. *Pruning* happens when the tree is fully grown. Starting from the terminal leaves and going backward, the code prunes branches when their presence accounts for little improvement in the overall information gain. By initially letting the tree expand, branches with little improvement are tolerated because they can unlock more interesting branches and leaves. Retracing from leaves to root and keeping only branches that have some predictive value makes the resulting model less complex and reduces the variance of the estimates.

Scikit-learn implements cost-complexity pruning, which computes different prunings and their resulting cost in terms of entropy or *total impurity*. The code begins by computing the pruning *alpha values* (a complexity parameter that specifies the importance to put on the size of the tree) and their cost in terms of *impurity* (which measures the total impurity across all terminal leaves). The higher the alpha, the simpler the tree and the lower the model variance, but this is offset by some bias. By using cross-validation or a validation set, it's possible to figure out the right balance in pruning for the best results, as shown in Figure 10-3:

```
import matplotlib.pyplot as plt

path = dt.cost_complexity_pruning_path(X_train, y_train)
(ccp_alphas, impurities) = (
    path.ccp_alphas, path.impurities)

fig, ax = plt.subplots(dpi=90)
ax.plot(ccp_alphas[:-1], impurities[:-1], marker="o",
        drawstyle="steps-post")
ax.set_xlabel("Effective alpha")
ax.set_ylabel("Total impurity of leaves")
ax.set_title("Total Impurity vs effective alpha")
plt.show()
```

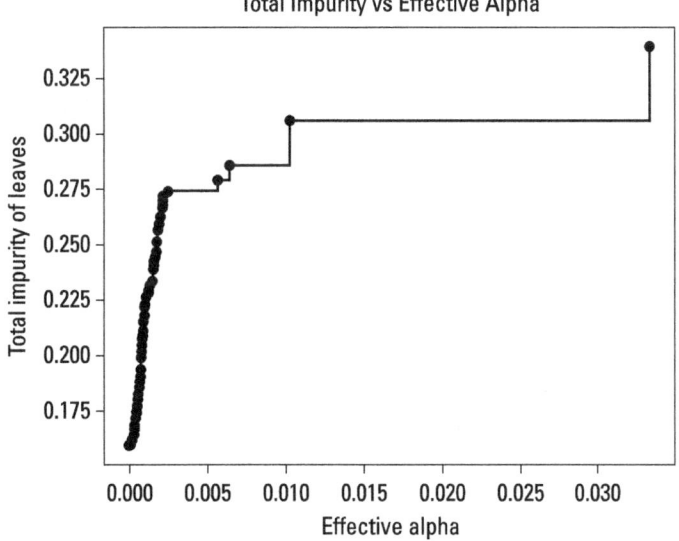

FIGURE 10-3: A visualization of the pruning alphas and their impurity cost.

As visualized in Figure 10-3, the total impurity grows quite fast for small changes in alpha. You can find the best values only by validating the alpha on the validation set:

```
best_pruning = list()
for ccp_alpha in ccp_alphas:
    if ccp_alpha > 0:
        dt = DecisionTreeClassifier(random_state=0,
            ccp_alpha=ccp_alpha)
        dt.fit(X_train, y_train)
        best_pruning.append([ccp_alpha,
            dt.score(X_test, y_test)])

best_pruning = sorted(best_pruning,
                    key=lambda x:x[1], reverse=True)

best_ccp_alpha = best_pruning[0][0]
dt = DecisionTreeClassifier(random_state=0,
                    ccp_alpha=best_ccp_alpha)
dt.fit(X_train, y_train)
accuracy = dt.score(X_test, y_test)

print(f"Test accuracy: {accuracy:.3f}")
print("Number of nodes in the last tree is: "
    f"{dt.tree_.node_count:.0f} with "
    f"ccp_alpha: {best_ccp_alpha:.3f}")
```

After finding the alpha with the best accuracy on the validation set, the code retrains the decision tree using that alpha for controlled pruning. The result is a clear set of rules that provides insight into factors influencing survival on the *RMS Titanic.*

```
import dtreeviz

viz = dtreeviz.model(dt, X, y,
                    target_name="survived",
                    feature_names=X.columns,
                    class_names=["No", "Yes"],)

viz.view(fontname="monospace", scale=1.5)
```

TIP

Think of building a decision tree like letting a bush grow wild: it gets huge and tangled (overfitting). Pruning is like bringing out the big scissors for the garden and trimming off the weak, scraggly branches that don't actually help produce good fruit (or predictions). You end up with a neater, healthier (and often better-predicting) tree.

A chart of the tree structure (Figure 10-4) reveals that only a few rules matter in survival, with the most important being gender (being male penalizes survival) and class (being in the third class, the poorest, likewise threatens survival).

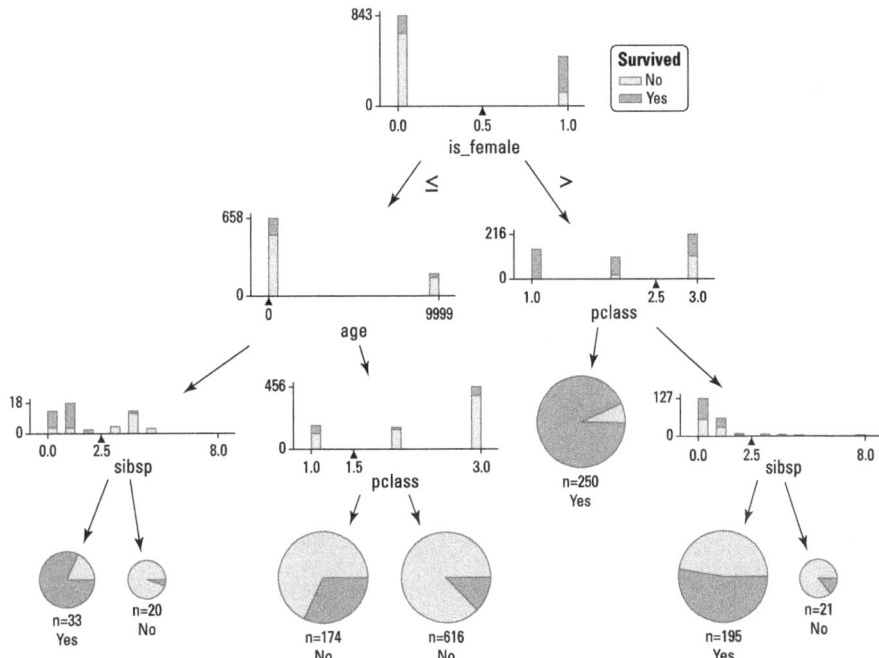

FIGURE 10-4:
A visualization of the pruned decision tree built from the Titanic dataset.

Taking a Probabilistic Turn

Naïve Bayes, another basic learning algorithm, is more similar to the previously discussed perceptron than the decision tree because it's based on a set of values used to obtain a prediction. As with the perceptron and decision trees, Naïve Bayes is a historical algorithm used since the 1950s, although under different names and forms. Moreover, Naïve Bayes is famed for being a practical algorithm for learning from text, and it clearly appeals to the Bayesian tribe. Given its simplicity and the fact that it works with little preprocessing, it has become the standard baseline for many text classification problems in machine learning before testing more complex solutions.

Understanding Naïve Bayes

As with the perceptron, Naïve Bayes requires values that are probabilities of an outcome given a certain context (a *conditional probability*). Moreover, you multiply the values instead of summing them. Naïve Bayes is powered by computations on probability, consequently requiring typical operations on probabilities.

REMEMBER

As seen in Chapter 7, when probabilities are multiplied, it means the events are independent and do not influence each other in any way. Though deemed simplistic and naïve, this assumption is common in many basic machine learning algorithms because it's unbelievably effective when working with a large amount of data. It's like assuming your choice of socks has absolutely zero connection to your choice of shoes or pants. In real life? Often wrong. In Naïve Bayes? Strangely, it often works surprisingly well, especially with lots of data!

By summing values or multiplying probabilities, you treat each piece of information as a separate contribution to the answer. It's an unrealistic assumption sometimes because reality points to a world of interconnections. However, in spite of the lack of realism, Naïve Bayes can sometimes outperform more complex techniques, as described by two researchers from Microsoft, Banko and Brill, in their memorable paper "Scaling to Very Very Large Corpora for Natural Language Disambiguation" (read the paper at https://aclanthology.org/P01-1005).

Naïve Bayes relates to the Bayes theorem discussed in Chapter 7. It represents a simplified form of the theorem itself. To determine the class of an example, the algorithm does the following:

1. Learns the probabilities connecting the features to each of the possible classes.

2. Multiplies all the probabilities related to each resulting class.

3. Normalizes the probabilities by dividing each of them by their total sum.

4. Takes the class featuring the highest probability as the answer.

For instance, in the previous example of the play tennis dataset, you observe that the different distributions of the sunny, overcast, and rainy outlooks connect to the positive and negative answers of whether to play tennis. Using the `crosstab` function from pandas can provide you with a quick check on that observation:

```
print("Frequency Table (Outlook vs Play):")
pd.crosstab(tennis.outlook,
            tennis.play.replace({0: "NO", 1: "YES"}))
```

The output shows nine positive responses and five negative ones:

Outlook	NO	YES
Overcast	0	4
Rain	2	3
Sunny	3	2

By analyzing the positive responses, you see that, given a positive response, the outlook is sunny two times out of nine (probability = 2/9 = 0.22); overcast four times out of nine (probability = 4/9 = 0.44); and rainy three times out of nine (probability = 3/9 = 0.33). You can repeat the same procedure using the negative responses with probabilities of 3/5, 0/5, and 2/5, respectively, for sunny, overcast, and rainy conditions when you can't play tennis. You can also use the crosstab function to return percentages based on the columns. This can save you from performing some computations:

```
print("Conditional Probability P(Outlook | Play):")
pd.crosstab(tennis.outlook,
            tennis.play.replace({0: "NO", 1: "YES"}),
            normalize="columns")
```

The output returns this table:

Outlook	NO	YES
Overcast	0.0	0.444444
Rain	0.4	0.333333
Sunny	0.6	0.222222

Using the Bayes theorem, you can determine that the probabilities that you calculated are actually P(E|B), which is the probability that, given a certain belief (such as whether to play tennis), you have certain evidence (which is weather, in this case):

```
P(B|E) = P(E|B)*P(B) / P(E)
```

The formula provides the answer you need, because it's the probability of a certain belief (to play or not to play) given certain evidence (the weather conditions). If you estimate the probabilities for every belief, you can choose the belief with the highest probability, thus minimizing the risk of mispredicting something. P(E|B) then becomes critical for estimating the probabilities because P(B) is the general probability of a positive or negative answer (the prior probability), and it's easy to determine. In this case, you have nine positive outcomes and five negative ones. Thus, P(B) is 9/(9 + 5) = 0.64 for positive and 0.36 for negative.

When you have many pieces of evidence, as in this example, P(E|B) is a compound of all the single P(E|B) probabilities on hand. This example has probabilities for outlook, temperature, humidity, and wind. Putting them together isn't easy unless you presume they affect the response separately. As mentioned previously, probabilities of independent events are multiplied, and the overall P(E|B) is the multiplication of all the P(E|B) for each feature.

TIP

It may happen that you don't have evidence for a response. For instance, in this example, you don't have cases of not playing tennis when the sky is overcast. The result is a zero probability. In a multiplication, a zero probability always returns zero, no matter what other probabilities are involved. A lack of evidence for a response can occur when you don't sample enough examples. A good practice to address the zero-probability problem and improve model robustness is to modify observed probabilities by a constant, called a *Laplace correction*. The method consists of adding 1 to the numerator count and k (the number of possible values for that feature) to the denominator count. Using such a correction in this example, the probability of 0/5 would become (0 + 1)/(5 + 3) = 0.125.

P(E) isn't a big deal for this example, and you should ignore it. The reason P(E) doesn't matter is that it represents the probability of seeing a certain set of features in reality, and it naturally varies from example to example (for instance, your location could make certain weather conditions rare). However, you're not comparing probabilities across examples. You're comparing probabilities within each example to determine the most likely prediction for that example. Within the same example, the likelihood of a certain set of evidence is the same because you have only that set for every possible outcome. Whether the set of evidence is rare doesn't matter; in the end, you have to predict that example in isolation from the others, so you can safely rule out P(E) by making it a value of 1. The following example uses basic Python commands to show how to get a prediction given certain weather conditions:

```
prob_outcomes = tennis.play.value_counts(sort=False,
    normalize=True)

outlook = pd.crosstab(tennis.outlook, tennis.play,
                    normalize="columns")
temperature = pd.crosstab(tennis.temperature,
            tennis.play, normalize="columns")
humidity = pd.crosstab(tennis.humidity,
            tennis.play, normalize="columns")
wind = pd.crosstab(tennis.wind,
            tennis.play, normalize="columns")
```

After running the previous code snippet, you have all the elements needed to make a prediction. Pretend that you need to guess the following condition:

```
Outlook = Sunny, Temperature = Mild, Humidity = Normal,
    Wind = Weak
```

To obtain the required information, you first compute the probability for an outcome based on the overall probability, and then you specify it by multiplying the conditional probabilities based on the specific evidence you have:

```
proba = prob_outcomes
proba *= outlook.loc["Sunny"]
proba *= temperature.loc["Mild"]
proba *= humidity.loc["Normal"]
proba *= wind.loc["Weak"]
print(proba)
```

The result in terms of probability for a positive response is 0.028219, more significant than the negative response, which is 0.006857. The higher likelihood of the positive result confirms that, given such conditions, the algorithm predicts that you can play tennis.

Estimating response with Naïve Bayes

Now that you know how it works, Naïve Bayes should be clear in its simplicity and strong assumptions. You should also know that multiplying probabilities is fine. You also need to consider these issues:

>> Fixing zero probabilities using the Laplace correction

>> Converting numeric into categorical features because estimating the probability for classes comprising ranges of numbers is easier (however, there is a variant of the algorithm, the *Gaussian Naïve Bayes*, that can handle numeric features without further processing)

>> Using counted features only (values equal to or above zero) — although some algorithm variants can deal with binary features and negative values

>> Imputing values in missing features (when you're missing an important probability in the computation), along with removing redundant and irrelevant features (keeping such features would make estimation by Naïve Bayes more difficult)

In particular, irrelevant features can affect the results a lot. When you're working with a few examples with many features, the noise that may be present in the data can really skew your results. As a solution, you can select a subset of the features, filtering only the most important ones. Chapter 12 discusses this technique using linear models (the presence of useless pieces of information also affects linear models). When you have enough examples and you spend some time fixing features, Naïve Bayes renders effective solutions to many prediction problems involving the analysis of textual input, such as:

>> **Email spam detection:** Allows you to place only useful information in your Inbox.

>> **Text classification:** No matter the source (online news, tweets, or other textual feeds), you can correctly arrange text into the correct category (sports, politics, economy, and so on).

>> **Text-processing tasks:** Lets you correct spelling or guess a text's language.

>> **Sentiment analysis:** Detects the sentiment behind written text (positive, negative, neutral, or another human emotion).

As an example of a practical application, since nobody likes emails about dubious princes or miracle cures cluttering their inbox, this section creates a spam detector.

First, download the spam dataset from the Internet in feather format. After doing so, you're ready to run the example code.

```
import pandas as pd

repository = \
            "https://github.com/lmassaron/ml4dummies_3ed/"
release = "releases/download/v1.0/"
filename = repository + release + "spam.csv"
spam = pd.read_csv(filename)

X = spam.iloc[:,:-1]
y = spam.iloc[:, -1]
```

Hewlett-Packard Labs collected the dataset and classified 4,601 emails as spam or nonspam, using 57 features, many of which were normalized counts of how many times certain words or symbols appear in the email. The free UCI machine learning repository at https://archive.ics.uci.edu/dataset/94/spambase also has the dataset.

If you download the spam dataset and check its features (using the command head(spam), for instance), you notice that some features are words, whereas others point to the presence of certain characters or writing styles (such as capital letters). More noticeably, some features aren't integer numbers representing counts but rather are floats ranging from 0 to 100. They represent the presence of each feature in the text as a percentage (such as the charDollar feature that represents the percentage of dollar sign characters in the phrase and ranges from 0 to 6).

Features expressed as percentages of certain words or characters in text represent a wise strategy to balance the higher likelihood of finding certain elements if the text is long. Using percentages instead of counts normalizes the texts and lets you view them as being of the same length.

Applying a Naïve Bayes model doesn't require fixing many hyperparameters at all. You can set the Laplace correction using the alpha parameter and defining different *a priori* probabilities, P(B), using the class_prior parameter and providing different probabilities from those learned from data.

```
from sklearn.model_selection import cross_val_predict
from sklearn.naive_bayes import MultinomialNB

nb = MultinomialNB()
preds = cross_val_predict(nb, X, y, cv=10, n_jobs=-1)
```

There are several Naïve Bayes models. The multinomial model just shown is suitable for occurrence counts and percentages. However, there is also a Bernoulli version (more suited for binary indicators) and a Gaussian version (which usually expects distributed features — that is, they have both positive and negative values). Python offers a complete range of Naïve Bayes models that can be found in the Scikit-learn package at https://scikit-learn.org/stable/modules/naive_bayes.html.

To test the model's efficacy and provide insights into its performance, besides the data in the training set, you use a helpful function from Scikit-learn, cross_val_predict (https://scikit-learn.org/stable/modules/generated/sklearn.model_selection.cross_val_predict.html). The dataset is automatically split according to the cross-validation scheme, and all the predictions of the out-of-sample validation sets are pooled together.

cross_val_predict is most useful when you want to predict the same test data and use multiple, different models together.

It's time to evaluate the cross-validation predictions using the `classification_report` command. This time, in addition to the usual accuracy measures, the example uses error measures that are more informative about how the spam model performs. Accuracy sounds like a good, intuitive measure, but sometimes it doesn't tell the whole story, especially with pesky problems like spam.

```
from sklearn.metrics import classification_report

cr = classification_report(y_true=y, y_pred=preds,
                target_names=["non spam", "spam"])
print(cr)
```

Precision and recall, and their conjoint optimization using the f1 score, can solve problems not addressed by accuracy. Precision is about being precise when guessing. When forecasting a class, it tracks the percentage of times that a class was right. For example, you can use precision when diagnosing cancer in patients after evaluating data about their exams. Your precision in this case is the percentage of patients who really have cancer among those diagnosed with cancer. Therefore, if you have diagnosed ten ill patients and nine are genuinely ill, your precision is 90 percent.

You face different consequences when you don't diagnose cancer in a patient who has it, or you do diagnose it in a healthy patient. Precision tells just a part of the story, because there are patients with cancer that you have diagnosed as healthy, and that's a terrible problem. The recall measure tells the second part of the story. It reports, among an entire class, your percentage of correct guesses. For example, when reviewing the previous example, the recall metric is the percentage of patients you correctly guessed have cancer. If there are 20 patients with cancer and you have diagnosed just nine of them, your recall will be 45 percent.

When using your model, you can be accurate but still have low recall, or have a high recall but lose accuracy in the process. Fortunately, precision and recall can be maximized together using the f1 score, which uses the formula: `f1 = 2 * (precision * recall) / (precision + recall)`. Using the f1 score ensures you always get the best precision and recall combined.

In the case of this example, you can see that the f1 signals that the model performs less well when dealing with the spam examples. This could be due to the small number of examples from that class. In fact, as often happens with real-world problems, it's difficult and costly to get all the examples you need in the right proportion. Spam emails are much less frequent than regular emails in this dataset, and the dataset is *imbalanced* because it doesn't have enough spam examples.

TIP

When you want to classify and your classes are imbalanced, meaning that they have a different number of examples per class, you need to rebalance your dataset, or the machine learning model could underperform. The package `imbalance-learn` (`https://github.com/scikit-learn-contrib/imbalanced-learn`) offers a set of possible state-of-the-art solutions, tutorials, and full compatibility with Scikit-learn algorithms.

Moreover, besides the two classes having a similar precision, the model has a lower recall for the spam emails, implying that it doesn't detect some kinds of spam. You can solve this problem by increasing the number of examples, tuning your algorithm (if possible), or testing a new algorithm type on the issue. Catching spam isn't that difficult in the end; the problem is avoiding discarding important emails in the process (false positives, where a positive is a spam email) and ignoring spam emails (false negatives). This is why evaluating both precision and recall is a key step after training your spam detector.

Chapter **11**

Leveraging Similarity

A rose is a rose. A tree is a tree. A car is a car. Even though you can make simple statements like this, one example of each kind of item doesn't suffice to identify all the items that fit into that classification. After all, many species of trees and many different types of roses exist. If you evaluate the problem under a machine learning framework in the examples, you find features whose values change frequently and features that are consistently present (a tree is always made of wood and has a trunk and roots, for instance). When you look closely for the features' values that repeat constantly, you can guess that certain observed objects are much the same.

So, children can figure out by themselves what cars are by looking at their features. After all, cars all have four wheels and run on roads. But what happens when a child sees a bus or a truck? Luckily, someone is there to explain the big cars and open the child's world to larger definitions. In this chapter, you explore how machines can learn by exploiting similarity in

» **A supervised way:** Learning from previous labeled examples to predict labels for new, similar examples. For example, if a new object is highly similar, in terms of features like size, shape, and number of wheels, to some other objects previously labeled as a car, we classify it as a car.

>> **An unsupervised way:** Inferring a grouping without any label to learn from. For example, a list of items all have roots and are made of wood, so they should go into the same group even though they lack a name.

Both algorithms discussed in this chapter — K-means, an unsupervised clustering algorithm, and K-Nearest Neighbors (KNN), a supervised regression and classification algorithm — work by leveraging similarities among examples. We use a series of experiments using Python programming to discover their advantages and disadvantages as they arrange the world into more or less similar items.

REMEMBER

You don't have to type the source code for this chapter manually. In fact, using the downloadable source code is a lot easier. You can find the source code for this chapter in the ML4D3E folder of the downloadable code file. The example files for this chapter will begin with ML4D3E-11-. See the Introduction for details on how to find these source files.

Measuring Similarity

If you consider each example from your data as a vector, you can easily compare them using calculations. The following sections describe how to measure similarity between vectors to perform tasks such as computing the distance between examples for learning purposes.

Understanding similarity

In a vector form, you can see each feature in your examples as a series of coordinates, with each component representing a value along a specific space dimension, as shown in Figure 11-1. If a vector has two elements, that is, it has two features, working with it is like checking an item's position on a map by using the first number for the position on the East-West axis and the second on the North-South axis.

For instance, the numbers between parentheses (1,2), (3,2), and (3,3) are all examples of points. Each example is an ordered list of values (called a tuple) that can be easily located and plotted on a chart using the first value of the list for x (the horizontal axis) and the second for y (the vertical axis). The result is a scatterplot, and you find examples of them in this chapter and the entire book.

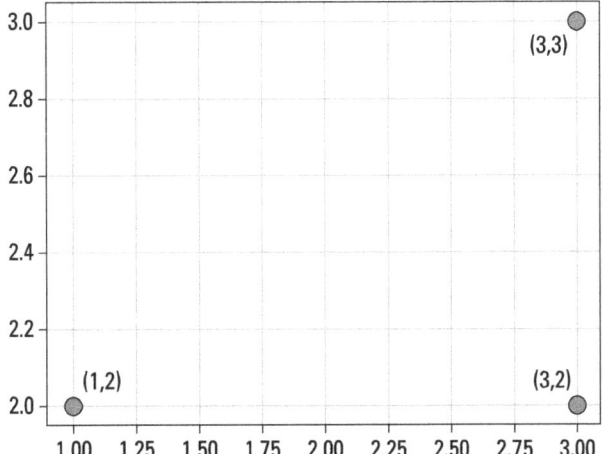

FIGURE 11-1:
Examples of
values plotted as
points on a chart.

Your dataset, in matrix form, has examples (the rows) and features (the columns). The number of features represents the dimensions of the data space, while the number of examples represents the number of points in that space. From a mathematical point of view, each example is a vector, often visualized as a point. If the data has two features, it can be plotted directly on a two-dimensional chart. Visualization becomes troublesome when your matrix has more than two columns because representing dimensionalities above the third isn't easy (after all, we live in a three-dimensional world). However, you can strive to convey more dimensionality using expedients, such as by using size, shape, or color for other dimensions. That's not an easy task, and often the result is far from intuitive. However, you can understand where the points would be in your data space by systematically printing many graphs while considering the dimensions two by two. Such plots are called scatterplot matrices.

Computing distances for learning

An algorithm can learn by using vectors of numbers and computing distances between them. Often, the space implied by your vectors is metric, a space whose distances satisfy certain specific conditions:

>> No negative distances exist, and your distance is zero only when the starting point and ending point coincide (called *nonnegativity*)

>> The distance is the same going from one point to another and vice versa (called *symmetry*)

>> The distance between an initial point and a final one is always less than, or, at worst, equal to, the distance going from the initial to a third point and from there to the final one (called the *triangle inequality*, which means that there are no shortcuts)

Distances that define a metric space are the Euclidean distance, the Manhattan distance, and the Chebyshev distance. These are all distances that can apply to numeric vectors.

Euclidean distance

The most common is the Euclidean distance, also described as the L2 norm of two vectors. In a bidimensional plane, the Euclidean distance corresponds to the length of the straight line connecting two points, and you calculate it as the square root of the sum of the squared differences between the elements of two vectors. In the previous plot, the Euclidean distance between points (1,2) and (3,3) can be computed in Python as `math.sqrt(math.pow((1-3),2)+math.pow((2-3),2))`, which results in a distance of about 2.236.

Manhattan distance

Another helpful measure is the Manhattan distance (also described as the L1 norm of two vectors). You calculate the Manhattan distance by summing the absolute value of the difference between the elements of the vectors. As the Euclidean distance marks the shortest route, the Manhattan distance measures the distance traveled along the axes, resembling the directions of a taxi moving between city blocks (a distance also known as taxicab or city-block distance). For instance, the Manhattan distance between points (1,2) and (3,3) is `abs(1-3) + abs(2-3)`, which results in 3.

Chebyshev distance

The Chebyshev distance or maximum metric takes the maximum of the absolute difference between the corresponding elements of the vectors. It is a distance measure representing how a king moves in chess or in warehouse logistics, the operations required by an overhead crane to move a crate from one place to another. In machine learning, the Chebyshev distance can prove helpful when you have many dimensions to consider. Most of them are irrelevant or redundant because they will use only the dimension whose absolute difference is the maximum. In the example used in previous sections, the distance is 2, or `max(abs(1-3), abs(2-3))`.

REMEMBER

Distance formulas extend easily from two or three dimensions to more dimensions. However, beware that geometric intuition about proximity and density tends to become unreliable in high dimensions because of the curse of dimensionality, as explained in the "Understanding the k parameter" section later in this chapter.

Using Distances to Locate Clusters

Working with a well-ordered space, you naturally find similar items next to each other, such as books about the same topic in a library. In a library, similar books stand in the same bookshelf, in the same bookcase, and in the same section. Imagine, for instance, being a librarian tasked with gathering all the books on the same topic without any helpful indication of a preexisting index or label. Grouping similar objects or examples, in this case, is *clustering.* In machine learning, it is an unsupervised task. It allows you to create labels when no labeling is available or when creating new labeling empirically is helpful.

With the library example, a good solution to the lack of an index or labels would be picking books here and there at random, each in a different bookcase and bookshelf, and then looking for similar books in all directions. You could go as far from the original book as it makes sense. In a short time, based on the books' locations, you could partition your library into homogeneous areas of books around similar topics. After reading a representative book from each area, you could easily and confidently label all the books by subject.

Based on this idea (starting from an example and looking in all directions within a given range), partitioning algorithms help explore data by grouping similar examples around initial starting points. Among partition algorithms, K-means is the most well-known and popular. It usually works out reasonable solutions by leveraging the nearness of similar examples in a data space, drawing the boundaries of classes, and ultimately recovering any unknown group structure. K-means allows labeling, summarization, and sometimes a deeper understanding of the hidden dynamics of data. K-means can help you achieve the following:

» Labeling examples into separate groups

» Creating new features (the labels of the groups) for use in supervised learning tasks (labels from a cluster analysis are very helpful as new features when learning from text and images)

» Grouping anomalous examples into groups of their own, thus helping you to locate them easily

K-means isn't the only algorithm capable of performing clustering tasks. Clustering (also known as cluster analysis) has a long history, and different algorithms exist to accomplish it. There are

» Hierarchical clustering methods that arrange examples into tree-like structures.

>> Methods looking for dense parts of the data space, such as DBSCAN, which is a computationally intensive density-based method.

>> Other methods that figure out whether any cluster is derivable from certain statistical distributions, such as a Gaussian. Gaussian mixture models are the most popular algorithm of this kind of distribution-based approach.

Among so many alternatives, which significantly diverge not only in approach but also in results, K-means has become a very successful algorithm in machine learning for good reasons:

>> It's easy and intuitive to understand.

>> It can be fast and scales nicely to large amounts of data.

>> It doesn't require keeping too much information in memory.

>> Its output is helpful as an input to other machine learning algorithms.

Checking assumptions and expectations

K-means relies on assumptions that some people dispute and that you need to know about. First, the algorithm assumes that your data has clusters (not all data is characterized by having clusters). It also assumes that such groups are made of similar examples, with the starting example, the *prototype* or the *centroid*, in the cluster's center. Finally, it assumes that groups in the data space have a rigorously spherical-like shape. Therefore, regretfully, K-means doesn't allow strange shapes, which can be a weakness of the technique because the real world isn't always geometrically shaped. These are all theoretical assumptions. The algorithm can work well when the data meets the conditions; otherwise, you must check the result closely.

K-means works with numeric measures because it is based on the Euclidean distance. All your data has to be in the form of a number representing a measure (technically called a metric measure; for instance, everyday metric measures are meters and kilos). You can't use features whose values are assigned arbitrarily; the measure should have some relation to reality. However, even though doing so is not ideal, you can use ordinal numbers (like 1st, 2nd, 3rd, and so on) because they have a measure-like order. Even if it is problematic, you may also use binary features (1/0), as described in the previous chapter.

The Euclidean distance is the root of a considerable sum, so your features have to be all on the same scale, or the features with the larger range will dominate the distance (and you'll create clusters on just those features). The same domination also occurs if some features are correlated. Correlated features share a part of their informative content (variance). Again, some features influence the result more than others. One solution is to transform your data before the K-means, for instance, by statistically standardizing all the features and transforming them into components by a dimensionality reduction algorithm such as *principal component analysis* (PCA). PCA finds out how to create artificial features (called the *components*), which are combinations of the original ones. By design, these components are uncorrelated and capture the maximum possible information (variance) from the original data. The components are ordered from the one that has captured the most information to the ones with the least (which can, therefore, be discarded). PCA effectively helps to reduce dimensions in data while retaining the essential information and removing any redundancy in data.

K-means also expects you to know already how many clusters your data contains. However, it isn't a big problem if you don't know, because you can guess or try many solutions, starting from the desirable ones. Because the algorithm makes so many theoretical and practical assumptions, it always comes up with a solution (which is why everyone loves it so much). When you work with data with no clusters or ask for the wrong number of clusters, it can provide misleading results. You can distinguish good results from bad ones based on the following:

>> **Heuristics:** You can measure the quality of the clustering.

>> **Reproducibility:** Random results cannot be replicated.

>> **Understandability:** Absurd solutions are seldom real solutions.

>> **Usability:** You care about how machine learning practically solves problems and aren't concerned about its correctness in terms of assumptions.

The K-means algorithm is unsupervised, so unless you know the cluster solution beforehand, you don't have any error to measure in terms of deviance or accuracy. After getting a solution, always do a reality check with the clustering quality measures to see whether the result

>> Is reproducible under different conditions.

>> Makes sense.

>> Can help with your problem.

Inspecting the gears of the K-means

The K-means algorithm performs tasks in a specific way. By understanding the algorithm's procedure to perform tasks, you can better understand how to employ the K-means algorithm. Here is the procedure that the classical algorithm uses (there are also improved versions, such as k-means++, which are slightly different):

1. After you instruct the algorithm that there are k clusters in the data (where k is an integer number), the algorithm picks k random examples as the original centroids of your k clusters (the cluster initialization).

2. The algorithm assigns the examples to one of the k clusters based on their Euclidean distance to each one's centroid. The nearest centroid wins the example, becoming part of its cluster.

3. After assigning all the examples to the clusters, the algorithm recalculates the new centroid of each one by averaging all the examples that are part of the group. After the first round, the new centroids likely won't coincide with a real example anymore. At this point, when thinking of centroids, consider them as ideal examples (actually, *prototypes*).

4. If it isn't the first round, after averaging, the algorithm checks how much the position of the centroids has changed in the data space. If it hasn't changed much from the previous round, the algorithm assumes a stable solution and returns the solution to you. Otherwise, the algorithm repeats Steps 2 and 3. Having changed the position of the centroids, the algorithm reassigns part of the examples to a different cluster, which likely leads to a change in the centroid position.

Given the jumps between Steps 4 and 2 until the output meets a specific convergence condition, the K-means algorithm is iterative. Iteration after iteration, the initial centroids, which the algorithm chooses randomly, move their position until the algorithm finds a stable solution. (The examples don't move anymore between clusters, or at least a few do.) At that point, after the algorithm has converged, you can expect that:

>> All your data is separated into clusters (so each example will have one and just one cluster label).

>> All the clusters tend to have the maximum internal cohesion possible. You can compute the cohesion for every cluster by subtracting the centroid position from the position of each example, then squaring the result of each subtraction (so you remove the sign), and finally summing all the results. Thus, you obtain the cohesion, which in a cluster analysis always tends to be the minimum possible (called the *within-cluster sum of squares* or *WSS*).

» All the clusters have the maximum external difference possible. This means that if you take the difference of each centroid with the average of the data space (the grand centroid), square each difference, multiply each of them by their respective cluster's number of examples, and then sum all results together, the result is the maximum possible (*between-cluster sum of squares* or *BSS*).

Because the between-cluster sum of squares is related to the result of the within-cluster calculation, you need to look at only one of them (usually WSS will suffice). Sometimes the starting position is unlucky, and the algorithm doesn't converge on a proper solution. The data is always partitioned, so you can only guess that the algorithm has performed the work acceptably by calculating the within-cluster sum of squares of the solution and comparing it with previous calculations.

TIP

If you run the K-means a few times and record the results, you can easily spot algorithm runs with a higher within-cluster sum of squares and a lower between-cluster result as the solution you can't trust. Depending on your computational power at hand and the dataset size, running many trials can consume a lot of time, and you have to decide how to trade time for safety in choosing a good solution.

Tuning the K-Means Algorithm

To get the best possible results from the K-means algorithm, you must tune it. Tuning a K-means algorithm requires clear ideas about its purpose:

» **If the purpose is explorative,** stop at the number of clusters that defines a solution that makes sense, and you can determine which clusters to use by naming them.

» **If you are working with abstract data,** looking at the within-cluster sum of squares or other tuning measures can help hint at the right solution.

» **If you need the cluster results to feed a supervised algorithm,** use cross-validation to determine the solution that brings more predictive power.

The next step requires you to decide on an implementation. The Python language offers two versions of the algorithm in the Scikit-learn package. The first one is the classical algorithm, `sklearn.cluster.KMeans`. You can also use a faster version, `sklearn.cluster.MiniBatchKMeans`, that differs from the standard K-means because it updates the cluster centroids incrementally using small random subsets (*mini-batches*) of the data. Instead of processing all the data at once, it works on small portions of it, updating its results as it goes. This allows for faster processing that can actually work even with large amounts of data that cannot fit into memory.

TIP

The advantage of the mini-batch is that it can process data that won't fit in your computer's available memory by fetching examples in small chunks from disk. The algorithm processes each chunk, updates the clusters, and loads the next chunk. The only possible bottleneck is the speed of data transfer. The process takes more time than the classical algorithm. Still, when it's finished computing (and it may take a few passages on all your data), you'll have a complete model that's not much different from the model you could have obtained using the standard algorithm.

REMEMBER

`sklearn.cluster.MiniBatchKMeans` has two fit methods:

» `fit`: Works with data in memory and stops after it processes the available information based on the batch size you set using the `batch_size` parameter.

» `partial_fit`: Processes the data in memory, but then remains open to start again when presented with new data, so it's perfect for streaming data in blocks from disk or from a network such as the Internet.

`sklearn.cluster.KMeans` offers all the standard parameters discussed earlier: the number of clusters (`n_clusters`) and the initialization method, which is the way the initial cluster centers are defined (`init`). Moreover, it provides the possibility to precompute distances (`precompute_distances`). If the number of effective iterations is high, `sklearn.cluster.KMeans` calculates the distances repetitively, wasting time. If you have memory and need speed, just set `precompute_distances` to `TRUE`, which stores all the calculations in advance. When the algorithm has to create many solutions simultaneously, because of different random initializations, you can also instruct it to work in parallel (setting `n_jobs` to –1 for using all the processors or –2 if you want to keep one processor free for other operations). Precomputing distances and parallel computation make the Python implementation execute very fast.

Experimenting with K-means reliability

The book's first experiment to demonstrate K-means nuances uses a new dataset, the Palmer Penguins dataset, whose data were collected and made available by Dr. Kristen Gorman and the Palmer Station, Antarctica LTER, a member of the Long Term Ecological Research Network (Horst AM, Hill AP, Gorman KB [2020]). Read about the Palmer Penguins dataset at `https://allisonhorst.github.io/palmerpenguins`.

The Palmer Penguins dataset is recent and, from an educational perspective, a suitable replacement for the older Iris dataset. The Iris dataset, introduced by statistician Ronald Fisher in one of his papers in 1936, is a popular example dataset about three species of iris flowers that had their petals and sepals (parts of the flower, supporting the petals when in bloom) measured. Because of its popularity, the Iris dataset appears in many books and tutorials, even though its data wasn't always suitable for many statistical and machine learning tasks.

The Palmer Penguins dataset records the gender, body mass, flipper length, and bill length and depth (called *culmen*) of three species of penguins (Adelie, Chinstrap, and Gentoo). See http://marinebio.net/marinescience/04benthon/AApenguins.htm for more information. These penguins live on islands in the Palmer Archipelago, in the Antarctic. The examples aren't balanced among classes (there are fewer Chinstrap), but they are balanced among genders (the count is for females and males).

The following example downloads the data from the book's dataset repository. It then divides the data among features (excluding the gender, but keeping all the numeric measures) and labels. Using LabelEncoder from Scikit-learn, the example converts the penguin species names into numbers and prints their encodings.

```
import numpy as np
import pandas as pd
from sklearn.preprocessing import LabelEncoder

repository = "https://github.com/lmassaron/"
release = "ml4dummies_3ed/releases/download/v1.0/"
filename = repository + release + "penguins.csv"
penguins = pd.read_csv(filename)

features = penguins.iloc[:,1:5]
le = LabelEncoder()
labels = le.fit_transform(penguins.species)
target_names = dict(zip(range(3), le.classes_))
```

The experiment uses both available K-means versions in Scikit-learn: the standard algorithm and the mini-batch version. In the Scikit-learn package, you must instantiate an estimator object for each learning algorithm in advance, specifying its parameters. Therefore, you define two features, k_means and mb_k_means, which require three clusters, a smart initialization procedure (called *k-means++*), and raising the number of maximum iterations to a high figure (don't worry, usually the algorithm is relatively fast). Because body size and the various measurements are on different scales, you first prepare a pipeline that will standardize the features and decorrelate them using PCA. By doing so, you can be confident that the Euclidean distance measurement that K-means computes works well. Finally, you transform the data and fit the features, and after a short delay, the computations complete.

```
from sklearn.pipeline import Pipeline
from sklearn.decomposition import PCA
from sklearn.preprocessing import StandardScaler
from sklearn.cluster import MiniBatchKMeans, KMeans

pca_pipeline = Pipeline([("scaler", StandardScaler()),
                         ("pca", PCA())])
pca_features = pca_pipeline.fit_transform(features)
explained_variance = (pca_pipeline.named_steps["pca"]
                      .explained_variance_)
print("Explained variance:", explained_variance)

k_means = KMeans(n_clusters=3, init="k-means++",
            max_iter=999, n_init=10, random_state=101)
mini_kmeans = MiniBatchKMeans(n_clusters=3,
                init="k-means++", max_iter=999, n_init=10,
                batch_size=30, random_state=101)

k_means.fit(pca_features)
mini_kmeans.fit(pca_features)
```

During execution, the code prints the variance explained by the PCA dimensions: 2.75, 0.78, 0.37, and 0.11. The first dimension is dominant, and the first two account for most variance. Plotting the results using the first two principal components allows you to understand how the cluster analysis worked. The following code prints a plot on your screen of how points are distributed on a map made of the first and second PCA dimensions, as shown in Figure 11-2.

```
import matplotlib.pyplot as plt

plt.scatter(pca_features[:,0], pca_features[:,1], s=50,
        c=labels, edgecolors="lightgrey", alpha=0.85,
        cmap="Spectral")

plt.xlabel("pca_0")
plt.ylabel("pca_1")
plt.grid()
```

```
km_centers = k_means.cluster_centers_
mkm_centers = mini_kmeans.cluster_centers_

plt.scatter(km_centers[:,0], km_centers[:,1],
            s=50, marker="s", c="orange",
            edgecolors="black")
plt.scatter(mkm_centers[:,0], mkm_centers[:,1],
            s=50, marker="*", c="yellow",
            edgecolors="black")

for class_no in range(0,3):
    plt.annotate(target_names[class_no],
            (pca_features[labels==class_no, 0].mean(),
             pca_features[labels==class_no, 1].mean()),
            fontsize=20)
plt.show()
```

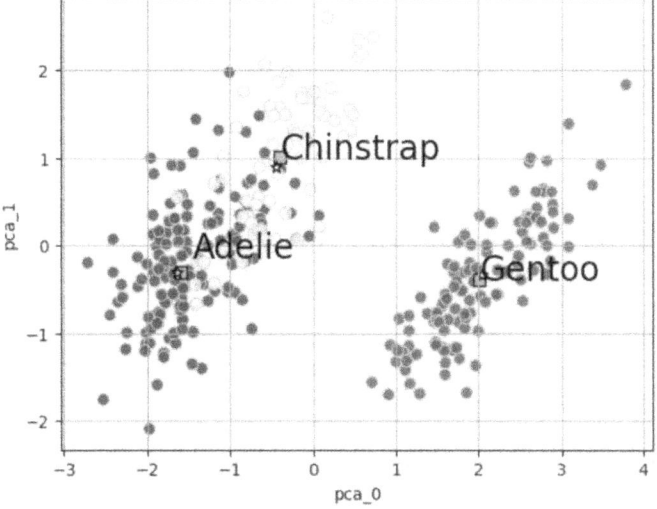

FIGURE 11-2:
Clusters of penguins plotted on a chart based on the first PCA dimensions.

Notice that the plot also displays the centroids — those from the standard algorithm as squares; those from the mini-batch version as stars — and they don't differ much. This fact demonstrates how the different learning procedures lead to almost identical conclusions. Sometimes it's amazing to see how different algorithms may arrive at the same conclusions. When that doesn't happen, you might have too much variance in the estimates, and each algorithm could have a very different learning strategy; yet, you'll notice that machine learning algorithms often tend to get the same strong signals (though in the end, they make different use of them).

All the information about the algorithm is now stored in the features, for instance, by typing **k_means.cluster_centers_**, you can get all the coordinates of the centroids calculated by the K-means procedure.

Experimenting with how centroids converge

Though you can now compute the result and know that the different versions and runs of K-means tend to arrive at similar solutions, you still need to grasp how you reach the result. In this section's experiment, you follow how a centroid (the second one) changes along iterations by visualizing its vector of coordinates step by step along the optimization.

```
import numpy as np

for iteration in range(1, 10):
    k_means = KMeans(n_clusters=3, init="random",
        max_iter=iteration, n_init=1, random_state=101)
    k_means.fit(pca_features)
    centroid = np.round(k_means.cluster_centers_[1], 3)
    print(f"Iteration: {iteration}", end= " ")
    print(f"- 2nd centroid: {centroid}")
```

At first, the coordinates of the centroid of the second cluster change quite rapidly, swinging from positive to negative values, and vice versa. This is the first phase of the optimization, when different examples are assigned to the cluster. After a few iterations, the centroid coordinates stabilize and change slightly at each iteration. Observing the adjusting values as iterations proceed, the rate of change diminishes until later iterations, when the change from each passage is so small that you can't see it without using many decimal places.

TIP

The clustering module in Scikit-learn contains all the presented versions of K-means, plus other clustering algorithms. You can find it at https://scikit-learn.org/stable/modules/clustering.html.

The following experiment, always based on Scikit-learn, aims to check how good the K-means algorithm is at guessing the real clusters in the Palmer Penguins dataset. Sometimes it's hard to reconstruct original clusters using an algorithm because you may be missing the right features for the task or have some irrelevant features that may lead the algorithm to a different solution.

```
from sklearn.metrics import confusion_matrix

pca = Pipeline([("scaling", StandardScaler()),
                ("pca", PCA())])
pca_features = pca.fit_transform(features)

k_means = KMeans(n_clusters=3, init="k-means++",
                 max_iter=999, n_init=10, random_state=101)
k_means.fit(pca_features)

cm = confusion_matrix(y_true=labels,
                      y_pred=k_means.labels_)
cm_str = str(cm).split("\n")
for row in range(3):
    print(f"{target_names[row]:15} {cm_str[row]}")
```

The code will print a confusion matrix, which is a handy tool in classifications for comparing your predictions against the correct labels (the so-called *ground truth*). In a confusion matrix, you read a table where the rows represent the proper classes and the columns the predicted ones:

```
Adelie          [[   0  22 124]
Chinstrap       [   0  63   5]
Gentoo          [119   0   0]]
```

In this cluster analysis, the Adelie and Gentoo species concentrate respectively on the last and first clusters. The second cluster (which can be read in the second column) has a prevalence of Chinstrap, but one-fourth of the elements are made of Adelie penguins. K-means wasn't able to recover the correct classes at this time. Usually, increasing the number of clusters solves such problems, although doing so may generate many clusters that differ only slightly from each other. From a machine learning point of view, having more clusters isn't a problem, but it may render understanding more complicated for humans. This experiment tests different clustering solutions in an iterative loop. The output is shown in Figure 11-3.

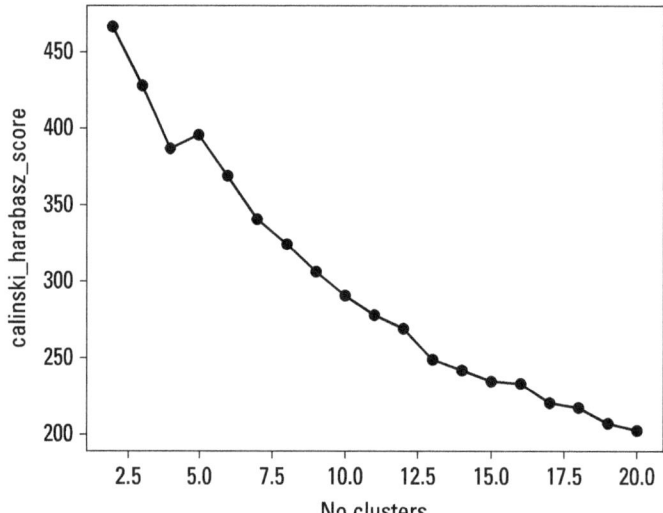

FIGURE 11-3:
Plot of the
Calinski and
Harabasz score
regarding
different cluster
solutions.

Because you don't want to measure the ideal clustering solution based on the original penguin labels (in many real-world problems, you apply cluster analysis when you don't have any ground truth labels), the example uses the *Calinski and Harabasz* score. The Calinski and Harabasz score (also known as *Variance Ratio*) provides an objective measure based on the ratio between how the cluster is homogeneous (the statistically called *within-cluster dispersion*) and how well the clusters are separated (the *between-cluster dispersion*). The core idea of the score is that your solution should present the best, well-separated, dense clusters.

```
from sklearn.metrics import calinski_harabasz_score

ch_scores = list()
max_clus = 20
for clus_no in range(2, max_clus+1):
    k_means = KMeans(n_clusters=clus_no,
                     init="k-means++", max_iter=999,
                     n_init=10, random_state=101)
    k_means.fit(pca_features)
    ch = calinski_harabasz_score(pca_features,
                                 k_means.labels_)
    ch_scores.append(ch)

plt.plot(range(2, max_clus+1), ch_scores, "o-")
plt.xlabel("no clusters")
plt.ylabel("calinski_harabasz_score")
plt.show()
```

A loop over many solutions allows you to plot the score of the different solutions. As you increase the number of clusters, the Calinski and Harabasz score usually improves. This happens because smaller clusters tend to be more cohesive and separated. Reasonable solutions aren't those with the highest score, but rather the ones where you notice a more or less abrupt discontinuity in the descent of the score (even just a change in the slope). A discontinuity means that the algorithm found some noticeable structural difference when looking for that number of clusters in the data. In this example, a good solution seems to go for five clusters, the only point where the downward trend reverses, as shown in Figure 11-3. The code then tests this value by computing a confusion matrix:

```
k_means = KMeans(n_clusters=5, init="k-means++",
            max_iter=999, n_init=10, random_state=101)
k_means.fit(pca_features)

cm = confusion_matrix(y_true=labels,
                    y_pred=k_means.labels_)
for row in range(3):
    print(f"{target_names[row]:10} {cm[row,:]}")
```

You now get a confusion matrix in which the penguin species are more neatly separated:

```
Adelie      [ 0 84  2  0 60]
Chinstrap   [ 0  5 63  0  0]
Gentoo      [62  0  0 57  0]
```

Plotting shows why a five-cluster solution is better than the previous solutions by helping you visualize the clusters' centroids on the first two PCA dimensions:

```
plt.scatter(pca_features[:,0], pca_features[:,1],
        s=50, c=k_means.labels_,
        edgecolors="white", alpha=0.85, cmap="winter")

km_centers = k_means.cluster_centers_
plt.scatter(km_centers[:,0], km_centers[:,1],
      s=50, marker="*", c="white", edgecolors="black")

plt.xlabel("pca_0")
plt.ylabel("pca_1")
plt.grid()
plt.show()
```

The solution depicted in Figure 11-4 shows how two extra centroids help to split the left cloud of points where the Adelie and Chinstrap species are quite adjacent, with no clear separation.

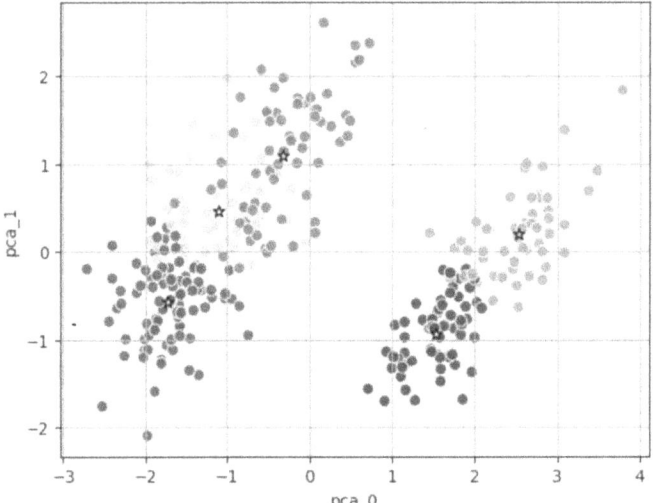

FIGURE 11-4:
Penguin species
represented by
five clusters.

You rarely have a ground truth to check when working with real data. Trust your intuition and the Calinski and Harabasz score if you can't rely on a test. If you're unsatisfied with the solutions, look for ways to add and remove one or more of your features.

REMEMBER

Finding Similarity by K-Nearest Neighbors

Whether the problem is to guess a number or a class, the idea behind the learning strategy of the K-Nearest Neighbors (KNN) algorithm is always the same. The algorithm finds the most similar observations to the one you have to predict, from which you derive a good intuition of the possible answer by averaging the neighboring values or by picking the most frequent answer class among them.

The learning strategy in a KNN is more like memorization. It's just like remembering what the answer should be when the question has specific characteristics (based on training examples) rather than knowing the answer, because you understand the question using particular classification rules. In a sense, KNN is often defined as a lazy algorithm because no real learning is done at the training time, just data recording.

Being a lazy algorithm implies that KNN is fast at training but very slow at predicting. (Most of the searching activities and calculations on the neighbors are done at that time.) It also implies that the algorithm is quite memory-intensive because you have to store your dataset in memory (which means there's a limit to possible applications when dealing with big data). Ideally, KNN can make the difference when working on classification and have many labels to deal with, such as when assigning tags on a social network or proposing a selling recommendation. KNN can easily deal with hundreds of labels, whereas other learning algorithms must specify a different model for each label.

Usually, KNN works out the neighbors of an observation after using a distance measure such as Euclidean (the most common choice) or Manhattan (works better when you have many redundant features in your data). No absolute rules exist concerning what distance measure is best to use. The optimal choice depends on the specific dataset and problem you have. Hence, experimentation is often required. You must also test each distance as a distinct hypothesis and verify by cross-validation which measure works better with your problem.

Understanding the k parameter

The k parameter is the one you can modify to make a KNN algorithm perform well in prediction and regression. The k value, an integer, is the number of neighbors the algorithm must consider to determine an answer. The smaller the k parameter, the more the algorithm will adapt to the data you present, risking overfitting but nicely fitting complex separating boundaries between classes. The larger the k parameter, the more it abstracts from the ups and downs of real data, which results in nicely smoothed curves between classes in the data. Still, it does so at the expense of accounting for irrelevant examples.

TIP

As a rule of thumb for the k parameter in KNN, first try the nearest integer of the square root of the number of examples. For instance, if you have 1,000 examples, start with k = 31 and then test values around this starting point (smaller and larger) using a grid search and cross-validation.

Using irrelevant features or choosing a too large k value increases the risk that the algorithm relies on unsuitable examples for its predictions. The previous illustration of the problem of data dimensions shows how to compute a well-ordered data space as a library in which you could look for similar books in the same bookshelf, bookcase, and section. However, things won't look so easy when the library has more than one floor. At that point, books upstairs and downstairs are not necessarily similar; therefore, being near but on a different floor won't ensure that the books are identical. Adding more dimensions weakens the role of useful ones, but that is just the beginning of your trouble.

Imagine having more than the three dimensions in daily life (four if you consider time). The more dimensions, the more space you gain in your library. (As in geometry, you multiply dimensions to get an idea of the volume.) You will have so much space at a certain point that your books will fit easily with space left over. For instance, if you have 20 binary features representing your library, you could have two raised to the 20th power combinations; that is, 1,048,576 possible different bookcases. It's great to have a million bookcases, but most of your library will be empty if you don't have a million books to fill them. So you obtain a book and then look for similar books to place it with. All your nearby bookcases are empty, so you must go far before finding another nonempty bookcase. Think about it: You start with *The Hitchhiker's Guide to the Galaxy* and have a book on gardening as its nearest neighbor. This is the *curse of dimensionality.* The more dimensions there are, the more likely you will experience some false similarity, misunderstanding far for near.

Using the right-sized k parameters alleviates the problem because the more neighbors you have to find, the further KNN has to look — but you have other remedies. PCA, where you remove the least significant dimensions, can compress the space, making it denser and eliminating noise and irrelevant, redundant information. In addition, feature selection can do the trick, selecting only the features that can help KNN find the right neighbors.

TIP

As explained in Chapter 9 about validating machine learning tasks, a stepwise selection, checked by cross-validation, can make a KNN work well because it keeps only the truly functional features for the task.

KNN is an algorithm that's sensitive to outliers. Neighbors on the boundaries of your data cloud in the data space could be outlying examples, causing your predictions to become erratic. You need to clean your data before using it. Running a K-means first can help you identify outliers gathered into their own groups. (Outliers love to stay in separate groups; you can view them as the hermit types in your data.) Also, keeping your neighborhood large can help you minimize (but sometimes not avoid altogether) the problem at the expense of a lower fit to the data (more bias than overfitting).

Experimenting with a flexible algorithm

The KNN algorithm is implemented in Scikit-learn (see `https://scikit-learn.org/stable/modules/neighbors.html`) for classification and regression tasks. The algorithm is particularly efficient when using the Euclidean distance because algorithms such as the Ball tree and the K-Dimensional (KD) tree are faster and less computationally intensive than a brute-force lookup for the nearest neighbor among the training examples.

The KNN algorithm is particularly popular for recommender systems because it derives the answer about a customer's preference by learning from similar customers. For instance, Spotify, a music streaming service, and Facebook, a social media company, have developed KNN algorithms for their business. Spotify has developed ANNOY (https://github.com/spotify/annoy), and Facebook has released FAISS (https://engineering.fb.com/2017/03/29/data-infra structure/faiss-a-library-for-efficient-similarity-search). Both are open-source libraries that implement highly efficient and fast approximate nearest neighbor search. They are often used in KNN-based recommender systems because they can work on massive datasets of terabytes of data.

The key to the algorithm is to choose the best k, the number of neighbors, to derive the prediction. A low k produces estimates with a higher variance and more sensitivity to outliers. On the other hand, higher k values generate more biased predictions. Finding the correct k value is possible only by systematically testing the effect of different values using a cross-validation. The following experiment uses a grid search on a KNN to classify the penguin species correctly. It looks for the best k value by cross-validation and then reports the result and the best k value. Learning the correct hyperparameters using cross-validation guarantees that you find the best value for the single analyzed data and any other possible data from the same source.

```
from sklearn.model_selection import GridSearchCV
from sklearn.neighbors import KNeighborsClassifier
from sklearn.model_selection import KFold


knn = KNeighborsClassifier(metric="euclidean")
kfold = KFold(n_splits=10, shuffle=True,
              random_state=0)
param_grid = {"n_neighbors": range(1, 16)}


experiment = GridSearchCV(knn, param_grid=param_grid,
                          cv=kfold)
```

Having set up the grid search parameters, we first test working on the original data (which presents features on different scales).

```
experiment.fit(features, labels)
print(f"best params: {experiment.best_params_}")
print(f"best cv accuracy: {experiment.best_score_:.3}")
```

With a cross-validated accuracy of 0.86, the ideal k is 1. We now repeat the test using the data after PCA normalization and transformation:

```
experiment.fit(pca_features, labels)
print(f"best params: {experiment.best_params_}")
print(f"best cv acc: {experiment.best_score:.3}")
```

The cross-validated search indicates that setting k to the value 3 scores the best, reaching a cross-validated accuracy of 0.99. As expected, initially, the Euclidean distance didn't perform well with the original data because of the different scales of the features. It worked, obtaining an almost perfect classification when we equalized the scales and removed correlations between features.

The second experiment with KNN demonstrates how such a simple algorithm is quite apt at learning shapes and nonlinear arrangements of examples in the data space. The block of code prepares a tricky dataset: Two classes are arranged in bull's-eye concentric circles in two dimensions, as shown in Figure 11-5.

```
import numpy as np
import matplotlib.pyplot as plt
from sklearn.datasets import make_circles, make_blobs
from sklearn.model_selection import train_test_split

X_circles, y_circles = make_circles(n_samples=500,
                         shuffle=True, noise=0.15,
                         random_state=101, factor=0.5)
X_blob, y_blob_generated = make_blobs(n_samples=100,
                            n_features=2, centers=1,
                            cluster_std=0.1,
                            center_box=(0, 0))

y_blob = np.zeros(100, dtype=int)
X_combined = np.vstack((X_circles, X_blob))
y_combined = np.concatenate((y_circles, y_blob))
X_train, X_test, y_train, y_test = train_test_split(
    X_combined, y_combined, test_size=0.5,
    shuffle=True, stratify=y_combined, random_state=101)

plt.scatter(X_train[:, 0], X_train[:, 1], s=50,
            c=y_train, edgecolors="white",
            alpha=0.85, cmap="winter")
plt.xlabel("Feature 1")
plt.ylabel("Feature 2")
plt.grid()
plt.show()
```

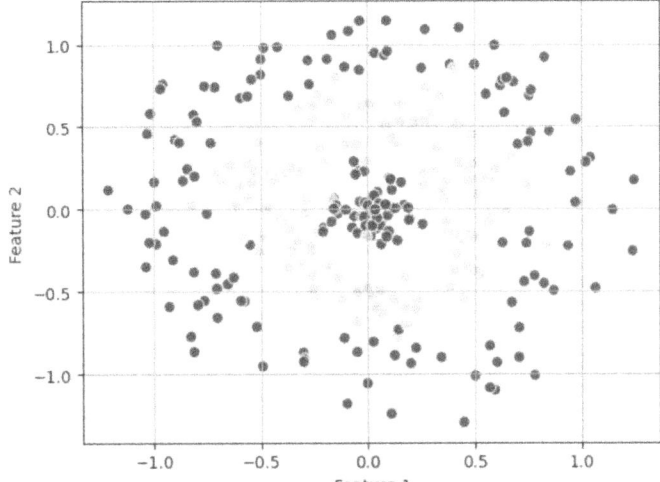

FIGURE 11-5:
The bull's-eye
dataset, a
nonlinear cloud
of points that is
difficult to learn.

You can experiment by setting the neighborhood to 3, the weights to be uniform, and the Euclidean distance as the metric. Scikit-learn allows you to weigh less distant observations when picking the reference examples. In addition, Scikit-learn KNN implementation enables you to perform both regression and classification using different metrics, such as Euclidean, Manhattan, or Chebyshev, as shown in this Python code:

```
from sklearn.neighbors import KNeighborsClassifier
from sklearn.metrics import accuracy_score

kNN = KNeighborsClassifier(n_neighbors=3,
                           weights="uniform",
                           algorithm="auto",
                           metric="euclidean")

kNN.fit(X_train, y_train)
preds = kNN.predict(X_test)
acc = accuracy_score(y_true=y_test, y_pred=preds)

print(f"Learning accuracy score: {acc:0.3}")
```

Chapter **12**

Working with Linear Models the Easy Way

You can't complete an overview of basic machine learning algorithms without exploring the linear models family, a common and often excellent starting point for making predictions from data. Linear models comprise a wide family of models derived from statistical science, although just two of them, linear regression and logistic regression, are frequently mentioned and used. (You can get an idea of how large the family of linear models is by glancing at the models offered by Scikit-learn at https://scikit-learn.org/stable/modules/linear_model.html.) The chapter explores how to work with linear models for both regression and classification.

Statisticians, econometricians, and scientists from many disciplines have long used linear models to confirm their theories using data validation and to obtain practical predictions. A vast body of literature discusses many applications, as well as the sophisticated tests and statistical measures devised to check and validate the applicability of linear models to many types of data problems in detail. This chapter helps you focus on limiting the influence of less useful and redundant features, selecting effective feature subsets, and using stochastic gradient descent (see the optimization procedure in Chapter 8) to work with large datasets.

You don't have to type the source code for this chapter manually. In fact, using the downloadable source code is a lot easier. You can find the source code for this chapter in the ML4D3E folder of the downloadable code file. The example files for this chapter will begin with ML4D3E-12-. See the Introduction for details on how to find these source files.

Starting to Combine Features

Regression boasts a long history in different domains: statistics, economics, psychology, social sciences, and political sciences. Apart from being capable of a large range of predictions involving numeric values, binary and multiple classes, probabilities, and count data, linear regression also helps you to understand group differences, model consumer preferences, and quantify the importance of a feature in a model. The following sections discuss how to combine features when working with various forms of regression.

Getting an overview of regression

Viewed primarily from a machine learning prediction perspective, regression is a simple, understandable, yet often effective algorithm for predicting values and classes. Fast to train, easy to explain to nontechnical people, and simple to implement in any programming language, linear and logistic regression are often the first choice of most machine learning practitioners when building models to compare, as *baseline* (meaning a basic standard) solutions, against more sophisticated ones. People also use linear models to figure out the key features in a problem, to experiment with feature combinations, and to obtain insight into new feature-creation procedures.

While robust and suitable for machine learning prediction, linear regression originates from statistics and is based on a few assumptions that guarantee important statistical properties: linearity, independence, and homoscedasticity. *Linearity* refers to the fact that the model can work only with situations that a line in two dimensions, or a hyperplane in multiple dimensions, can represent. *Independence* and *homoscedasticity* refer to characteristics of its errors (residuals): they should be independent of each other and have constant variance (homoscedasticity). However, you will still have a working predictive model even when these assumptions are violated or ignored.

Linear regression works by combining numeric features through a weighted summation. Adding a constant number, called the *bias,* completes the summation. The bias represents the prediction baseline when all the features have zero values. Bias can play an essential role in producing default predictions, especially when some of your features are missing (and so have a zero value). Here's the standard formula for a linear regression:

$$y = \beta X + \alpha$$

In this expression, y is the vector of the response values. Possible responses include the prices of houses in a city or product sales, which are simply any numeric target variable, such as a measure or quantity. The X symbol represents the matrix of features used to predict the y vector. X is a matrix that contains only numeric values. The Greek letter alpha (α) represents the bias (or intercept), which is a constant. In contrast, the letter beta (β) is a vector of coefficients that a linear regression model uses with the bias to create the prediction. Using Greek letters alpha and beta in regression is widespread to the point that most practitioners refer to the vector of coefficients for the regression as *betas*.

You can make sense of this expression in different ways. To simplify things, you can imagine that X is composed of a single feature (described as a *predictor* in statistical practice), so you can represent it as a vector named x. The calculation is a *simple linear regression* when only one predictor is available. Now that you have a simpler formulation, your high school algebra and geometry tell you that the formulation $y = \beta x + \alpha$ is a line in a coordinate plane made of an x-axis (the abscissa) and a y-axis (the ordinate).

When you have more than one feature (a *multiple linear regression*), you can't use a simple coordinate plane made of x and y anymore. The space now spans multiple dimensions, with each dimension being a feature. Now your formula involves multiple x values (features), each weighted by its own corresponding beta coefficient. For instance, if you have four features (so that the overall space is five-dimensional because you have four features and a target), the regression formulation, as explicated from matrix form, is

$$y = \beta_1 x_1 + \beta_2 x_2 + \beta_3 x_3 + \beta_4 x_4 + \alpha$$

This complex formula, which exists in a multidimensional space, isn't a line anymore but a plane within the multidimensional space defined by the features and the target. This is called a *hyperplane*, whose surface identifies the predicted response values for every possible combination of values in the feature dimensions.

This discussion explains regression in its geometrical interpretation, but you can also view it as just a large, weighted summation. You can decompose the response into many parts, each referring to a feature and contributing to a certain portion. The geometric meaning is particularly useful for discussing regression properties, but the weighted summation meaning helps you understand practical examples better. For instance, if you want to predict a model for advertising expenditures, you can use a regression model and create a model like this:

$$sales = \beta_{adv} * advertising + \beta_{shop} * shops + \beta_{price} * price + \alpha$$

In this formulation, sales are the weighted sum of advertising expenditures, the number of shops distributing the product, and the price. You can quickly demystify linear regression by explaining its components. First, you have the bias, the constant α, which acts as a starting point. Then you have three feature values, each one expressed in a different scale (advertising is a lot of money, price is some affordable value, and shops are a positive number), each one rescaled by its respective beta coefficient.

Each beta coefficient represents a numeric value that describes the intensity of the relationship to the response. It also has a sign that shows the effect of a change in the feature. When a beta coefficient is near zero, the effect of the feature on the response is weak, but if its value is far from zero, either positive or negative, the effect is significant and the feature is important to the regression model.

TIP

The model scales each feature by its corresponding beta coefficient to estimate the target value. A high beta provides a greater effect on the response, either positive or negative, depending on the scale of the feature. A good habit is to standardize the features (by subtracting the mean and dividing by the standard deviation) to avoid being fooled by high beta values on small-scale features and to compare different beta coefficients. The resulting beta values are comparable, allowing you to determine which ones impact the response most (those with the largest absolute value).

If beta is positive, increasing the feature will increase the response, whereas decreasing the feature will reduce the response. Conversely, if beta is negative, the response will act contrary to the feature: When one increases, the other decreases. Each beta in a regression represents an impact. Using the gradient descent algorithm discussed in Chapter 8, linear regression can find the best set of beta coefficients (and bias) to minimize a cost function given by the squared difference between the predictions and the real values:

$$J(w) = \frac{1}{2n}\Sigma(Xw - y)^2$$

This formula, called the *cost function*, tells you the cost J as a function of w, the vector containing the model's parameters (coefficients and possibly the bias term). The cost is the summed squared difference of response values from predicted values (the multiplication Xw) divided by two times the number of observations (n). The algorithm strives to find the parameter values (w) that minimize this cost function.

You can graphically express the result of the optimization as the vertical distances between the data points and the regression line. The regression line represents the response variable well when the distances are small. If you sum the squares of the distances, the sum is always the minimum possible when calculating the regression line correctly. (No other combination of beta will result in a lower error.)

Solving problems with a machine learning approach

In statistics, practitioners often refer to linear regression as *ordinary least squares (OLS)*. Another difference in statistics is the way of estimating the solution, which is based on matrix calculus (solving the estimation by using an analytical approach, the closed-form normal equations, called the *normal equation*, as explained by Sebastian Raschka in this post: `https://sebastianraschka.com/faq/docs/closed-form-vs-gd.html`). Using this approach may become computationally infeasible because it depends on the computation involving the inverse of a matrix derived from the features, which isn't always possible. In addition, matrix inverse computations are quite slow when the input matrix is large. In machine learning, you obtain the same results using the *gradient descent optimization,* which handles larger amounts of data more easily and quickly, thus estimating a solution from any input matrix (also for logistic regression, which lacks a simple closed-form solution).

A key requirement for gradient descent is to standardize (zero mean and unit variance) or normalize (feature values bound between +1 and −1) the features because the optimization process is sensitive to differently scaled features. While some specialized implementations might handle scaling implicitly (so, you don't have to remember this detail) implementations like Stochastic Gradient Descent, SGD, in Scikit-learn: `https://scikit-learn.org/stable/modules/sgd.html` require an explicit scaling procedure that you have to remember to apply. As a result, it's prudent to say that you should always standardize the predictors. Gradient descent calculates the solution by optimizing the coefficients slowly and systematically. It bases its update formula on the mathematical derivative of the cost function:

$$w_j = w_j - a * \frac{1}{n} \Sigma (Xw - y) * x_j$$

The single weight w_j, relative to the feature j, is updated by subtracting from it a term consisting of a difference divided by the number of examples (n) and a learning factor alpha, which determines the impact of the difference in the resulting new w_j. (A small alpha reduces the update effect.) The part of the formula that reads (Xw − y) calculates the difference between the prediction from the model and the value to predict. By calculating this difference, you tell the algorithm the size of the prediction error. The difference is then multiplied by the value of the feature j. The multiplication of the error by the feature value enforces a correction on the coefficient of the feature proportional to the value of the feature itself. Because the features contribute to a summation, the correction process by gradient descent won't work effectively if you're mixing features of different scales — features with larger scales will dominate the gradient calculation and the updates. For instance, mixing measures expressed in kilometers and centimeters usually isn't a good idea, unless you transform them using standardization.

TIP

Math is part of machine learning, and sometimes you can't avoid learning formulas because they prove helpful in understanding how algorithms work. After demystifying complex matrix formulas into sets of summations, you can determine how algorithms work under the hood and act to ensure that the algorithm engine works better by having the right data and correctly set parameters.

The following Python example uses the California Housing dataset from Scikit-learn to try to guess housing prices at the block group level using a linear regression. Block group levels are the smallest geographic units analyzed and published by the U.S. Census Bureau (approximately 300 to 6,000 people live in a block group). The dataset contains information collected by the U.S. Census Bureau about housing in California in 1990. The dataset was initially published by Pace, R. Kelley, and Ronald Barry in "Sparse Spatial Autoregressions" in the *Statistics and Probability Letters* journal in 1997.

The dataset contains 20,640 cases and eight attributes; it has no missing values and is typically used as a benchmark for regression tasks and as an example for exploratory analysis. The target variable represents the median house value in each block group, expressed in hundreds of thousands of dollars. The predictive features represent characteristics of each block group:

>> **MedInc:** Median income in the block group

>> **HouseAge:** Median house age in the block group

>> **AveRooms:** Average number of rooms per household

>> **AveBedrms:** Average number of bedrooms per household

>> **Population:** Block group population

>> **AveOccup:** Average number of household members

>> **Latitude:** Block group latitude

>> **Longitude:** Block group longitude

The dataset has to be fetched from the Scikit-learn repository, hence you need an internet connection the first time you use it.

```
import pandas as pd
from sklearn.datasets import fetch_california_housing

housing = fetch_california_housing(as_frame=True)
X = housing.data
y = housing.target.values
```

The following code graphically represents the geographic distribution of data, and we can recognize California's regions and geography, as shown in Figure 12-1.

```
import matplotlib.pyplot as plt

plt.figure(figsize=(10, 8))
scatter = plt.scatter(X["Longitude"], X["Latitude"],
    c=y, cmap="viridis", alpha=0.5, s=20)
plt.xlabel("Longitude")
plt.ylabel("Latitude")
plt.title(
    "California Housing: Median House Value by Location")
plt.colorbar(scatter,
            label="Median House Value ($100k)")
plt.show()
```

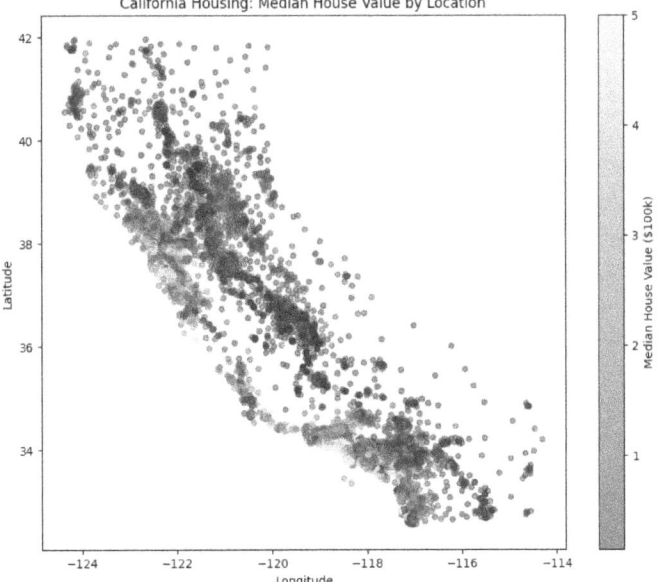

FIGURE 12-1: Plotting median house value in California, using latitude and longitude features.

The code then randomly splits the data into training and test sets, comprising 20 percent of the available data, shuffling each set's order:

```
from sklearn.model_selection import train_test_split

X_train, X_test, y_train, y_test = train_test_split(
    X, y, shuffle=True, test_size=0.2, random_state=11)
```

The regression class in Scikit-learn is part of the `linear_model` module. Standardizing the predictors, that is, subtracting their mean and dividing by their standard deviation, proves quite useful if you want to determine the influential features and helps during the optimization, as explained when discussing the gradient descent in Chapter 8. We wrap both the standardization procedure and the linear regression model into a single algorithm using Scikit-learn's `Pipeline` function (https://scikit-learn.org/stable/modules/generated/sklearn.pipeline.Pipeline.html).

```
from sklearn.linear_model import LinearRegression
from sklearn.preprocessing import StandardScaler
from sklearn.pipeline import Pipeline

lm = Pipeline([
    ("scaler", StandardScaler()),
    ("regression", LinearRegression())])
lm.fit(X_train, y_train)
```

Now that the algorithm is fitted, you can use the `score` method to report the R^2 measure and a Scikit-learn function to compute the root mean squared error, a common metric used in regression problems that is strictly connected with the regression loss.

```
from sklearn.metrics import root_mean_squared_error

fitted = lm.predict(X_train)
preds = lm.predict(X_test)
rmse_train = root_mean_squared_error(y_train, fitted)
rmse_test = root_mean_squared_error(y_test, preds)
print(f"train R2: {lm.score(X_train, y_train):0.3f}")
print(f"train RMSE: {rmse_train:0.3f}")
print(f"testR2: {lm.score(X_test, y_test):0.3f}")
print(f"test RMSE: {rmse_test:0.3f}")
```

The output of the scoring method (which by default in regression provides the R^2 value) and the root mean squared error for the train and the test are:

```
train R2: 0.606
train RMSE: 0.723
testR2: 0.606
test RMSE: 0.728
```

Understanding R-squared and RMSE

R^2, also known as the *coefficient of determination*, is a measure ranging from 0 to 1. It shows how using a regression model better predicts the response than using a simple mean. The coefficient of determination derives from statistical practice and directly relates to the sum of squared errors (which implies that fewer errors result in a higher R^2 measure). You can calculate the R^2 value by hand using the following formula:

$$R^2 = 1 - \frac{\Sigma(Xw - y)^2}{\Sigma(\bar{y} - y)^2}$$

The upper part of the division represents the usual difference between response and prediction. In contrast, the lower part represents the difference between the mean of the response and the response itself. You square and sum both differences across the examples. Squaring the errors has solid reasons: it makes the formula easier to optimize using calculus and heavily penalizes large errors.

As for the root mean squared error (shortened as RMSE), it is calculated as:

$$RMSE = \sqrt{\frac{1}{m}\Sigma(Xw - y)^2}$$

Here, before the root operation, you take the mean (by dividing by m, the number of cases) of the squared difference between response and prediction. The squared difference tends to give more importance to large errors. Noticeably, since you have the squared difference between response and prediction in both R^2 and RMSE, you can optimize either for one or the other and obtain the same results, although using RMSE is more common in machine learning whereas R^2 is more typical of statistical analysis and provides an immediate idea of how well you are fitting or predicting because it can be interpreted as a percentage.

In terms of code, you can easily translate the formulations into programming commands and then compare the result with what the Scikit-learn model reports:

```
import numpy as np

mean_y = np.mean(y_train)
squared_errors_mean = np.sum((y_train - mean_y)**2)
squared_errors_model = np.sum((y_train -
                        lm.predict(X_train))**2)
R2 = 1 - (squared_errors_model / squared_errors_mean)
RMSE = np.sqrt(np.mean((y_train -
    lm.predict(X_train))**2))

print (f"Computed R2: {R2:.3f}")
print (f"Computed RMSE: {RMSE:.3f}")
```

In this case, the R^2 on the previously fitted data is around 0.606, which, from an absolute point of view, is quite good for a linear regression model (values over 0.90 are rare and are sometimes indicators of serious problems, such as data snooping or leakage).

Because R^2 relates to the sum of squared errors and represents how data points can represent a line in a linear regression, it also relates to the statistical correlation measure. Correlation in statistics is a measure ranging from +1 to –1 that tells how two features relate linearly (that is, if you plot them together, it tells how the lines resemble each other). When you square a correlation, you get a proportion of how much variance two features share. In the same way, no matter how many predictors you have, you can also compute R^2 as the quantity of information the model explains (the same as the squared correlation), so getting near 1 means explaining most of the data using the model.

REMEMBER

Calculating the R^2 on the same data used for training is common in statistics. In data science and machine learning, you're always better off testing scores on data that isn't used for training. Complex algorithms can memorize the data rather than learn from it. This problem can also happen in certain circumstances when using simpler models, such as linear regression.

The RMSE calculated on the train data, which is around 0.723, gives us an idea of how much the model has fitted the data. RMSE is easy to understand because it is in the same measurement unit as the target variable (in our case, hundreds of thousands of dollars). When RMSE is applied to test data, it provides an estimate of the model's errors when applied to new data and helps to compare different models.

To understand what drives the estimates in the multiple regression model, you have to look at the `coefficients_` attribute, which is an array containing the regression beta coefficients. In our example, we can extract it from the pipeline we previously created by referring to the label in the assembly, which will point to the regression model:

```
print([f"{feat} : {coef:0.2f}" for feat, coef in
       zip(X.columns, lm["regression"].coef_)])
```

You obtain this output:

```
['MedInc : 0.82', 'HouseAge : 0.12', 'AveRooms : -0.26',
 'AveBedrms : 0.31', 'Population : -0.01',
 'AveOccup : -0.04', 'Latitude : -0.91', 'Longitude : -0.88']
```

Based on the largest absolute unit change expressed by the coefficients, the most predictive features are latitude and longitude, that is, the geographical position of the Census block. Based on the signs of the coefficients, since latitude values decrease when moving South, the model has figured out that the target variable tends to increase as we go toward southern California. As for longitude, the model has interpreted that block values generally increase as we move West and approach the ocean. The other crucial predictive feature is the median income (MedInc): blocks where families have more income are associated with more expensive blocks for housing.

REMEMBER

If the block is costly, hence more affluent families inhabit it, or if being inhabited by wealthier families made the block more expensive, is something that the model cannot tell, given the fact that, by formulation, a linear regression expects the target to be determined, that is, to be caused by the predictors. It is up to us and our understanding of how the world works to decide the target and its predictors.

Mixing Features of Different Types

Quite a few problems arise with the effective yet simple linear regression tool. Sometimes, depending on the data you use, these problems may arise at the same time. This section tells you about ways to deal with as many of them as possible in an easy and effective way.

Linear regression can model responses only as quantitative data. When you need to model categories as a response, you must turn to logistic regression, which will be covered later in the chapter. When working with predictors, you do best using continuous numeric features, although you can fit ordinal numbers and qualitative categories with some transformations.

A *qualitative feature* (also known as a *categorical feature*) might express a color, such as the color of a product or a person's profession. Each qualitative feature has unique values for each class, such as the different colors or occupations. You have a number of options for transforming a qualitative feature by using a technique such as binary encoding (the most common approach). When making a qualitative feature binary, you create as many features as classes in the feature. Each feature contains zero values unless its class appears in the data, when it takes the value of one. This procedure is called *one-hot encoding*. A simple Python example using the Scikit-learn preprocessing module shows how to perform one-hot encoding:

```
from sklearn.preprocessing import OneHotEncoder
from sklearn.preprocessing import LabelEncoder

lbl = LabelEncoder()
enc = OneHotEncoder(sparse_output=False)
qualitative = ["red", "red", "green", "blue",
               "red", "blue", "blue", "green"]

labels = lbl.fit_transform(qualitative).reshape(-1, 1)

print(enc.fit_transform(labels))
```

As a result, you obtain a matrix with three columns made of zeros and ones. Each column corresponds to one of the "red", "green", or "blue" labels. The code first encoded the string labels into numbers. If you print the lbl.classes_ attribute, you will get the sequence ["blue", "green", "red"], implying that the first label, "blue", got the value 0; the second, "green", got 1; and the last one, "red", got 2. This same numeric order is then encoded into the resulting three binary columns because the first represents the presence of the label "blue" in the original data, the second the label "green", and the third the label "red". You can confirm this by checking the correspondence between the original and corresponding values in the matrix.

In statistics, when you want to make a binary feature out of a categorical one, you transform all the levels but one because using all levels would introduce perfect multicollinearity (each level can be perfectly predicted by the others), making the matrix inversion required by the Normal Equation impossible. In machine learning, you use gradient descent, which isn't based on the matrix inversion operation; hence, you instead transform all the levels.

TIP

The presented California Housing dataset does not have categorical features to be transformed, but we could create some. For instance, since blocks near the ocean seem more expensive, a binary feature telling if a block is near the sea would be very helpful for helping the model predict.

Dealing with a categorical feature isn't one of the necessary data transformations you have to apply if you want to run a linear model (as well as many other machine learning algorithms). If a data matrix is missing data and you don't deal with it correctly, the model will stop working. Consequently, you need to impute the missing values (for instance, by replacing a missing value with the mean value calculated from the feature itself). A solution specific to linear models is to use a zero value for the missing case and create an additional binary feature whose unit values point out missing values in the feature.

In addition, *outliers* (values outside the normal range) disrupt linear regression because the model tries to minimize the square value of the errors (also called *residuals*). Outliers have large residuals, thus forcing the algorithm to focus more on them than on regular points. You can use the indications provided in Chapter 11 to detect and deal with any outlying value that could influence your linear model.

The greatest linear regression limitation is that the model is a summation of independent terms, because each feature stands alone in the summation, multiplied only by its own beta. This mathematical form is perfect for expressing a situation in which the features are unrelated. For instance, a person's age and eye color are unrelated terms because they don't influence each other. Thus, you can consider them independent terms, and in a regression summation, it makes sense that they stay separated. On the other hand, a person's age and hair color aren't unrelated, because aging causes hair to whiten. When you put these features in a regression summation, it's like summing the same information. Because of this limitation, you can't determine how to represent the effect of feature combinations on the outcome.

In other words, you can't represent complex situations with your data. Because the model is made of simple combinations of weighted features, it expresses more bias than variance in its predictions. In fact, after fitting the observed outcome values, the solution proposed by linear models is always a proportionally rescaled mix of features. Unfortunately, you can't represent some relations between a response and a feature faithfully by using this approach. On many occasions, the response depends on features in a nonlinear way: Some feature values act as hurdles, after which the response suddenly increases or decreases, strengthens or weakens, or even reverses.

As an example, consider how human beings grow in height from childhood. If observed in a specific age range, the relationship between age and height is somehow linear: The older the child gets, the taller the child becomes. However, some children grow more (overall height) and some grow faster (in a certain amount of time). This observation holds when you expect a linear model to find an average answer. However, after a certain age, children stop growing, and their height remains constant for a long period of life, slowly decreasing at a later age. Clearly, a linear regression can't grasp such a nonlinear relationship. (In the end, you can represent it as a kind of parabola.)

Another age-related example is the amount spent on consumer products. People in the earliest phases of their lives tend to spend less. Expenditures increase during the middle of life (maybe because of the availability of more income or larger expenses because of family obligations). Still, they decrease again in the latter part of life (clearly another nonlinear relationship). Observing and thinking more intensely of the world around us shows that many nonlinear relationships exist.

Because the relation between the target and each predictor feature is based on a single coefficient, you don't have a way to represent complex relations like a parabola (a unique value of x maximizing or minimizing the response), an exponential growth, or a more complex nonlinear curve unless you enrich the feature. The easiest way to model complex relations is by employing mathematical transformations of the predictors using *polynomial expansion.* Given a certain degree d, polynomial expansion creates powers of each feature up to the dth power and dth combinations of all the terms. For instance, if you start with a simple linear model such as the following Python code:

```
y = β₁x₁ + β₂x₂ + α
```

and then use a polynomial expansion of the second degree, so that the model becomes

```
y = β₁x₁ + β₂x₂ + α + β₃(x₁)² + β₄(x₂)² + β₅x₁x₂
```

You make the addition to the original formulation (the expansion) using powers and combinations of the existing predictors. As the degree of the polynomial expansion grows, so does the number of derived terms. The following Python example uses the California Housing dataset (in continuation of previous examples) to check the technique's effectiveness. If successful, the polynomial expansion may catch nonlinear relationships in data and possibly resolve initial problems of nonseparability between classes (the problem seen with the perceptron algorithm in Chapter 10) at the expense of an increased number of predictors.

```
from sklearn.preprocessing import PolynomialFeatures

lm = Pipeline([
    ("scaler", StandardScaler()),
    ("polynomial", PolynomialFeatures(degree=2)),
    ("regression", LinearRegression())])

lm.fit(X_train, y_train)
r2 = lm.score(X_train, y_train)
rmse = root_mean_squared_error(y_train,
    lm.predict(X_train))

print(f"train R2: {r2:.3f}")
print(f"train RMSE: {rmse:.3f}")
```

The resulting R^2 of the model on the fitted data is now 0.690, a noticeable improvement compared to the previous 0.606, implying that polynomial expansion has provided more features that can better fit the target. However, when you try to use the polynomial expansion on the test set, you notice that the R^2 result significantly worsens to 0.423, pointing out that overfitting is happening because there are too many features at play:

```
r2 = lm.score(X_test, y_test)
rmse = root_mean_squared_error(y_test,
    lm.predict(X_test))
print(f"test R2: {r2:0.3f}")
print(f"test RMSE: {rmse:0.3f}")
```

REMEMBER

Polynomial expansion doesn't always benefit the test set. Expanding the number of features reduces the bias of the predictions at the expense of increasing their variance. Expanding too much may hinder the model's ability to represent general rules, making it unable to make predictions using new data.

Switching to Probabilities

Up to now, the chapter has considered only regression models, which express numeric values as outputs from data learning. Most problems, however, also require classification. The following sections discuss how you can address both numeric and classification output.

Specifying a binary response

A solution to a problem involving a binary response (the model has to choose from between two possible classes) would be to code a response vector as a sequence of ones and zeros (or positive and negative values, just as the perceptron does). The following Python code proves both the feasibility and limits of using a binary response.

```
from sklearn.linear_model import LinearRegression
import numpy as np

y = np.array([0, 0, 0, 0, 1, 1, 1, 1])
X = np.array([1, 2, 3, 4, 5, 6, 7, 8]).reshape(8,1)

lm = LinearRegression()
lm.fit(X, y)
preds = lm.predict(X)

for y_true, y_pred in zip(y, preds):
    print(f"{y_true} -> {y_pred:+0.3f}")
```

The results range from negative values to values greater than one, but most are far from the target values of zero and one:

```
0 -> -0.167
0 -> +0.0238
0 -> +0.214
0 -> +0.405
1 -> +0.595
1 -> +0.786
1 -> +0.976
1 -> +1.17
```

In statistics, linear regression can't solve classification problems because doing so would create a series of violated statistical assumptions. So, for statistics, using regression models for classification is mainly a theoretical problem, not practical. In machine learning, the problem with linear regression is that it serves as a linear function that's trying to minimize prediction errors; therefore, depending on the slope of the computed line, it may not be able to solve the data problem.

When a linear regression is given the task of predicting two values, such as 0 and +1, representing two classes, it will try to compute a line that provides results close to the target values. In some cases, even though the results are precise, the output is too far from the target values, which forces the regression line to adjust to minimize the summed errors. The change results in fewer summed squared errors but potentially more misclassified cases.

Contrary to the perceptron example in Chapter 10, linear regression doesn't produce acceptable results when the priority is classification accuracy, as demonstrated by the previous example. Therefore, it won't work satisfactorily in many classification tasks. Linear regression works best on a continuum of numeric estimates. However, you need a more suitable measure for classification tasks, such as the probability of class ownership.

The solution is transforming linear regression into *logistic regression,* a regression model that uses a transformation called the Sigmoid function (or standard logistic function):

$$f(x) = \frac{1}{\left(1 + e^{-x}\right)}$$

This formula takes any value and squashes it in the range from zero to one, thus effectively transforming any output from a regression model into probabilities. Hence, thanks to the Sigmoid formula, you can transform linear regression numeric estimates into probabilities that are more apt to describe how a class fits an observation:

$$p(y = 1) = \frac{\exp(r)}{1 + \exp(r)}$$

In this formula, the target is the probability that the response y will correspond to the class 1. The letter r is the *regression result,* the sum of the features weighted by their coefficients. The exponential function, $\exp(r)$, corresponds to Euler's number e elevated to the power of r. A linear regression using this transformation formula (also called a *link function*) for changing its results into probabilities is a logistic regression.

Logistic regression is the same as a linear regression except that the y data contains integer numbers indicating the class relative to the observation, and a different cost function is optimized by gradient descent (the cross-entropy cost function that is specific to probabilities). In statistics, logistic regression also uses a different optimization process, a process not addressed to minimize the sum of squared errors but based on maximizing the probability of seeing the expected outcomes, which is called *maximum likelihood.*

As an example, using the California Housing dataset from the Scikit-learn datasets module, you can try to guess which block groups contain the most expensive houses (the top 25 percent corresponds to median values above or equal to 264,000 USD 1990 prices):

```
from sklearn.linear_model import LogisticRegression
from sklearn.metrics import accuracy_score

lr = Pipeline([
```

```
    ("scaler", StandardScaler()),
    ("logistic", LogisticRegression())])

topQ_train = y_train >= np.percentile(y_train, 75)
topQ_test = y_test >= np.percentile(y_train, 75)
lr.fit(X_train, topQ_train)

in_sample_acc = accuracy_score(topQ_train,
                               lr.predict(X_train))
out_sample_acc = accuracy_score(topQ_test,
                                lr.predict(X_test))

print(f"Training accuracy: {in_sample_acc:.3f}")
print(f"Testing accuracy: {out_sample_acc:.3f}")
```

The example tests the efficacy of the logistic regression in terms of accuracy (per-centage of correct predictions) of both training and testing sets, resulting in about 0.871 for the training sample and 0.863 for the testing. The computed coefficients tell you the probability of a particular class being in the target class (which is any class encoded using a value of 1). If a coefficient increases the likelihood, it will be positive; otherwise, it will be negative.

```
for var, coef in zip(X_train.columns,
                     lr["logistic"].coef_[0]):
    print(f"{var:10} : {coef:+0.3f}")
```

The sequence of coefficients will appear on screen:

```
MedInc     : +2.28
HouseAge   : +0.443
AveRooms   : -0.705
AveBedrms  : +0.904
Population : +0.0714
AveOccup   : -5.12
Latitude   : -3.8
Longitude  : -3.54
```

Reading the results, as in the regression model, the block's latitude, longitude, and median income are crucial in determining if the block is in the top 25 percent in terms of cost, similar to the regression model. In addition, average occupancy (AveOccup) has a very large negative coefficient, implying that block groups with higher average household sizes are less likely to be in the higher price ranks because more crowded places seem less desirable. You can interpret how these coefficients impact probability by exponentiating the coefficient values. For instance, MedInc has a coefficient of 2.28, which, after applying the exponential function, becomes 9.8. This indicates that a single unit increase in median income (in tens of thousands of dollars) increases the odds of a block group being in the top price quartile by nearly tenfold.

Finally, we have to notice that the model also has less intuitive coefficients. For instance, the Average Rooms (AveRooms) has a negative coefficient, implying that more rooms are not necessarily associated with more luxury. In addition, house age has a positive coefficient because older houses are in more established, richer areas. Population, instead, has little impact (a small positive coefficient), pointing out that block group population has little effect on the value of a property.

TIP

Don't be fooled by the coefficients of a linear model and take them for pure gold. The coefficients of a linear model are visible and interpretable, but they are the product of mathematical optimization, and how features correlate with each other may confound their role in the model. Therefore, the coefficients you get may reflect only a side effect of the model optimization, whereas other correlated features have the right sign and value. Always use your judgment and knowledge to determine whether the coefficients you get are reasonable and make sense.

Moreover, contrary to linear regression, logistic regression doesn't simply output the resulting class (in this case a 1 or a 0) but also estimates the probability of the observation being part of one of the two classes.

```
print("classes: ", lr.classes_)
print("\nProbs:\n", lr.predict_proba(X_test)[:3,:])
```

You get the labels of the classes and the corresponding probabilities for the first three cases in the test set:

```
classes: [False True]

Probs:
 [[0.99200156 0.00799844]
  [0.85857244 0.14142756]
  [0.78629948 0.21370052]]
```

In the test set, the first example has a 98 percent probability of not being an expensive housing area. When you perform predictions using this approach, you also know the likelihood that your forecast is accurate and can act accordingly, choosing only predictions with the right level of accuracy. For instance, you might pick only predictions that exceed an 80 percent likelihood, though usually the logistic regression works with the 50 percent probability threshold.

TIP

Using probabilities, you can guess a class (the most probable one), but you can also order all your predictions as part of that class. This is especially useful for medical purposes, ranking a prediction in terms of likelihood with respect to other cases.

Handling multiple classes

In a previous problem, K-Nearest Neighbors (KNN) automatically determined how to handle a multiclass problem. (Chapter 11 presents an example showing how to guess a single solution from three species of Antarctic penguins.) Most algorithms that predict probabilities or a score for a class automatically handle multiclass problems using two different strategies:

>> **One Versus Rest (OvR):** The algorithm compares every class with the remaining classes, building a model for every class. The class with the highest probability is the chosen one. So if a problem has three classes to guess, the algorithm also uses three models. This book uses the OneVsRestClassifier class from Scikit-learn to demonstrate this strategy.

>> **One Versus One (OvO):** The algorithm compares every class against every remaining class, building a number of models equivalent to $n * (n-1) / 2$, where n is the number of classes. So if a problem has five classes to guess, the algorithm uses ten models. This book uses the OneVsOneClassifier class from Scikit-learn to demonstrate this strategy. The class that wins the most is the chosen one.

The default multiclass strategy with logistic regression is OvR.

Guessing the Right Features

Having many features to work with may address the need for machine learning to understand a problem thoroughly. However, just having more features doesn't solve anything; you need the right features to solve problems. A good practice is to explore the relationships between your predictor variables before starting to build your model. Plotting each variable against the others (a set of plots called a *scatterplot*) may reveal that some features are very similar because their points resemble the distribution of points of the other variables. That's a strong hint that you are not adding new information to your model, as we will see. The following sections discuss ensuring you have the right features when performing machine learning tasks.

Defining the outcome of features that don't work together

As previously mentioned, having many features and making them work together may incorrectly indicate that your model is working well when it really isn't.

Without cross-validation, error measures such as R^2 can be misleading because the number of features can easily inflate it, even if the feature doesn't contain relevant information. The following example shows what happens to R^2 when you add just random features.

```
r2_train = list()
r2_test = list()
X_train_extra = X_train.copy()
X_test_extra = X_test.copy()

np.random.seed(42)
for i in range(1, 50):

    X_train_extra[f"rand_{i}"] = (
                X_train["MedInc"].sample(frac=1.).values)
    X_test_extra[f"rand_{i}"] = (
                X_test["MedInc"].sample(frac=1.).values)

    lm = Pipeline([
      ("scaler", StandardScaler()),
      ("regression", LinearRegression())])

    lm.fit(X_train_extra, y_train)
    r2_train.append(lm.score(X_train_extra, y_train))
    r2_test.append(lm.score(X_test_extra, y_test))
```

In this example, the code trains a linear regression model on the California Housing data after adding some new random features to both the training and test sets. The example records the R^2 for both sets as the number of random features increases. If you plot the results, increasing in-sample predictive capability seems just an illusion. By checking the test set, you see that the model performance has decreased, as shown in Figure 12-2.

```
import matplotlib.pyplot as plt

fig, ax = plt.subplots(dpi=120)
plt.plot(r2_train, label="train")
plt.plot(r2_test, label="test")
plt.xlabel("additional random features")
plt.ylabel("R2")
plt.legend()
plt.show()
```

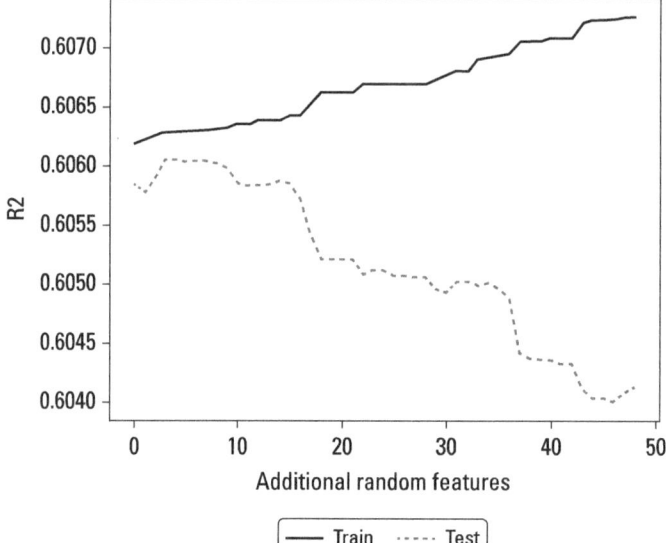

FIGURE 12-2:
Adding random
features
increases
in-sample
performance but
degrades the
test results.

Solving overfitting by greedy selection

Not only irrelevant features, such as random noise, but also redundant features may play a role in the model's predictive performance and your ability to understand a linear model. Previous sections acknowledge that having too much information in your linear model could be a problem:

>> Irrelevant features may worsen the prediction capabilities of a model.

>> Polynomial expansion may produce a good training fit, but poor test results signal that overfitting has occurred because of the expansion of many redundant features.

>> Logistic regression shows that some features have a counterintuitive coefficient, indicating a possible correlation with other features.

As a solution to these issues, it's possible to simplify the training set by choosing only the most predictive set of features. In doing so, you can approach the problem using cross-validation (a guarantee that your choice should be optimal) and a series of tools that Scikit-learn provides. The first one is recursive selection, where you test removing the least effective features from the training set one by one. As a heuristic, the recursive selection uses the absolute value of the regression coefficient to eliminate the features with the least impact progressively. Another commonly used algorithm is the sequential feature selection, which can work forward and backward. When proceeding forward, you start with an empty model and add iteratively the feature that increases the predictive power the most.

In the backward approach, you start from a model containing all the features, and you remove the features that do not affect, or negatively affect, the predictive power of the model. In this example, you start from an expanded dataset containing all the feature interactions (features are multiplied by each other) and determine whether it's possible to build a model with forward selection that works with a smaller, more predictive set of features. First, we proceed to create the expanded train and test datasets:

```
from itertools import combinations

features = ["MedInc", "HouseAge", "AveRooms",
            "AveBedrms", "Population", "AveOccup"]
feature_pairs = combinations(features, 2)

for f1, f2 in feature_pairs:
  X_train[f"{f1}_{f2}"] = X_train[f1] * X_train[f2]
  X_test[f"{f1}_{f2}"] = X_test[f1] * X_test[f2]

lm.fit(X_train, y_train)

r2_train = lm.score(X_train, y_train)
rmse_train = root_mean_squared_error(y_train,
    lm.predict(X_train))
print(f"R2 train: {r2_train:0.3f}")
print(f"RMSE train: {rmse_train:0.3f}")

r2_test = lm.score(X_test, y_test)
rmse_test = root_mean_squared_error(y_test,
    lm.predict(X_test))
print(f"test R2: {r2_test:0.3f}")
print(f"test RMSE: {rmse_test:0.3f}")
```

After having taken note of the results (test R^2 is a disappointing 0.562), now we are ready to attempt to reduce the number of features by requiring Scikit-learn `SequentialFeatureSelection` to build a model starting from zero features and increasing the number of features involved as long as doing so improves (or doesn't significantly hurt) the model's cross-validated performance:

```
from sklearn.feature_selection import (
                        SequentialFeatureSelector)
lm = Pipeline([
  ("scaler", StandardScaler()),
  ("regression", LinearRegression())])
```

```
selector = SequentialFeatureSelector(estimator=lm,
                                     direction="forward",
                                     cv=5, scoring="r2")
selector.fit(X_train, y_train)
n_features = selector.n_features_to_select_
selection = X_train.columns[selector.support_].tolist()
print(f"Features reduced from {X_train.shape[1]}"
      f" to {n_features}")
print(selection)
```

After the selection is complete, only 11 features remain out of the 23 potential features (original + interactions). The selection comprises six of the original features and a selection of five interactions between them. You can test applying the selection on both the training and test sets. After retraining only on the selection, notice how much the prediction performance has improved just by removing some features, now reaching a test R^2 of 0.61 as compared to the starting value of around 0.562:

```
lm.fit(X_train[selection], y_train)

r2_train = lm.score(X_train[selection], y_train)
rmse_train = root_mean_squared_error(y_train,
    lm.predict(X_train[selection]))
print(f"R2 train: {r2_train:0.3f}")
print(f"RMSE train: {rmse_train:0.3f}")

r2_test = lm.score(X_test[selection], y_test)
rmse_test = root_mean_squared_error(y_test,
    lm.predict(X_test[selection]))
print(f"test R2: {r2_test:0.3f}")
print(f"test RMSE: {rmse_test:0.3f}")
```

Addressing overfitting by regularization

Regularization is an effective, fast, and easy solution to implement when you have many features and want to reduce the variance of the estimates due to multicollinearity between your predictors. Regularization works by adding a penalty to the cost function. The penalty term is based on the sum of the magnitudes of the coefficients. If the coefficients are squared (so that positive and negative values can't cancel each other), it's an *L2 regularization* (also called the *Ridge*). When you use the absolute value of the coefficient, it's an *L1 regularization* (also called the *Lasso*).

However, regularization doesn't always work perfectly. L2 regularization keeps all the features in the model and balances the contribution of each of them. In an L2 solution, if two features correlate well, each one contributes equally to the solution for a portion, whereas without regularization, their shared contribution would have been unequally distributed.

Alternatively, L1 tends to select one feature from a group of highly correlated features and set the coefficients of the others to zero, thus proposing a selection among features. Setting the coefficient to zero is just like excluding the feature from the model. When multicollinearity is high, the choice of which predictor to set to zero can seem somewhat arbitrary, and you can get various solutions characterized by different excluded features. Such solution instability may prove a nuisance, making the L1 useful for feature selection, although the selection can be unstable in the presence of many correlated features.

TIP

Scholars have found a fix by creating various solutions based on L1 regularization and then looking at how the coefficients behave across solutions. In this case, the algorithm picks only the stable coefficients (the ones that are seldom set to zero). You can read more about this technique and its details on the Scikit-learn compatible projects website at `https://github.com/scikit-learn-contrib/stability-selection` as well as in the blog at `https://thuijskens.github.io/2018/07/25/stability-selection`.

The following example modifies the polynomial expansions example using L2 regularization (Ridge regression) and reduces the influence of redundant coefficients created by the expansion procedure. Because the degree of regularization is controlled by the `RidgeCV` alpha parameter (the higher the alpha, the more the regularization), the example validates which alpha is better for your model using an internal cross-validation procedure. You only have to provide a set of alpha values to test:

```
from sklearn.linear_model import RidgeCV

ridge = Pipeline([
  ("scaler", StandardScaler()),
  ("regression", RidgeCV(alphas=[0.1, 1, 10, 50,
      70, 100, 300, 500, 1000], cv=5, scoring="r2"))])

ridge.fit(X_train, y_train)

best_alpha = ridge["regression"].alpha_
r2_test = ridge.score(X_test, y_test)
rmse_test = root_mean_squared_error(y_test,
    ridge.predict(X_test))
```

```
print(f"best alpha is: {best_alpha}")
print(f"test R2: {r2_test:0.3f}")
print(f"test RMSE: {rmse_test:0.3f}")
```

Here's the output from this code:

```
best alpha is: 300.0
test R2: 0.615
test RMSE: 0.719
```

The following example uses L1 regularization, which tends to bring coefficients to zero when redundant (L2 just reduces them). The results do not differ much in this case from L2. This time, the example uses the Scikit-learn LassoCV class, which is analogous to RidgeCV but applies L1 regularization instead of L2:

```
from sklearn.linear_model import LassoCV
from sklearn.metrics import r2_score

lasso = Pipeline([
    ("scaler", StandardScaler()),
    ("regression", LassoCV(n_alphas=300,
                    max_iter=10_000, cv=5))])
lasso.fit(X_train, y_train)

best_alpha = lasso["regression"].alpha_
r2_test = lasso.score(X_test, y_test)
rmse_test = root_mean_squared_error(y_test,
    lasso.predict(X_test))

print(f"best alpha is: {best_alpha:0.5f}")
print(f"test R2: {r2_test:0.3f}")
print(f"test RMSE: {rmse_test:0.3f}")
```

Learning One Example at a Time

Finding the correct coefficients for a linear model is just a matter of time and memory. However, sometimes a system won't have enough memory to store a huge dataset. In this case, you must resort to other means, such as learning from one example at a time rather than having all of them loaded into memory. The following sections help you understand the one-example-at-a-time approach to learning.

Using gradient descent

The gradient descent finds the right way to minimize the cost function one iteration at a time. After each step, it accounts for all the model's summed errors and updates the coefficients to reduce the error even further during the next data iteration. The efficiency of this approach derives from considering all the examples in the sample. The drawback of this approach is that you must load the entire dataset into memory.

Unfortunately, you can't always store all the data in memory because some datasets are massive. In addition, learning using simple learners requires large amounts of data to build effective models (more data helps to disambiguate multicollinearity correctly). Getting and storing chunks of data on your hard disk is always theoretically possible, but in reality, it may not be feasible because of the need to perform matrix multiplication, which would require lots of data swapping between disk and memory. Scientists who have worked on the problem have found an effective solution. Instead of learning from all the data after seeing it all (called an *iteration*), the algorithm learns from one example at a time, as picked from storage using sequential access, and then learns from the following example. When the algorithm has learned all the examples, it starts again from the beginning unless some stopping criterion is met (for instance, completing a predefined number of iterations).

REMEMBER

A *data stream* is the data that flows from disk, one example at a time. *Streaming* is the action of passing data from storage to memory. The *out-of-core learning* style (online learning) occurs when an algorithm learns from a stream, a viable learning strategy discussed at the end of Chapter 8.

Some typical sources of data streams are web traffic, sensors, satellites, and surveillance recordings. An intuitive example of a stream is, for instance, the data produced instant by instant by a sensor installed on machinery, or the posts generated by a social media network. You can also stream common data you're used to keeping in memory. For example, if a data matrix is too big, you can treat it as a data stream and start learning one row at a time, pulling it from a text file or a database. This is the *online-learning* style.

Understanding how SGD is different

Stochastic gradient descent (SGD) is a slight variation on the gradient descent algorithm. It provides an update procedure for estimating beta coefficients. Linear models are perfectly at ease with this approach.

In SGD, the formulation remains the same as in the standard version of gradient descent (called the batch version, in contrast to the online version), except for the update. In SGD, the update is executed on a single instance at a time, allowing the algorithm to leave core data in storage and place just the single observation needed to change the coefficient vector in memory:

$$w_j = w_j - a(Xw - y)x_j$$

As with the gradient descent algorithm, the algorithm updates the coefficient, w, of feature j by subtracting the difference between the prediction and the real response. It then multiplies the difference by the value of the feature j and by a learning factor (which can reduce or increase the effect of the update on the coefficient).

There are other subtle differences when using SGD rather than gradient descent. The most important difference is the stochastic term in the name of this online-learning algorithm. In fact, SGD expects an example at a time, drawn randomly from the available examples (random sampling). The problem with online learning is that example ordering changes how the algorithm guesses beta coefficients. This means the order in which examples are processed can influence the final set of coefficients, unlike batch gradient descent.

TIP

As a practical example, keep in mind that SGD can learn the order in which it sees the examples. So if the algorithm performs any kind of ordering (historical, alphabetical, or, worse, related to the response variable), it will invariably learn it. Only random sampling (meaningless ordering) allows you to obtain a reliable online model that works effectively on unseen data. When streaming data, you need to reorder your data (data shuffling) randomly.

The SGD algorithm, contrary to batch learning, needs a much larger number of iterations to get the right global direction despite noisy updates derived from individual examples. In fact, the algorithm updates after each new example, and the consequent journey toward an optimal set of parameters is more erratic than an optimization made on a batch, which immediately tends to get the right direction because it's derived from data as a whole.

The learning rate is lower when using SGD because it helps the optimization procedure be less sensitive to outliers or noisy examples. If the learning rate is high, an outlying example could derail the algorithm completely, preventing it from reaching a good result. On the other hand, higher learning rates help the algorithm learning faster from new examples. A good strategy is to use a flexible learning rate, starting with a higher learning rate and decreasing it as the number of examples it has seen grows (optimal or inverse strategies) or if the algorithm doesn't seem to learn (adaptive strategy).

TIP

If you think about it, SGD is a learning strategy. In that case, the flexible learning rate is similar to the one adopted by your brain: flexible and open to learning as a child, and more difficult (but not impossible) to change as an adult.

Python offers two SGD implementations in Scikit-learn, one for classification problems (SGDClassifier) and one for regression problems (SGDRegressor). Both of these methods, apart from the fit method (used to fit data in memory), feature a partial_fit method that keeps previous results and learning schedule in memory, and continues learning as new examples arrive. With the partial_fit method, you can partially fit small chunks of data, or even single examples, and continue feeding the algorithm data until it finds a satisfactory result.

Both SGD classification and regression implementations in Scikit-learn feature different loss functions that you can apply to the stochastic gradient descent optimization. Only two of those functions refer to the methods discussed in this chapter:

>> loss="squared_loss": Ordinary least squares (OLS) for linear regression

>> loss="log": Classical logistic regression

The other implementations (hinge, huber, epsilon-insensitive) optimize a loss function different from the perceptron. Chapter 13 explains them in more detail when discussing support vector machines.

To demonstrate the effectiveness of out-of-core learning, the following example sets up a brief experiment in Python using regression and squared_loss as the cost function. It illustrates how beta coefficients change as the algorithm sees more examples. The example also passes the same data multiple times to reinforce data pattern learning. Using a test set guarantees a fair evaluation, providing measures of the algorithm's capability to generalize to out-of-sample data.

The example reports the coefficient vector and the error measures after it sees a variable number of examples in powers of two (to represent learning at different steps). The experiment shows how long it takes before R^2 increases and the values of the coefficients stabilize. Running this example can take a long time depending on your system, so it might be a good time to get a cup of coffee. In this case, a few iterations are enough to reach almost the maximum R^2 possible. It is hard to see in the figure, but the R2 is slightly worse in the training set (see Figure 12-3), whereas you might have expected it to be better than the test one. This is because of regularization (the example uses L2), which makes fitting the data more difficult.

```python
import numpy as np
import matplotlib.pyplot as plt
from sklearn.linear_model import SGDRegressor
from sklearn.preprocessing import StandardScaler

scaler = StandardScaler()
scaled_X_train = scaler.fit_transform(X_train)
scaled_X_test = scaler.transform(X_test)

SGD = SGDRegressor(penalty="l2",
                   alpha=0.00001,
                   learning_rate="adaptive",
                   eta0=0.00004,
                   random_state=0)
r2_train = list()
r2_test = list()
rmse_train = list()
rmse_test = list()

iterations = 37
np.random.seed(0)

for i in range(iterations):
    n = np.random.permutation(len(scaled_X_train))
    for j in n:
        SGD.partial_fit(scaled_X_train[[j], :],
                        y_train[[j]])

    r2_train.append(SGD.score(scaled_X_train, y_train))
    r2_test.append(SGD.score(scaled_X_test, y_test))
    rmse_train.append(root_mean_squared_error(y_train,
        SGD.predict(scaled_X_train)))
    rmse_test.append(root_mean_squared_error(y_test,
        SGD.predict(scaled_X_test)))

print(f"Last R2 score on train: {r2_train[-1]:0.3f}")
print(f"Last R2 score on test: {r2_test[-1]:0.3f}")
```

```
fig, axs = plt.subplots(1, 2, figsize=(10, 4), dpi=120)
axs[0].plot(r2_train, label="Train R2")
axs[0].plot(r2_test, label="Test R2")
axs[0].set_ylabel("R2")
axs[0].legend()
axs[0].set_title("R2 over iterations")
axs[1].plot(rmse_train, label="Train RMSE")
axs[1].plot(rmse_test, label="Test RMSE")
axs[1].set_xlabel("Number of iterations")
axs[1].set_ylabel("RMSE")
axs[1].legend()
axs[1].set_title("RMSE over iterations")
plt.tight_layout()
plt.show()
```

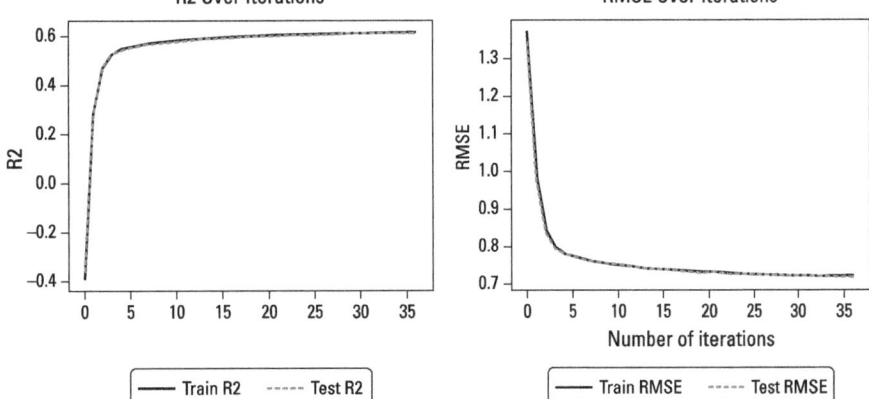

FIGURE 12-3: How R^2 varies in training and test sets as iterations increase in an SGD regression model.

REMEMBER

No matter the amount of data, you can always fit a simple but effective linear regression model using SGD online-learning capabilities.

Chapter **13**

Going Beyond the Basics with Support Vector Machines

This chapter presents an idea that sprouted from rigorous mathematical and statistical learning theory work by Vladimir Vapnik and others: using *support vector machines* (SVMs) to solve problems in image recognition and language processing. We start by revisiting the nonseparability problem in classification and explain how SVMs have been precisely devised for solving such a problem by exploring how they work mathematically (don't worry — it won't be as boring as those high school math lessons!). We then list the method's strengths and weaknesses and present a few practical examples, through experiments, to better understand it all.

Two decades ago, support vector machines emerged as the next big thing in machine learning. Initially met with skepticism, they left many scholars wondering whether they'd work. Many questioned whether the kind of representation SVMs were capable of could perform helpful tasks. To reprise a concept from Chapter 11, the *representation* is the capability of a machine learning algorithm to approximate certain types of target functions and correctly represent the data problem. Having an algorithm with a good representation of a problem means being able to produce reliable predictions on any new data related to that problem.

SVMs demonstrate not only an incredible capability for representation but also a useful one, allowing the algorithm to be applied across the large (and growing) world of machine learning applications. You use SVMs today for linear and nonlinear classification, regression, or even unsupervised detection of outliers. This chapter helps you discover how versatile SVMs are by presenting you with a mind-blowing algorithm that uses sophisticated calculations to solve key problems in image recognition, medical diagnosis, and textual classification.

REMEMBER

You can find the source code for this chapter in the ML4D3E folder of the downloadable code file. The example files for this chapter will begin with ML4D3E-13-. See the Introduction for details on how to find these source files.

Revisiting the Separation Problem

As discussed in Chapter 10, when talking about the perceptron, nonseparability occurs when classes cannot be perfectly divided by a straight line in a two-dimensional space or by a hyperplane in higher dimensions. The set of machine learning algorithms and techniques that you have available offers some options in such occurrences:

>> **K-Nearest neighbors:** Adapts to nonlinear boundaries, especially when using a small k.

>> **Logistic regression:** Solves the problem by estimating a probability of being in a particular class, thus allowing an estimate even if it isn't possible to distinguish correctly between classes due to partial overlap.

>> **Feature transformations:** Solves the problem by employing feature engineering (adding human creativity and prior knowledge to the learning process) and automatic polynomial expansion (creating power transformations and interactions from features). It finds a new set of features capable of distinguishing classes using a separating line or plane.

Decision trees (discussed in Chapter 10) naturally adjust to nonlinearity because the algorithm builds its classification boundaries using multiple splits on key features to approximate complex, nonlinear separating boundaries.

Given such an extensive range of options, one might wonder why another algorithm like SVM was necessary to solve the nonseparability problem. The lack of success people have had in searching for a master algorithm that learns most problems and the no-free-lunch theorem explain everything. You can't deem one algorithm universally superior across all possible problems. On the contrary, you need a palette of algorithms to tackle a large variety of problems from the real world. The kind of features you're dealing with and the kind of problem you need to solve are what determine which algorithms work better. Accessing another effective learning technique is like getting an extra weapon to fight complex data problems. Moreover, SVMs feature a range of characteristics that can make the algorithm quite appealing for many data problems:

>> They are versatile, being applicable to binary and multiclass classification, regression, and detection of outliers or novelty patterns.

>> They offer generally robust handling of overfitting, noisy data, and outliers.

>> They are effective in handling many features (SVMs are still effective when you have more features than examples).

>> They offer an implicit transformation of the data into a space where a linear separation might be possible, thus handling effectively and automatically nonlinearity in data without applying direct transformations to features.

In particular, the last characteristic is effective thanks to the availability of special functions, the kernel functions. Kernel functions have the exceptional capability of mapping the original feature space into a new feature space reconstructed to achieve better classification or regression results. This is similar to the polynomial expansion principle (one available kernel function provides polynomial expansion support). Still, the mathematics behind it requires fewer computations, allowing the algorithm to map complex response functions faster and more precisely.

Explaining the Algorithm

SVMs are a kind of algorithm that performs well and historically rivaled neural networks on many classification tasks, especially with structured data. SVMs were created by mathematician Vladimir Vapnik and some of his colleagues (Boser, Guyon, and Cortes) who worked at AT&T Laboratories in the 1990s. Even though many machine learning experts were initially skeptical of the algorithm because it didn't resemble any other then-existing approach, SVMs quickly gained momentum and success thanks to their performance in many image-recognition problems, such as handwritten digit (number) input that was challenging the machine learning community of the time.

Today, SVMs are widely used by data scientists, who apply them to an incredible array of problems, from medical diagnosis to image recognition and textual classification. However, the technique is limited in applicability to big data because it lacks scalability when examples and features are too numerous.

The mathematics of the algorithm is a bit complex, but the idea that started everything is quite simple. With this in mind, the chapter uses easy examples and demonstrations to illustrate its workings based on simple mathematical intuitions.

Start by looking at the problem of separating two groups with a line. You rarely see a similar situation in real-life data, but it's a fundamental classification problem in machine learning, and many algorithms, such as the perceptron, are built from it. Depending on the data arrangement, a classification problem can be challenging. For instance, without transforming the feature space of a hypothetical data matrix (made of two features, x1 and x2), Figure 13-1 shows how to solve the problem using (clockwise from upper left) a perceptron, a logistic regression, and an SVM.

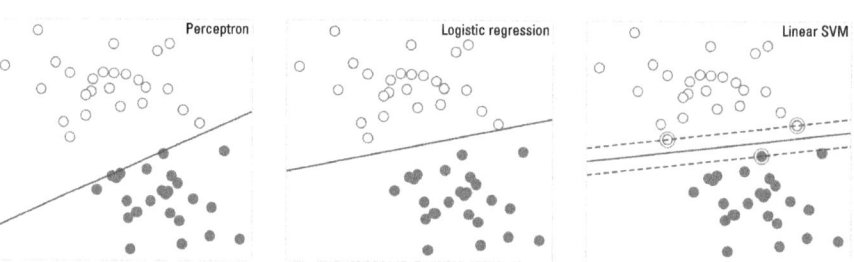

FIGURE 13-1: Comparing different approaches: perceptron, logistic regression, and SVM.

Interestingly, although the perceptron aims only at separating the classes, and the mass of the points influences the logistic regression, the separating line drawn by an SVM has clear and defined characteristics. By observing the line differences, you can see that the best line separating the classes is the one with the largest space between the line itself and the examples on the fringes of the classes, which is the solution from SVM. Using SVM terminology, the separating line is the one with the largest *margin* (the space between the boundaries of the classes). SVM places the separating line in the middle of the margin (described in textbooks as *maximum margin* or *optimal margin hyperplane*), and the examples lying exactly on the margin boundaries, or within the margin, are *support vectors.*

REMEMBER

Support vectors are actually examples represented as vectors in the feature space. In fact, to define a point's position in a space, you have to state its coordinates in each dimension as a series of numbers, which is a vector. Moreover, you can view them as support vectors because the largest margin hyperplane depends on them, and changing the position of any support vector potentially changes the margin and the hyperplane. Non-support vectors do not influence the hyperplane.

REMEMBER

Margin, separating hyperplane, and support vectors are key terms used to define how an SVM works. Support vectors decide the best margin possible for linearly separable and nonseparable classes.

The strategy of an SVM is quite simple: By looking for the largest separating margin, it provides robustness against possible variations in data, making the model generalize better. Sampled values do change, sometimes even greatly, from sample to sample. Consequently, you can't rely on a *just-fit* approach based on a single sample to understand all possible data variations (the way a perceptron does, for example). Keeping the fattest margin allows SVM flexibility in the feature space when working with successive samples because you can't know whether a successive sample will be similar to the one used for learning. In addition, by looking at the class boundaries, SVM isn't influenced by distant points (contrary to a linear regression). The algorithm determines the margin using only the examples placed on the boundaries.

REMEMBER

Even though they are created for classification, SVMs can also perform well in regression problems. You use the prediction error as distance and the separating hyperplane surface values to determine the right prediction value for each feature value combination.

Avoiding the pitfalls of nonseparability

You need to consider a final issue concerning the SVM optimization process previously described. Because you know that classes are seldom linearly separable, it may not always be possible for all the training examples to force the distance to be equal or exceed the threshold value delimiting the margin upward and downward. Using slack variables and a penalty, we can actually move from a hard-margin solution to a soft-margin SVM. Both values influence how the SVM reacts to misclassified examples by softening its constraints to find the maximum margin while minimizing the classification errors.

Going into more mathematical details, in figuring out the best margin, the standard SVM optimization minimizes an objective function like:

$$(1/2)||w||^2 + C * \Sigma\xi i$$

where

>> w is a vector containing the coefficients assigned to each feature in your dataset. The L2 norm (discussed in Chapter 11) is applied to the vector (it is the root of the sum of squares of its elements).

>> ξ (pronounced ksi) is a value associated with each training example, taking a different value if the example is misclassified or not.

>> C is a hyperparameter that controls the trade-off between the first part of the term related to the coefficients and the second part associated with the misclassifications.

In the optimization process, minimizing the norm of the coefficients (w) maximizes the margin. However, this may conflict with the second part of the term, the sum of slack variables ξ (ksi). Each example gets a specific slack value (a value equal to or greater than zero). If an example is correctly classified, the assigned ξ (ksi) is 0. Values between 0 and 1 indicate that the example is still correctly classified, although it falls inside the margin. Finally, when the assigned value is above 1, the case is misclassified and is located on the wrong side of the optimal separating hyperplane.

When there are too many misclassifications, the sum of the slack variables is high, and the C hyperparameter can make it even larger. C is a positive number, and it is referred to as the regularization term. When it is very large, the optimization process will try to minimize the sum of the slack variables by making the margin smaller and by having a more complex, nonlinear margin. This can lead to over-fitting when C is too large. When C is smaller, instead, the optimization will accept a greater sum of slack variables and make the margin larger and smoother. This can lead to underfitting if C is actually too small.

Applying nonlinearity

SVMs are mathematically demanding. Up to now, you've seen some formulations that help you understand that SVMs are an optimization problem that strives to classify all the examples of two classes. When solving optimization in SVMs, you use a partitioning hyperplane having the largest distance from the class boundaries. If classes aren't linearly separable, searching for the optimal separating hyperplane allows for errors and a soft boundary (controlled by the value of C).

Despite allowing a small cost for errors, the SVM's linear hyperplane can't recover nonlinear relationships between classes unless you transform the features appropriately. For instance, you can correctly classify only a part of the examples like the ones depicted on the left in Figure 13-2 if you don't transform the existing two dimensions into other dimensions using some other operations such as multiplication or exponentiation.

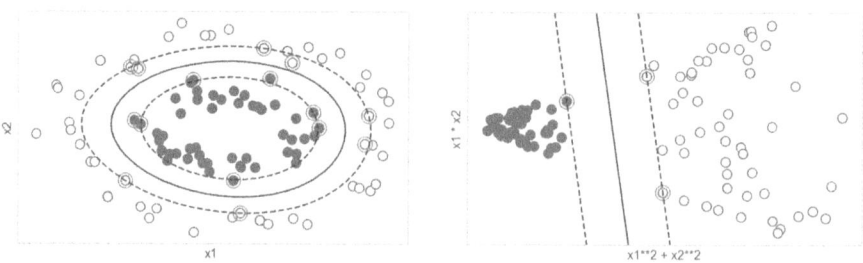

FIGURE 13-2: A case of nonlinearly separable points requiring feature transformation (left) to be fit by a line (right).

In other words, you map the existing features onto a different feature space (often characterized by a higher dimensionality) in hopes of finding a way to separate the classes linearly. This is the same process shown in Chapter 12 when trying polynomial expansion (where you discovered how a linear model automatically captures nonlinear relationships between features). Automatic feature creation using polynomial expansion, which is also possible for SVMs, has some limits:

>> The number of potential features increases exponentially, making computations cumbersome and saturating the in-memory dataset. (Some datasets can't be expanded beyond a power of 2 or 3.)

>> The expansion creates many redundant features, causing overfitting.

>> It's difficult to determine the level of expansion where the classes will become linearly separable, thus requiring many iterations of expansion and testing.

Because of these limitations, SVM has adopted a different way, called *kernel functions,* to redefine the feature space without occupying more memory or increasing the number of computations too much. Kernel functions aren't magic; they rely on algebraic calculations and are the more mathematically demanding part of an SVM. To understand how they work, you could say that kernel functions project the original features into a higher-dimensional space by combining them nonlinearly. They do so implicitly because they don't provide SVM with a new feature space to use for learning (as a polynomial expansion would do). Instead, they return the computed values from the dot product of the features in the high-dimensional space. The SVM can directly use the calculated values to fit a nonlinear separating hyperplane on the original data.

Therefore, kernel functions provide the result of a combination of features (precisely a dot product, a multiplication between vectors), without calculating all the combinations involved in such a result. They act as a translator, converting implicitly the original data into a higher-dimensional space, finding a linear separator, and then returning the information of that linear separator in higher dimensions into the original space (where it is nonlinear). This is called the *kernel trick.*

Explaining the kernel trick by example

Kernel functions are convenient mapping functions that allow SVMs to operate as if in a high-dimensional space without the more complicated and data-intensive nonlinear transformation. Computationally accessible by most computers in terms of processing and memory, kernel functions allow solving a data problem using a nonlinear separating hyperplane automatically, without requiring human intervention for feature creation.

In its implementations in Python, SVM offers quite a large range of nonlinear kernels. Here is the list of all the kernels and their parameters:

>> **Linear:** No extra parameters

>> **Radial Basis Function:** Shape parameters: gamma

>> **Polynomial:** Shape parameters: gamma, degree, and coef0

>> **Sigmoid:** Shape parameters: gamma and coef0

>> **Custom-made Kernels:** You can code and provide your own kernel

Even though the choice of kernels is large (and possibly larger if you design your own custom kernels), you usually use the Radial Basis Function (RBF). RBF is the most popular kernel because it's more effective than other kernels, as it can map and approximate almost any nonlinear function if you tweak its shape parameter, gamma.

The RBF works in a simple but clever way. It creates a margin around every support vector — drawing bubbles in the feature space, as Figure 13-3 shows. According to the gamma hyperparameter value, the radius of the bubbles is larger or smaller, and, pooled together, they shape the classification areas. When the gamma value is high, the radius of influence of each support vector is smaller, and the resulting margin of the entire classification area is wiggly and closer to the training data distribution. When the gamma value is low, on the contrary, the influence of each vector can reach farther, and the resulting classification margin is smoother. The resulting margin and the hyperplane passing through it will consequently show soft curvy boundaries, demonstrating that it can be pretty flexible, as in the examples provided by Figure 13-3.

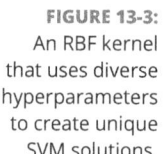

FIGURE 13-3:
An RBF kernel that uses diverse hyperparameters to create unique SVM solutions.

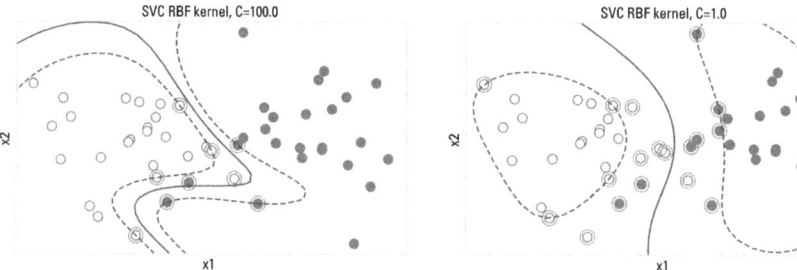

The RBF kernel can adapt to different learning strategies by blending different values of C and gamma. A good choice of parameters can also fit complex shapes, such as the bull's eye, when a class is placed inside another. All this flexibility may come at the expense of a more considerable variance, but SVMs with RBF kernels can detect complex classification rules that other algorithms may fail to find.

REMEMBER

When tuning an RBF kernel, first fix the C parameter, the regularization term, to define how bent the separating hyperplane should be. Then, tune gamma to make the margin shape rough and broken when the hyperparameter gamma is high, or regular and fused into large bubble-shaped areas when it is low.

The polynomial and sigmoid kernels aren't as adaptable as RBF, thus showing more bias, yet they are both nonlinear transformations of the separating hyperplane. In particular, the polynomial function can create more complex decision boundaries based on its degree. However, the higher the degree, the longer it takes to compute.

REMEMBER

When using the sigmoid and polynomial kernels, you have many shape values to fix: gamma and coef0 for both, and degree for the polynomial. Because determining the effects of different values on these parameters is difficult, you need to test different value combinations, using a grid search, for instance, and evaluate the results practically. Figure 13-4 visually represents what you can do with the polynomial and the RBF kernels.

FIGURE 13-4:
A polynomial
(left) and an RBF
kernel (right)
applied to the
same data.

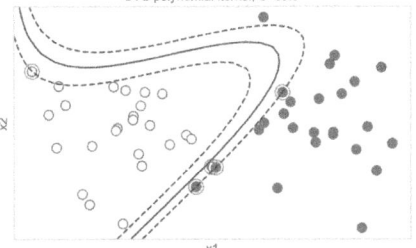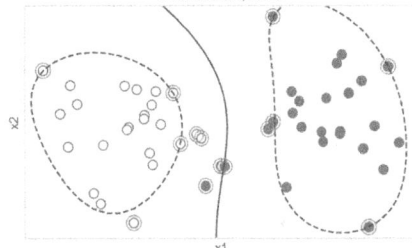

TIP

Despite the possibility of creating your own kernel function, most data problems can easily be solved using the RBF. Look for the right combination of C and gamma by trying different values systematically until you achieve the best result for your validation set or cross-validation procedure.

Classifying and Estimating with SVM

Although SVMs are complex learning algorithms, they are versatile and easy to use when implemented in Python. The Scikit-learn implementation relies on an external C++ package, LIBSVM, developed at National Taiwan University. You can find more on the shared LIBSVM for SVM classification and regression at www.csie.ntu.edu.tw/~cjlin/libsvm. The Scikit-learn implementation also uses the LIBLINEAR C package, which specializes in classification problems using linear methods on large and sparse datasets. This package is from the same authors at National Taiwan University who produced the LIBSVM package (see more at `www.csie.ntu.edu.tw/~cjlin/liblinear`).

TIP

SVM optimization is complex, which hinders the algorithm's scalability. Using LIBSVM and handling large datasets may result in long processing times. The GPU manufacturer NVIDIA has developed the RAPIDS package (`https://developer.nvidia.com/rapids`) that can make SVMs work with GPUs and become blazing fast, 25 times faster or even more, according to our tests.

As an example of how you can use an SVM to solve a complex problem, this section demonstrates a handwritten digit recognition task and solves it using a nonlinear kernel, the RBF. This is one of the first real-world applications to use an SVM, and this application created a renewed interest in the algorithm. The SVM algorithm learns from the digits dataset available from the module `datasets` in the Scikit-learn package. The digits dataset contains 8x8 grayscale pixel images of hand-written numbers ranging from 0 to 9. The problem is quite simple compared to many issues that image recognition engines solve today through deep learning, but it helps you grasp the potential of the learning approach. As a first step, the code loads the dataset from Scikit-learn:

```
import numpy as np
from sklearn.datasets import load_digits

digits = load_digits()
X, y = digits.data, digits.target
```

This dataset contains just 1797 examples. The y variable contains numeric labels from 0 to 9. The X variable contains one example per row, and each example contains the pixels for each digit in 64 features (flattening the 8x8-pixel matrix). The SVM algorithm learns that if certain pixels activate together in the data, the represented image corresponds to a particular number.

This example demonstrates the idea espoused by the Analogizers tribe: Certain patterns correspond to answers based on an analogy. SVMs hide this fact because they seem to provide a linear combination of weighted features, just as linear regression does. However, when applying kernel functions, optimization is based on the dot products of examples, expressed as coordinate vectors. Dot products are a way to estimate the distance between points to divide the feature space into homogeneous partitions with the same class inside. Distance is a way to establish similarities in a space made of features. SVMs work on similarity, associating points and patterns based on distance.

The next code snippet divides the available data into training and test parts. To verify the results from the model correctly, the code extracts 20 percent of the examples to use later as a test set (an out-of-sample test):

```
from sklearn.model_selection import train_test_split
from sklearn.model_selection import cross_val_score

X_train, X_test, y_train, y_test = train_test_split(X,
                        y, test_size=0.2, random_state=42)
```

As a third step, the code prepares the SVM algorithm as a Scikit-learn pipeline combining the scaling of the data in the range (–1, +1) and the support vector classification algorithm. The code doesn't tune any hyperparameters, but the gamma parameter can adapt to data: it is set to 'auto', which uses the result of one divided by the number of features.

```
from sklearn.preprocessing import MinMaxScaler
from sklearn.pipeline import make_pipeline
from sklearn.svm import SVC

svm = make_pipeline(MinMaxScaler(
                    feature_range=(-1, 1)),
                    SVC(gamma='auto'))
```

TIP

Scaling is a critical action to take before feeding the data into an SVM. *Scaling* transforms all the values to the range between –1 and +1 (or from 0 to 1, if you prefer). Scaling transformation avoids the problem of having only some features influence the algorithm's optimization process and helps make the computations converge faster and more reliably.

The training phase begins by cross-validating (based on 10 folds using cv=10) the performance of the SVM on the training data. To check the usefulness of the algorithm representation, the example uses the accuracy score (the percentage of correct guesses) as a measure of how good the model is. The resulting accuracy is 0.9847 on the cross-validation and 0.9806 on the out-of-sample test sample.

```
cv_acc = cross_val_score(svm, X_train, y_train, cv=10)
test_acc = (svm.fit(X_train, y_train)
                    .score(X_test, y_test))
print(f"CV accuracy: {np.mean(cv_acc):0.3f}")
print(f"Test accuracy: {test_acc:0.3f}")
```

After verifying the cross-validation and test scores using the default hyperparameters, the code uses a systematic search to find better settings that could provide more exact answers. During the search, the code tests different combinations of linear and RBF together with C and gamma parameters (the example can require some time to run).

```python
from sklearn.model_selection import GridSearchCV

search_space = [{"svc__kernel": ["linear"],
                 "svc__C": np.logspace(-3, 3, 7)},
                {"svc__kernel": ["rbf"],
                 "svc__C": np.logspace(-3, 3, 7),
                 "svc__gamma": np.logspace(-3, 2, 6)}]
gridsearch = GridSearchCV(svm,
                          param_grid=search_space,
                          refit=True, cv=10,
                          n_jobs=-2)
gridsearch.fit(X_train, y_train)
print(f"Best parameter: {gridsearch.best_params_}")
cv_acc = gridsearch.best_score_
test_acc = gridsearch.score(X_test, y_test)
print(f"CV accuracy: {np.mean(cv_acc):0.3f}")
print(f"Test accuracy: {test_acc:0.3f}")
```

The computations may take a few minutes, after which the computer reports the best kernel, C, and gamma parameters, with an improved cross-validation (CV) score reaching almost 99 percent accuracy. The high accuracy indicates that the computer can nearly distinguish all the different ways to write numbers from 0 to 9.

TIP

The dataset provided by Scikit-learn is just a portion of the real MNIST dataset, available at the repository for datasets provided by the French company Hugging Face (https://huggingface.co/datasets/ylecun/mnist). The full dataset consists of 60,000 training examples and 10,000 test examples. Using the same SVC algorithm and code, the SVC can also learn the original dataset, allowing your solution to predict any handwritten number you may present to it.

Chapter **14**

Tackling Complexity with Neural Networks

As you journey into the world of machine learning, you often see metaphors from the natural world to explain the details of algorithms. This chapter presents a family of learning algorithms directly inspired by the brain's functioning. They are neural networks, the core algorithms of the connectionists' tribe (see Chapter 2 for a listing of the various tribes).

Starting with the idea of reverse-engineering how the brain processes signals, connectionists base neural networks on biological analogies and their components, using terms derived from neuroscience, such as neurons. However, when you check their mathematical formulations, you'll discover that neural networks resemble nothing more than a sophisticated, complex, nonlinear kind of linear regression. Yet, these algorithms are extraordinarily effective against complex problems such as image and sound recognition, or machine translation. They can also execute quickly when predicting, depending on their size, as some recent neural network models are quite large.

The chapter starts by revising how the perceptron worked and its limitations. It then goes on to demonstrate how neural networks overcome such limits. We then detail the core components of a neural network, such as neurons, weights, and layers, and discuss how the feed-forward process effectively manipulates data in a neural network architecture. Next, the chapter introduces the backpropagation algorithm and how it enables neural networks to adjust to errors and learn to predict. Finally, we discuss deep learning, illustrating its advancements over standard neural networks and introducing its application in image, sound, and text due to specific architectures such as convolutional neural networks (CNNs) and recurrent neural networks (RNNs). At the closing of the chapter, we will mention the transformer architecture and the attention mechanism, the foundational technology behind many generative AI models.

Well-devised, large neural networks, also known as deep learning, are behind such powerful chatbot tools as OpenAI, ChatGPT, and Google Gemini. They are also behind some of the more astonishing machine learning applications, such as generating highly realistic images and art from descriptive text inputs (for instance, DALL-E, Midjourney), achieving breakthroughs in scientific research like predicting protein structures with AlphaFold, or powering increasingly sophisticated autonomous vehicles. If we are on the verge of an AI revolution, the ever-advancing learning capabilities of neural networks will likely drive it.

Revising the Perceptron

The core neural network building block is the *neuron* (also called a *unit*). A neural network consists of many neurons arranged in an interconnected structure, with each neuron linking to the inputs and outputs of other neurons. Thus, a neuron can input features directly from examples or the results of different neurons, depending on its location in the network.

Something similar to the neuron, the perceptron, appears earlier in this book, although it uses a simpler structure and function. When the psychologist Rosenblatt conceived the perceptron, he considered it a simplified mathematical version of a brain neuron. A perceptron follows these steps:

1. Takes values as inputs from the nearby environment (the dataset).

2. Weighs these values (as brain cells do with electric signals, based on the strength of the incoming connections).

3. Sums all the weighted values.

4. Activates when the sum exceeds a threshold (using a step function, operating as an on/off switch).

The activation function outputs a value of 1 if the sum exceeds a threshold; otherwise, its prediction is 0. This on/off function is called a step function. Unfortunately, a perceptron can't learn when the classes it tries to process aren't linearly separable. However, scholars discovered that even though a single perceptron couldn't represent the logical operation XOR shown in Figure 14-1 (the exclusive or, which is true only when the inputs are dissimilar), a network of perceptrons working together could.

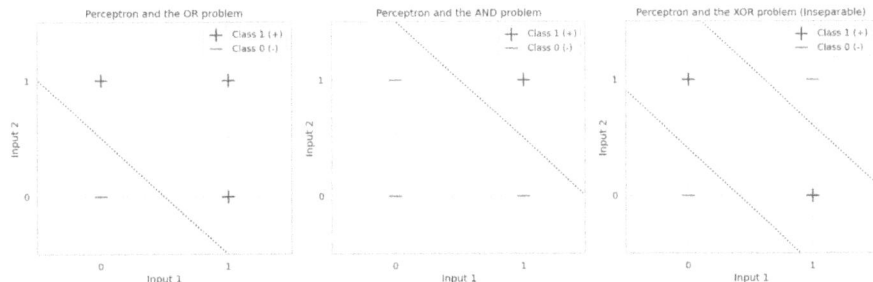

FIGURE 14-1:
Learning logical
XOR using a
single separating
line isn't possible.

Neurons in a neural network are a further evolution of the perceptron: They take many weighted values as inputs, sum them, and provide the summation as the result, just as a perceptron does. However, they also apply a nonlinear transformation of the summation, which is also differentiable, that is, you can take a mathematical derivative of it and use it for optimization (something we discussed in Chapter 9 when talking about the Gradient Descent). This is something that the perceptron couldn't do because its step function wasn't differentiable at the threshold point. In observing nature, scientists noticed that neurons receive signals but don't always release a signal of their own. It depends on the amount of signal received. When a neuron acquires enough stimuli, it fires an answer; otherwise, it remains silent. Similarly, after receiving weighted values, algorithmic neurons sum them and use an *activation function* to process the sum, which is nonlinearly transformed. For instance, the activation function can release a zero value unless the input achieves a certain threshold, or it can dampen or enhance a value by nonlinearly rescaling it, thus transmitting a rescaled signal.

A neural network can use different activation functions, as Figure 14-2 shows. The linear function applies a linear transformation and is sometimes used, but not as the only type of activation in a neural network, because a neural network composed of only linear activations collapses into a single linear transformation, equivalent to a linear regression with no interactions. Neural networks commonly use and derive their predictive capabilities from nonlinear transformations through activation functions, such as the sigmoid (also known as logistic), the hyperbolic tangent (labeled TanH), or the ReLU (which is by far the most common today) activation functions.

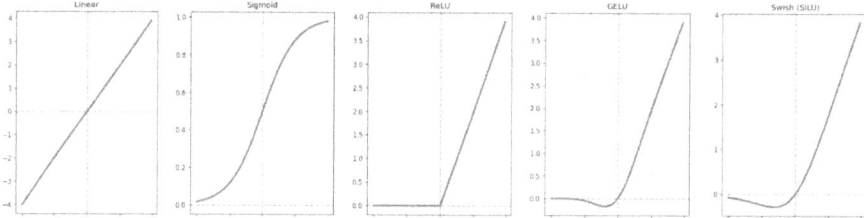

FIGURE 14-2:
Plots of different activation functions.

The figure shows how an input (expressed on the horizontal axis) can be transformed into an output (represented on the vertical axis). The examples illustrate linear, logistic, hyperbolic tangent, ReLU, GELU, and Swish activation functions. GELU and Swish activation functions are commonly used in the most recent deep learning architectures.

TIP

You learn more about activation functions later in the chapter, but note that some activation functions, such as sigmoid and TanH, work well in a specific input range. When values are too high, the output from the neuron tends to be the same value (a phenomenon called *saturation*). In contrast, others, such as ReLU, can take any positive values and produce a related output (as for negative values, it always produces zero). As you can see from Figure 14-2, sigmoid and TanH activations output end-of-scale values outside certain input boundaries. For this reason, you should always rescale inputs to a neural network using statistical standardization (zero mean and unit variance) or normalize the input in the range from 0 to 1 or from –1 to +1.

Pushing forth with feed-forward

In a neural network, you must first consider the architecture, which is how the neural network components are arranged. Contrary to other algorithms, which have a fixed pipeline that determines how the algorithm receives and processes data, neural networks require you to decide how information flows by fixing the number of units (the neurons) and their distribution in layers, as shown in Figure 14-3.

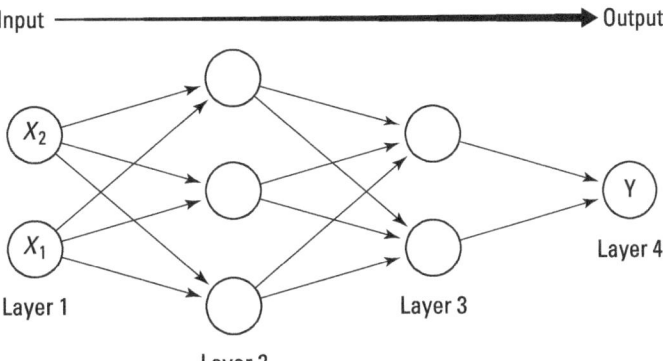

FIGURE 14-3:
An example of
the architecture
of a neural
network.

Input ————————————————→ Output

X_2

X_1

Layer 1

Layer 2

Layer 3

Layer 4

Y

The figure shows a simple neural architecture. Note how the layers progressively filter information. This is a feed-forward network because data feeds forward through the network in a single direction. Connections exclusively link the units in one layer with those in the subsequent layers (information flows from left to right). In a standard feed-forward neural network, no connections exist between units in the same layer or with units outside the next layer. The information usually pushes forward to the next layer, but it can skip to additional layers forward (this is called a skip connection, and it is an advanced concept — let's stick to the fact that the information just goes to the immediately subsequent layer). The example in Figure 14-3 shows the connections from left to right, but in other representations, you may find connections from top to bottom or bottom to top. Processed data never returns to the previous neuron layers.

REMEMBER

Neural networks are also seen as graphs. A *graph* is simply a set of vertices, nodes, or points connected by edges, arcs, or lines. In the case of neural networks, the graph is called a directed acyclic graph (DAG) because:

» Using any route, you can't get from one vertex to another and back to the beginning vertex.

» A predictable set of routes moves from one vertex to the next.

REMEMBER

There are kinds of neural networks that actually allow loops, though the loops occur inside certain neurons (not between layers), and they're limited to the size of the input they receive. Such networks are called *recurrent neural networks* (RNNs), and they are briefly illustrated at the end of this chapter.

Using a neural network is like using a stratified filtering system for water: You pour the water from above, and the water is filtered at the bottom. The water has no way to go back; it just goes forward and straight down, and never laterally. In the same way, neural networks force data features to flow through the network and mix only according to the network's architecture. Using the best architecture to combine features, the neural network creates new composite features at every layer and helps achieve better predictions. Unfortunately, there is no way to determine the best architecture without empirically (or systematically) trying different solutions and testing whether output data helps predict your target values after flowing through the network.

The first and last layers play an important role. The first layer, called the *input layer*, picks up the features from each data example the network processes. The last layer, called the *output layer*, releases the results.

A neural network can process only numeric (continuous, discrete, or binary) information. It can't directly process qualitative features, such as labels indicating a quality, or words in a text. You can process qualitative features by transforming them into continuous numeric or binary values. This transformative process of qualitative features is called *encoding*, and it is done using one-hot-encoding functions or embedding layers, whose purpose is to assign numeric values to features. When a neural network processes a binary feature, the neuron treats the feature as a generic number. It turns the binary values into other values, even negative ones, by processing across units.

Note the limitation of dealing only with numeric values, because you can't expect the last layer to output a non-numeric label prediction. When dealing with a regression problem, the final layer is a single unit. Likewise, when you're working with a classification and you have output that must choose from a number of classes, you should have an equivalent number of terminal units, each representing a score linked to the probability of the represented class. Therefore, the final layer has as many units as classes when classifying a multiclass problem (as discussed in Chapter 12). For example, we can refer to the classification of penguin species, as we discussed when reviewing the Palmer Penguins dataset demonstration in Chapter 11. In such a case, in a neural network, you would have three units representing one of the three Penguin species: Adelie, Chinstrap, or Gentoo. For each example, the predicted class gets the highest score at prediction time.

If the classes you predict can coexist (where a training example can be a member of multiple classes), you have a *multilabel classification,* and your terminal output neurons will provide probability estimates for each class independently of the others. A typical example of multilabel classification occurs when a neural network has to guess all the objects in a photo. All the possible objects are classes for the neural network, and each one receives a probability score of being in the image. All the objects whose score exceeds a threshold are thus deemed to be in the photo.

In contrast to multilabel classification, when the classes you predict are mutually exclusive (your problem is *multiclass classification*, as in the Penguins dataset), the sum of the probabilities derived from your output neurons should equal 100 percent. An activation function is applied to the final layer, called *Softmax*, which can adjust the output values of the neurons associated with each class so that their sum equals 1.0 (100 percent).

In classification, the final layer may represent both a partition of probabilities thanks to a Softmax layer (and you have a multiclass problem in which total probabilities sum to 100 percent) or an independent probability prediction (because an example can have more classes, which is a multilabel problem in which summed probabilities do not result in 100 percent). When the classification problem is a binary classification, a single node suffices.

Contrary to other algorithms discussed so far, neural networks can have multiple output units as part of a regression problem, with each one representing a different regression problem. (For instance, in forecasting, you can have different predictions for the next day, week, month, and so on.)

Going even deeper down the rabbit hole

Neural networks have different layers, each one having its own weights. Because the neural network segregates computations by layers, knowing the *reference layer* (the one used for the calculation) is important for accounting for certain units and connections. Thus, you can refer to every layer using a specific number and generically talk about each layer using the letter h (so that the first layer would be h1, the second h2, and so on).

Each layer can have a different number of units, and the number of units between two layers dictates the number of connections. By multiplying the number of units in the starting layer with the number in the following layer, you can determine the total number of connections between the two: *number of connections*$^{(h)}$ = *units*$^{(h)}$ * *units*$^{(h+1)}$.

A matrix of weights, usually named with the uppercase Greek letter theta (Θ), represents the connections. For ease of reading, the book uses the capital letter W. Thus, you can use W^1 to refer to the connection weights from layer 1 to layer 2, W^2 for the connections from layer 2 to layer 3, and so on.

You may see references to the layers between the input and the output as *hidden layers* and count layers starting from the first hidden layer. This is just a different convention from the one used in the book. The examples in the book always start counting from the input layer, so the first hidden layer is layer number 2.

Weights represent the strength of the connection between neurons in the network. When the weight connecting two neurons is small, it means that the network dumps values flowing between them and signals that taking this connection is unlikely to influence the final prediction. On the contrary, a considerable positive or negative weight affects the values that the next layer receives, thus determining specific predictions. This approach is clearly analogous to brain cells, which don't stand alone but are connected with other cells. As someone grows in experience, connections between neurons tend to strengthen or weaken to activate or deactivate certain cell regions of the brain network, causing additional neural processing or an activity with strong connections (a reaction to a danger, for instance, if the processed information signals a life-threatening situation).

Now that you know some conventions regarding layers, units, and connections, you can start examining the operations that neural networks execute in detail. To begin, you can call inputs and outputs in different ways:

>> **a:** The result stored in a unit in the neural network after being processed by the activation function (called g). This is the final output that is passed from one layer to the next in the network.

>> **z:** The multiplication between a, the output from the previous layer, and the weights from the W matrix, followed by the addition of bias values (one for each neuron). z represents the signal going through the connections, analogous to water in pipes that flows at a higher or lower pressure depending on the pipe thickness. In the same way, the values received from the previous layer get higher or lower because of the connection weights used to transmit them.

Each successive layer of units in a neural network progressively processes the values taken from the features. Think of it as a conveyor belt. As data transits the network, it arrives in each unit as a value produced by the summation of the values present in the previous layer and weighted by connections represented in the matrix W. When the data with added bias exceeds a certain threshold, the activation function increases the value stored in the unit; otherwise, it extinguishes the signal by reducing or cancelling it. After processing by the activation function, the result is ready to be pushed forward to the connections linked to the next layer. These steps repeat for each layer until the values reach the end and you have a result, as shown in Figure 14-4.

FIGURE 14-4:
A detail of the feed-forward process in a neural network.

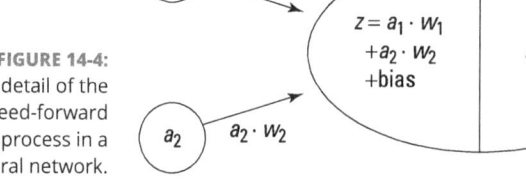

The figure shows details of the process that involves two units pushing their results to another unit. This event happens in every part of the network. When you understand the passage from two neurons to one, you can understand the entire feed-forward process, even when more layers and neurons are involved. For more explanation, here are the seven steps used to produce a prediction in a neural network made of four layers (like the one shown earlier in Figure 14-3):

1. The first layer (notice the superscript 1 on a) loads the value of each feature in a different unit:

$$a^{(1)} = X$$

2. The weights of the connections bridging the input layer with the second layer are multiplied by the values of the units in the first layer. A matrix multiplication weights and sums the inputs for the second layer. The algorithm adds a bias vector to layer two before running the activation function in the following step. Bias are values that, like the intercept in linear regression, shift the activation function's operating point, increasing the capabilities of the neurons to model their response.

$$z^{(2)} = W^{(1)}a^{(1)} + bias^{(2)}$$

3. The activation function transforms the second-layer inputs. The resulting values are ready to pass to the connections.

$$a^{(2)} = g(z^{(2)})$$

4. The outputs of layer two are weighted and summed by the connections of the third layer. Before running the activation function on the result, the algorithm adds a bias vector.

$$z^{(3)} = W^{(2)}a^{(2)} + bias^{(3)}$$

5. The activation function transforms the layer-three inputs.

$$a^{(3)} = g(z^{(3)})$$

6. The layer-three outputs are weighted and summed by the connections to the output layer. Finally, the algorithm adds a bias vector to layer four before running the activation function in the next step.

$$z^{(4)} = W^{(3)}a^{(3)} + bias^{(4)}$$

7. The output units receive their inputs and transform the input using the activation function. After this final transformation, the output units are ready to release the resulting neural network predictions.

$$a^{(4)} = g(z^{(4)})$$

The activation function plays the role of a signal filter, helping to select the relevant signals and avoid the weak and noisy ones (because it discards values below a certain threshold). Activation functions also provide nonlinearity to the output because they enhance or damp the values passing through them in a nonproportional way.

REMEMBER

From another perspective, the weights of the connections provide a way to mix and compose the features in a new way, creating new features in a manner similar to a polynomial expansion. The activation function makes the resulting recombination of the features by the connections nonlinear. Both of these neural network components enable the algorithm to learn complex target functions that represent the relationship between the input features and the target outcome.

Feeding data forward from the input to the output layer is what exclusively happens when you predict. When you train a neural network, you have both a feed-forward and a backpropagation phase. The backpropagation phase helps you refine the weights in your network. Because the feed-forward phase depends on weight multiplication, you have to start with some weights, or you won't be able to learn effectively with your network. *Initialization* provides some initial, randomly estimated weights.

How such initial weights are set matters because you can't use values that are too small — there will be too little signal for the network to work. However, you must also avoid values that are too large because the calculations become too cumbersome to handle. Sometimes they fail, which causes the exploding gradient problem or, more generally, causes *saturation of the neurons*, which means that you can't correctly train a network because all the neurons are always activated (or deactivated, the *vanishing gradients* problem).

REMEMBER

Initializing the weights of your network using all zeros is always a bad idea because all the neurons have the same value; hence, they'll learn the same thing from the training input, and you won't progress with the learning. No matter how many neurons the architecture contains, they will operate like a single neuron. A simple solution is to start with initial random weights in the range required for the activation functions, which are the transformation functions that add flexibility to solving problems using the network. Another possible solution is to initialize weights from a distribution with zero mean and unit standard deviation (a *standard normal distribution*, in statistics).

TIP

There are smarter weight initializations for more complex networks. The Keras package (https://keras.io/api/layers/initializers), which we discuss later in the chapter, contains most of them.

Pulling back with backpropagation

From an architectural perspective, a neural network does a great job of mixing signals from examples and turning them into new features to approximate complex nonlinear functions (functions that you can't represent as a straight line in the feature space). To create this capability, neural networks work as *universal approximators*, meaning they can approximate any target function. However, you must consider that one aspect of this feature is the capacity to model complex functions *(representation capability)*, and another is the capability to learn from data effectively. Learning occurs in the brain because of the formation and modification of synapses between neurons, based on stimuli received by trial-and-error experience. Neural networks provide a way to replicate this process thanks to an algorithm called *backpropagation* and an optimizer, such as gradient descent.

Since its early appearance in the 1970s, the backpropagation algorithm has been given many fixes. Each neural network learning process improvement resulted in new applications and a renewed interest in the technique. In addition, the current deep learning revolution, a revival of neural networks that were abandoned at the beginning of the 1990s, is the result of key advances in the way neural networks learn from their errors. As seen in other algorithms, the cost function signals when it is necessary to learn specific examples better (large errors correspond to high costs). When an instance with a significant error occurs, the cost function outputs a high value that is minimized by changing the parameters in the algorithm.

In linear regression, finding an update rule to apply to each parameter (the vector of beta coefficients) is straightforward; you can manage it using gradient descent or an analytical approach. However, in a neural network, things are a bit more complicated. The architecture is variable, and the parameter coefficients (the connections) relate to each other because the connections in a layer depend on how the connections in the previous layers recombined the inputs. The solution to this problem is the backpropagation algorithm. Backpropagation is specifically the algorithm for calculating the gradients of the loss function with respect to the weights distributed in the various layers of the network. Gradient descent (or some other optimizer) then uses these gradients to adjust the weights. If you initially feed-forward propagated information through the network, it's time to go backward and give feedback on what went wrong in the forward phase.

Discovering how backpropagation works isn't complicated, even though demonstrating how it works using formulas and mathematics requires derivatives and the proving of some formulations, which is quite tricky and beyond the scope of this book. To get a sense of how backpropagation operates, start from the end of the network, just at the moment when an example has been processed and you have a prediction as an output. At this point, you can compare it with the real result and, by subtracting the two results, get an offset, which is the error (for classification tasks, it is a bit more complicated — the difference is between predicted probabilities and true labels). Now that you know the mismatch of the results at the output layer, you can progress backward in order to distribute the error responsibility along all the units in the network.

The cost function of a neural network for classification is based on cross-entropy (as seen in logistic regression):

$$Cost = y * \log(h_w(X)) + (1-y) * \log(1 - h_w(X))$$

This is a formulation involving logarithms. It refers to the prediction produced by the neural network and expressed as $h_w(X)$ (which reads as the result of the network given connections W and X as input). To make things easier, when pondering the cost, it helps to simply think of the formulation as computing the offset between the expected results and the neural network output.

The first step in transmitting the error back into the network relies on backward multiplication. Because the values fed to the output layer are made of the contributions of all units, proportional to the weight of their connections, you can redistribute the error according to each contribution. For instance, the vector of errors of a layer n in the network, a vector indicated by the Greek letter delta (δ), is the result of the following formulation:

$$\delta^{(n)} = W^{(n)T} * \delta^{(n+1)}$$

This formula says that, starting from the final delta, you can continue redistributing delta going backward in the network and using the weights you used to push forward the value to partition the error to the different units. In this way, you can get the terminal error redistributed to each neural unit and use it to recalculate a more appropriate weight for each network connection to minimize the error. To update the weights W of layer l, you just apply the following formula:

$$W^{(1)} = W^{(1)} + \eta * \delta^{(1)} * g'(z^{(1)}) * a^{(1)}$$

It may appear to be a puzzling formula at first sight, but it is a summation, and you can discover how it works by looking at its elements. First, look at the function g'. It's the first derivative of the activation function g, evaluated at the input values z. In fact, derivatives are a key component of the gradient descent optimization method. Gradient descent determines how to reduce the error measure by finding, among the possible combinations of values, the weights that most reduce the error.

The Greek letter eta (η), sometimes also called alpha (α) or epsilon (ε), depending on the textbook you consult, is the learning rate. As found in other algorithms, using similar learning strategies, it reduces the effect of the update suggested by the gradient descent derivative. In fact, the direction provided by the weight updates may be only partially correct or just roughly correct (because of noise or errors in the data or because of the composition of the processed batch of examples). By taking multiple small steps in the descent, the algorithm can take a more precise direction toward the global minimum error, which is the target you want to achieve (that is, a neural network producing the least possible prediction error).

Different methods are available for setting the correct eta value, because the optimization largely depends on it. One method, called *learning rate scheduling,* sets the eta value starting high and reduces it according to a function based on the iterations during the optimization process. Other adaptive methods, like Adam and AdaGrad, variably increase or decrease eta based on the improvements obtained by the algorithm: large improvements call for a larger eta (because the descent is easy and straight); more minor improvements call for a smaller eta so that the optimization will move slower, looking for the best opportunities to descend. Think of it as being on a torturous path in the mountains: You slow down and try not to fall or be thrown off the road as you descend.

TIP

Most implementations offer an automatic setting of the correct eta. This setting is relevant when training a neural network because it's one of the important parameters to tweak to obtain better predictions, along with the layer architecture.

Weight updates can happen in different ways with respect to the training set of examples:

>> **Online mode:** The weight update happens after every example traverses the network. In this way, the algorithm treats the learning examples as a stream from which to learn in real time. This mode is perfect when you have to learn *out-of-core,* that is, when the training set can't fit into RAM memory. However, this method is sensitive to outliers, so you must keep your learning rate low. (Consequently, the algorithm is slow to converge to a solution.)

>> **Batch mode:** The weight update happens after seeing all the examples in the training set. This technique makes optimization fast and less subject to having too much process variance because of variability in the example stream. On the other hand, in batch mode, you need to keep all your examples *in-memory* (actually in RAM, rather than being streamed). In fact, in batch mode, the backpropagation considers the summed gradients of all examples.

>> **Mini-batch mode:** The weight update happens after the network has processed a subsample of randomly selected training set examples. This approach mixes the advantages of online mode (low memory usage) and batch mode (rapid convergence), while introducing a random element (the subsampling) to avoid having the gradient descent become stuck in a local minimum (a drop in the cost function that isn't the actual minimum).

Understanding Network Learning and Overfitting

Given the neural network architecture, you can imagine how easily the algorithm could learn almost anything from data, especially if you add too many layers. In fact, the algorithm does so well that its predictions are often affected by a high variance, a phenomenon called *overfitting*. Overfitting causes the neural network to learn every detail of the training examples, which makes it possible to replicate them in the prediction phase. However, apart from the promising results obtained using the training set, it will perform poorly on new, unseen data in case of overfitting.

Understanding the problem with overfitting

When you use a neural network for a real problem, you have to take some cautionary steps in a much stricter way than you do with other algorithms. Neural networks are more susceptible to overfitting and more sensitive to hyperparameter choices than other machine learning solutions.

First, you carefully split your data into training, validation, and test sets. Before the algorithm learns from data, you must make some crucial choices for your neural network and its hyperparameters:

» **Architecture (the number of layers and neurons):** Using a larger architecture for the problem offers increased opportunities to create powerful predictive models, but at a higher risk of overfitting.

» **Initialization:** It affects whether a network can learn effectively and influences how the neural network is optimized (different initializations lead to different solutions).

» **Activation functions:** Transform the data in a nonlinear way. Also, choosing the correct activation for each layer can make a difference in the predictive power of the neural network.

» **Learning parameters:** Controlling how fast a network learns from data, but it may not suffice in preventing overfitting of the training data.

» **Number of epochs:** Defining the number of useful epochs (an epoch marks a complete pass over the data by the neural network). The more times this happens, the higher the risk that overfitting may occur.

You have a few possible solutions to solve overfitting issues. Here we will mention two primary ones. The first is regularization, as in linear and logistic regression. You can sum all connection coefficients, squared or in absolute value, to penalize models with too many coefficients with high values (achieved by L2 regularization) or values different from zero (achieved by L1 regularization). The second solution is also effective because it controls when overfitting happens. It's called *early stopping* (as shown in Figure 14-5) and works by checking the cost function on the validation set as the algorithm learns from the training set.

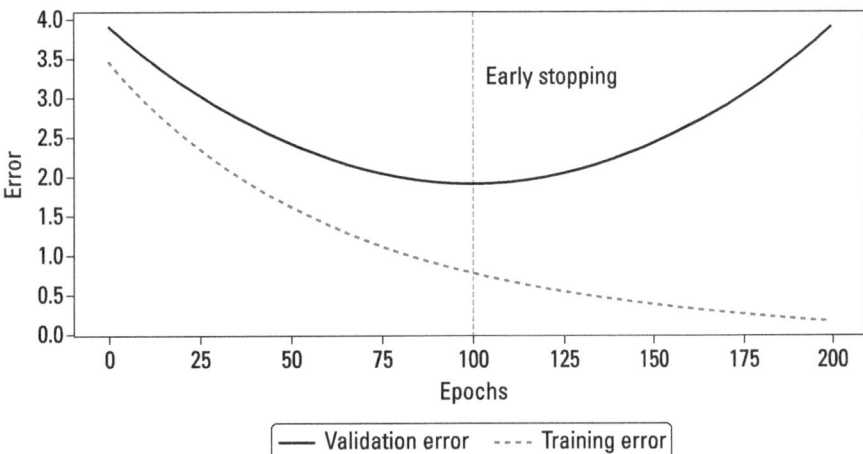

FIGURE 14-5: Overfitting also occurs when too many epochs are performed on the data.

TIP

You may not realize when your model starts overfitting. The cost function calculated using the training set keeps improving as optimization progresses. However, as soon as you start receiving noise from the data and stop learning general rules, you can check the cost function on *out-of-sample* (the validation sample) data. At some point, you'll notice that it stops improving and starts worsening, which means that your model has reached its learning limit.

Choosing a framework

The best way to learn how to build a neural network is to build one, and if you are going to get your hands dirty, especially with deep learning, the most straightforward way is to leverage the functionalities offered by a framework. Using a deep learning framework can significantly reduce the time, cost, and complexity of developing a deep learning solution. Even though deep learning frameworks have many characteristics of frameworks in general (consistent domain solutions), they also provide specific functionality: specialized hardware access for GPUs or TPUs, and including computations designed for use in deep learning.

Python offers a wealth of possible frameworks for neural networks and deep learning. At the time of the publication of this book, there were quite a few deep learning frameworks around, such as

>> **TensorFlow (`www.tensorflow.org`):** This product is one of the most widely adopted deep learning frameworks. TensorFlow's success stems from many reasons, mainly from providing a comprehensive and flexible programming environment, strong production deployment capabilities, and a relatively easy-to-use API through Keras (`www.tensorflow.org/guide/keras`). TensorFlow is used in both industry and research.

>> **JAX (`https://github.com/jax-ml/jax`):** Developed by Google Research, JAX is a library for high-performance numerical computation. It is particularly employed in research, where custom calculations and building new architectures are paramount. It features a familiar NumPy-like API with powerful differentiation, vectorization, compilation, and parallelization functions. Commonly, neural network libraries like Keras, Flax (from Google), and Haiku (from DeepMind) are built on top of JAX to provide higher-level abstractions for model building.

>> **PyTorch (`https://pytorch.org`):** Initially developed by Facebook (now Meta) AI Research (previously called FAIR, now Meta AI), PyTorch is used by many other organizations today, including Salesforce and the University of Oxford. PyTorch is renowned for its Pythonic feel, dynamic way of defining neural networks as graphs, and ease of use for rapid prototyping and experimentation, making it a particularly popular choice with academics and scientists.

>> **MXNet (`https://mxnet.apache.org`):** An Apache Incubator product that supports various languages, including Python, Julia, C++, R, and JavaScript, MXNet is designed for both flexibility and efficiency. Numerous large organizations, including Microsoft, Intel, and Amazon Web Services, continue to use it, although its user base has not grown significantly in recent years.

The Keras 3 package (`https://keras.io`) has been designed to make deep learning accessible and accelerate the development of neural networks. It allows you to build complex neural networks using simple command sequences. Keras's most significant selling point is that it puts the process of creating deep learning applications into a paradigm that most people can understand well. Keras started a few years ago as a stand-alone package developed by François Chollet. Over the years, it has enjoyed an enormous popularity among practitioners because of its practicality and ease of use, making it an easy solution for reducing the complexity of building a deep learning solution. Although a framework itself, it relies on other frameworks for its computations, and you can decide what Keras runs behind the scenes (the back-end engine), among TensorFlow, JAX, or PyTorch. Although using the Keras API, it makes little difference what back-end you decide on (except for some slight performance differences in certain situations), it is still a relevant choice because if you have to write custom functions or layers, you will rely on the syntax and functions of the back-end framework.

REMEMBER

Originally, Keras was less of a framework and more of an API, a set of interface specifications you can use with multiple frameworks as backends, like TensorFlow, Theano, or CNTK. For a certain period, the development focus shifted, and Keras's multi-backend capabilities were discontinued. At the time, Keras was bundled within TensorFlow (tf.keras). Recently, with the release of Keras 3, Keras reverted to its initial multi-backend vision, offering support for TensorFlow, JAX, and PyTorch.

Opening the black box

It's time to see how to use the Keras framework (with JAX as its backend for this example) to work through a problem. For this example, you start with a very simple bidimensional problem inspired by the TensorFlow Neural Network Playground, trying to divide two clouds of points shaped as opposing half-moons positioned in a Cartesian plane:

```
import numpy as np
from sklearn.datasets import make_moons
from sklearn.model_selection import train_test_split
import matplotlib.pyplot as plt

np.random.seed(0)
coord, cl = make_moons(500, noise=0.05)
X, Xt, y, yt = train_test_split(coord, cl,
                                test_size=0.30,
                                random_state=0)
cmap_set1 = plt.cm.Set1
fig, ax = plt.subplots(dpi=90)
ax.scatter(X[:,0], X[:,1], s=25, c=y, cmap=cmap_set1)
plt.show()
```

Looking at Figure 14-6, the task requires formulating a nonlinear separation because no straight line can exactly separate the two clouds of points.

TIP

Experimenting with the TensorFlow Neural Network Playground can help you visualize how a neural network works and learn how the different parameters of a network impact the generated results.

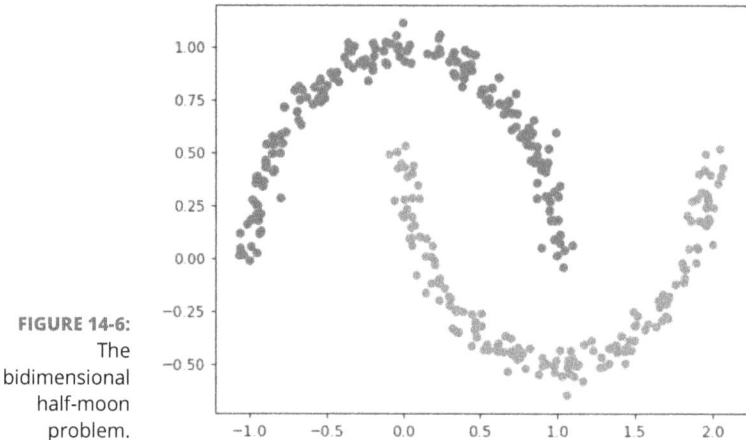

FIGURE 14-6:
The
bidimensional
half-moon
problem.

After setting up the data for the example, the code creates a neural network solution with Keras by defining the network architecture that processes the data. As a preference, we use JAX as the backend for Keras, but you could also choose TensorFlow ("tensorflow") or PyTorch ("torch") — in our example, the choice is quite uninfluential.

```
import os
os.environ["KERAS_BACKEND"] = "jax"
```

Then we proceed to define the architecture of the network using the sequential procedure that operates by adding layers in sequence:

```
import keras

model = keras.models.Sequential()
model.add(keras.layers.Input(shape=(2,)))
model.add(keras.layers.Dense(8, activation='relu'))
model.add(keras.layers.Dense(8, activation='relu'))
model.add(keras.layers.Dropout(0.2))
model.add(keras.layers.Dense(1, activation='sigmoid'))

model.compile(optimizer='adam',
              loss='binary_crossentropy',
              metrics=['accuracy'])
model.summary()
```

In some cases, importing the required package will generate warning messages you can safely ignore because the code will run as expected. The warnings are generated by the back-end you choose, not by the example code. When you run this code, you see the following output, which shows the neural network makeup:

```
Model: "sequential"

_____

Layer (type)            Output Shape            Param #
=======================================================

dense (Dense)           (None, 8)                  24

_____

dense_1 (Dense)         (None, 8)                  72

_____

dropout (Dropout)       (None, 8)                   0

_____

dense_2 (Dense)         (None, 1)                   9

=======================================================

Total params: 105
Trainable params: 105
Non-trainable params: 0

_____
```

After importing Keras, the code specifies a model using the `Sequential()` function. The function works as a pipeline of layers and operations to execute from the first to the last. To define these layers, you call `add()` to define the next operation, as you would do with building blocks stacked one upon the other. You start with the `Input` layer, which feeds your data into the neural network. The only requirement for this layer is to define the expected shape of your data. Because the network normally expects the data to be divided into smaller chunks, called *batches,* the input layer's shape argument defines the dimensions of a single sample, excluding the batch size. However, it can handle as many dimensions as needed, marking a difference from other machine learning algorithms that accept only matrices of cases by features as an input.

REMEMBER

The `Input` layer handles the input without applying any transformation. Because neural networks rely on gradient descent, you usually standardize (by subtracting the mean and dividing by the standard deviation) or normalize the inputs (forcing them into a specific range of values such as between 0 and +1 or between −1 and +1) beforehand. Also, you have to test which procedure, standardization or normalization, works the best with your data and your network.

Two dense layers, activated by ReLU activation function, follow the input layer. Here, the inputs combine, and the activation functions produce nonlinear mappings between the inputs and the results. A ReLU, or Rectified Linear Units, whose function is $(A(x) = max(0, x))$, provides an output in the range of zero to infinity: When the input is above zero, it behaves similarly to a linear function, except for the flat zero output when the inputs are zero or negative. This activation function is simple enough to approximate even complex nonlinear functions if you stack enough layers of ReLU-activated neurons.

An advantage of ReLU is that it requires less processing power because fewer neurons fire a nonzero number. However, this advantage can also become a disadvantage because when you have too many inactive neurons, you get a problem called the dying ReLU. In fact, you can't backpropagate any error to a neuron whose output is zero, and the network stops learning or even working if there are many dying ReLUs.

The two dense layers are followed by a dropout layer, which prevents overfitting by randomly switching off some neurons from the previous layer. This implementation randomly excludes 20 percent of the incoming signals at each training iteration, as shown in Figure 14-7.

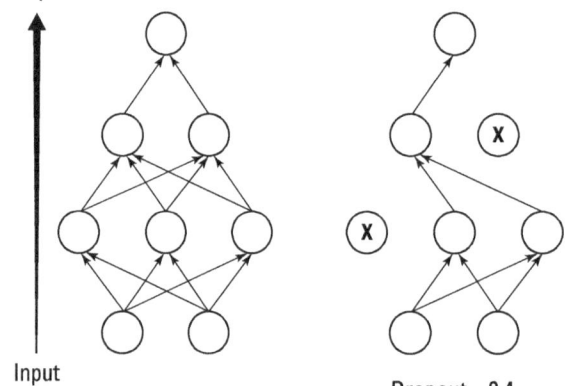

FIGURE 14-7:
Dropout temporarily rules out a proportion of the neurons from the training.

As depicted on the left side of Figure 14-7, the weights normally operate by multiplying their inputs into outputs for the activations. To switch off activation, the code multiplies a mask of a random mix of ones and zeros with the results. If the neuron is multiplied by one, the network passes its signal. When a neuron is multiplied by zero, the network stops its signal, forcing other neurons not to rely on it in the process.

Finally, the network is completed with an output neuron, activated by a sigmoid function, which releases results in the range 0 to 1 that can be interpreted as probabilities. (If the output is over 0.5, there is more than 50 percent probability that the example is of the positive class.) The model is finally compiled (the final preparation step) using an optimizer, in this case, the Adam optimizer, a general-purpose and automatic optimizer based on gradient descent, a cost function (or loss function), and an error measure to monitor.

Even if there seem to be too many parameters for the number of examples you have prepared for training (the rule of thumb in statistics is to have at least 10 or more examples of every model parameter), techniques such as dropout help keep overfitting under control. As a general approach, you shouldn't be afraid of using complex architectures when using neural networks. You start with medium-sized networks, then determine whether reducing or increasing the complexity of the architecture of the layers improves your results.

At this point, you can start the training by specifying the number of complete epochs through the data. The more epochs, the more the neurons will acquire information from the data, which risks overfitting. You also specify the batch, which is the size of the data chunks to feed the optimizer, and you decide whether you want to shuffle the input data at each epoch to inject randomization into the process that may help the optimization.

```
history = model.fit(X, y, epochs=1000, batch_size=64,
                    shuffle=True, verbose=0)
```

The training may take a while, but it shouldn't be excessively long (on a Google Colab instance, using an L4 GPU runtime, it takes about 13 seconds). When completed, you can ask for the accuracy on the train and test sets and see that the neural network will work perfectly because the accuracy (that is, the ratio of correct to incorrect classifications) is 1.0, meaning that it's a perfect fit.

First, we ask for the training fitted accuracy:

```
fitted_acc = history.history['accuracy'][-1]
print(f"Final training accuracy: {fitted_acc:0.3f}")
```

Then, we proceed to check the accuracy score also on the test set:

```
from sklearn.metrics import accuracy_score

predictions = (model.predict(Xt)>=0.5).astype(int)
test_accuracy = accuracy_score(yt, predictions)
print(f"Accuracy on test set: {test_accuracy:0.3f}")
```

Given the simplicity of the problem, which is the mapping of clouds of points on a Cartesian plane, you can also visualize the decision boundaries that separate one cloud from the other, as produced by the neural network (see Figure 14-8).

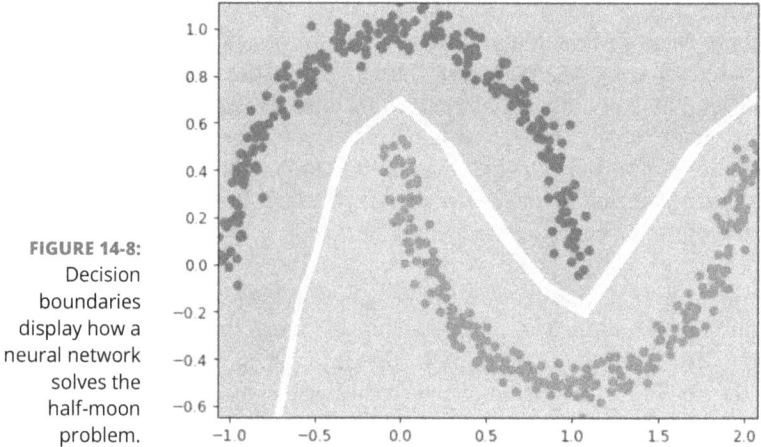

FIGURE 14-8:
Decision
boundaries
display how a
neural network
solves the
half-moon
problem.

To produce the chart in Figure 14-8, representing how the neural network mapped a function that cuts through the plane, separating the two clouds of points, you have to test the neural network across a range of possible input values and then plot the results using different colors:

```
x_min, x_max = coord[:,0].min(), coord[:,0].max()
y_min, y_max = coord[:,1].min(), coord[:,1].max()

x_range = np.linspace(x_min, x_max, 100)
y_range = np.linspace(y_min, y_max, 100)

xx, yy = np.meshgrid(x_range, y_range)
xy = np.stack([np.ravel(xx), np.ravel(yy)], axis=1)
zz = model.predict(xy)
zz = zz.reshape(xx.shape)
```

The NumPy functions `linspace()` and `meshgrid()` help you produce a range of input abscissa and ordinate values and combine them thoroughly. You then pass the combinations to the evaluation of the neural network and get a vector of predictions. Finally, you print the results as a contour plot, combined with your original scatterplot of the data points:

```
cmap_rb = plt.get_cmap('RdBu')
fig, ax = plt.subplots(dpi=90)
ax.contourf(xx, yy, zz, cmap=cmap_rb,
            alpha=0.3, levels=3)
ax.scatter(coord[:,0], coord[:,1],
           s=25, c=cl, cmap=cmap_set1)
plt.show()
```

TIP

For all your experiments on bidimensional toy datasets, you can visualize the decision boundaries. To apply this approach to other machine learning algorithms, adapt and utilize the previous two code snippets.

Introducing Deep Learning

After backpropagation, the next improvement in neural networks led to deep learning. Research continued in spite of AI winter, and neural networks started to take advantage of the developments in CPUs and GPUs, graphics processing units better known for their application in gaming, which are actually powerful computing units for matrix and vector calculations. These technologies make training larger neural networks an achievable task in a shorter time and accessible to more people. Research also opened a world of new applications. Neural networks can learn from vast amounts of data. Because deep neural networks are highly flexible (low-bias models), they're more prone to high variance than bias. They can take advantage of big data, creating models that continuously perform better, depending on how much data they ingest. The following sections provide you with an overview of deep learning.

Understanding some deep learning essentials

If you perceive deep learning to be only something that involves using larger networks than before, you miss an important point. Deep learning isn't simply a rebranding of an old technology; it works better than that older technology because of the extra sophistication it adds through the use of powerful computers and the availability of better (not just more) data. Deep learning also implies a profound qualitative change in the capabilities the technology offers, along with new and astonishing applications. These capabilities modernize old but good neural networks, transforming them into something new.

Because it uses many layers, deep learning can map more complex target functions and solve problems that are out of reach of preexisting machine learning techniques. These problems include image recognition, machine translation, and speech recognition. Given enough units, enough hidden layers, and a suitable nonlinear activation, a neural network can recreate, with a minimal degree of approximation, any continuous mathematical function, proving itself a *universal function approximator*. When fitted with many more layers, a neural network can autonomously create sophisticated target functions and a system of feature representations suitable to solve complex problems inside its internal chain of matrix multiplications.

One of the earliest deep learning achievements that made the public aware of its potential is the cat neuron. The Google Brain team, run by Andrew Ng and Jeff Dean at that time, put together a cluster with 16,000 CPU cores to calculate a deep learning network with more than a billion weights, thus enabling unsupervised learning from YouTube videos. The computer network could even determine, without human intervention, what a cat is, and Google scientists managed to dig out of the network a representation of how the network itself expected a cat to look (see the *Wired* article at www.wired.com/2012/06/google-x-neural-network). However, you need large, complex networks to successfully tackle certain applications (to learn complex features, such as the characteristics of a series of images). Therefore, previous neural networks incurred problems like the vanishing gradient as soon as people tried to make them larger.

A vanishing gradient occurs when, during backpropagation, you try to transmit a signal through a neural network, and the signal quickly fades to near-zero values; it can't get through the activation functions. This happens because neural networks are chained multiplications. Multiplication by values with magnitude less than one shrinks the gradient rapidly, and activation functions need large enough values to let the signal pass. The farther the neuron layers are from the output, the more likely they will get locked out of updates because the signals are too small; the activation functions will stop them. Consequently, your network stops learning as a whole, or it learns at an incredibly slow pace.

In fact, when training a large network, the error redistributes among the neurons, favoring the layers nearest to the output layer. Layers that are further away receive smaller gradients and consequent minor corrections, sometimes too small to effectively change the weights, making training slow if not impossible. Today, deep networks are possible thanks to the studies of scholars from the University of Toronto in Canada, such as Geoffrey Hinton (https://www.utoronto.ca/news/artificial-intelligence-u-t), who insisted on working on neural networks even when they seemed to most to be an old-fashioned machine learning approach.

Professor Hinton, a veteran of the field of neural networks (he contributed to defining the backpropagation algorithm), and his team in Toronto devised a few methods to circumvent the problem of vanishing gradients. He opened the field to rethinking new solutions that made neural networks a crucial tool in machine learning and AI again. The chapter has already examined some of his ideas, such as ReLU activation and dropout. He also introduced smarter initializations and presented the idea of pretraining — a way of using the weights computed by a neural network trained for a similar problem — as a way to bootstrap a better solution.

TIP

Deep learning is a complex and fascinating part of machine learning that is just now blooming. *Artificial Intelligence For Dummies* by John Paul Mueller and Luca Massaron (Wiley) thoroughly examines the concepts and practicalities of deep learning and its applications in artificial intelligence.

Explaining the magic of convolutions

Given the high reliance on neural networks for image-recognition tasks, deep learning has achieved significant momentum thanks to a particular type of neural network, the convolutional neural network (CNN), which you also see referenced as a ConvNet. The French scientist Yann LeCun and other notable scientists devised the idea of CNNs at the end of the 1980s, and they fully developed their technology during the 1990s. But only about 25 years later are such networks starting to deliver astonishing results, even achieving better performance than humans do in particular recognition tasks. The change has come because it's possible to configure such networks into complex architectures that can refine their learning from lots of valuable data.

To understand the concept behind CNNs, consider convolutions as operations that apply learnable filters to a matrix of pixel values, which are part of a larger image. The CNN learns how to filter images using a dot product and a sliding filter or kernel (a small matrix of weights) that computes dot products across the image. Image filtering, as learned by CNNs, can transform specific parts of the pixel matrix, make other parts disappear, and make other parts stand out. You can use convolution filters for borders or particular shapes. Such filters are also helpful in finding details in images that determine what the image shows. Humans know a car is a car because it has a particular shape and features, not because they have previously seen every type of car possible. A standard neural network is tied to its input, and if the input is a pixel matrix, it recognizes shapes and features based on their position on the matrix. CNNs can elaborate images better than a standard neural network because

>> The network specializes particular neurons to recognize specific shapes (thanks to convolutions), so the same capability to recognize a shape doesn't need to appear in different parts of the network.

>> By sampling parts of an image into a single value (a task called *pooling*), you don't need to strictly tie shapes to a certain position (which would make rotating them impossible). The neural network can recognize the shape in every rotation or distortion, thus ensuring a high capacity for generalization of the convolutional network.

In more technical terms, an image in a computer is composed as a three-dimensional matrix consisting of height, width, and the number of channels, which is typically three for an RGB image. Still, it could be just one for a black-and-white image. (Grayscale is a special sort of RGB image for which each of the three channels is the same number.)

A convolution operates by processing small image chunks across all image channels simultaneously. As an analogy, picture a slice of layer cake, with each piece showing all the layers. Image chunks are simply a moving image window. The convolution window can be a square or a rectangle, and it starts from the upper left of the image, moving from left to right and from top to bottom. Applying a single kernel across the entire image produces a *feature map* or *activation map*. The kernel itself is often referred to as a *filter*. Also important to note is that when the window frames a new chunk, the window then shifts a certain number of pixels; the amount of the slide is called a *stride*. A stride of 1 means that the window is moving one pixel toward the right or bottom; a stride of 2 implies a movement of two pixels; and so on.

Every time the convolution window moves to a new position, a filtering process occurs to create part of the filter described in the previous paragraph. In this process, the values in the convolution window are multiplied by the values in the kernel, a small matrix used for blurring, sharpening, embossing, edge detection, and more — you choose the kernel you need for the task in question. The article at `https://setosa.io/ev/image-kernels` tells you more about various kernel types. The kernel is the same size as the convolution window. The dot product between the kernel and each corresponding image patch generates a new value, forming the output feature map, which can be viewed as a new processed feature of the image. The convolution outputs the pixel value, and when the sliding window has completed its tour across the image, the image has been filtered. As a result of the convolution, you find a new image having the following characteristics:

» If you use a single filtering process, the result is a transformed image of a single channel.

» If you use multiple kernels, the new image has as many channels as the number of filters, each containing specially processed new feature values. The number of filters is the filter depth of a convolution.

» If you use a stride of 1, you get an image of the exact dimensions as the original.

» If you use strides of a size greater than 1, the resulting convoluted image is smaller than the original; a stride of size two implies halving the image size.

The resulting image may be smaller, depending on the kernel size, because the kernel must start and finish its tour on the image borders. A kernel will eat up its size minus one when processing the image. For instance, a kernel of 3-by-3 pixels processing a 7-by-7 pixel image will eat up 2 pixels from the height and width of the image, and the result of the convolution will be an output of size 5 x 5 pixels. You can pad the image with zeros at the border (in essence, to put a black border on the image) so that the convolution process won't reduce the final output size. This strategy is referred to as *same padding*. If you just let the kernel reduce the size of your starting image, it's called *valid padding*.

Thanks to their characteristics, convolution filters can detect edges or enhance specific features of an image. Specifically, thanks to the learned weights obtained through backpropagation, each filter specializes in identifying particular aspects of an image. For example, a kernel specialized in filtering features typical of cats can see a cat no matter where it is positioned in an image and, if you use enough kernels, every possible variant of an image of a kind (resized, rotated, translated) is detected, rendering your neural network an efficient tool for image classification and recognition. Figure 14-9 provides an example of some convolutions transforming an image.

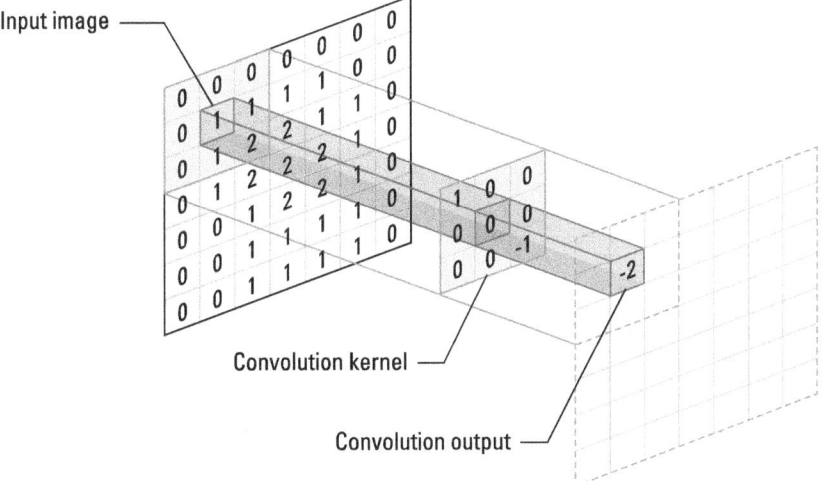

FIGURE 14-9: A convolution processes a chunk of an image at a time.

The following example demonstrates how convolutional layers work by classifying images from the *Fashion-MNIST dataset* (https://github.com/zalandoresearch/fashion-mnist), which comprises clothing items from

Zalando, an online fashion retailer. The dataset contains 60,000 training examples and 10,000 test examples. Each example is a 28-by-28 pixel image representing an article from ten groups of clothing apparel, like those shown in Figure 14-10.

```
import keras
import matplotlib.pyplot as plt

loader = keras.datasets.fashion_mnist.load_data
(x_train, y_train), (x_test, y_test) = loader()

class_names = {
    0: 'T-shirt/top', 1: 'Trouser', 2: 'Pullover',
    3: 'Dress', 4: 'Coat', 5: 'Sandal', 6: 'Shirt',
    7: 'Sneaker', 8: 'Bag', 9: 'Ankle boot'}

fig, axes = plt.subplots(5, 5, figsize=(10, 10), dpi=90)
for i in range(25):
    ax = axes[i // 5, i % 5]
    ax.imshow(x_train[i], cmap=plt.cm.binary)
    ax.set_xticks([])
    ax.set_yticks([])
    ax.set_xlabel(class_names[y_train[i]])
    ax.grid(False)
plt.tight_layout()
plt.show()
```

After loading the dataset and plotting some examples, the code divides the pixel values in the images by 255, so that the values of the pixels now range from 0 to 1. The code then reshapes the image format to have only one color channel.

REMEMBER

Images typically have a 3D matrix form, with the third dimension being a color channel. (Usually, there is one channel each for red, green, and blue in the RGB format.) CNNs expect to receive images in a 3D matrix format, so you have to reshape the 2D image matrices.

```
num_classes = 10
x_train = (x_train / 255.).reshape(-1, 28, 28, 1)
x_test = (x_test / 255.).reshape(-1, 28, 28, 1)
```

FIGURE 14-10:
Some images
from the
Fashion-
MNIST dataset.

After preparing the data, the code instantiates the model, which consists of two layers of convolutions (one with 32 filters and another with 64 filters) that will analyze the images using a 3-by-3-pixel kernel. The expectation is that the large number of filters and the small kernel will pick up many image details. Next, the code uses a max pooling layer to reduce the size of the resulting input by half before passing it through several dense layers.

```
model = keras.models.Sequential([
    keras.layers.Input(shape=(28, 28, 1)),
    keras.layers.Conv2D(32, (3, 3), activation='relu'),
    keras.layers.Conv2D(64, (3, 3), activation='relu'),
    keras.layers.MaxPooling2D(pool_size=(2, 2)),
    keras.layers.Flatten(),
    keras.layers.Dense(32, activation='relu'),
    keras.layers.Dropout(0.2),
```

```
      keras.layers.Dense(num_classes,
          activation='softmax')])

model.compile(optimizer='adam',
              loss='sparse_categorical_crossentropy',
              metrics=['accuracy'])
model.summary()
```

You can see the organization of the model from this output:

```
Model: "sequential_1"
_____
Layer (type)            Output Shape             Param #
=========================================================
conv2d (Conv2D)          (None, 26, 26, 32)        320

_____
conv2d_1 (Conv2D)        (None, 24, 24, 64)        18496

_____
max_pooling2d (MaxPooling2D)(None, 12, 12, 64) 0

_____
flatten (Flatten)        (None, 9216)              0

_____
dense_3 (Dense)          (None, 32)                294944

_____
dropout_1 (Dropout)   (None, 32)                0

_____
dense_4 (Dense)          (None, 10)                330
=========================================================
Total params: 314,090
Trainable params: 314,090
Non-trainable params: 0
_____
```

The code now uses sparse categorical cross-entropy as a loss function because it accepts a multiclass target expressed as class numbers, without any further transformation.

```
model.fit(x_train, y_train,
          batch_size=64,
          epochs=11,
          verbose=1,
          validation_split=0.2)

score = model.evaluate(x_test, y_test, verbose=0)
print(f"Accuracy on test set: {score[1]:.3f}")
```

Given the numerous examples and 11 epochs through the data, the neural network requires some amount of time to process everything (On Google Colab running with an L4 GPU, it takes about 27 seconds). The code reserved 20 percent of the examples for validation purposes during training, allowing verification that the validation loss and measures never deteriorate, a sign of overfitting. The code also compares the validation loss with the training loss; a large difference between the training and validation losses is another, more subtle sign of overfitting.

The process should complete with a training accuracy of approximately 95 percent, a validation accuracy of roughly 92 percent, and a test accuracy of 91.5 percent (note that the test accuracy is only displayed in the printed output, which may vary slightly from 91.5 percent). Because the differences between training, validation, and test are minor, you have confirmation that the model can correctly guess nine examples out of ten in the Fashion-MNIST test set, thanks to the implemented and trained convolution layers.

Understanding recurrent neural networks

The kind of neural architectures discussed up to this point in this chapter don't allow you to process a sequence of elements simultaneously using a single input. For instance, when you have a series of monthly product sales, you input the sales figures using twelve inputs, one for each month, and let the neural network analyze them simultaneously. It follows that when you have more extended sequences, you need to accommodate them using a larger number of inputs, and your network becomes quite huge because each input should connect with every other input in the next layer. You end up with a network characterized by a large number of connections, which translates into many weights.

Recurrent neural networks (RNNs) first emerged in the 1980s, and various researchers have continued to work on improving them until they recently gained popularity due to advancements in deep learning and computational power. The idea behind RNNs is simple: they examine each element of the sequence one at a time and retain a memory of it, allowing them to reuse it when reviewing the next component of the sequence. The process is akin to how the human mind works when reading text: A person reads the text letter by letter but understands words by remembering each letter in the word. Similarly, an RNN can associate a word with a result by remembering the sequence of letters it receives, as shown in Figure 14-11.

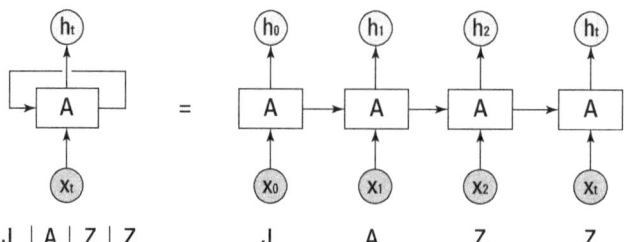

FIGURE 14-11:
A folded and
unfolded RNN cell
processing a
sequence input.

You represent an RNN graphically as a neural unit, also known as a cell, that connects an input to an output and also connects to itself (refer to Figure 14-11). This self-connection represents the concept of recursion, which is a function applied to itself until it achieves a particular output. One of the most commonly used examples of recursion is the computation of a factorial, as described at https://realpython.com/python-recursion. The figure shows a specific RNN example using a letter sequence to make the word *jazz*. The right side of the figure depicts a representation of the RNN unit behavior receiving the word *jazz* as input, but there is actually only one unit, as shown on the left. The figure shows a recursive cell on the left and expands it as an unfolded series of units that receives the single letters of the word *jazz* on the right. It starts with *j*, followed by the other letters. As this process occurs, the RNN emits an output and modifies its internal parameters. By modifying its internal parameters, the unit learns from the data it receives and from the memory of the previous data.

TIP

RNNs are useful for sequences, and are therefore useful for learning sequences of letters or words as well as a time series of economic data.

However, RNNs initially suffered from the vanishing gradient problem until two scientists studied the issue and published a milestone paper in 1997 that proposed a solution. Sepp Hochreiter, a computer scientist who made many contributions to the fields of machine learning, deep learning, and bioinformatics, and Jürgen Schmidhuber, a pioneer in the field of artificial intelligence, published "Long Short-Term Memory" in the MIT Press journal *Neural Computation* (https://direct.mit.edu/neco/article-abstract/9/8/1735/6109/Long-Short-Term-Memory).

The article introduced a new recurrent cell concept that now serves as the foundation of all deep learning applications using sequences. Originally rejected because it was too innovative (ahead of its time), the new cell concept proposed in the article, named LSTM (short for long short-term memory), has been used to perform billions of neural operations per day, and is considered the standard for machine translation and chatbots.

The core idea behind LSTM is for the RNN to discriminate between the short-term and long-term states. The state is the memory of the cell, and LSTM maintains distinct memory components: the cell state (long-term) and the hidden state (short-term, also the output):

>> **Short term:** Input data directly mixes with data arriving from the sequence

>> **Long term:** Picks up from short-term memory only the elements that need to be retained for a long time

LSTMs are arranged around gates, which are internal mechanisms that use summation, multiplication, and an activation function to regulate the flow of information inside the LSTM cell. By controlling the flow, a gate can maintain, enhance, or discard the information that has arrived from a sequence in both short- and long-term memory, which is reminiscent of an electric circuit. Figure 14-12 illustrates the internal structure of an LSTM.

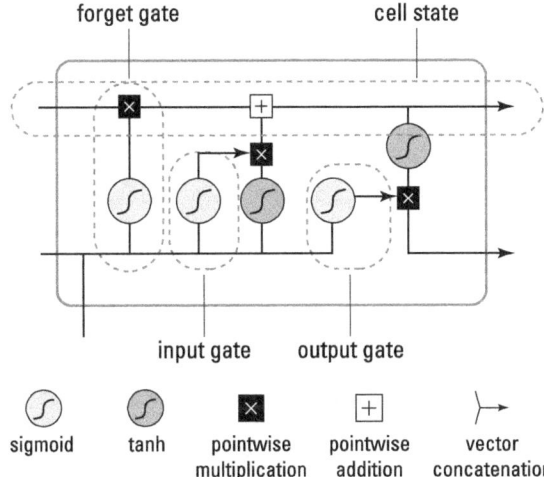

FIGURE 14-12: The internal structure of an LSTM, with the two memory flows and gates.

The different roots and gates may seem a bit complicated at first, but the following sequence of steps helps you understand them:

1. The short-term memory arriving from a previous state (or from random values) meets the newly inputted part of the sequence, and they mix, creating a first derivation.

2. The short-term memory signal, carrying both the existing signal and the newly input signal, tries to reach the long-term memory by passing through the forget gate, which is used to forget specific data. (Technically, you see branching where the signal is duplicated.)

3. The forget gate determines which short-term information to discard before passing it to the long-term memory. A sigmoid activation cancels the signals that aren't useful and enhances what seems essential to keep and remember.

4. Information passing through the forget gate arrives at the long-term memory channel, carrying the information from the previous states.

5. The values of the long-term memory and the output from the forget gate are multiplied together.

6. The short-term memory that didn't pass through the forget gate is duplicated again and takes another branch; that is, one part proceeds to the output gate, and the other one faces the input gate.

7. At the input gate, the short-term memory data passes through a sigmoid function and a TanH function separately. The outputs of these two functions are then first multiplied together and then added to the long-term memory. The effect on long-term memory depends on the sigmoid, which determines whether to forget or remember a signal based on its importance.

8. After the addition of the outputs from the input gate, the long-term memory remains unchanged. Being composed of selected inputs from short-term memory, long-term memory retains information for a more extended period and doesn't react to a temporal gap between inputs.

9. Long-term memory provides information directly to the next state. It's also sent to the output gate, where the short-term memory also converges. This last gate normalizes the data from long-term memory using TanH activation and filters the short-term memory using the sigmoid function. The two results are multiplied together and then sent to the next state.

TIP

LSTM has variants, such as the Gated Recurrent Units (also known as GRUs), which are a simplification of the LSTM architecture. GRUs are less complex than LSTMs, thus less capable of remembering past signals. However, they train faster than LSTMs (they have fewer parameters to adjust) and perform better than LSTMs when there is less training data, as they are less likely to overfit the information they receive.

REMEMBER

Google, Apple, Facebook, Microsoft, and Amazon have all previously developed products based on Hochreiter and Schmidhuber's long short-term memory (LSTM) technology. The introduction of a new deep learning technology, the transformers (not discussed by this book), has challenged LSTM's dominance in natural language processing (NLP). However, LSTM remains a viable solution for other types of data, such as time series and language processing, particularly when large models are unsuitable or uneconomical.

This example shows the capabilities and performance of LSTMs by utilizing a well-known time series problem: the Air Passengers Dataset. This example was first introduced in the classic book *Time Series Analysis, Forecasting and Control* by Box, Jenkins, and Reinsel (Wiley, 1976), and it has since become widely known, appearing in all books and software on time series analysis.

The figures in the Air Passengers Data represent the monthly totals of international airline passengers from 1949 to 1960 for an American airline company. The interesting aspect of such statistics is that they exhibit a growing trend that is not linear, and they display some seasonal recurrence, such as increased travel during the summer, as shown in Figure 14-13. The following code loads and plots the raw data:

```python
import pandas as pd
import numpy as np
import matplotlib.pyplot as plt

repository = (
        "https://github.com/lmassaron/ml4dummies_3ed/")
release = "releases/download/v1.0/"
filename = repository + release + "air_passengers.csv"
passengers = pd.read_csv(filename)
passengers = passengers.set_index("Month")

passengers.plot()
plt.show()
```

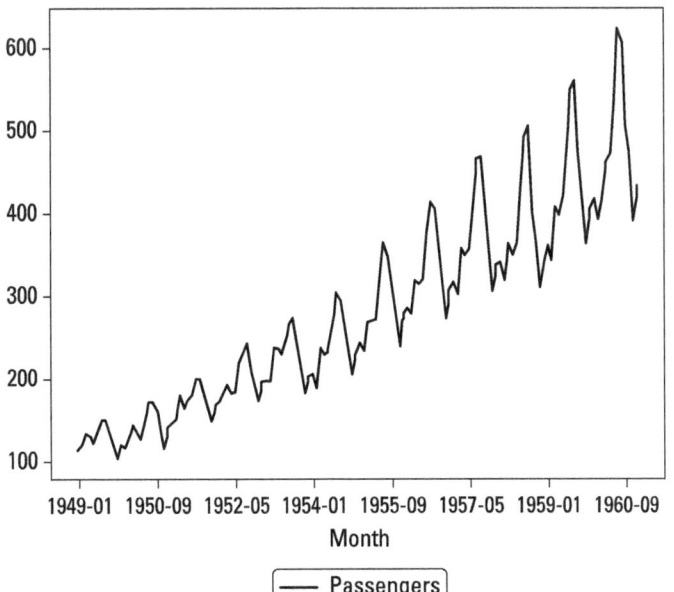

FIGURE 14-13: The Air Passengers Data.

In forecasting problems, you try to find a model that can predict the future by knowing the past. As a first step, decide how far into the future you want to predict, and then determine how far back in the past you can look for information. The example aims to predict the number of passengers for the next month using information from the previous twelve months. The .shift method from pandas can take the original series and create shifted versions to present the values of passengers in the past. In this way, it's possible to align the target value with its 12 previous values.

```
lookback = 12
sequence = pd.DataFrame(
    {"shift_" + str(s):
        passengers["Passengers"].shift(s)
        for s in range(lookback + 1)}
)[lookback:]
```

The first 12 examples are incomplete (the dataset lacks all the past information), so the code discards them. The data manipulation then follows these steps:

1. Separate the target variable from the predictors.

2. Record the maximum value in the data.

3. Use the maximum value to transform the data by division (ensuring that the data values won't exceed 1.0).

4. Reshape the data because LSTM expects sequences of data; their inputs should also be 3D:

   ● The first dimension is for the cases (the batch size)

   ● The second dimension is for the number of past time steps you want to consider for your prediction (the sequence)

   ● The last dimension is for the number of variables you're using to predict the future value (the features)

Here's the code used to perform these tasks.

```
y = sequence.iloc[:, 0]
X = sequence.iloc[:, 1:]

max_value = np.max(y)
y /= max_value
X /= max_value

X = X.values.reshape((X.shape[0], X.shape[1], 1))
```

This code also divides the data into training and test sets by selecting the last two years of data to verify that the model performs as expected. Selecting the latter part of the data is a best practice when dealing with time series (the last part is used as a *hold-out set*) because it accurately simulates what happens when you start predicting the future after training your model on a portion of the past.

TIP

Never use cross-validation for time series; use the latter part of the data as a hold-out set, or the time-split cross-validation from Scikit-learn: https://scikit-learn.org/stable/modules/generated/sklearn.model_selection.TimeSeriesSplit.html. When you train your model using examples from the time you want to predict, you can leak some information and generate overfitting that will prevent you from having a useful predictor:

```
y_train = y[:-24]
y_test = y[-24:]


X_train = X[:-24]
X_test = X[-24:]
```

At this point, you instantiate the model and use the LSTM as a processing layer before passing the information to one or more dense layers. Setting the random seed enables us to reproduce the same results, as the neural network is initialized randomly in the same manner each time, based on the provided seed number. Also, notice that as input, the network receives the number of time steps (lookback, set to 12), and the number of features, which is set to 1 since we are working with an univariate time series:

```
import keras

seed = 0
keras.utils.set_random_seed(seed)

model = keras.models.Sequential()
model.add(keras.layers.Input(shape=(lookback, 1)))
model.add(keras.layers.LSTM(units=4))
model.add(keras.layers.Dense(4, activation="relu"))
model.add(keras.layers.Dense(1))
model.compile(loss="mean_squared_error",
              optimizer="adam")
model.summary()
```

The next step is then fitting the model, passing the information to the network enough times. To further help make the optimization process reproducible, we also do not shuffle the data at each epoch (so the sequence of information always stays the same):

```
history = model.fit(X_train, y_train,
                    epochs=300,
                    batch_size=8,
                    shuffle=False,
                    verbose=0)
```

When the training is complete (on Google Colab running a L4 GPU runtime it should take about 9 seconds), you can test your model by predicting on the test data. Because you previously transformed the data by dividing it by the maximum value in the series, you now need to multiply the results for the same maximum value to restore the values as they should be, thereby creating the result shown in Figure 14-14.

```
from sklearn.metrics import mean_squared_error

preds = model.predict(X_test) * max_value
real = y_test * max_value

rmse = np.sqrt(mean_squared_error(y_true=real,
                                  y_pred=preds))
print(f"RMSE for test set: {rmse:0.3f}")

fig, ax = plt.subplots(dpi=90)
real.plot(label="Actual", ax=ax)
ax.plot(preds, label="Predicted")
ax.set_title("Air Passenger Forecast vs Actual")
ax.set_ylabel("Monthly Passengers")
ax.set_xlabel("Time")
ax.legend()
plt.show()
```

You can examine the model's fit (the lighter, bottom line) in Figure 14-14. The prediction is not perfect (predictions can't ever be entirely exact because the future is inherently uncertain). Deep neural networks, powered by RNNs such as LSTM, can easily identify patterns in a sequence, approximating functions that, using classical forecasting approaches, would typically require extensive experimentation and trials.

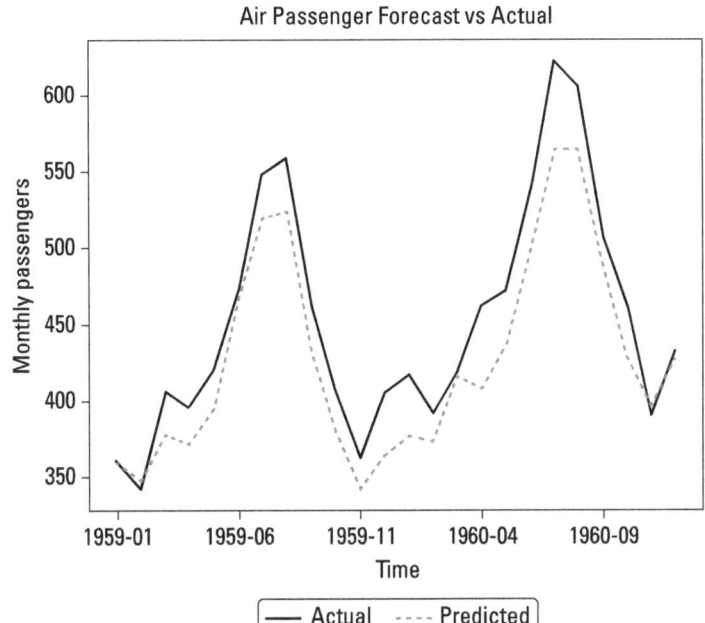

FIGURE 14-14:
Predictions
on the last two
years of the Air
Passengers Data.

TIP

Convolutional layers and recurrent neural networks are complex topics that require additional examples to be fully understood. In Part 5 of this book, you find some more basic examples of deep learning models.

Chapter **15**

Resorting to Ensembles of Learners

After discovering so many complex and powerful algorithms, you might be surprised that a combination of simpler machine learning algorithms can often outperform the most sophisticated solutions. Such is the power of *ensembles*, groups of models made to work together to produce better predictions.

At the beginning of this chapter, we revisit the foundations of ensembles and decision trees. Then, we review the different models that combine multiple models: Bagging, Random Forests, AdaBoost, Gradient Boosting, and approaches such as heterogeneous blending and stacking ensembles. We will explore these concepts through the lens of the Wine dataset, comparing approaches and performances and highlighting strengths and weaknesses, with particular attention to the state-of-the-art gradient boosting implementations, XGBoost, LightGBM, and CatBoost.

REMEMBER

You don't have to type the source code for this chapter manually. In fact, using the downloadable source code is a lot easier. You can find the source code for this chapter in the ML4D3E folder of the downloadable code file. The example files for this chapter will begin with ML4D3E-15-. See the Introduction for details on how to find these source files.

Leveraging Decision Trees

Ensembles don't work much differently from the collective intelligence of crowds, through which a set of approximate estimations, if averaged, often provides a more correct answer. Sir Francis Galton, the English Victorian age statistician known for having formulated the idea of correlation, narrated an anecdote about a crowd in a county fair that could correctly guess the weight of an ox after all individual answers were averaged. You can find similar examples everywhere and easily recreate the experiment by asking friends to guess the number of sweets in a jar and averaging their answers. The more friends participating in the game, the more precise the average answer.

Luck isn't what's behind the result — it's simply the law of large numbers in action. The law of large numbers, a fundamental theorem in statistics and probability, states that when you average the results from many trials, you get an estimate near the value you expected. Hence, even though an individual has a slight chance of getting the correct answer, the guess is little better than a random choice. By accumulating more and more guesses, the average of the guesses will slowly converge toward the right answer, and this is true even if you are trying to guess a categorical choice because the correct category will tend to appear most frequently. Machine learning ensembles are based on a recent idea (formulated around 1990), but they leverage older tools, such as decision trees, which have been part of machine learning since the mid-twentieth century. As covered in Chapter 10, decision trees initially looked quite promising to practitioners because of their ease of use and interpretability. A decision tree can easily do the following:

>> Handle mixed types of target variables and predictors, with very little or no feature preprocessing

>> Specific mechanisms within the tree algorithm can handle missing values, or they can be addressed beforehand by imputation, using a specific placeholder or a statistical value like the mean or the median

>> Ignore redundant features and select only the relevant features

>> Often work out-of-the-box, with relatively simple hyperparameters to set and tune

>> Visualize the prediction process as a set of recursive rules arranged in a tree with branches and leaves, thus offering ease of interpretation

Given the range of positive characteristics, you may wonder why practitioners slowly started losing confidence in this algorithm after a few years. The main reason is that the resulting models often have high variance in the estimates.

To better grasp the critical problem of decision trees, you can consider the problem visually. Think of the tricky situation of the bull's-eye problem that requires a machine learning algorithm to approximate nonlinear functions (as neural networks do) or to transform the feature space (as when using a linear model with polynomial expansion or kernel functions in support vector machines). Figure 15-1 shows the rectangular decision boundary of a single decision tree (on the left) compared to an ensemble of decision trees (on the right).

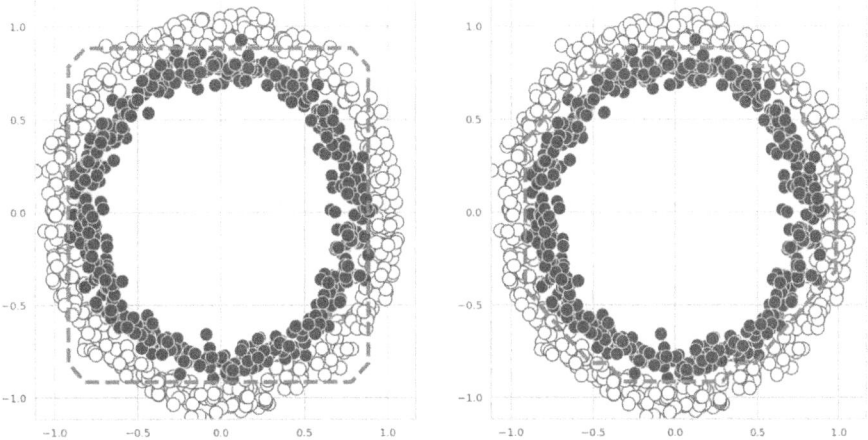

FIGURE 15-1: Comparing a single decision tree output (left) to an ensemble of decision trees (right).

Decision trees partition the feature space into delimited areas and then use such areas for classification or regression purposes. When the decision boundary that separates classes in a bull's-eye problem is an ellipse, decision trees can approximate it by combining a certain number of areas.

Even if a decision tree performs fine in separating two classes, it may perform poorly on the test set at the boundaries between classes. In fact, in the proximity of the boundary, the characteristics of the data may differ significantly from the training set. The decision boundary of the decision tree is very imprecise and typically follows rough, axis-aligned steps. The issue is clearly visible on two-dimensional visualizations. Overfitting can occur even with data with few features. It can get even worse as feature dimensions increase and in the presence of noisy observations, that is, observations that are scattered (noisy observations) around the feature space. But you can improve decision trees using some interesting heuristics that stabilize results from trees, such as simplifying the structure of the tree by pruning the less effective rules or building separate trees for misclassified examples (a technique related to boosting, a method we will illustrate in the following paragraphs).

Apart from these heuristics, the best trick is to build multiple trees using different samples, then compare and average their results. The example in Figure 15-1 indicates that the benefit is immediately visible. As you build an ensemble of more trees, the decision boundary gets smoother, slowly resembling the hypothetical target shape of the class separator.

Growing a forest of trees

Improving a decision tree by replicating it many times and averaging results to get a more general solution sounded like such a good idea that it spread, and both academics and practitioners derived various solutions. When the problem is a regression, the technique averages results from the ensemble. However, when the trees deal with a classification task, the method can use the ensemble as a voting system, choosing the most frequent response class as an output for all its replications. The following sections discuss how using trees for an ensemble creates a superior solution.

Creating the Random Forests ensemble

TIP

When using an ensemble for regression, the standard deviation, calculated from all the ensemble's estimates for an example, can provide an estimate of how confident you can be about the prediction. The standard deviation shows how good the mean of the forecast is. For classification problems, the percentage of trees predicting a particular class is indicative of the level of confidence in the prediction. Still, you can't use it as a probability estimate because it's the outcome of a voting system.

Deciding on how to compute the solution of an ensemble happened quickly; finding the best way to replicate the trees in an ensemble required more research and reflection. The first solution is *pasting,* that is, sampling a portion of your training set. Initially proposed by Leo Breiman, pasting reduces the number of training examples. This can become a problem for learning from complex data because you get fewer examples to feed to the learning algorithm. It shows its usefulness by reducing the learning sample noise (sampling fewer examples minimizes the number of outliers and anomalous cases). After pasting, Professor Breiman also tested the effects of *bootstrap sampling* (sampling with replacement), which not only leaves out some noise (when you bootstrap, on average, you leave out 37 percent of your initial example set) but also, thanks to sampling repetition, creates more variation in the ensembles, improving the results. This technique is called *bagging* (also known as *bootstrap aggregation*).

Bootstrapping appears in Chapter 9 as part of validation alternatives. In bootstrapping, you sample the examples from a set to create a new set, allowing the code to extract the same examples multiple times. Therefore, in a bootstrapped sample, the same example is repeated from one to many times.

Breiman noticed that an ensemble of trees improves when the trees differ significantly from each other (statistically, we say that they're *uncorrelated*), which led to the last key technique — the creation of mostly uncorrelated ensembles of trees using different subsets of features.

The law of large numbers works because you make many independent trials of an event (for example, testing whether a coin is loaded on one side). When you count the distribution of trials, you get the correct probability distribution of the event. Similarly, when you create a forest of decision trees, if they are independent of each other and tend not to make the same errors, aggregating their estimates produces a more accurate overall prediction. Breiman found that decision trees become independent of each other if you randomize them by sampling both the training examples and the features used. This sampling approach performs predictions better than bagging. The approach samples both features and examples. In collaboration with Adele Cutler, Breiman named the new ensemble Random Forests (RF).

Random Forests is a trademark of Leo Breiman and Adele Cutler. For this reason, open source implementations may use variations of the name. For instance, Python's Scikit-learn provides `RandomForestClassifier` and `Random ForestRegressor`, also following its naming conventions (see `https://scikit-learn.org/stable/modules/generated/sklearn.ensemble.RandomForest Classifier.html` for details).

RF is a classification (naturally multiclass) and regression algorithm that uses a large number of decision tree models built on different sets of bootstrapped examples and subsampled features. Its creators strove to make the algorithm easy to use (with little preprocessing and few hyperparameters to try) and understandable (because based on the decision tree) in order to democratize access to machine learning. In other words, RF can allow a broader range of users to apply machine learning effectively because of its simplicity and immediate usage. The algorithm works through a few repeated steps:

1. Bootstrap the training set multiple times. The algorithm obtains a new set to build a single tree in the ensemble during each bootstrap.

2. Randomly pick a partial feature selection in the training set to find the best split feature every time you split the sample in a tree.

3. Create a complete tree using the bootstrapped examples. At each split, evaluate how to perform the split using only the randomly selected subset of features. Grow each tree fully without limitations to allow the algorithm to work better.

4. Compute the performance of each tree using examples you didn't choose in the bootstrap phase (out-of-bag estimates, or OOB). OOB examples provide performance metrics without cross-validation or using a test set (equivalent to out-of-sample).

5. Produce feature importance statistics and compute how examples are associated in the tree's terminal nodes.

6. Compute an average or a vote on new examples when you complete all the trees in the ensemble. Declare the average estimate or the winning class for each of them as a prediction.

All these steps reduce the variance of the predictions at the expense of an increase in bias (because you use fewer features simultaneously). The solution builds each tree to its maximum possible extension, thus allowing an acceptable approximation of even complex target functions. Moreover, you increase the chance that each tree in the forest differs from the others because it's built by fitting different samples. It's not just a matter of building on different bootstrapped example sets: Each split taken by a tree is strongly randomized — the solution considers only a feature from a set defined by a random selection. Consequently, even if an important feature dominates the others in terms of predictive power, the times a tree doesn't contain the selection allow the tree to find different ways of developing its branches and terminal leaves effectively.

The main difference with bagging is the opportunity to limit the number of features to consider when splitting the tree branches. If the number of selected features is small, the complete tree will differ from others, thus adding uncorrelated trees to the ensemble. On the other hand, if the selection is small, the bias increases because the fitting power of the tree is limited. As always, determining the correct number of features to consider for splitting requires that you use cross-validation or OOB estimate results.

TIP

There is a variant of RF called Extremely Randomized Trees (ERT) that is even more randomized because it not only randomly picks the features for the splits but also randomly decides the splits (see https://scikit-learn.org/stable/modules/ensemble.html#extremely-randomized-trees). In this version, randomness introduces slightly more bias but reduces the variance of the estimates, a solution that, in some data problems, may work better than RF. In addition, it is always faster because ERT requires fewer computations. No problem arises when growing a large number of trees in the ensemble. The more trees, the more precise and stable your estimates will become. You need to consider the cost of the computational effort; completing a large ensemble takes a long time. RF is an algorithm you can run in parallel on multiple CPU processors.

TIP

Each tree in the RF ensemble is independent from the others (after all, they should be uncorrelated), meaning you can build each tree parallel to the others. Given that all modern computers have multiprocessor and multithread functionality, they can perform computations on many trees simultaneously, which is a real advantage of RF over other machine learning algorithms.

Demonstrating the RF algorithm

A simple demonstration conveys how an RF algorithm can solve a problem using a growing number of trees. This example uses the wine quality dataset, which models wine preferences by data mining *physicochemical* (physical and chemical) properties, combining white and red wines. This dataset is described in "Modeling wine preferences by data mining from physicochemical properties," by P. Cortez, A. Cerdeira, F. Almeida, T. Matos, and J. Reis, in *Decision Support Systems* at `https://www.sciencedirect.com/science/article/abs/pii/S0167923609001377?via%3Dihub`. The data associates physicochemical tests (alcohol concentration, density, acidity, and so on) with the quality evaluation of experts on some Portuguese wines. The dataset offers the opportunity to treat it both as a regression and a classification problem. This example works it out as a regression problem. It begins by loading the data and creating both training and test sets.

```
import numpy as np
import pandas as pd
import matplotlib.pyplot as plt
import seaborn as sns
from sklearn.model_selection import train_test_split

sns.set(style='whitegrid', palette='deep',
        font='sans-serif')

repository = "https://github.com/lmassaron/"
release = "ml4dummies_3ed/releases/download/v1.0/"
filename = repository + release + "wine_quality.csv"
wine = pd.read_csv(filename)
```

```
X_train, X_test = train_test_split(
    wine,
    test_size=0.3,
    stratify=wine['quality'],
    random_state=42)

y_train = X_train.iloc[:, 0]
X_train = X_train.iloc[:, 1:]
y_test, X_test = X_test.iloc[:, 0], X_test.iloc[:, 1:]
```

After loading the dataset from the book's Internet repository at GitHub (see the Introduction for details), the code uses the `train_test_split` function from Scikit-learn to apply stratified sampling, so that the response variable, `quality`, is distributed equally in the train and test data. As the test set, we reserve 30 percent of the observations.

The next step is to model the problem by testing Random Forest using a growing number of trees for their ensemble, as shown here:

```
from sklearn.metrics import mean_absolute_error
from sklearn.ensemble import RandomForestRegressor

n_range = [10, 25, 50, 100, 150, 200, 250, 300, 500]
test_scores = []

for n in n_range:
    rf = RandomForestRegressor(
        n_estimators=n,
        max_depth=14,
        random_state=42,
        n_jobs=-1)

    rf.fit(X_train, y_train)
    predictions = rf.predict(X_test)
    error = mean_absolute_error(y_test, predictions)
    test_scores.append(error)
```

The example begins by importing functions and classes from Scikit-learn: `mean_absolute_error`, for measuring, and `RandomForestRegressor`, for modeling the problem. The last item is Scikit-learn's implementation of Random Forests for regression problems. After defining some possible values for the `n_estimator` parameter, which specifies the number of decision trees in the RF, the code iterates over the values. It tests each one by training the regressor and then evaluating the result on the test set.

TIP

To make the example run faster, the code sets the n_jobs parameter to –1, allowing the algorithm to use all available CPU resources. Alternatively, you can set the parameter to –2, thus leaving one processor free for other tasks.

After completing the computations, the code outputs a plot that reveals how the Random Forests algorithm converges to a reasonable accuracy after building a few trees, as shown in Figure 15-2. It also shows that adding more trees isn't detrimental because the error tends to stabilize and even improve slightly after reaching a certain number of trees.

```python
import matplotlib.pyplot as plt

fig, ax = plt.subplots(dpi=120)
plt.plot(n_range, test_scores, '-o')
plt.xlabel('number of trees')
plt.ylabel('mean absolute error')
plt.show()
```

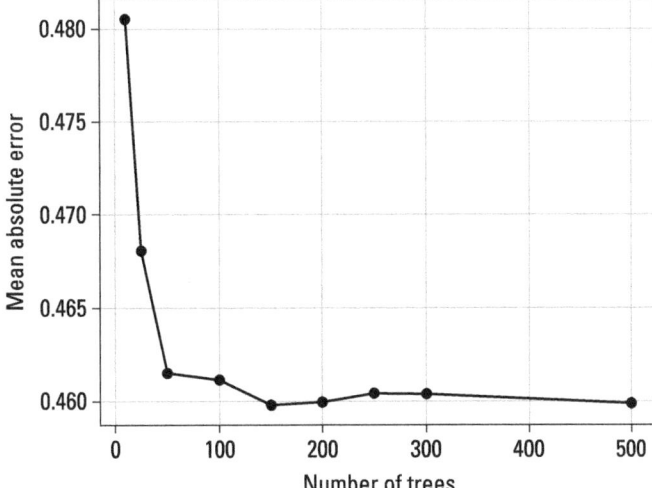

FIGURE 15-2:
Seeing the accuracy of ensembles of different sizes.

Understanding the importance measures

RF has these benefits:

>> Fit complex target functions well, with reduced risk of overfitting compared to single trees

>> Select the features they need automatically (although the random subsampling of features in branch splitting influences the process)

>> They are easy to tune-up because they have a limited number of hyperparameters

>> Offer OOB error estimation, saving you from setting up verification by cross-validation or test set

An RF ensemble can also provide additional output, which is helpful when learning from data. For example, it can tell you which features are more important than others. You can build trees by optimizing a purity measure (entropy or Gini index) so that each split chooses the feature that improves the measure the most. When the tree is complete, you check which feature the algorithm uses at each split and sum the improvement related to each feature. When working with an ensemble of trees, average the improvements that each feature provides in all the trees. The result shows you the ranking of the most important predictive features.

Among practitioners, this kind of importance evaluation is known as *Gini importance* or *mean decrease impurity.* The method is not faultless; it tends to favor categorical features with many unique values (the high-cardinality features) because they need many splits compared to other features, which implies that they have more importance in the evaluation. Another way to estimate feature importance, which is considered fairer, is *permutation importance,* and you obtain it by using the `permutation_importance()` function (see `https://scikit-learn.org/stable/modules/generated/sklearn.inspection.permutation_importance.html`) on a fitted RF model. In this case, each feature is randomly permuted, and the performance difference on a validation set is considered a measure of the feature importance.

TIP

An interesting experiment in the Scikit-learn documentation illustrates the limits of the mean decrease impurity method: A random feature can increase in importance in an RF model when randomly chosen to split more times during training. Permutation importance can provide more reliable estimates in similar cases. See `https://scikit-learn.org/stable/auto_examples/inspection/plot_permutation_importance.html#sphx-glr-auto-examples-inspection-plot-permutation-importance-py`.

To provide an interpretation of important measures derived from RF, this example tests the implementation of permutation importance on the wine quality dataset tested earlier using the optimal number of estimator trees. The example starts by training the RF regressor using 500 trees.

```
from sklearn.inspection import permutation_importance

rf = RandomForestRegressor(n_estimators=500,
                           max_features='sqrt',
                           random_state=42)
rf.fit(X_train, y_train)
preds = rf.predict(X_test)
mae = mean_absolute_error(y_test, preds)
print(f"Test mean absolute error for rf: {mae:0.3f}")
```

The resulting mean absolute error is 0.435, quite a good result considering that the code estimates values on a scale ranging from 0 to 5. Having trained the RF, you can test the importance of the feature by permutation and plot the outcome, as shown in Figure 15-3.

```
result = permutation_importance(
    rf, X_test, y_test,
    n_repeats=10,
    random_state=42,
    n_jobs=-1)

sorted_idx = result.importances_mean.argsort()

fig, ax = plt.subplots(dpi=120)
ax.boxplot(
    result.importances[sorted_idx].T,
    vert=False,
    tick_labels=X_test.columns[sorted_idx])
ax.set_title("Permutation Importances (Test Set)")
ax.set_xlabel("Decrease in MAE")
fig.tight_layout()
plt.show()
```

Alcohol is by far the most decisive factor in impacting quality. Volatile acidity and density are also significant aspects. The rest of the features contribute in almost the same way. Still, the binary feature, indicating whether the wine is red or white, is not a key, given the other physical and chemical characteristics.

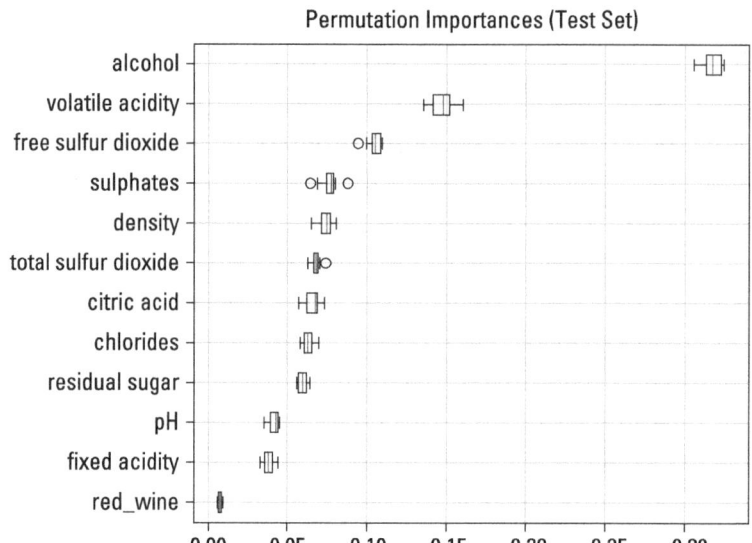

Permutation Importances (Test Set)

FIGURE 15-3:
Permutation
importance of
features
computed on
the test set.

Learning from Mistakes and Weak Learners

Thanks to bootstrapping, bagging reduces variance by inducing some variations in otherwise similar predictors. Bagging is most effective when the models created are different from each other, and though it can work with various kinds of models, it is mainly used with decision trees.

Bagging and its evolution, RF, aren't the only ways to leverage an ensemble. Instead of keeping ensemble elements independent, the opposite strategy is to create interrelated ensembles of simple machine learning algorithms to solve complex target functions. This approach is called *boosting*, which works by building models sequentially and training each model using information from the previous one.

Contrary to bagging, which prefers working with fully grown trees, boosting uses biased models, which are models that can predict simple target functions well. Simpler models include decision trees with a single split branch (*stumps*), linear models, perceptrons, and Naïve Bayes algorithms. These models may not perform well when the target function to guess is complex (they're also called *weak learners*), but they can be trained fast and perform at least slightly better than a random lucky guess (meaning they can model a part of the target function).

Each ensemble algorithm guesses part of the function well, so they can approximate the entire function when combined together. The situation differs from the story of the blind men and the elephant (https://americanliterature.com/author/james-baldwin/short-story/the-blind-men-and-the-elephant). In the story, a group of blind men needs to discover the shape of an elephant, but each man can feel only a part of the whole animal. One man touches the tusk, one the ears, one the trunk, one the body, and one the tail, which are different parts of the elephant. They can only figure out the real elephant's shape when they combine their individual findings. Such an approach has a relevant advantage compared to bagging: Each model depends on the others because it specializes in guessing parts of the target function where other models failed, thus simplifying the global task of the ensemble.

Boosting predictors with AdaBoost

The first boosting algorithm, formulated in 1995, is AdaBoost (short for Adaptive Boosting) by Yoav Freund and Robert Schapire. Here is the AdaBoost formulation:

$$H(X) = sign\left(\sum_{m=1}^{W}\alpha_m h_m(X)\right)$$

You may think that the AdaBoost formulation is quite complicated at first sight, but you can make it simpler by examining it piece by piece. The function H(X) represents the prediction function, which transforms the features, the X matrix, into predictions. As an ensemble of models, the prediction function is a weighted summation of models, in a way that resembles the linear models that you examine in Chapter 13.

The H(X) function provides results as a vector of signs (positive or negative) that indicate classes in a binary prediction. (AdaBoost is a binary prediction algorithm.) The signs derive from the summation of M models, each distinguishable by a different m index (the generic model is $h_m(X)$). M is an integer that you determine when training from data. You decide M by testing on a validation set or, even better, using cross-validation. You need testing for M because, in principle, each model fits a portion of the data, and having too many models means fitting the data too well, which is a kind of memorization that leads to overfitting, high variance of estimates, and, consequently, bad predictions. The number of added models is therefore a critical hyperparameter.

Note that the algorithm multiplies each model $h_m(X)$ by an alpha value, which differs for each model. This is the weight of the model in the ensemble, and alpha is devised smartly because its value is related to the capacity of the model to produce the fewest prediction errors possible. You calculate alpha as follows:

According to this formulation, Field Alpha gets a larger value as the error of the model $h_m(X)$, pointed out by the notation err_m, gets smaller. The algorithm multiplies models with fewer errors by larger alpha values, and thus, such models play a more critical role in the summation at the core of the AdaBoost algorithm. Models that produce more prediction errors are weighted less.

The role of the coefficient alpha doesn't end with model weighting. Errors output by a model in the ensemble don't simply dictate the importance of the model in the ensemble itself but also modify the relevance of the training examples used for learning. AdaBoost learns the data structure by using a simple algorithm, a little at a time; the only way to focus the ensemble on different parts of the data is to assign weights. Assigning weights tells the algorithm to count an example according to its weight; therefore, a single example can count the same as two, three, or even more examples. You can also make an example disappear from the learning process by making it count less and less. When considering weights, it becomes easier to reduce the cost function of the learning function by working on the examples that weigh more (more weight = more cost function reduction). Using weights effectively guides the learning process.

Initially, as in all the other learning algorithms seen so far, the examples have the same contribution in constructing the model. The optimization happens as usual. After creating the first model and estimating a total error, the algorithm checks each example to determine whether the prediction is correct. If correctly predicted, nothing happens; each example's weight remains the same as before. If misclassified, each example has its weight increased. In the next iteration, examples with larger weights influence the model, placing a greater emphasis on finding a solution for the larger example.

At each iteration, the AdaBoost algorithm is guided by weights to work on the less predictable part of the data. You don't need to work on data that the algorithm can predict well. Weighting is an innovative solution for conditioning learning and gradient boosting machines. For the following algorithm you explore, refine, and improve the process. Notice that the strategy here is different from RF. In RF, the goal is to create independent predictions; here, the predictors are chained together because earlier predictors determine how later predictors work. Because boosting algorithms rely on a chain of calculations, you can't easily parallelize the computations, so they're slower. You can express the formulation of the weight update in this way:

$$w_i = w_i * \exp(\alpha_m * I(y_i \neq h_m(X_i)))$$

The $I(y_i \neq h_m(X_i))$ function outputs zero if the inequality is false and one if true. When true, the previous example weight is multiplied by the exponential of alpha. The algorithm modifies the resulting vector w by overweighting misclassified cases using the ensemble's most recent learning algorithm. Figuratively, learning in such a way is like taking a small improvement step each time toward the goal of a working predictive ensemble, and doing so without looking back, because after learning algorithms are summed, you can't change them anymore.

The kinds of learning algorithms that work well with AdaBoost are weak learners, which means they don't have much predictive power. Because AdaBoost approximates complex functions using an ensemble of its parts, using machine learning algorithms that train quickly and have a particular bias makes sense, so the parts are simple. It's just like drawing a circle using a series of lines: Even though the line is straight, you have to draw a polygon with as many sides as possible to approximate the circle. Commonly, decision stumps are the favorite weak learner for an AdaBoost ensemble, but you can also successfully use linear models or Naïve Bayes algorithms. The following example leverages the AdaBoost function provided by Scikit-learn to determine whether decision trees, ridge regression, or the K-Nearest Neighbor (KNN) algorithm is best for predicting from the wine quality dataset. This example uses the wine quality data (X_train, y_train, X_test, y_test) we previously prepared at the start of the chapter. The example may run for some time (on Google Colab, it takes about 23 seconds). The best performing algorithm is the KNN, with a mean absolute error of 0.694, which is worse than the performance of the previously seen RF algorithm.

```python
import numpy as np
from sklearn.ensemble import AdaBoostRegressor
from sklearn.tree import DecisionTreeRegressor
from sklearn.linear_model import LinearRegression
from sklearn.neighbors import KNeighborsRegressor

dt = DecisionTreeRegressor(max_depth=1)
lr = LinearRegression ()
knn = KNeighborsRegressor(n_neighbors=10)

labels = ['Decision Tree', 'Linear Regression', 'KNN']
base_models = [dt, lr, knn]

for label, base_model in zip(labels, base_models):
    model = AdaBoostRegressor(
        estimator=base_model,
        n_estimators=300,
        random_state=42)
    model.fit(X_train, y_train)
    predictions = model.predict(X_test)
    mae = mean_absolute_error(y_test, predictions)
    print(f"Test MAE for {label}: {mae:.3f}")
```

You can improve the performance of AdaBoost by increasing the number of elements in the ensemble until the cross-validation performance stops improving or starts worsening. The parameter you can grow is n_estimators, and it's currently set to 300. The weaker your predictor is, the larger your ensemble should be to perform the prediction well.

Boosting via Gradient Descent

The AdaBoost discussed in this chapter explains how the learning procedure creates a function after moving systematically toward a target, an analogy similar to the gradient descent described in Chapter 8. This section describes the gradient boosting machines (GBM) algorithm, proposed by Jerome Friedman in 1999, which uses gradient descent optimization to determine the correct weights for learning in the ensemble. The resulting performance is impressive, making GBM one of the most powerful and widely used predictive tools that you can learn to use in machine learning. Here is the GBM formulation:

$$H(X) = \sum_{m=1}^{M} v * h_m(X, w_m)$$

As in AdaBoost, you start from the formulation. The GBM formulation requires a weighted sum of multiple models from the algorithm. What changes the most is not the principle of how boosting works but rather the optimization process used in the summed functions.

In the preceding formula, M represents the number of total models, and H represents the final function, which is the sum of a series of M models. Each model is different, hence the notation h_m, which translates into h_1, h_2, and so on. The difference between the learning functions of the series occurs because the models depend on the features X and the examples weighted by the values of the vector w, which changes for every model.

Meeting again with gradient descent

Up to now, things aren't all that different from AdaBoost. However, note that the algorithm weights each model by a constant factor, v, the shrinkage factor. This is where you start noticing the first difference between AdaBoost and GBM. The fact is that v (often called the learning rate) is analogous to alpha in AdaBoost because it scales the contribution of each model; however, unlike alpha, which changes for each model, here v is a fixed hyperparameter fixed through all the iterations. Because v is fixed, a GBM is forced to take into the ensemble a fixed number of models equally contributing to the solution, regardless of the performance of the previously added ones. Considering this difference, the algorithm builds the chain by iterating the following sequence of operations:

$$H_m(X) = H_{m-1}(X) + v * h_m(X, w_m)$$

Look at the formula as it develops during training. After each iteration m, the algorithm sums the result of the previous models with a new model built on the same features, but on a differently weighted series of examples. This is represented as the function $h_m(X, w)$. Another key difference compared to AdaBoost resides in how GBM determines what the next model will learn. Instead of weighting the misclassified examples, the GBM algorithm, based on the chosen loss function, trains each next model in the series on the *pseudo-residuals* of the ensemble. The pseudo-residuals are the *negative gradient of the loss function* — that is, in other words, the adjustments necessary for the predicted values of the ensemble to be correct. In an optimization process, taking at each step the negative gradient is the gradient descent procedure seen in Chapter 8.

Since the negative gradients are based on the loss function, by changing the loss function, GBM can take on different problems: regression, classification, and ranking (for ordering examples, such as in the results from a search engine). Gradient descent is used to calculate the target for each new base learner. The secret of GBM's performance lies in using a procedure reminiscent of gradient descent (hence the name, "gradient" boosting), as well as in these three clever technical solutions:

» **Shrinkage:** Acts as a learning rate in the ensemble. As in gradient descent, you must fix an adequate learning rate to avoid jumping too far from the solution, which is the same as in GBM. Small shrinkage values lead to better predictions.

» **Subsampling:** Emulates the pasting approach. If each subsequent tree builds on a subsample of the training data, the result is a stochastic gradient descent. For many problems, the pasting approach helps reduce noise and influence by outliers, thus improving the results.

» **Trees of fixed size:** Fixing the tree depth used in boosting is like fixing a complexity limit to learning functions that you put into the ensemble, yet relying on more sophisticated trees than the stumps used in AdaBoost. Depth acts somewhat like the degree in a polynomial expansion: deeper trees can capture more complex patterns and interactions between features, although increasing the risk of overfitting.

Scikit-learn implements GBM using all the characteristics described in the chapter so far. You can find GBM discussed at `https://scikit-learn.org/stable/modules/ensemble.html#gradient-boosting`. The following example continues the previous test. In this case, you create a GBM classifier for the wine quality dataset and test its mean absolute error performance, which is now lowered to 0.395. Also, this example may run for some time (about 18 seconds on Google Colab):

```
from sklearn.ensemble import GradientBoostingRegressor

gbm = GradientBoostingRegressor(
    n_estimators=550,
    learning_rate=0.05,
    max_depth=15,
    subsample=0.6,
    random_state=42)

gbm.fit(X_train, y_train)
predictions = gbm.predict(X_test)
mae = mean_absolute_error(y_test, predictions)
print(f"Test Mean Absolute Error for GBM: {mae:.3f}")
```

Considering the state of the art in tabular data

The Scikit-learn implementation of gradient boosting (one of the first available for Python and closely resembling Jerome Friedman's original proposal) is not the only option for creating high-performing models. You can improve gradient boosting by upgrading how the optimization process works, what type of decision trees and split-finding strategies to use, and the algorithm's treatment of missing data and categorical features.

A prominent alternative gradient boosting package is XGBoost, initially developed by Tianqi Chen and contributors (https://github.com/dmlc/xgboost). This solution first became popular in Kaggle competitions, and later it became globally renowned for its versatility, speed, and performance over the existing Scikit-learn version.

In particular, XGBoost effectively utilizes multicore processing. Even though the overall boosting procedure remains a sequential algorithm, XGBoost parallelizes the computationally intensive parts of building each tree, that is, finding the best splits across the multiple features in the data. However, the secret ingredient of the algorithm is not only multiprocessing. XGBoost can feature increased performance because of its enhanced gradient optimization, which uses both gradients and Hessians (in simple words, the curvature of the gradients), achieving faster convergence.

XGBoost is preinstalled on Google Colab. On a different system, you can install XGBoost using the command pip install XGBoost. You can try the previous example on the Wine dataset using an XGBoost regressor and notice an even better mean absolute error, now decreased to 0.389:

```
import xgboost as xgb

xg_reg = xgb.XGBRegressor(
    n_estimators=550,
    learning_rate=0.05,
    max_depth=15,
    subsample=0.6,
    colsample_bytree=0.7,
    random_state=42)

xg_reg.fit(X_train, y_train)
predictions = xg_reg.predict(X_test)
mae = mean_absolute_error(y_test, predictions)
print(f"Test Mean Absolute Error for XGBoost: "
    f"{mae:.3f}")
```

Analogous to XGBoost, in 2017, Microsoft researchers created LightGBM (https://github.com/Microsoft/LightGBM), which is even faster than XGBoost (because it uses even more approximations) and performs better on specific problems because it builds its decision trees differently. LightGBM uses a *leaf-wise* search strategy, creating very deep and asymmetric trees because it splits insistently on the most predictive feature until it works. This contrasts with the common decision trees, which are built with a level-wise strategy, where the trees are balanced and symmetric because the splits are evaluated level after level. Applying the leaf-wise approach can make LightGBM shine in certain situations. In contrast, it tends to underperform in others, especially with smaller datasets, because it can easily overfit the data. Here is our example using LightGBM. Light-GBM is preinstalled on Google Colab (if you need to install the package on a different system, use the command pip install lightgbm):

```
import lightgbm as lgb

lgb_reg = lgb.LGBMRegressor(
    n_estimators=2000,
    learning_rate=0.12,
    max_depth=18,
    subsample=0.6,
    colsample_bytree=0.85,
```

```
        random_state=42,
        verbose=-1)
lgb_reg.fit(X_train, y_train)
predictions = lgb_reg.predict(X_test)
mae = mean_absolute_error(y_test, predictions)
print(f"Test Mean Absolute Error for LightGBM: "
      f"{mae:.3f}")
```

Finally, there is another solution: CatBoost (https://catboost.ai) from the Russian search engine Yandex. Claimed to be the algorithm behind the search engine itself, CatBoost is particularly effective when dealing with numerous and complex categorical data like geographical addresses or product identifiers, because it can effectively map categorical values into numeric ones. CatBoost is not available on Google Colab. First, you need to install it using the command pip install catboost. Then, here is an example using CatBoost on the Wine dataset (it may be slower than other examples in this chapter: on Google Colab, it takes about one minute to execute):

```
from catboost import CatBoostRegressor

cat_reg = CatBoostRegressor(
    iterations=900,
    learning_rate=0.07,
    depth=12,
    subsample=0.55,
    colsample_bylevel=0.6,
    random_state=42,
    thread_count=-1,
    verbose=0)
cat_reg.fit(X_train, y_train)
predictions = cat_reg.predict(X_test)
mae = mean_absolute_error(y_test, predictions)
print(f"Test Mean Absolute Error for CatBoost: "
      f"{mae:.3f}")
```

Together with Scikit-learn's new implementation of gradient boosting (inspired by LightGBM's solutions, anyway), these three algorithms are leading the way in data modelling. They are considered the state of the art in machine learning regarding predictive performance and feature handling capabilities when dealing with structured data in matrices (whereas deep learning reigns uncontested in unstructured data, such as text and images).

Averaging Different Predictors

Until this section, the chapter has discussed ensembles composed of the same kind of machine learning algorithms (homogeneous ensembles). Still, both averaging and voting systems can also work fine when you use a mix of different machine learning algorithms. This is the *averaging* approach, and it's widely used when you can't otherwise reduce the variance of the estimates.

As you try to learn from data, you try different solutions, thus modeling your data using various machine learning solutions. It's good practice to compare solutions by looking for the best validation fit. Still, you can also take advantage of the work done by checking whether you can successfully put some of these solutions into ensembles using prediction averages or by counting the predicted classes. The principle is the same as in bagging noncorrelated predictions; when diverse models are combined, they can produce less variance-affected predictions. To achieve effective averaging, you have to

1. Divide your data into training, validation, and test sets.

2. Use the training data with different machine learning algorithms.

3. Record predictions from each algorithm and evaluate the viability of the result using the validation set.

Average the results for a regression task (also using different weights) or pick the most frequent result for classification. Your averaging is like a second-level model. Once you have produced your final predictions, you can still verify them on the validation set before trying the test set.

Blending solutions

Averaging different solutions is also called *blending,* and the process you use to blend them is often called *blender.* Scikit-learn provides `VotingClassifier` and `VotingRegressor` classes that can arrange blending for you. This example combines the best previous model, the gradient boosting regressor, with a completely different support vector regressor model because you're usually more successful when you blend different models. After running the code, you find that blending a GBM and an SVR works best for the wine quality data.

```
from sklearn.ensemble import VotingRegressor
from sklearn.svm import SVR
```

```
gbm = GradientBoostingRegressor(n_estimators=500,
            learning_rate=0.1, max_depth=8,
            subsample=0.65, random_state=42)
svr = SVR(C=2.5, gamma=0.7, epsilon=0.0005)

blender = VotingRegressor(
    estimators=[("gbm", gbm), ("svm", svr)], n_jobs=-1)
blender.fit(X_train, y_train)
predictions = blender.predict(X_test)
mae = mean_absolute_error(y_test, predictions)
print(f"Test mean absolute error for blender: "
    f"{mae:0.3f}")
```

TIP

Blending can provide better results than blended elements when you blend different models that perform almost equally well. Averaging adjusts some of their weaknesses while maintaining their performances.

With `VotingRegressor` and `VotingClassifier`, you can decide to perform a weighted average by providing the weights in the weights parameter. In addition, `VotingClassifier` allows you to count majority classifications (`voting="hard"`) or blend probabilities of the different classes (`voting="soft"`).

Stacking diverse solutions

Blending isn't the only possible approach to integrate multiple models. Another approach is to use the predictions of your models as input features to another model. This is *stacking*, which requires careful preparations. Scikit-learn has made the process easier by providing `StackingRegressor` and `StackingClassifier` classes that handle all the processes for you. As in the example, you provide a valid cross-validation approach, estimators, and a final model. The result in this case might not be the absolute best for the problem. However, stacking multiple solutions often provides some of the best results at the price of increased complexity. This example may take a while to complete (On Google Colab, we timed a minute of execution), returning a fair result with a mean absolute error of 0.431.

```
from sklearn.ensemble import StackingRegressor
from sklearn.model_selection import KFold

gbm = GradientBoostingRegressor(n_estimators=200,
            learning_rate=0.05, max_depth=3,
            subsample=0.85, random_state=42)
```

```
svr = SVR(C=20.0, gamma=0.001, epsilon=0.004)
rf = RandomForestRegressor(n_estimators=150,
                                random_state=42)

cv = KFold(n_splits=10, shuffle=True, random_state=42)
stacker = StackingRegressor(
    estimators=[("svm'", svr), ("rf", rf)],
    final_estimator=gbm,
    passthrough=True,
    cv=cv,
    n_jobs=-1)

stacker.fit(X_train, y_train)
predictions = stacker.predict(X_test)
mae = mean_absolute_error(y_test, predictions)
print(f"Test mean absolute error for stacker: "
      f"{mae:0.3f}")
```

TIP

In real-world practice, always remember that technical debt — trading off unnecessary complexity for some tiny extra performance — will have to be repaid eventually. As a general suggestion, it is worth adopting blending and stacking only when there is a significant performance difference compared to simpler solutions.

5

Applying Learning to Real Problems

Chapter **16**

Classifying Images

Among the five senses, sight is undoubtedly the most powerful in conveying knowledge and information derived from the world outside. Many people believe that the gift of sight enables children to learn about the various things and people around them. In addition, humans receive and transmit knowledge across time by means of pictures, visual arts, and textual documents. The first part of this chapter helps you understand how Python can help your computer transform digital images and derive new images from other ones, which can help you build richer datasets for computer vision tasks (a process called *image augmentation*).

Because sight is so important, granting machines a form of sight is invaluable for machine learning, opening up new capabilities for algorithms. In recent years, one of the more important uses of vision in machine learning is to classify images for all sorts of reasons. For example, robots need to know which objects to avoid and which objects to work with. Humans also rely on image classification to perform tasks such as handwriting recognition and finding particular individuals in a crowd. Other vital functions of image classification include conducting medical scans, detecting pedestrians (a crucial feature to implement in cars that could save thousands of lives), and helping farmers determine where fields require the most water. The final two sections of this chapter demonstrate techniques for processing image information and then using that information to perform classification tasks.

REMEMBER

You don't have to type the source code for this chapter manually. In fact, using the downloadable source code is a lot easier. You can find the source code for this chapter in the ML4D3E folder of the downloadable code file. The example files for this chapter will begin with ML4D3E-016-. See the Introduction for details on how to find these source files.

Learning the Magic of Data Augmentation

Even if you have access to large image datasets for your deep learning model, that may not be enough because of the vast number of parameters in complex neural architectures. Even if you use techniques such as dropout (as explained in Chapter 14), overfitting is still possible. Overfitting occurs when the network memorizes the input data but fails to learn any generally useful patterns in the data. Apart from dropout, other techniques that can help a network combat overfitting include L1, L2, and ElasticNet regularization. However, nothing is as effective for enhancing your neural network's predictive capabilities as adding more examples to your training data.

REMEMBER

Originally, L1 (LASSO), L2 (Ridge), and ElasticNet were ways to constrain the weights of a linear regression model, as we discussed in Chapter 12. In a neural network, they work similarly by adding a penalty to the loss function based on the magnitude of the weights. This nudges the network to learn smaller weights, preventing overfitting, without harming the accuracy of predictions. L1 strives to set many weights to zero, thereby achieving a selection of the features. By contrast, L2 tends to dampen all the weights, avoiding larger weights that can lead to overfitting. Finally, ElasticNet is a combination of the L1 and L2 approaches, resulting in a trade-off between the selection and weight shrinkage strategies.

Image augmentation provides a solution to the problem of a lack of training examples, enabling a neural network to create new images from existing ones artificially. Image augmentation involves various image processing operations that are performed separately or in combination to create an altered image distinct from the original one. The result helps the neural network learn its recognition task better.

For instance, if you have training images that are too bright or too blurry, image processing can modify them into darker and sharper versions. These augmented versions help the neural network generalize by exposing it to a wider variety of visual conditions. This makes the model less sensitive to specific variations (like brightness or blur) and more focused on learning the invariant features of the objects themselves. In addition, rotating, cropping, or otherwise transforming the image, as shown in Figure 16-1, could help because, again, they force the network to learn general and invariant image features, no matter how the object appears.

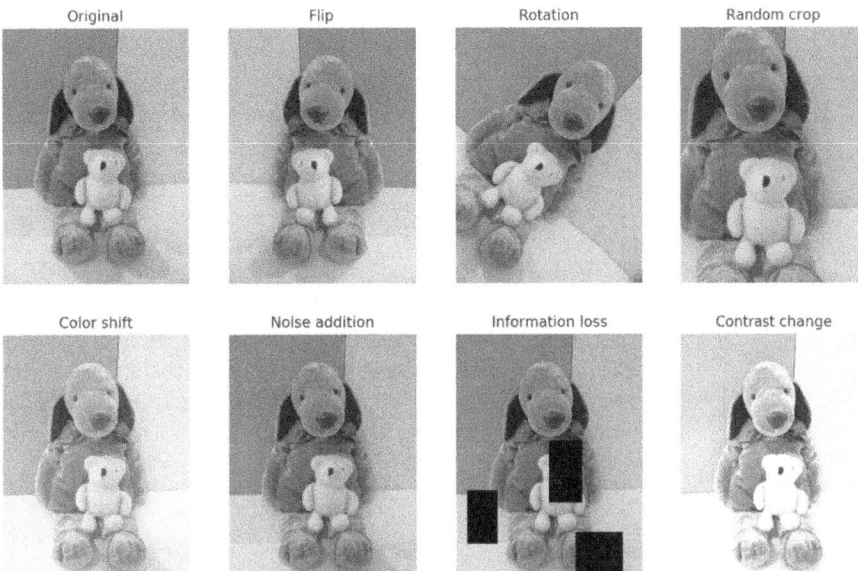

FIGURE 16-1:
Some common
image
augmentations.

The most common image augmentation procedures, as shown in Figure 16-1, are:

>> **Flip:** Flipping your image on its axis tests the algorithm's capability to find it regardless of perspective. The overall meaning of your image should hold even when flipped. Some algorithms can't see objects when upside down or even mirrored, especially if the original contains words or other specific symbols.

>> **Rotation:** Rotating your image allows algorithm testing at certain angles, simulating different perspectives or imprecisely calibrated cameras.

>> **Random crop:** Cropping your image forces the algorithm to focus on an image component. Cutting an area and resizing it to the original input dimensions enables you to test for recognition of partially hidden image features.

>> **Color shift:** Changing aspects like hue, saturation, or brightness of image colors generalizes your example because the colors can change or be recorded differently in the real world.

>> **Noise addition:** Adding random noise tests the algorithm's capability to detect an object even when the image quality is less than perfect.

>> **Information loss:** Randomly removing parts of an image simulates visual obstruction. It also helps the neural network rely on general image features, not on specific details (which could be randomly eliminated).

>> **Contrast change:** Adjusting the contrast makes the neural network less sensitive to variations in light conditions (for instance, between daylight and artificial light).

You don't need to specialize in image processing to leverage this powerful image-augmentation technique. Keras 3, the deep learning framework we will be using in this chapter and that we previously presented in Chapter 14, offers a way to incorporate augmentation into any training using some specialized layers that can be directly integrated into a neural network. You can find a complete list of Keras image augmentation layers at `https://keras.io/api/layers/preprocessing_layers/image_augmentation/`.

TIP

You can get an even more varied set of powerful image augmentations using a package such as albumentations (`https://github.com/albumentations-team/albumentations`). Alexander Buslaev, Alex Parinov, Vladimir I. Iglovikov, and Eugene Khvedchenya created it based on their experience with many image-detection challenges. The package offers an incredible array of possible image processing tools, depending on the task to be accomplished and the type of neural network used.

Revising the State of the Art in Computer Vision

One of the applications of working with images that affects nearly everyone today is *computer vision*, which is a set of techniques for analyzing individual objects within a frame from a camera or other source. When you look at an image, you see objects — perhaps individual people, stoplights, cars, and other items. Whatever the image contains, you see the objects and understand what they are. A computer, however, sees pixels — a 2D image that contains numeric values that translate into color when presented on a screen. For a computer to see the objects that you know, it requires some deep learning technology, such as a convolutional neural network (CNN).

Devising the CNN architecture

The concept of computer vision started in 1966 (yes, that long ago) when Seymour Papert and Marvin Minsky launched the Summer Vision Project (`https://dspace.mit.edu/handle/1721.1/6125`), a two-month, ten-person effort to create a computer system using symbolic AI that could identify objects in images. To accomplish this task, the computer would have to move from working with pixels to identifying which pixels belonged to a particular object. Given the technology of the time, the Summer Vision Project made limited progress.

The next attempt came from a Japanese scientist, Kunihiko Fukushima, in 1979, who proposed the Neocognitron. This project was based on neuroscience research conducted on humans, and it attempted to perform its task in a manner that mimicked human behavior. The Neocognitron was successful in a very basic way, but it, too, failed at tasks of any complexity. However, it introduced ideas and concepts that were later reprised, such as processing images through hierarchical layers, working with images in small portions, and utilizing the same weights in different parts of the architecture.

The first success came in the 1980s with the CNN architecture, which took inspiration from some of the initial ideas of the Neocognitron. The renowned French computer scientist, Yann LeCun (currently Vice President and Chief AI Scientist at Meta, professor at New York University, and recipient of the ACM Turing Award), along with a team of researchers at AT&T Labs, pioneered modern CNN architectures for image recognition. At the time, AT&T implemented the result of their work, LeNet-5, a neural network designed for recognizing handwritten numbers, into ATM check readers.

A complex and revolutionary CNN architecture, such as LeNet-5, which had to work within the computer technology and limitations of the time, had little opportunity to showcase its true power. Its invention didn't prevent the AI winter that started in the 1990s, when many researchers and investors lost faith in neural network technologies. However, it laid the groundwork for the future revival of the technology, establishing the foundations for the success of today's computer vision, which is based on deep learning.

Witnessing a renaissance

Only a handful of researchers, such as Geoffrey Hinton, Yann LeCun, Jürgen Schmidhuber, and Yoshua Bengio, continued to develop neural network technologies, striving to achieve a breakthrough that would have ended the AI winter. Meanwhile, in 2006, Fei-Fei Li, a computer science professor at the University of Illinois at Urbana-Champaign (currently a professor of computer science at Stanford University and codirector of the Stanford Institute for Human-Centered AI), initiated an effort to provide more real-world datasets to test computer vision algorithms more effectively. She began amassing an incredible number of images, representing a vast array of object classes.

She and her team performed such a massive task by using Amazon's Mechanical Turk, a service that you use to ask people to do microtasks for you (such as classifying an image) for a small fee. The resulting dataset, completed in 2009, was called ImageNet and initially contained 3.2 million labeled images (it now includes more than 14 million images) arranged into 5,247 hierarchically organized categories. If interested, you can explore the dataset at `https://image-net.org` or read the original paper at `www.image-net.org/static_files/papers/imagenet_cvpr09.pdf`.

ImageNet soon appeared at a 2010 competition, in which neural networks, utilizing convolutions (hence the revival and further development of the technology developed by Yann LeCun in the 1990s), demonstrated their capability in correctly classifying images arranged into 1,000 classes. In seven years of competition (the challenge closed in 2017), the winning algorithms in the top-5 accuracy challenge improved the accuracy of predicting images from 71.8 percent to 97.3 percent, which surpasses human capabilities (even humans make mistakes in classifying objects). Generally speaking, by utilizing this vast image dataset for training, many researchers observed that their neural network architectures began to perform more effectively (there had been no comparable dataset like ImageNet before that time), and subsequently, they began testing new ideas and refining neural network architectures.

Here are some notable CNN architectures that were devised by researchers for the competition and that later became available to everyone:

>> **AlexNet (2012):** Created by Alex Krizhevsky from the University of Toronto. It utilized CNNs with an 11x11-pixel filter, won the competition, and introduced the use of GPUs for training neural networks, along with the ReLU activation to speed up training and avoid the vanishing gradient problem, and techniques like dropout to control overfitting.

>> **VGGNet (2014):** This appeared in two versions, 16 and 19. It was created by the Visual Geometry Group at Oxford University and defined a new 3×3 standard in filter size for CNNs.

>> **ResNet (2015):** Created by Microsoft. This CNN not only extended the idea of different versions of the network (50, 101, 152), but also introduced skip layers, a way to connect deeper layers with shallower ones to prevent the vanishing gradient problem (see Chapter 8 for more about this problem) and allow much deeper networks that are more capable of recognizing patterns in images.

The impact and importance of the ImageNet competition (also known as ImageNet Large Scale Visual Recognition Challenge, or ILSVRC; `https://image-net.org/challenges/LSVRC`) on the development of deep learning solutions for image recognition can be summarized in three key points:

>> Helping establish a deep neural network renaissance: The AlexNet CNN architecture (developed by Alex Krizhevsky, Ilya Sutskever, and Geoffrey Hinton) won the 2012 ILSVRC challenge by a large margin over other solutions.

» Pushing various teams of researchers to develop more sophisticated solutions, ILSVRC advanced the performance of CNNs. VGG16, VGG19, ResNet50, Inception V3, Xception, and NASNet are all neural networks tested on ImageNet images that you can find in the Keras package (`https://keras.io/api/applications`). Each architecture represents an improvement over the previous architectures and introduces key deep learning innovations.

» Making *transfer learning* (which we will explain in the next section) possible: The ImageNet competition helped make the pre-trained weights of successful models publicly available. The 1.2 million ImageNet training images, distributed across 1,000 separate classes, helped create convolutional networks whose lower convolutional layers can generalize to problems beyond ImageNet.

Discussing transfer learning

Deep learning models that distinguish objects and correctly classify them require a large number of images, considerable processing time, and substantial computational capacity to learn what to do. Adapting a network's capability to new image types that weren't part of the initial training means transferring existing knowledge to the target problem. This process of adapting a network's capability is called *transfer learning*, and the network being adapted is often referred to as a *pre-trained model*. Sometimes, when transfer learning is not working perfectly because the problem you want to solve is too specific, you can still continue training a pre-trained model, refining its network to achieve performance in a new task. This process of further training is called *fine-tuning*.

You can't easily apply transfer learning to other machine learning algorithms, such as linear regression or gradient boosting. Due to its architecture, deep learning is well-suited for transferring knowledge learned on one problem to another. Apart from vision problems, transfer learning has been successfully applied to language models. Large language models such as ChatGPT, Anthropic Claude, or Google Gemini are all pre-trained models.

REMEMBER

Recently, considerable research has been conducted to develop pre-trained models that can also be applied to structured tabular data tasks such as TabPFN (read this *Nature* article for an overview: `www.nature.com/articles/s41586-024-08328-6`). However, we are still in the early stages of this new solution, and the algorithms we have seen so far in the book remain the most effective approach.

For instance, you can transfer a network that's capable of distinguishing between dogs and cats to perform a job that involves spotting dishes of macaroni and cheese. From a technical point of view, you achieve this task in different ways, depending on how similar the new image problem is to the previous one and how many new images you have for training. (A small image dataset amounts to a few thousand images, sometimes even less.)

Convolutional layers learn features like edges (in the early layers), textures, and more complex patterns/object parts (in deeper layers) that can be reused if your new image problem is similar to the one they have been trained for. In this case, you don't need to include too many images in training, add excessive computational power, or modify your pre-trained network too deeply. This type of transfer is the most common application of transfer learning, and you usually apply it by leveraging a network trained for the ImageNet competition, because there are so many images that the convolutions have acquired the capability to process a vast, different set of images. In this case, you freeze the values of the coefficients of the convolutions of the pre-trained model, so that they are not affected by any additional training, and the network won't overfit to the data you have, if your dataset is too small. You simply add a new *head*, which is a new terminal layer with nodes suitable for performing your task. During fine-tuning, the head will adjust to the correct weights.

If you cannot get good results from this approach, maybe because dogs and macaroni are too dissimilar, some alternatives require retraining part of the network, not just the classification head:

>> If you have limited data for the new task, you can freeze the weights of the early convolutional layers (the layers that extract the image features) of the pre-trained network and train only a new classification head, or perhaps fine-tune a few of the later convolutional layers as well.

>> If you have lots of data, you add a suitable output layer to the pre-trained network, but you don't freeze the convolutional layers. You use the pre-trained weights as a starting point and let the network fit your problem in the best way because you can train on lots of data. Typically, you retrain using a small learning rate, so you adapt the pre-trained weights, but you do not change them too much, or the pre-trained knowledge embedded there will be lost (a situation known as *catastrophic forgetting*).

In this chapter, we will present how to leverage a pre-trained model effectively on an image classification problem that has a strong affinity with ImageNet. Hence, we won't need to retrain the entire model, but rather add a suitable classification head.

Going beyond classification

CNNs are the building blocks of deep learning–based image recognition. Yet, they answer only a basic classification need: Given a picture, they can determine whether its content can be associated with a specific image class learned through previous examples. Therefore, when you train a deep neural network to recognize dogs and cats, you can feed it a photo and obtain output that tells you whether the photo contains a dog or a cat. The outputs generally come in two forms:

>> If the last network layer is a softmax layer (see the discussion in the "Pushing forth with feed-forward" section of Chapter 14), the network outputs the probability of the photo containing a dog or a cat (the two classes you trained it to recognize), and the output sums to 100 percent.

>> When the last layer is a sigmoid-activated layer, you obtain scores that you can interpret as probabilities of content belonging to each class, independently.

The scores won't necessarily sum to 100 percent. In both cases, the classification may fail when the following occurs:

>> The main object isn't what you trained the network to recognize. You may have presented the example neural network with a photo of a raccoon. In this case, the network will output an incorrect answer, either "dog" or "cat".

>> The main object is partially obstructed. For instance, your cat is playing hide-and-seek in the photo you show the network, and the network can't spot it.

>> The photo contains many different objects to detect, perhaps including animals other than cats and dogs. In this case, the output from the network will suggest a single class rather than include all the objects.

Figure 16-2 shows image 47780 (https://cocodataset.org/#explore?id=47780) taken from the MS Coco dataset (released as part of the open source Creative Commons Attribution-ShareAlike 4.0 International License). The series of three outputs shows how a CNN has detected, localized, and segmented the objects appearing in the image (a kitten and a dog standing on a field of grass). A plain CNN can't reproduce the examples in Figure 16-2 because its architecture will output the entire image as being of a particular class. To overcome this limitation, researchers extend the basic CNNs' capabilities to make them capable of the following:

>> **Detection:** Determining when an object is present in an image. Detection differs from classification because it involves only a portion of the image, implying that the network can detect multiple objects of the same type and of different types. The capability to spot objects in partial images is called *instance spotting*.

>> **Localization:** Defining exactly where a detected object appears in an image. You can have different types of localizations. Depending on granularity, they distinguish the part of the image that contains the detected object.

>> **Segmentation:** Classification of objects at the pixel level. Segmentation takes localization to the extreme. This kind of neural model assigns each pixel of the image to a class or even a specific instance. For instance, the network identifies all the pixels in a picture that relate to dogs and assigns a distinct label (called *instance segmentation*) to each one.

Among the various applications of CNNs, facial recognition is one of the most well-known. However, new technologies such as self-driving cars rely extensively on CNNs. In addition, you see CNNs used in places like content moderation, in which an organization must remove unwanted uploads from a website (for example). However, the most interesting applications of computer vision are in helping people perform tasks more effectively. For instance, by using computer vision to monitor how a person is moving their limbs, it becomes possible to provide a better level of physical therapy for patients (https://arxiv.org/ftp/arxiv/papers/1901/1901.10435.pdf).

It is essential to recognize that deep learning networks can perform tasks beyond classification. In the next section, we will explore how to code a CNN image classification model from scratch. If you're curious to see examples of detection or segmentation tasks, you can find more examples of computer vision with neural networks in *Deep Learning For Dummies* (Wiley) by John Paul Mueller and Luca Massaron.

  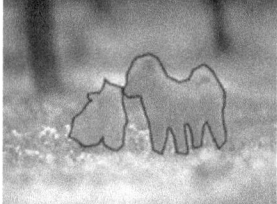

FIGURE 16-2: Detection, localization, and segmentation example from the Coco dataset.

Multiple detection   Localization by bounding boxes   Semantic Segmentation

Classifying Images with CNNs

After discussing the theoretical grounds and characteristics of CNNs, you can try building one. The Keras framework can construct an image classifier for a specific delimited problem. Solving specific, delimited problems often doesn't require learning a vast range of image features. Therefore, you can easily solve them using simple architectures, building them from scratch.

In our example, we try to distinguish between dogs and cats in a series of images. The dataset we will use is the Oxford-IIIT Pet Dataset III (www.robots.ox.ac. uk/~vgg/data/pets). This is a dataset created by the Visual Geometry Group at the University of Oxford. It consists of 37 pet breeds (12 cat breeds and 25 dog breeds) with roughly 200 images per class. The photos display different scales, poses, and lighting conditions, making the dataset quite effective for learning from scratch how a cat or a dog should look. Moreover, the images are annotated, allowing for the simple classification of pet type (dog vs. cat) or breed, as well as complex tasks such as object detection (using bounding boxes) and image segmentation, including foreground-background separation. The dataset is typically used for computer vision research, but it is also suitable for other educational or commercial uses, thanks to its Creative Commons Attribution-ShareAlike 4.0 International License (https://creativecommons.org/licenses/by-sa/4.0/ deed.en). For our examples, we will use a version where the number of images of dogs equals the number of images of cats. Moreover, the images have already been separated into training, validation, and test sets, and we simplified the target from specific breeds to being a dog or a cat.

REMEMBER

You can find plenty of information about the dataset in the article "Cats and Dogs" by Omkar Parkhi, Andrea Vedaldi, Andrew Zisserman, and C.V. Jawahar (www. robots.ox.ac.uk/~vgg/publications/2012/parkhi12a/parkhi12a.pdf).

Building a classifier from scratch

Because our data is hosted on Hugging Face's infrastructure, a French tech company that provides a popular platform for sharing machine learning models and datasets (we will discuss Hugging Face further in the next chapter), we utilize their datasets package to download the data we will be using. Before doing that, we need to update the package in Google Colab to the latest version in order to avoid problems during access:

```
pip install -U -q datasets
```

TIP

We recommend using a GPU on your Google Colab instance to accelerate the calculations. The matrix computations required by deep learning are handled much faster by GPUs than by CPUs. An NVIDIA L4 GPU is an excellent choice for our examples.

As previously done in Chapter 14, we then proceed to set up Keras. This framework will help build the image classifier on a JAX backend (JAX is another Google framework for deep learning). Then we import all the packages that will help us in the task, in addition to Keras: datasets for downloading the data, NumPy for processing arrays, `matplotlib` for charts and plots, and `tqdm` for monitoring the progress of the tasks:

```
import os
os.environ["KERAS_BACKEND"] = "jax"
os.environ["HF_HUB_DISABLE_IMPLICIT_TOKEN"] = "1"

import keras
from keras import layers, optimizers
from datasets import load_dataset
import numpy as np
import matplotlib.pyplot as plt
from tqdm import tqdm
```

We now proceed to download the data by simply providing the address of the data on the Hugging Face platform. In return, we receive a data structure, divided into separate sets (training, validation, and test), comprising images, labels, and additional useful metadata:

```
ds = load_dataset("lmassaron/dogs-cats-openimages")
```

By indexing the split we want to use, we can check the size of each dataset:

```
print(f"Train set size: {len(ds['train'])}")
print(f"Validation set size: {len(ds['validation'])}")
print(f"Test set size: {len(ds['test'])}")
```

Our training data consists of 3,360 images. In addition, there are two sets of 720 images, allocated for validation and testing purposes. The target is binary, with 1 labeling cats and 0 labeling dogs. We then set a few constants that we will use during data preparation and training. Since the images in the dataset can vary in size, we resize all of them to a standard image size of 256 x 256. This image resolution provides a good balance between image detail and computational requirements. A lower resolution may require less memory, but it may also result in poorer performance. The batch size is suitable for the GPUs available on Google Colab, and it should provide a balanced training, neither too noisy nor too smooth.

```
IMAGE_WIDTH = 256
IMAGE_HEIGHT = 256
BATCH_SIZE = 32
EPOCHS = 25
```

Our next step is to process the data from the Hugging Face dataset structure into a list of NumPy arrays. To achieve this, we utilize a function that extracts the images and labels one by one, resizes them, and converts them into float32 arrays, a numeric format that GPUs are optimized for:

```
def process_images(data):
  all_images_list = []
  all_labels_list = []

  for example in tqdm(data):
    pil_image = example['image']
    label = example['label']
    img_rgb = pil_image.convert("RGB")
    img_resized = img_rgb.resize((IMAGE_WIDTH,
                                  IMAGE_HEIGHT))
    img_array = keras.utils.img_to_array(img_resized,
                    dtype='float32')

    all_images_list.append(img_array)
    all_labels_list.append(label)

  x_np = np.array(all_images_list)
  y_np = np.array(all_labels_list)
  return x_np, y_np

x_train, y_train = process_images(ds['train'])
x_valid, y_valid = process_images(ds['validation'])
x_test, y_test = process_images(ds['test'])
```

Once the processing has been completed, we define a data augmentation procedure, which, as previously discussed, should allow for more diverse inputs during the training phase, thereby reducing overfitting and enabling the network to generalize more effectively. The two image processing operations that we have implemented are:

» Randomly flipping the image horizontally (left-to-right) with 50 percent probability

» Randomly rotating the image by an angle between –0.05 and 0.05 radians (approximately ±2.9 degrees)

The operations are handled by Keras layers, which can be inserted directly into the network later. In this way, you don't have to preprocess the images, but the augmentation process is done on the fly on the batch of images that is sent into the network at each iteration for training.

```
data_augmentation = keras.Sequential(
    [
        layers.RandomFlip("horizontal"),
        layers.RandomRotation(factor=(-0.05, 0.05) )
    ],
    name="data_augmentation")
```

We also define a block of convolutions that we can use repeatedly within our image recognition network. Two identical convolutional layers process the image. The `filters` parameter dictates the number of feature maps produced, while the kernel size defines the convolution window to be used. The resulting output is then downsampled by a factor of two using a max pooling function (the function selects the max value in each 2 x 2 window region of the output):

```
def conv_block(filters, kernel_size, name):
    params = {
        "filters": filters,
        "kernel_size": kernel_size,
        "activation": "relu",
        "padding": "same"}
    block = [
        layers.Conv2D(**params),
        layers.Conv2D(**params),
        layers.MaxPooling2D((2, 2))
    ]
    return keras.Sequential(block, name=name)
```

Before proceeding with creating the neural network, we set all the random seeds using the `set_random_seed` function. This helps ensure a certain degree of replicability of the process. Then we proceed to define the blocks that constitute the network.

```
keras.utils.set_random_seed(0)

model = keras.Sequential(
    [
        keras.Input(shape=(IMAGE_HEIGHT,
                           IMAGE_WIDTH, 3)),
        layers.Rescaling(1.0 / 255),
        data_augmentation,
```

```
        conv_block(32, 5, name="conv_block1"),
        layers.BatchNormalization(),
        conv_block(32, 4, name="conv_block2"),
        conv_block(64, 4, name="conv_block3"),
        layers.BatchNormalization(),
        conv_block(64, 3, name="conv_block4"),
        conv_block(128, 3, name="conv_block5"),
        layers.BatchNormalization(),
        conv_block(128, 2, name="conv_block6"),
        conv_block(256, 2, name="conv_block7"),
        layers.GlobalAveragePooling2D(),
        layers.BatchNormalization(),

        layers.Dropout(0.2),
        layers.Dense(128, activation="relu"),
        layers.Dropout(0.2),
        layers.Dense(64, activation="relu"),
        layers.Dropout(0.1),
        layers.Dense(1, activation="sigmoid"),
    ],
    name="simple_cat_dog_classifier")
```

We can inspect the result by observing the summary in Figure 16-3. The architecture is designed to progressively extract higher-level features while reducing computational complexity at each stage. By increasing the filters and reducing the kernels, the architecture transforms the data as it flows through the layers from low-level features, such as edges, lines, texture, and simple shapes, to mid-level features, such as object parts and geometric patterns, to finally high-level features, which are complex representations that help to distinguish a dog from a cat.

TIP

Creating a similar architecture is a matter of trial and error. It also helps a lot to mimic successful examples that can be found in blogs or GitHub open-source repositories because you can learn from other practitioners' mistakes and successes.

Batch normalization layers, by normalizing activations, and dropout layers, by randomly deactivating neurons, aim to stabilize the learning process and avoid overfitting (the network has over one million parameters).

```
model.summary()
```

```
Model: "simple_cat_dog_classifier"
```

Layer (type)	Output Shape	Param #
rescaling (Rescaling)	(None, 256, 256, 3)	0
data_augmentation (Sequential)	(None, 256, 256, 3)	0
conv_block1 (Sequential)	(None, 128, 128, 32)	28,064
batch_normalization (BatchNormalization)	(None, 128, 128, 32)	128
conv_block2 (Sequential)	(None, 64, 64, 32)	32,832
conv_block3 (Sequential)	(None, 32, 32, 64)	98,432
batch_normalization_1 (BatchNormalization)	(None, 32, 32, 64)	256
conv_block4 (Sequential)	(None, 16, 16, 64)	73,856
conv_block5 (Sequential)	(None, 8, 8, 128)	221,440
batch_normalization_2 (BatchNormalization)	(None, 8, 8, 128)	512
conv_block6 (Sequential)	(None, 4, 4, 128)	131,328
conv_block7 (Sequential)	(None, 2, 2, 256)	393,728
global_average_pooling2d (GlobalAveragePooling2D)	(None, 256)	0
batch_normalization_3 (BatchNormalization)	(None, 256)	1,024
dropout (Dropout)	(None, 256)	0
dense (Dense)	(None, 128)	32,896
dropout_1 (Dropout)	(None, 128)	0
dense_1 (Dense)	(None, 64)	8,256
dropout_2 (Dropout)	(None, 64)	0
dense_2 (Dense)	(None, 1)	65

```
Total params: 1,022,817 (3.90 MB)
Trainable params: 1,021,857 (3.90 MB)
Non-trainable params: 960 (3.75 KB)
```

FIGURE 16-3: Summary of the neural network we created from scratch.

Before launching the training, we must compile the network, specifying the optimizer, loss, and metric we want to monitor. Adam (Adaptive Moment Estimation) is a gradient descent-based optimization method that is usually relatively stable and performs well, as it automatically adapts its learning rate. The loss is the binary cross-entropy, a loss function that is specifically designed for binary classification tasks. Finally, we use accuracy, which is the percentage of correct predictions, because it is an easy-to-understand, human-readable metric that relates well to performance, given that our target is balanced (we have the same number of dogs and cats).

```
model.compile(
    optimizer=optimizers.Adam(),
    loss = "binary_crossentropy",
    metrics = ["accuracy"])
```

Everything is now ready for the training time. We set an early stopping callback, which is a function that is executed after each training epoch. The function helps us stop training if the performance on the validation set does not improve for 10 epochs, and it also helps us recover the state of the network at the epoch that performed best on the validation set. The idea is that if we take the model with the best performance on the validation set, that model should also generalize well to unseen test data.

The training is then launched by providing the training set, validation set, maximum number of epochs, batch size (the number of images processed simultaneously by the network), an option for shuffling the input, and the callback function. The training may take a long time, even on an NVIDIA L4 GPU (on Google Colab powered by a L4 GPU runtime, it takes about 25 minutes), so consider grabbing a coffee or a cup of tea.

```
early_stopping = keras.callbacks.EarlyStopping(
    monitor='val_loss',
    patience=10,
    restore_best_weights=True)

history = model.fit(
    x_train,
    y_train,
    batch_size=BATCH_SIZE,
    epochs=EPOCHS,
    validation_data=(x_valid, y_valid),
    shuffle=True,
    callbacks=[early_stopping])
```

Once the training is complete, we can plot the training and validation performances to determine how well it performed. You can see an example plot in Figure 16-4.

Even though we tried to seed for replicability, the training may vary in trajectory and results, hence you may have a different path on your chart. However, you should also see a quite smooth training line, with our chosen evaluation metric, accuracy, constantly increasing, and a validation line following in a wavy fashion (there can be times when the network's performance in validation collapses and then recovers).

```
def plot_history(history):
    plt.plot(history.history["accuracy"])
    plt.plot(history.history["val_accuracy"])
    plt.title("model accuracy")
```

```
        plt.ylabel("accuracy")
        plt.xlabel("epoch")
        plt.legend(["train", "validation"],
                    loc="upper left")
        plt.show()

plot_history(history)
```

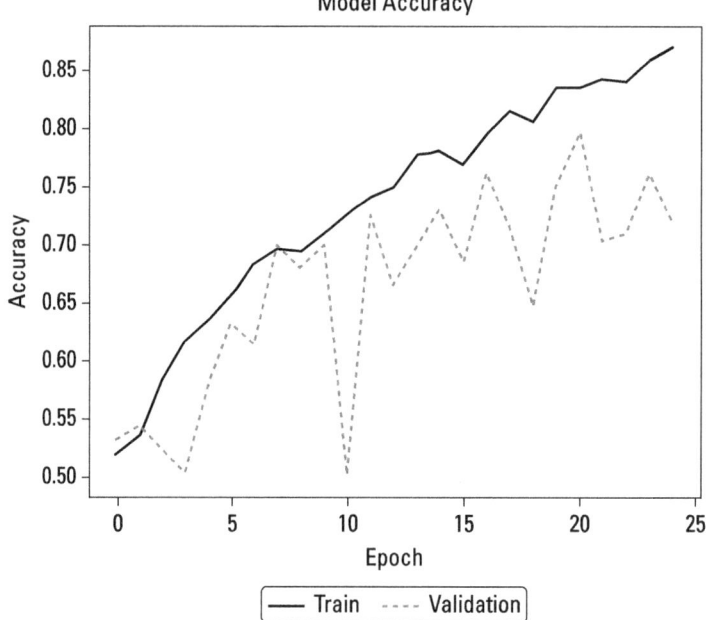

FIGURE 16-4:
The training
and validation
accuracy
plotted across
the epochs.

The final performance is estimated on the test set. It should result in an accuracy of about 0.84, implying that the network correctly classifies an image as a dog or a cat more than 8 times out of 10.

```
loss_value, accuracy_value = model.evaluate(
    x_test, y_test, batch_size=BATCH_SIZE)
print(f"test accuracy {accuracy_value:0.3f}")
```

In the next section, we will try to improve this result by leveraging a pre-trained neural network, which gives you a clearer idea of why transfer learning has become so successful nowadays.

Leveraging pre-trained solutions

In the following example, which builds on the previous one, we replace the network we built from scratch with a pre-trained model. Our strategy is to leverage the model's previous training on ImageNet and fine-tune only the weights of the classification head. The model we will use, EfficientNetV2B0, is a CNN architecture designed for image classification tasks, whose weights have been pre-trained on large datasets like ImageNet, enabling transfer learning for various computer vision problems. It is the smallest and lightest variant in the EfficientNetV2 family, making it the right choice if you are looking for a computationally less demanding model compared to more cumbersome architectures, while still delivering sufficiently high accuracy. It achieves a top-1 accuracy of approximately 78.7% and a top-5 accuracy of 94.3% on ImageNet, with about 7.1 million parameters. It is part of the model garden of pre-trained models available from Keras (`https://keras.io/api/applications`).

After setting a seed for replicability, we load the model, excluding its classification head, and provide our image shape as the input shape. We then freeze its weights, rendering them non-trainable.

```
keras.utils.set_random_seed(0)

transfer_model = keras.applications.EfficientNetV2B0(
    include_top=False,
    weights="imagenet",
    input_shape=(IMAGE_HEIGHT, IMAGE_WIDTH, 3))

transfer_model.trainable = False
```

We then place the pre-trained model (`transfer_model`) after the input and data augmentation layers, and add a new prediction head consisting of a single neuron. After the `transfer_model`, we add a global average pooling layer (which flattens the output of `transfer_model`'s final layers), followed by batch normalization and a dropout layer for stabilization and to reduce overfitting.

```
model = keras.Sequential(
    [
        keras.Input(shape=(
                IMAGE_HEIGHT, IMAGE_WIDTH, 3)),
        data_augmentation,
        transfer_model,
        layers.GlobalAveragePooling2D(),
```

```
            layers.BatchNormalization(),
            layers.Dropout(0.2),
            layers.Dense(1, activation="sigmoid")
    ], name="EffNetV2_cat_dog_classifier")
```

As before, we compile the model at this point.

```
model.compile(
    optimizer=optimizers.Adam(),
    loss = "binary_crossentropy",
    metrics = ["accuracy"])
```

In Figure 16-5, you can observe the new architecture, much simpler than before, and notice how the architecture proceeds almost directly from the output of the pre-trained model to the final classification output, and how the trainable weights constitute a tiny portion of the total (3,841 weights out of a total of 5,921,972).

```
model.summary()
```

Model: "EffNetV2_cat_dog_classifier"

Layer (type)	Output Shape	Param #
data_augmentation (Sequential)	(None, 256, 256, 3)	0
efficientnetv2-b0 (Functional)	(None, 8, 8, 1280)	5,919,312
global_average_pooling2d_1 (GlobalAveragePooling2D)	(None, 1280)	0
batch_normalization_4 (BatchNormalization)	(None, 1280)	5,120
dropout_3 (Dropout)	(None, 1280)	0
dense_3 (Dense)	(None, 1)	1,281

Total params: 5,925,713 (22.60 MB)
Trainable params: 3,841 (15.00 KB)
Non-trainable params: 5,921,872 (22.59 MB)

FIGURE 16-5: Summary of the neural network using the pre-trained EfficientNetV2B0 base.

This time, the training is set to a single epoch, to provide the model with a chance to process all the data at least once.

```
history = model.fit(
    x_train,
    y_train,
```

```
    batch_size=BATCH_SIZE,
    epochs=1,
    validation_data=(x_valid, y_valid),
    shuffle=True)
```

The results are quite fast and very promising, but the evaluation on the test set reveals excellent performance.

```
loss_value, accuracy_value = model.evaluate(
    x_test,
    y_test,
    batch_size=BATCH_SIZE)
print(f"test accuracy {accuracy_value:0.3f}")
```

With an accuracy of over 0.99 in the test set, the model achieves excellent performance. The pre-training on the ImageNet data provided it with highly effective processing layers for accurately detecting whether an image is of a cat or a dog. Of course, in a much more complex classification problem, this network may not perform as well. Still, the present example demonstrates how pre-trained models have revolutionized computer vision tasks by simplifying solutions and providing models with advanced feature extraction capabilities.

Chapter **17**

Scoring Opinions and Sentiments

Thanks to widely available chatbots such as OpenAI, ChatGPT, or Google Gemini, many people have formed the idea that computers can understand text and converse in a human-like fashion. The fact is that computers have their own way of representing and manipulating text. It's all numbers to computers. They do not understand text in a human sense, yet they still process it and produce meaningful results. This chapter helps you understand how natural language processing (NLP) works, and the examples will provide insight into current large language models (LLMs) and how they approach language.

We begin by exploring how NLP is used to parse text and understand it through various approaches, from simpler methods like bag-of-words to more sophisticated ones, including transformer-based models. This specialized neural network architecture is particularly adept at understanding sequences of text, placing words and phrases in their proper context, and generating human-like discourse. The transformer architecture is the foundation of LLMs — those incredible chatbots that seem to converse and reason like humans. This chapter concludes with an example of working with text to score opinions and sentiments using recurrent neural networks and a transformer-based architecture.

REMEMBER

You don't have to type the source code for this chapter manually. In fact, using the downloadable source code is a lot easier. You can find the source code for this chapter in the ML4D3E folder of the downloadable code file. The example files for this chapter will begin with ML4D3E-17-. See the Introduction for details on how to find these source files.

Introducing Natural Language Processing

As human beings, understanding language is one of our first achievements, and associating words with their meaning seems natural. It's also automatic for humans to handle discourses that are ambiguous, unclear, or simply have a strong reference to the context in which we live or work (such as dialect, jargon, or terms that family or associates understand). In addition, humans can catch subtle references to feelings and sentiments in text, enabling people to understand polite speech that hides negative feelings and irony. Computers don't have this ability; they are number crunchers, but can rely on NLP to bridge between human language and numerical representations. NLP is a field of computer science concerned with language understanding and language generation between machines and humans. Since Alan Turing first devised the Turing Test in 1950, which aims to distinguish between artificial intelligence and human intelligence based on how it communicates with humans (https://plato.stanford.edu/entries/turing-test), NLP experts have developed a series of techniques that define the state of the art in computer–human interaction through text.

A computer powered by NLP can successfully identify spam in emails, tag parts of speech in a conversation (such as identifying verbs or nouns), and recognize entities, such as a person's name or a company's name (a task called *named entity recognition,* or NER). All these achievements have found applications in tasks such as spam filtering, predicting stock market trends using news articles, and deduplicating redundant information in data storage.

Things become more challenging for NLP with tasks like translating text from one language to another or determining the referent of a pronoun in an ambiguous phrase. For example, consider the sentence, "John told Luca he shouldn't do that again." In this case, you can't really tell whether "he" refers to John or Luca. Disambiguating words with multiple meanings, such as determining whether the word *mouse* in a phrase refers to a mouse as an animal or a computer device (a task known as word-sense disambiguation) can prove challenging. Still, recent advancements appear to have narrowed even this gap. The core difficulty in all these problems often arises from the need to understand context.

As humans, we can easily resolve ambiguity by examining the text for hints about elements like place and time that express the details of the conversation (such as understanding what happened between John and Luca, or whether the conversation is about a computer when mentioning the mouse). Relying on additional information for understanding is part of the human experience. This sort of analysis is somewhat tricky for computers. Moreover, if the task requires critical contextual knowledge or demands that the system (or AI) resort to common sense and general expertise, the task becomes daunting. Until the recent advances in transformer architectures, effectively extracting meaningful summaries or completing missing information in text (text-infilling) was very challenging. As all these tasks now seem easy for recent LLMs, new, unexpected challenges have emerged for the field, ranging from mitigating plausible-sounding but incorrect outputs (so-called "hallucinations") to the deeper challenge of understanding how these massive neural networks operate and why they generate specific text over other alternatives.

Revising the State of the Art in NLP

NLP consists of a series of procedures that enable computers to understand, interpret, and generate human language. These techniques prepare textual data for statistical analysis, machine learning algorithms, and deep learning models. NLP owes its roots to computational linguistics, which provided the foundations for rule-based AI systems, such as expert systems. These early systems made decisions based on a codification of human knowledge, experience, and ways of converting text into rules that the computer can understand.

NLP transforms unstructured textual information into more structured data, enabling computational systems to manipulate and evaluate it more easily. Historically, and for many years, statistical algorithms have performed most of the work in NLP, along with simple computational procedures such as TF-IDF (explained in detail later in this chapter) or the hashing trick (a system that maps words to a fixed-size vector using a hash function).

Recently, deep learning has emerged as the dominant paradigm in NLP. While traditional statistical methods and even rule-based approaches, such as expert systems, are still employed in specific applications when computational resources are limited or where interpretability and control of decision processes are paramount, deep learning models have achieved state-of-the-art performance across a vast range of tasks. Recurrent neural networks (RNNs), mentioned in Chapter 14, marked a significant advancement in NLP compared to previous approaches, such as the bag-of-words (BoW) method, another NLP technique explained later in this chapter. RNN variants like long short-term memories (LSTMs) and gated recurrent units (GRUs) enabled models to process words in their exact order, capturing dependencies across sequences.

Further advancements in neural networks led to the development of *word embeddings,* such as Google's Word2Vec or Facebook's fastText. These methods can represent words as dense, meaningful vectors of values, as they are trained on and capture the semantic information from millions of texts. These embeddings, rich in semantic meaning, can be used as input features to feed machine learning algorithms, helping practitioners obtain significantly better results in many NLP activities.

Embeddings were an essential building block for another approach, the transformer-based architectures, which have become the current state-of-the-art in NLP. They were introduced in the foundational paper "Attention Is All You Need" (Vaswani et al., 2017), and they revolutionized the NLP field because they processed word inputs in parallel, abandoning the previous recurrent approach of dealing with words one by one, and they also weighted the importance of different words in a sequence thanks to a sophisticated mechanism, the *attention mechanism.* Thanks to the attention mechanism, even complex relationships of various and distant words in phrases were captured and processed more effectively than with RNNs. Initially devised for automatic translation tasks, the transformer models were later divided into two large families: *encoder models*, which specialize in comprehending the meaning of phrases deeply, and *decoder models*, which specialize in generating language. A key example of encoder models is Google's BERT (Bidirectional Encoder Representations from Transformers). As for decoder models, the most notable example is OpenAI's GPT (Generative Pre-trained Transformer) series (for example, GPT-3, GPT-4, GPT-5), but there are also other quite popular models such as Google's Gemini, Claude by Anthropic, Meta's Llama models, the models from DeepSeek, and many others. Applications powered by such models are capable of generating meaningful text on the fly, producing coherent text that can include reasoning steps, generated plans, or powering the most advanced personal conversational AI systems and personal assistants.

Despite all these incredible advances, classic NLP processing and technology remain relevant, especially when computational resources are limited, there is insufficient training data, and interpretability of the resulting model is required. This is the reason why, in the following sections, we will first help you understand how a computer can read words, and then we will discuss how methods, such as tokenization, bag of words, TF-IDF, and n-grams, work.

Understanding How Machines Read

Before a computer can do anything with text, it must be able to read the text in some manner. Categorical data is a type of short text that you typically represent using binary features, that is, features coded using one and zero values according to whether a certain value is present in the categorical feature. Not surprisingly, you can represent complex text using the same logic.

REMEMBER

Text data is usually represented as strings, but strings are also typical of categorical data and for structured data such as addresses or directory entries. What makes textual data distinct is the richness of meaning and information it presents in an unstructured way.

Chapter 12 presents a technique named *one-hot encoding* that shows how you can transform a categorical color feature, having values such as red, green, and blue, into three binary features, each one representing one of the three colors. In a similar way, you can transform a phrase like "The quick brown fox jumps over the lazy dog" using nine binary features, one for each word that appears in the text ("The" is considered distinct from "the" because of its initial capital letter). This is the BoW form of representation. In its simplest form, BoW indicates whether a specific word is present in the text by setting a corresponding feature's value in the dataset. The following sections show an example using Python and its Scikit-learn package.

Defining the input data

The input data is three phrases, `text_1`, `text_2`, and `text_3`, placed in a list, `corpus`. A *corpus* is a set of homogeneous documents put together for NLP analysis:

```
text_1 = "The quick brown fox jumps over the lazy dog."
text_2 = "My dog is quick and can jump over fences."
text_3 = \
        "Your dog is so lazy that it sleeps all the day."
corpus = [text_1, text_2, text_3]
```

TIP

When you need to analyze text using a computer, you load the documents from disk or scrape them from the web and place each of them into a string variable. If you have multiple documents, you store them all in a list, the corpus. When you have a single document, you can split it using chapters, paragraphs, or simply the end of each line. After splitting the document, place all its parts into a list and apply analysis as if the list were a corpus of documents.

Now that you have a corpus, you use a class from the `feature_extraction` module in Scikit-learn, `CountVectorizer`, which easily transforms texts into BoW, like this:

```
from sklearn.feature_extraction.text import (
    CountVectorizer)

vectorizer = CountVectorizer(binary=True,
                             lowercase=False)
vectorizer.fit(corpus)
vectorized_text = vectorizer.transform(corpus)
print(vectorized_text.todense())

[[0 1 0 0 0 1 0 0 1 0 1 0 0 0 1 1 1 1 0 0 0 1]
 [1 0 0 0 1 0 1 0 1 1 0 1 0 1 0 0 1 1 0 0 0 0]
 [0 0 1 1 0 0 0 1 1 0 0 1 1 0 0 1 0 0 1 1 1 1]]
```

The `CountVectorizer` class learns the corpus content using the `fit` method and then turns it (using the `transform` method) into a list of lists. As discussed in Chapter 7, a list of lists is nothing more than a matrix in disguise, so what the class returns is actually a matrix made of three rows (the three documents, in the same order as the corpus) and 21 columns, each representing a unique word from all the text data you're using.

The BoW representation converts words into column features of a document matrix, and these features have a nonzero value when the word is present in the processed text. For instance, consider the word *dog.* The following code shows its representation in the BoW:

```
print(vectorizer.vocabulary_)

{'The': 1, 'quick': 17, 'brown': 5, 'fox': 10, 'jumps': 14,
    'over': 16,
 'the': 21, 'lazy': 15, 'dog': 8, 'My': 0, 'is': 11, 'and':
    4, 'can': 6,
 'jump': 13, 'fences': 9, 'Your': 2, 'so': 19, 'that':
    20, 'it': 12,
 'sleeps': 18, 'all': 3, 'day': 7}
```

It uses the `CountVectorizer()` function to print the vocabulary learned from text reports, and returns a dictionary where the keys are the words and the values are their indices. In our example, it associates *dog* with the number 8, meaning that *dog* is the feature at index 8 (the ninth column) in the BoW matrix representations. In fact, in the obtained BoW, the element at index eight of each document list always has a value of 1 because *dog* is the only word present in all three documents.

REMEMBER Storing documents in a document matrix form can be memory-intensive because you must represent each document as a vector of the same length as the dictionary that created it. The dictionary in this example is quite limited, but when you use a larger corpus, you discover that a dictionary of the English language contains well over a million terms. The solution is to use sparse matrices. A sparse matrix is a way to store a matrix in your computer's memory without having zero values occupy memory space. You can read more about sparse matrices in Python here: `https://cmdlinetips.com/2018/03/sparse-matrices-in-python-with-scipy`.

Processing and enhancing text

Marking whether a word is present or not in a text is indeed a good start, but sometimes it's not enough. The BoW model has its own limits. As if you were putting stuff randomly into a bag, in a BoW, words lose their order and relationship with each other. For instance, in the phrase *My dog is quick and can jump over fences*, you know that *quick* refers to *dog* because it is glued to it by the verb *"is."* In a BoW, however, everything is mixed, and some syntactic and semantic relationships between words are lost. Further processing can help prevent such a situation. The following sections discuss how to process and enhance text.

Considering basic processing tasks

Instead of marking the presence or absence of an element of the phrase (technically called a *token*), you can instead count how many times it occurs, as shown in the following code:

```
text_4 = \
    "A black dog just passed by but my dog is brown."
corpus.append(text_4)
vectorizer = CountVectorizer()
vectorizer.fit(corpus)
vectorized_text = vectorizer.transform(corpus)
print(vectorized_text.todense()[-1])


[[0 0 1 1 1 0 0 2 0 0 1 0 0 0 1 0 1 0 1 0 0 0 0 0 0]]
```

This code modifies the previous example by adding a new phrase with the word *dog* repeated two times. The code appends the new phrase to the `corpus` and retrains the `vectorizer`, but it omits the `binary=True` setting this time. The resulting vector for the last inserted document clearly shows a 2 value at index 8 (the ninth position), indicating the vectorizer counted the word *dog* twice in the new document. Note that the vocabulary (and thus the indices) can change when new documents are added and the language used by the BoW has expanded.

Counting tokens helps make important words stand out. Yet, it's easy to repeat phrase elements, such as articles, that aren't important to the meaning of the expression. In the next section, you discover how to exclude less important elements, but for the time being, the example down-weights them using the Term Frequency-Inverse Document Frequency (TF-IDF) transformation.

The TF-IDF transformation is a technique that weights terms based on their frequency in a document (term frequency, or TF) and their rarity across the entire corpus (inverse document frequency, or IDF). Using this technique, the vectorizer deems a word less critical, even if it appears many times in a text, when it also finds that word in other texts. In the example corpus, the word *dog* appears in every text. In a classification problem, you can't use the word to distinguish between texts because it occurs everywhere in the corpus. The word *fox* appears in only one phrase, making it a key classification term.

You commonly apply several transformations when applying TF-IDF. For instance, for the IDF part, a standard adjustment involves taking the logarithm of the total number of documents in the corpus divided by the number of documents containing the term. The operation down-weights more commonly occurring words and highlights rarer, more distinctive words. Regarding the TF, the most significant adjustment is normalizing the text length.

Clearly, a longer text has more chances to have more words that are distinctive when compared to a shorter text. For example, when the word *fox* appears in a brief text, it can be relevant to the meaning of that expression because *fox* stands out among a few other words. However, when the word *fox* appears once in a long text, its presence might not matter much because it's a single word among many others. For this reason, the TF component often undergoes a normalization operation where you divide the count of each token by the total number of tokens in that document. This turns raw counts into percentages, so TF-IDF no longer considers how many times the word *fox* appears, but instead takes into account the percentage of times the word *fox* occurs among all the tokens. The following example demonstrates how to complete the previous example by combining normalization and TF-IDF.

```
from sklearn.feature_extraction.text import (
    TfidfTransformer)

tfidf = TfidfTransformer(norm="l1")
tfidf_mtx = tfidf.fit_transform(vectorized_text)
```

```
phrase = 3 # choose a number from 0 to 3

total = 0
for word in vectorizer.vocabulary_:
    pos = vectorizer.vocabulary_[word]
    value = list(tfidf_mtx.toarray()[phrase])[pos]
    if value !=0.0:
        print(f"{word:7s}: {value:0.3f}")
        total += value
print(f"\nSummed values of a phrase: {total:.1f}")

brown   : 0.095
dog     : 0.126
my      : 0.095
is      : 0.077
black   : 0.121
just    : 0.121
passed  : 0.121
by      : 0.121
but     : 0.121

Summed values of a phrase: 1.0
```

Using this new TF-IDF model rescales the values of important words and makes them comparable between each text in the corpus. To recover part of the ordering of the text before the BoW transformation, adding n-grams is also useful. An *n-gram* is a continuous sequence of tokens in the text that you use as a single token in the BoW representation. For instance, in the phrase, "The quick brown fox jumps over the lazy dog," a *bigram* — that is, a sequence of two tokens — transforms *brown fox* and *lazy dog* into single tokens. A *trigram* may create a single token from *quick brown fox*. An n-gram is a powerful tool, but it has a drawback because it doesn't know which combinations are important to the meaning of a phrase. N-grams create all the contiguous sequences of size N. The TF-IDF model can upweight or underweight the n-grams for a specific task, but only projects like Google's NGram viewer (you learn more about this viewer later in the chapter) can tell you which n-grams are generally more helpful than others in NLP, because it is calculated on a massive corpus of books and other texts. The following example uses CountVectorizer to model n-grams in the range of (2, 2), that is, bigrams.

```
bigrams = CountVectorizer(ngram_range=(2, 2))
print(bigrams.fit(corpus).vocabulary_)

{'the quick': 30, 'quick brown': 24, 'brown fox': 3,
 'fox jumps': 9, 'jumps over': 15, 'over the': 21,
```

```
'the lazy': 29, 'lazy dog': 17, 'my dog': 19, 'dog is': 7,
 'is quick': 11, 'quick and': 23, 'and can': 1,
 'can jump': 6, 'jump over': 14, 'over fences': 20,
 'your dog': 31, 'is so': 12, 'so lazy': 26,
 'lazy that': 18, 'that it': 27, 'it sleeps': 13,
 'sleeps all': 25, 'all the': 0, 'the day': 28,
 'black dog': 2, 'dog just': 8, 'just passed': 16,
 'passed by': 22, 'by but': 5, 'but my': 4, 'is brown': 10}
```

TIP

Setting different ranges lets you use both *unigrams* (single tokens) and n-grams in your NLP analysis. For instance, the setting `ngram_range=(1,3)` creates all tokens, all bigrams, and all trigrams. As a general heuristic, you often don't need to consider beyond trigrams in an NLP analysis. Increasing the number of n-grams tends to be slightly beneficial after trigrams and sometimes even just after bigrams, depending on the corpus size (on smaller ones, it can even turn out to be detrimental to performance) and the NLP problem.

Stemming and removing stop words

Stemming is the process of reducing words to their stem (or root) word. This task isn't the same as understanding that some words come from Latin or other roots, but instead makes similar words equal to each other for the purpose of comparison or sharing. For example, the words *cats, catty,* and *catlike* all have the stem *cat.* The act of stemming helps you analyze sentences when tokenizing them because words having the same stem often share a core meaning, allowing them to be represented by a single feature and improving performance in your NLP task. On the other hand, stemming is not always a solution for everything, and sometimes it can group words with distinct meanings, which can be detrimental.

Creating stem words by removing suffixes to make tokenizing sentences easier isn't the only way to make the document matrix simpler. Languages include many glue words that don't mean much to a computer but have significant meaning to humans, such as *a, as, the, that,* and so on in English. They make the text flow and concatenate in a meaningful way. Yet, the BoW approach doesn't care much about how you arrange words in a text. Thus, removing such words is legitimate. These short, less useful words are called *stop words.*

The act of stemming and removing stop words simplifies the text and reduces the number of textual elements so that only the essential elements remain. By reducing the number of tokens, a computational algorithm can work faster and process the text more effectively when the corpus is large. However, keep in mind that using these techniques may simplify your text too much, and some essential nuances may be lost in the process.

This example requires the use of the Natural Language Toolkit (NLTK), which Anaconda doesn't normally install by default. (You can check for an NLTK installation by opening an Anaconda prompt, typing **conda list nltk**, and pressing Enter. If the output doesn't show that you have version 3.5 or above installed, then you must install it.) To use this example, you must download and install the NLTK using the instructions found at `www.nltk.org/install.html` for your platform. Make certain that you install the NLTK for whatever version of Python you're using for this book when you have multiple versions of Python installed on your system. After you install the NLTK, you must also install the packages associated with it. The instructions at `www.nltk.org/install.html` tell you how to perform this task. (Install all the packages to ensure that you have everything.) Here is the code necessary for downloading the packages we need for our next example:

```
import nltk
nltk.download("punkt")
nltk.download("punkt_tab")
nltk.download("stopwords")
```

The following example demonstrates how to perform stemming and remove stop words from a sentence. It begins by training an algorithm to perform the required analysis using a test sentence. Afterward, the example checks a second sentence for words that appear in the first.

```
from sklearn.feature_extraction.text import (
    CountVectorizer)

from nltk import word_tokenize
from nltk.stem.porter import PorterStemmer
from nltk.corpus import stopwords

stemmer = PorterStemmer()
stop_words = stopwords.words("english")

def stem_tokens(tokens, stemmer):
    stemmed = []
    for item in tokens:
        stemmed.append(stemmer.stem(item))
    return stemmed

def tokenize(text):
    tokens = word_tokenize(text)
    tokens = [token for token in tokens
                if token not in stop_words]
```

```
    stems = stem_tokens(tokens, stemmer)
    return stems

docs = ["Sam loves swimming so he swims all the time"]
vect = CountVectorizer(tokenizer=tokenize)
vec = vect.fit(docs)

sentence1 = vec.transform(
    ["George loves swimming too! "])

print(vec.get_feature_names_out())
print(sentence1.toarray())
```

At the outset, the example creates a CountVectorizer, vect, to hold a list of stemmed words, but it excludes the stop words. The tokenizer parameter defines the function used to stem the words. The stop_words parameter refers to a pickle file that contains stop words for a specific language, which is English in this case. There are also files for other languages, such as French and German. (You can see other parameters for the CountVectorizer() at https://scikit-learn.org/stable/modules/generated/sklearn.feature_extraction.text.CountVectorizer.html.) The vocabulary is fitted into another CountVectorizer, vec, which is used to perform the actual transformation on a test sentence using the transform() function. Here's the output from this example (you can safely ignore warning messages, if any).

```
['love', 'sam', 'swim', 'time']
[[1 0 1 0]]
```

The first output shows the stemmed words. Notice that the list contains only *swim*, not *swimming* or *swims*. All the stop words are missing as well. For example, you don't see the words *so, he, all, or the.*

The second output shows how many times each stemmed word appears in the test sentence. In this case, a *love* variant appears once, and a *swim* variant appears once as well. The words *sam* and *time* don't appear in the second sentence, so those values are set to 0.

Handling problems with raw text

While raw text files might seem straightforward, and even structured formats like HTML pages have their own parsing rules, both can present challenges, especially concerning character encoding. Character encoding is the method by which computers internally assign numbers to letters and symbols, enabling them to understand and display these characters. The multiple forms of encoding used for texts and web pages can present interpretation problems that you need to consider as you work through the text.

For example, the way the text is encoded can vary due to differences in operating systems, languages, and geographical regions. Be prepared to encounter a variety of different encodings as you retrieve data from the web or other repositories. Human language is complex, and the original ASCII encoding of unaccented English letters can't represent every alphabet. That's why so many encodings appeared with special characters. For example, a character can use either seven or eight bits for encoding purposes. The use of special characters can differ as well. In short, the interpretation of bits used to create characters differs from encoding to encoding. You can see a host of encodings at `www.i18nguy.com/unicode/codepages.html`.

When working with Python, it's highly recommended to handle text files using the Universal Transformation Format 8-bit (UTF-8) as the encoding for reading and writing files. Setting UTF-8 explicitly every time you load or save a text ensures consistent behavior across different environments and avoids potential errors. However, sometimes you need to work with encodings other than the default encoding set within the Python environment (and the list of possible encodings is really long: `https://docs.python.org/3/library/codecs.html#standard-encodings`).

TIP

If you already know the encoding you are working with, the best strategy is to specify it explicitly when reading your file.

The internal string representation in Python 3 is Unicode. When you read a file with a specified encoding (for instance, Latin-1) into Python, the strings are stored in memory as Unicode. When you write them out, you then select the output encoding, and Python will make the conversion of your data to the preferred encoding, which is commonly UTF-8. For instance, the pandas `read_csv()` function has an encoding parameter that lets you specify the encoding of your textual data. In addition, the method `to_csv()` attached to `DataFrames` has the same parameter that defaults to converting all the text in the output to UTF-8.

Resorting to neural network technology

Text processed as a bag of words (BoW) can be used with various machine learning models, commonly with regularized linear models like logistic regression (for classification) or linear regression (for regression tasks), as discussed in Chapter 12. However, understanding text is understanding sequences of words, and sequences are challenging to incorporate in a BoW (n-grams can provide some support). A new type of neural network, the recurrent neural network (RNN), offered a significant advancement in better understanding sequences because it processes new inputs while retaining information about past ones. The network takes in sequences of inputs, capturing and retaining information from each element of the sequence. In this way, the network can model complex relationships between the elements in the sequence, making it particularly suitable for handling textual inputs.

As we have previously seen in Chapter 14, if you feed an RNN a sequence of words, the network will learn that when it sees a word, preceded by certain other words, it can learn to predict the following words or understand the contextual meaning of words in the sequence, something that previous natural language processing techniques, such as the bag-of-words model, could not easily achieve. RNNs represented a significant step forward for sequence modeling. When researchers and practitioners experienced the considerable advantages of RNNs over the previous statistical approach of analyzing text as a bag of words, they began to adopt them en masse. As they tested more applications, they also discovered limitations that they attempted to overcome.

As initially devised, the RNN had limits. First of all, it often requires large amounts of data for effective training. In addition to this, due to unresolved problems such as the vanishing gradient problem (which we discussed in Chapter 12), it struggled to recall information from earlier in a sequence. Moreover, many researchers realized that the fact that an RNN can only process text one token at a time from start to end was a much more serious limitation than initially estimated. The look-back approach of an RNN can be a problem, as understanding often requires considering future context to interpret present and earlier words fully. Thus, to cope with the memory limitations of the RNN and the multiple relations between words in a phrase, researchers devised the long short-term memory (LSTM) and the gated recurrent unit (GRU) neural architectures, which can both remember and forget previous words. To better address the problem that an RNN cannot look forward in a phrase but only back, researchers developed bidirectional RNNs (including BiLSTMs and BiGRUs), which process text in both forward and backward directions, allowing each step to consider information from both past and future words in the text sequence.

RNNs, along with their LSTM and GRU variations, have dominated the field of natural language processing until recently, when a new approach, pioneered by Google researchers, known as the attention mechanism, emerged. This breakthrough technology is at the core of the current large language models such as ChatGPT and Google Gemini. An attention model processes text sequences in a different way, thanks to a mechanism called self-attention, which helps the model focus on the essential parts of the discourse, no matter where they're placed in a phrase. This contrasts with the unidirectionality of an RNN that can process the words of a phrase in only one direction, has limited memory, can't retrace if a word appearing later in the phrase modifies the initial meaning of the discourse, and generally, the sequential way of proceeding of an RNN in text proves to be a bottleneck.

Take, for instance, a phrase such as "The bird perched on the branch, and it sang a song that echoed through the forest." A RNN model progresses word by word, and it cannot refer back to words in the phrase or figure out whether the word *it* refers to the bird or the branch. An LSTM or GRU architecture could potentially resolve this, especially with bidirectional processing, but an approach based on the self-attention mechanism does it more directly and often more effectively by explicitly calculating relevance scores between *it* and all other words. The self-attention mechanism would highlight words such as *bird* and *sang* and correctly identify that *it* refers to the bird singing the song. This mechanism is indeed more effective in problems such as machine translation, text summarization, and sentiment analysis, and it is at the root of recent GenAI models, including OpenAI ChatGPT, Google Gemini, and Meta's Llama.

Employing self-attention models

Before explaining what makes the attention mechanism special in a neural network, we first need to clarify what tokenization and embeddings are. The idea is to convert words into numbers, but you start from phrases or entire texts represented as strings, not numbers. A tokenizer is a piece of code that performs the initial transformation, the tokenization, of your text into a format that a neural network can process.

Tokenizing means splitting the text into smaller chunks, called tokens, based on some predefined rules — for instance, based on spaces, punctuation, and special characters such as the newline character. The process isn't just getting the words out of the text. Most advanced tokenizers can handle numbers and emojis, and they're proficient in multiple languages at once, from Arabic to French and from Chinese to Indian Devanagari and beyond. Even with English, the more sophisticated tokenizers don't simply split words, but they distinguish between the meaningful sub-units of a word (known as subword tokenization).

Tokenization is also a standard procedure in NLP to split text into tokens (elements of a phrase or subwords). The tokenized text is then processed using statistical operations or machine learning. Once a tokenizer has split the text, it's not yet ready to be fed into a neural network — it has to be converted into numbers first. The best way to do this is to choose arbitrary integers mapping to the vocabulary derived from the text. Embedding layers further transform these numbers, mapping them to vectors of values in a meaningful way. For example, you can assign the names of various foods to vectors of values in such a way that the words that show fruits can have a similar score in a particular vector. In the same column, vegetables can score different values, but not too far from those of fruit. Finally, the names of meat dishes can be far removed in value from those of fruits and vegetables. The values are similar when the words are synonymous or refer to a similar concept. This is called semantic similarity, where the term semantic refers to the meaning of words.

This process of converting words into numerical representations is called *word embedding.* Embeddings aren't new; they have a long history. The concept of embeddings appeared in statistical multivariate analysis under the name of "multivariate correspondence analysis." In the 1970s, Jean-Paul Benzécri, a French statistician and linguist, along with colleagues from the French School of Data Analysis, developed a method for mapping a limited set of words into low-dimensional spaces, typically 2D representations, such as visual maps. This process turns words into meaningful numbers and projections. This discovery, which has led to numerous applications in linguistics and the social sciences, paved the way for recent advancements in language processing using deep learning.

REMEMBER

The word *embedding* refers to a mapping operation that transforms tokens into numeric vectors meaningful for a deep learning architecture. Using embeddings, a text can be converted into a multidimensional numeric matrix.

Initially, embeddings were standalone solutions. Popular word embeddings were Google's Word2Vec, Stanford's Global Vectors (GloVe), and Facebook's fastText, which were used to transform words into numeric vectors for RNNs. Then, a series of networks appeared, making modeling language problems even easier. One of the earliest and most influential models was the Google Bidirectional Encoder Representations from Transformers (BERT). Here's a link to the Google AI blog post describing the technique: `https://blog.google/products/search/search-language-understanding-bert`. Google's development of the Transformer architecture was fundamental for the GenAI revolution.

Like Word2Vec, GloVe, and fastText embeddings, these new transformer-based models were also pre-trained, meaning they were trained in a self-supervised fashion on massive amounts of text, such as books, text documents, and web pages scraped from the Internet. This enabled the models to gain a comprehensive understanding of language, including syntax rules and semantic relationships between words. Analogous to transfer learning with neural networks for image recognition, pre-training enabled language models to handle general tasks related to text understanding and be flexible enough to adapt to new tasks after further supervised training (a phase called *fine-tuning*) on limited amounts of labeled textual data suitable for specific problems.

The interesting aspect of BERT was that it produced even more useful embeddings because it could map words into numbers differently based on the other words that appear with it in the phrase. Even though embeddings were just numbers, such developments demonstrated how machines could take an approach similar to how humans understand the meaning of words based on their context. BERT managed to understand the context of a word because it employed the attention mechanism — that is, it could focus on the most essential parts of the sequence to understand the meaning of a phrase. In contrast to RNNs, the attention mechanism operates on the entire sequence of words at once and can be applied multiple times to capture all nuances in the text. (This is referred to as the attention mechanism being *multi-head*.) In BERT, as well as in a series of improved models that followed, such as Meta's RoBERTa, Google's DistilBERT and ALBERT, and Microsoft's DeBERTa, the attention mechanism is part of a more complex architecture called the *transformer architecture*. That's why you may hear all these models commonly referred to as transformers.

TIP

You can read an illustrated explanation of how transformers work from the Financial Times Visual Storytelling team at `https://ig.ft.com/generative-ai`.

Based on the same philosophy, the GPT neural network, developed by OpenAI, can achieve highly competitive results, particularly in text generation tasks. Even the first GPT models could answer questions, write and summarize essays, generate adventure games, translate languages, and even write computer code. Essentially, the recipe from the first GPT to the most recent GPT-5 remains the same: tokenization of a text and transformation of the tokens into a matrix of embeddings, followed by the data passing through multiple layers based on the attention mechanism (utilizing trillions of parameters). All this architecture is then trained for a long time and on massive amounts of text to predict the likelihood of the next word in a sequence of words. To give an example, if the neural network is exposed to many documents where the article "the" is followed by the word "world," it will associate a high probability with the word "world" after the article "the." A GPT model learns what a word should be, given the other words preceding it.

The next-word prediction mechanism in a GPT model, as well as in the other LLMs, is the key to explaining why they can chat with you and solve complex problems. Being trained on massive amounts of data with sophisticated training techniques, along with their incredible number of parameters and remarkable neural architecture, contributes to all such technology performing exceptionally well in determining the next word, given a starting text, which is referred to as the prompt. After the initial input, the LLMs then continue predicting the next word, after having appended the previously predicted words, and they continue to do so until a stopping criterion is met. Even if some researchers still debate the nature and extent of LLMs' reasoning abilities, at their core, LLMs are just sophisticated machines that can complete a phrase in the best way possible based on the text they have been trained on.

Using Scoring and Classification

The previous NLP discussions in this chapter discussed how a machine learning algorithm can read text using the BoW representation and how NLP can enhance its understanding of text through text length normalization, the TF-IDF model, and n-grams. We have also discussed how deep learning has revolutionized the NLP field through recurrent neural network architectures, such as LSTM and GRU, as well as the introduction of the self-attention mechanism and the transformer architecture. The following sections demonstrate how to solve a common problem in textual analysis: sentiment analysis, first using a built-from-scratch neural network based on embeddings trained on the fly and a few bidirectional LSTM layers. We will then solve the same problem using a pre-trained model based on the BERT architecture, modernBERT, demonstrating how to fine-tune a pre-trained language model for solving a specific text problem.

Analyzing reviews from e-commerce

Sentiment is challenging to detect because humans can use the same words to express even opposite sentiments. For example, in "Before making bread, dust off the work table and then dust the dough with flour," the word "dust" has two opposite meanings (words with opposite meanings are called contronyms). The sentiment conveyed depends on how thoughts are constructed within a phrase, not simply the individual words used. Even though dictionaries of positive and negative words do exist and are helpful, they aren't solely decisive because word context matters. Usually, you look up the words in a phrase, find their values in the dictionary, and sum them to get a sentiment score. You can use these dictionaries as a way to score your texts quickly, but in the end, you have to rely more on machine learning if you want to achieve good results.

TIP

It's a good idea to see how positive and negative word dictionaries work. The AFINN-111 dictionary contains 2,477 positive and negative words and phrases (`www2.imm.dtu.dk/pubdb/pubs/6010-full.html`). Another good choice is the larger *opinion lexicon* (a special dictionary designed for sentiment analysis containing opinion-based words; see `http://sentiment.christopherpotts.net/lexicons.html` for details) by Hu and Liu that appears at `www.cs.uic.edu/~liub/FBS/sentiment-analysis.html#lexicon`. Both dictionaries contain English words.

Using machine learning with labeled examples where phrases are associated with sentiments can yield more effective predictions. In this example, you create a deep learning model based on a dataset released by Stanford University, the Large Movie Review Dataset. The dataset (`https://ai.stanford.edu/~amaas/data/sentiment`) was presented in the 2011 paper "Learning Word Vectors for

Sentiment Analysis" (https://ai.stanford.edu/~amaas/papers/wvSent_acl2011.pdf). It collects 50,000 movie reviews from the Internet Movie Database (IMDb), an online database of information related to movies, TV programs, and video games. The dataset contains an even number of positive and negative reviews. Sixty percent of the reviews are for training purposes, and the remaining are for validation and testing purposes. You can directly download the dataset into memory by reading it from a GitHub repository containing the data in the CSV format:

```
import pandas as pd

repository = \
    "https://github.com/lmassaron/ml4dummies_3ed/"
release = "releases/download/v1.0/"
filename = repository + release + "imdb_50k.csv"
reviews = pd.read_csv(filename)
```

The target variable is a binary variable signaling whether the sentiment toward the film is favorable or not. The target is balanced because the number of positive cases equals the number of negative ones:

```
reviews.sentiment.value_counts()

          count
sentiment
1    25000
0    25000
```

Directly exploring the textual data is quite interesting. Taking a look, especially when the problem involves text, can offer valuable hints and insights. You can use this command to pick a random review from the data:

```
print(reviews.review.sample(1).values[0])
```

Depending on the example you picked, you may find phrases such as "Wasted two hours" or "It was so cool." Some are clearly ambiguous for a computer, such as "This movie was sick!" Although "sick" has a negative connotation (literally meaning "unwell"), the context makes the phrase sound positive because it refers to the slang usage of the word (meaning "excellent"). A machine learning algorithm can learn to decipher ambiguous phrases like these only after seeing many variants. The task can be much easier for a pre-trained model because it has examined large amounts of text before, focusing on learning general relationships between words.

The next step is to build the model by splitting the data into training, validation, and test sets. The code utilizes the `train_test_split` function available in Scikit-learn; it first divides the data into 60 percent for training and a residual 40 percent for further splitting. The remaining data is then split equally, with one part assigned for validation (to check the expected performance during training) and the other for testing (to evaluate the model's final performance). The entire procedure allows replication because of the fixed `random_state` value:

```
from sklearn.model_selection import train_test_split

train, temp = train_test_split(
    reviews, test_size=0.4, random_state=0)
valid, test = train_test_split(
    temp, test_size=0.5, random_state=0)

print(f"Train size: {len(train)}")
print(f"Validation size: {len(valid)}")
print(f"Test size: {len(test)}")
```

The data is divided into a training set of 30,000 examples and two sets of 10,000 examples each, for validation and testing purposes, respectively. The following steps will then create the neural network and train it on the available training dataset. For this purpose, we will be using the Keras 3 framework with a JAX backend, although TensorFlow and PyTorch backends are also excellent choices if you are running the code on a Google Colab notebook:

```
import os
os.environ["KERAS_BACKEND"] = "jax"
os.environ["HF_HUB_DISABLE_IMPLICIT_TOKEN"] = "1"
```

After splitting the data, the code applies most of the NLP techniques described in this chapter to transform the text. We can find all such transformations conveniently incorporated into Keras layers, such as `TextVectorization` (https://keras.io/api/layers/preprocessing_layers/text/text_vectorization), a preprocessing layer that maps text features to integer sequences. Using the `.adapt()` method from `TextVectorization`, the layer can analyze the provided text, determine the frequencies of the various tokens, and build a vocabulary that maps them. After the `TextVectorization` layer has built its vocabulary using the training set (via the `.adapt()` method), it can immediately be used to convert text into numeric sequences. The provided `vectorize_text_data` function applies this transformation. In doing so, it normalizes the texts by converting them to lowercase, removing punctuation, splitting the text into tokens based on whitespace, trimming the sequences that are too long, and padding those that are too short with a specific padding value. Thus, in the end, all the sequences will have the same number of elements. This process is called *padding*. The code applies the function to the training, validation, and test sets, and we obtain the transformed sequences and our target sentiment in return.

```
import keras

maxlen = 256
vocab_size_limit = 10000

text_vectorization = keras.layers.TextVectorization(
    max_tokens=vocab_size_limit,
    output_mode='int',
    output_sequence_length=maxlen,
    pad_to_max_tokens=True)

text_vectorization.adapt(train.review.values)

def vectorize_text_data(df, vectorizer):
    sequences = vectorizer(df.review.values)
    return sequences, df.sentiment.values

X, y = vectorize_text_data(train, text_vectorization)
Xv, yv = vectorize_text_data(valid, text_vectorization)
Xt, yt = vectorize_text_data(test, text_vectorization)
```

After converting the text into sequences of numeric codes of the same length for the training, validation, and test sets, the code sets a suitable deep learning architecture. This example uses an embedding layer that maps each integer token ID to a dense vector of `embedding_dim` features before feeding them to a couple of bi-directional LSTM layers. The network ends with a dropout to reduce overfitting, and with a final output neuron with sigmoid activation that will return the probability that our text has a positive sentiment:

```
keras.utils.set_random_seed(0)

model = keras.models.Sequential()
vocab_size = text_vectorization.vocabulary_size()
embedding_dim = 64

model.add(keras.layers.Input(shape=(maxlen,)))
model.add(keras.layers.Embedding(input_dim=vocab_size,
                                 output_dim=embedding_dim))
model.add(keras.layers.Bidirectional(
    keras.layers.LSTM(32, return_sequences=True)))
```

```
model.add(keras.layers.Bidirectional(
    keras.layers.LSTM(32, return_sequences=False)))
model.add(keras.layers.Dropout(0.25))
model.add(keras.layers.Dense(1, activation='sigmoid'))

model.compile(optimizer='adam',
              loss='binary_crossentropy',
              metrics=['accuracy'])
model.summary()
```

TIP

When instantiating a neural network, its layers are initially filled with random numbers (*random initialization*). Using the command `keras.utils.set_random_seed` before building the neural network will reproduce the same initialization every time we run the code.

The summary method, reproduced in Figure 17-1, describes, from top (input) to bottom (output), the layers, their characteristics, the dimensions of their output tensors, and the number of parameters employed.

Model: "sequential"

Layer (type)	Output Shape	Param #
embedding (Embedding)	(None, 256, 64)	640,000
bidirectional (Bidirectional)	(None, 256, 64)	24,832
bidirectional_1 (Bidirectional)	(None, 64)	24,832
dropout (Dropout)	(None, 64)	0
dense (Dense)	(None, 1)	65

Total params: 689,729 (2.63 MB)
Trainable params: 689,729 (2.63 MB)
Non-trainable params: 0 (0.00 B)

FIGURE 17-1:
Summary of the layers and total parameters.

Guided by the summary method, we can now visualize the neural network architecture that we have built, showing that as the sequence (which is always made of 256 numeric entries) entirely enters the network, it is first transformed by the embedding layer, which widens each element of the sequence, turning it into a vector of length 64. Hence, for a batch input of 8 texts, the resulting tensor after embedding will be 8 x 256 x 64. The tensor will then be processed twice by the first bi-directional LSTM layer, first starting from the first element of the sequence to the last, and then vice versa.

The first bidirectional LSTM layer processes the sequence, and since `return_sequences=True`, it outputs a value for each element in the sequence. These output values, which are called the *hidden states of the network,* are usually not taken into account, as you typically care only for the last one, the final output. The outputs from the forward and backward passes are concatenated, resulting in a tensor of shape (batch_size, 256, 64) since LSTM units are 32, 2*32 = 64. The second bidirectional LSTM layer processes this sequence of 64-dimensional vectors. Since `return_sequences=False`, it returns only the final output (concatenated from both directions), resulting in a tensor of shape (batch_size, 64). For a batch of 8, this would be 8 x 64.

A dropout is then applied to this tensor, randomly setting 25 percent of its input units to zero during training at each update step. Finally, the tensor is fed into the output dense layer with a single neuron and sigmoid activation. For each element of the batch, the result will be a value ranging from zero to one, which can be interpreted as a probability of the sentiment being positive.

By training the model for a couple of epochs and validating it using the validation set, you can obtain a validation accuracy of about 0.84:

```
history = model.fit(X, y, epochs=2, batch_size=8,
                    validation_data=(Xv, yv))
```

As a final step, the code tests the deep learning model on the test set using the `accuracy_score()` function offered by Scikit-learn. Because the model outputs a probability for the positive class, the code uses a 0.50 threshold to assign a prediction to the positive class or the negative one:

```
from sklearn.metrics import accuracy_score

predictions = (model.predict(Xt)>=0.5).astype(int)
test_accuracy = accuracy_score(yt, predictions)
print(f"Accuracy on test set: {test_accuracy}")
```

The evaluation of the test set confirms that the accuracy is about 0.84, as indicated by the validation set during the training.

Improving your analysis using a pre-trained model

The accuracy we obtained using a neural network we defined using Keras 3, based on a couple of stacked LSTM bi-directional recurrent layers, was a good result. However, the neural network learned to accomplish the task from scratch using the available training data, without any prior knowledge of language and contextual understanding of how reviews work. A host of pre-trained language models have an advantage in this sense because they have been pre-trained on numerous previous text documents. Hence, they can leverage a basic understanding of how language works, and they need to be taught just the necessary additional information to accomplish the specific required task (a further training procedure called fine-tuning). It is the principle that standing on the shoulders of giants (large amounts of text) should allow you to see farther and reach higher heights.

Among the pre-trained models based on the transformer architecture, the encoder models are the best kind of models for tasks such as sentiment classification because they can grasp the structure of the text all at once. Decoder models excel at generating language, but they may prove limited in their understanding of complex phrases because they tend to analyze the text progressively, capable of looking behind their reading point, rather than ahead.

Among the transformer-based encoder models, we decided to resort to a very recent model, modernBERT (research paper: `https://arxiv.org/pdf/2412.13663`; code repository: `https://github.com/AnswerDotAI/ModernBERT`). The model builds upon the legacy of BERT, the initial model from Google that initiated the transformer revolution. This new version of BERT, however, has been trained on a massive amount of 2 trillion tokens of English Web documents, code, and scientific literature, and it utilizes many new architectural innovations that have emerged over the years and were not available in 2018, the year BERT was launched. Thanks to these innovations, the model is significantly more performant and memory-efficient. ModernBERT is the result of a collaboration involving Benjamin Warner, Antoine Chaffin, Benjamin Clavié, affiliated with Answer. AI, and additional contributors from LightOn, Johns Hopkins University, NVIDIA, and Hugging Face.

In the following code snippet, we define the model we will use from the Hugging Face repository, ensure the correct tokenizer is loaded, and then proceed to tokenize all the data to be processed by our model. For all these steps and the following, you will need an Internet connection and wait to receive all the necessary data from the Hugging Face repositories.

Hugging Face is a French company and an open-source community that provides tools and platforms for machine learning, mainly focused on natural language processing, but not exclusively, because recently they have also been involved in image recognition and robotics. One of their major contributions is the `transformers` package, which makes it incredibly easy to download, use, and share pre-trained state-of-the-art models (like the ModernBERT model we are using in our example). The Hugging Face `transformers` package also offers straightforward procedures for fine-tuning pre-trained models, making it easy and accessible to perform a transformative operation on an existing neural network (to train it further for a specific task) that would have otherwise been quite complicated.

```
from datasets import Dataset
from transformers import AutoTokenizer


model_name = "answerdotai/ModernBERT-base"


tokenizer = AutoTokenizer.from_pretrained(model_name)

def tokenize_function(examples):
    return tokenizer(examples["text"],
                     padding="max_length",
                     truncation=True,
                     max_length=256)

def tokenize_dataset(data):
  data_dict = {'text': data['review'].values,
               'labels': data['sentiment'].values}
  dataset = Dataset.from_dict(data_dict)
  return dataset.map(tokenize_function, batched=True)

tokenized_train_dataset = tokenize_dataset(train)
tokenized_valid_dataset = tokenize_dataset(valid)
tokenized_test_dataset = tokenize_dataset(test)
```

In the previous code, the `tokenize_dataset` function transforms the data in two ways: first, it converts the data into the `Dataset` format from Hugging Face, and then it maps the text data in it into tokens suitable for modernBERT. The next step involves loading the model moderBERT from the Hugging Face repository and specifying that our task is a classification task with just two labels: positive and negative sentiments. Everything is then done automatically by the `AutoModel ForSequenceClassification` function from the `transformers` package.

```
from transformers import (
    AutoModelForSequenceClassification as AutoModel)

model = AutoModel.from_pretrained(model_name,
                                  num_labels=2)
```

The `model` variable now contains our model, and we can print its structure by a simple `print(model)` command. We can also estimate the number of parameters (neurons and biases) that it contains by iterating through its layers and counting the trainable elements in them. The count returns a whopping 149,606,402 parameters for the modernBERT model, and that should suffice to hint at its complexity compared to our previous model, built from scratch, that accounted for 689,729 parameters, a considerable number but just a small fraction of the present model.

Once the model has been uploaded into memory and prepared for the classification task, we can proceed to fine-tune it. This is done by the `Trainer` function, instructed by a series of parameters defined using the `TrainingArguments` function. In particular, we can define the number of epochs to train, the batch size to use (the number of examples sent to the training procedure at once), the learning rate, and the weight decay (to slow down the learning process as we progress). The method `.train()` starts the training based on these parameters, and we just have to wait for it to complete. Please note that, depending on the GPU type you are running on Google Colab, you may get some warnings when the training starts. You can safely ignore such warnings, as they are related to performance, but they do not hinder the process or its results.

```
from transformers import TrainingArguments, Trainer

training_args = TrainingArguments(
    output_dir="./results",
    num_train_epochs=1,
    per_device_train_batch_size=8,
    per_device_eval_batch_size=8,
    learning_rate=2e-5,
    weight_decay=0.01,
    report_to="none",
    eval_strategy="steps")

trainer = Trainer(
    model=model,
    args=training_args,
    train_dataset=tokenized_train_dataset,
    eval_dataset=tokenized_valid_dataset)

train_result = trainer.train()
```

After the training is completed, we can read the training loss at different steps. Of course, the training loss will indicate that the model, which is massive, fits the training data in an increasingly better manner. However, what we care about is that our training resulted in a model that can generalize to our problem. The validation loss, while fluctuating during training, generally tended to decrease. The definitive word is returned by checking the accuracy on our test set:

```
import numpy as np
from sklearn.metrics import accuracy_score

predictions = trainer.predict(tokenized_test_dataset)
predicted_labels = np.argmax(predictions.predictions,
                             axis=1)
test_accuracy = accuracy_score(test['sentiment'].values,
                               predicted_labels)
print(f"Accuracy on test set: {test_accuracy}")
```

The accuracy results in approximately 0.94, representing a notable improvement over our previous 0.84 result. As previously noted, pre-trained models have a strong advantage in many tasks, albeit at a complexity and time cost, because they are much larger. Consequently, they require more powerful computers to run and take more time for inference. It is up to you to consider whether, for your specific use of the model, you can trade off accuracy against model size.

Chapter **18**

Recommending Products and Movies

O ne of the oldest and most common sales techniques is to recommend a product or service to a customer based on what you know about their needs and wants. If people buy one product, they might buy another associated product if given a good reason to do so. They may not have even considered the need for the second product until the salesperson recommends it, yet they do need it to use the primary product. For this reason, most people prefer to get recommendations. Given that web pages now serve as salespeople in many cases, recommender systems are a necessary part of any serious sales effort on the web. This chapter helps you better understand the significance of the recommender revolution in various settings.

Recommender systems serve all sorts of other needs. For example, you might see an interesting movie title, read the synopsis, and still not know whether you're likely to find it a good movie. Watching the trailer might prove equally fruitless. Only after you see reviews provided by others do you feel that you have enough information to make an informed decision. You also find methods for obtaining and using rating data in this chapter.

Gathering, organizing, and ranking such information is hard, though, and information overload is the bane of the Internet. A recommender system can perform all the required work for you in the background, making the work of getting to a decision a lot easier. You may not even realize that search engines are, in fact, huge recommender systems. The Google search engine, for instance, can provide personalized search results based on your previous search history.

This chapter also considers the role of behaviors in performing machine learning tasks. By understanding behaviors, it becomes possible to consider how behaviors should affect the outcome of an analysis. Behavioral data is a crucial component of machine learning today. To illustrate how to effectively utilize behavioral data, this chapter also explores the integration of behavioral data with text.

Recommender systems do more than make recommendations. After reading images and texts, machine learning algorithms can infer a person's personality, preferences, and needs and act accordingly. This chapter helps you understand how all these activities take place by exploring techniques such as singular value decomposition (SVD).

REMEMBER

You don't have to type the source code for this chapter manually. In fact, using the downloadable source code is a lot easier. You can find the source code for this chapter in the ML4D3E folder of the downloadable code file. The example files for this chapter will begin with ML4D3E-18-. See the Introduction for details on how to find these source files.

Realizing the Revolution of E-Commerce

A recommender system can suggest items or actions of interest to a user after learning the user's preferences over time. The technology, which is based on data and machine learning techniques (both supervised and unsupervised), has been available on the Internet for approximately two decades. Today, you can find recommender systems almost everywhere, and they're likely to play an even larger role in the future under the guise of personal assistants powered by chatbots such as ChatGPT.

The drivers for users and companies to adopt recommender systems are different but complementary. Users have a strong motivation to reduce the complexity of the modern world (regardless of whether the issue is finding the right product or a place to eat) and avoid information overload. Companies, on the other hand, find that recommender systems provide a practical way to communicate in a personalized way with their customers and successfully push sales.

REMEMBER

As companies have invested more effort in understanding how recommender systems work, they have come to realize that a combination of product attributes and review ratings has a significant impact on the effectiveness of a recommender system.

There is a correlation between product type and the effectiveness of a recommender:

>> The effect is greater on utilitarian products (such as a hammer) than hedonic products (such as perfume).

>> The effect is greater on products that can only be judged based on use (such as movies) and less on products that are easily judged by seeing a picture or reading a description (such as a poster or a t-shirt where the fit and feel aren't paramount and visual is key).

In addition, the effectiveness of a recommender is complemented by the user reviews. This type of recommender works with user reviews that a product receives, which is why you often receive several invitations to review a product after making a purchase. The star rating and terms used in the written part of the review help change the recommender's behavior to encourage others to make a purchase more effectively.

Recommender systems originated as a means to manage information overload. The Xerox Palo Alto Research Center built the first recommender in 1992. Named Tapestry, it handled the increasing number of emails received by the center researchers. The idea of collaborative filtering was born (learned from users by leveraging similarities in preferences), and the GroupLens project soon extended it to news selection and movie recommendations (the MovieLens project, whose data you use in this chapter).

When major players in the e-commerce sector, such as Amazon, began adopting recommender systems, the idea went mainstream and spread widely across e-commerce. Netflix did the rest by promoting recommenders as a business tool and sponsoring a competition to improve its recommender system (`www.thrillist.com/entertainment/nation/the-netflix-prize`), which involved various teams for quite a long time. The result is an innovative recommender technology that utilizes singular value decomposition (SVD) and Restricted Boltzmann Machines (a now less popular method for unsupervised learning).

However, recommender systems aren't limited to promoting products. Since 2002, a new type of Internet service has emerged: social networks, including YouTube, Instagram, WhatsApp, TikTok, Facebook, and LinkedIn. These services facilitate link exchanges between users and share information, including posts, pictures, and videos. In addition, search engines such as Google amassed user response information to offer more personalized services and better match users' desires when responding to users' queries (https://backlinko.com/google-rankbrain-seo).

Recommendations have become so pervasive in guiding people's daily lives that experts now worry about their impact on our ability to make independent decisions and perceive the world in freedom. You can read about this concern in the article at https://edu.gcfglobal.org/en/digital-media-literacy/how-filter-bubbles-isolate-you/1. The history of recommender systems is one of machines striving to learn about our minds and hearts, making our lives easier, and promoting the businesses of their creators. However, like any other technology, there are unexpected secondary effects and rogue uses.

Downloading Rating Data

Getting good rating data can be complex. Later in this chapter, you use the MovieLens dataset to see how SVD can help you create movie recommendations. However, you have other databases at your disposal. The following sections describe the MovieLens dataset and the data logs contained in MSWeb — both of which work pretty well when experimenting with recommender systems.

Trudging through the MovieLens dataset

The MovieLens site (https://movielens.org) is all about helping you find a movie you might like. After all, with millions of movies out there, finding something new and interesting could take time that you don't want to spend. The setup works by asking you to input ratings for movies that you already know about. The MovieLens site then makes recommendations for you based on your ratings. In short, your ratings teach an algorithm what to look for, and then the site applies this algorithm to the entire dataset.

You can obtain the MovieLens dataset used in this section at http://files.grouplens.org/datasets/movielens/ml-1m.zip. The interesting thing about this site is that you can download all or part of the dataset based on your interaction needs. You can find downloads in the following sizes:

>> 100,000 ratings from 1,000 users on 1,700 movies

>> 1 million ratings from 6,000 users on 4,000 movies

>> 10 million ratings and 100,000 tag applications applied to 10,000 movies by 72,000 users

>> 20 million ratings and 465,000 tag applications applied to 27,000 movies by 138,000 users

>> MovieLens's latest dataset in small or full sizes (at this writing, the full size contained 21,000,000 ratings and 470,000 tag applications applied to 27,000 movies by 230,000 users)

This dataset presents you with an opportunity to work with user-generated data using both supervised and unsupervised techniques. Large datasets present special challenges that only big data can effectively address. You can find some starter information for working with supervised and unsupervised methods in Chapter 8. The first step is to obtain the dataset. In Google Colab, you can run this command in the first cell to easily get the files you need:

```
URL = "http://files.grouplens.org/datasets/"
URL += "movielens/ml-1m.zip"
!wget {URL}
!unzip ml-1m.zip
```

The wget command will download the zipped file, and the unzip command will unpack all the datasets in the ml-1m folder, which are three .dat files: movies.dat, ratings.dat, and users.dat. To work with the MovieLens dataset as a whole, you must combine these three files into a single pandas DataFrame, like this:

```
import pandas as pd

users_column_names = [
    "user_id", "gender", "age",
    "occupation", "zip"]
users = pd.read_table(
    "ml-1m/users.dat",
    sep="::",
    header=None,
    names=users_column_names,
    engine="python")
ratings_column_names = [
    "user_id", "movie_id", "rating",
    "timestamp"]
ratings = pd.read_table(
    "ml-1m/ratings.dat",
    sep="::",
    header=None,
```

```
    names=ratings_column_names,
    engine="python")

movies_column_names = [
    "movie_id", "title", "genres"]
movies = pd.read_table(
    "ml-1m/movies.dat",
    sep="::",
    header=None,
    names=movies_column_names,
    engine="python",
    encoding="latin-1")

movie_lens = (ratings
    .merge(users, on="user_id")
    .merge(movies, on="movie_id"))
```

To see the resulting number of reviews, you use `print(movie_lens.head())`. Figure 18-1 shows what you can expect to see.

```
   user_id  movie_id  rating  timestamp gender  age  occupation    zip  \
0        1      1193       5  978300760      F    1          10  48067
1        1       661       3  978302109      F    1          10  48067
2        1       914       3  978301968      F    1          10  48067
3        1      3408       4  978300275      F    1          10  48067
4        1      2355       5  978824291      F    1          10  48067
```

FIGURE 18-1:
The output shows
some sample
cases and the
features from
the dataset.

```
                                         title                          genres
0        One Flew Over the Cuckoo's Nest (1975)                           Drama
1            James and the Giant Peach (1996)  Animation|Children's|Musical
2                        My Fair Lady (1964)                Musical|Romance
3                    Erin Brockovich (2000)                           Drama
4                      Bug's Life, A (1998)  Animation|Children's|Comedy
```

Now that you have a single dataset to use, you might want to figure out how people voted. In this case, you perform a count of the ratings, like this:

```
rating_counts = (movie_lens
    .groupby("rating")["user_id"]
    .count())
print(rating_counts)
```

The output shows that the ratings aren't spread equally; people are more likely to provide a rating of 3, 4, or 5:

```
rating
1       56174
2      107557
3      261197
4      348971
5      226310
```

A disparity in the number of ratings for each level often happens with rating data: It has some imbalance in favor of positive data because users tend to buy or watch what they believe they will like. Disappointment mostly motivates negative ratings because expectations aren't satisfied. You can also use the following code to report how many films each user has rated on average and how many users have rated each film:

```
reviews_per_user = (movie_lens
    .groupby("user_id")["title"]
    .count())

print("Average movie reviews per user:", end=" ")
print(f"{reviews_per_user.mean():.1f}")

reviews_per_movie = (movie_lens
    .groupby("title")["movie_id"]
    .count())

print("\nNumber of Reviews Per Movie:")
print(reviews_per_movie)
```

The results shown in Figure 18-2 tell you that each user reviewed 165.6 movies on average. Some movies, such as *eXistenZ* (1999), have quite a few reviews, while other movies, such as *Zero Kelvin* (*Kjærlighetens kjøtere*) (1995), have almost none. Knowing these details helps you understand whether the results you obtain from specific queries are statistically valid.

It is also quite easy to go into deeper details and discover how users rank a particular film.

```
selected_movie = movie_lens[
    movie_lens["movie_id"] == 260]

num_ratings_for_movie = len(selected_movie)
average_rating_for_movie = (
    selected_movie["rating"].mean())
```

```
print(
    f"{num_ratings_for_movie} users gave an "
    f"average rating of {average_rating_for_movie:.2f}")
```

```
Average movie reviews per user: 165.6

Number of Reviews Per Movie:
title
$1,000,000 Duck (1971)                                    37
'Night Mother (1986)                                      70
'Til There Was You (1997)                                 52
'burbs, The (1989)                                       303
...And Justice for All (1979)                            199
                                                         ...
Zed & Two Noughts, A (1985)                               29
Zero Effect (1998)                                       301
Zero Kelvin (Kjærlighetens kjøtere) (1995)                 2
Zeus and Roxanne (1997)                                   23
eXistenZ (1999)                                          410
Name: movie_id, Length: 3706, dtype: int64
```

FIGURE 18-2:
You can obtain a
wealth of
statistics about
the movies.

In this example, 2,991 users have rated movie number 260, the original *Star Wars* from 1977, which scored an average rating of 4.45.

Encountering the limits of rating data

For recommender systems to work well, they need to know about you as well as other people, both those who are like you and those who are different from you. Acquiring rating data allows a recommender system to learn from the experiences of multiple customers. Rating data could derive from a judgment (such as rating a product using stars or numbers) or a fact (a binary 1/0 that states that you bought the product, saw a movie, or stopped browsing at a specific web page).

REMEMBER

No matter the data source or type, rating data is always about behaviors. To rate a movie, you have to decide to see it, watch it, and then rate it based on your experience of seeing the movie. Actual recommender systems learn from rating data in different ways:

>> **Collaborative filtering:** Matches raters based on movie or product similarities used in the past. You can get recommendations based on items liked by people similar to you or on items similar to those you like.

>> **Content-based filtering:** Goes beyond the fact that you watched a movie. It examines the features relative to you and the movie to determine whether a match exists based on the larger categories that the features represent.

For instance, if you are a female who likes action movies, the recommender will look for suggestions that include the intersection of these two categories.

>> **Knowledge-based recommendations:** Based on metadata, such as preferences expressed by users and product descriptions. It relies on machine learning and is effective when you do not have enough behavioral data to determine user or product characteristics. This is called a *cold start* and represents one of the most difficult recommender tasks because you don't have access to either collaborative filtering or content-based filtering.

The example that follows demonstrates collaborative filtering. It locates the movies that are the most similar to *Young Frankenstein*.

Considering collaborative filtering

When using collaborative filtering, you need to calculate similarity. See Chapter 11 for a discussion of the use of similarity measures. Apart from Euclidean, Manhattan, and Chebyshev distances, the remainder of this section discusses cosine similarity. *Cosine similarity* measures the angular cosine distance between two vectors, which may seem like a difficult concept to grasp, but it is just a way to measure angles in data spaces.

The idea behind the cosine distance is to use the angle created by the two points connected to the space origin (the point where all dimensions are zero) instead. If the points are near, the angle is narrow, no matter how many dimensions there are. If they are far away, the angle is quite large. Cosine similarity results in a score between –1 and +1, where **+1** means the vectors point in the same direction (very similar), 0 means they are orthogonal (no similarity), and –1 means they point in opposite directions (strong dissimilarity). Cosine distance is then defined as 1 cosine similarity, which gives it a range from 0 (for identical vectors) to +2 (for opposite vectors). Cosine similarity is effective in determining whether a user is similar to another or whether a film can be associated with another, as users who tend to favor the same content often share similar preferences.

Massaging the data

The current MovieLens dataset is vast and cumbersome, yet it is not yet ready for analysis. Massaging the data is an essential part of performing data science tasks because you may not have good data. This section explores methods for refining the MovieLens dataset to achieve optimal results.

As a first step, you can reduce the memory requirements for working with the data by removing items that are not relevant to the analysis. For this analysis, you can safely drop these columns: movie_id, timestamp, genres, gender, age, occupation, and zip. In addition, a person would need to think enough of a movie to give it at least three out of five stars. Consequently, you can also get rid of the lesser value reviews using the following code:

```
reduced_movie_data = movie_lens[
    movie_lens["rating"] >= 3.0]

columns_to_drop = [
    'movie_id', 'timestamp', 'genres', 'gender',
    'age', 'occupation', 'zip']
reduced_movie_data = reduced_movie_data.drop(
    columns=columns_to_drop)

print(reduced_movie_data.head(), "\n")

original_shape = movie_lens.shape
new_shape = reduced_movie_data.shape

print(
    f"Original Shape: {original_shape}, "
    f"New Shape: {new_shape}")
```

The reduction primarily removes movies with very few ratings or those that received predominantly low ratings. The aim is to focus our analysis on more frequently rated and generally well-received films, which should lead to clearer patterns. The size of the `reduced_movie` dataset is significantly smaller than the original `movie_data` dataset, as shown here:

```
   user_id rating                            title
0        1      5  One Flew Over the Cuckoo's Nest (1975)
1        1      3        James and the Giant Peach (1996)
2        1      3                      My Fair Lady (1964)
3        1      4                 Erin Brockovich (2000)
4        1      5                   Bug's Life, A (1998)

Original Shape: (1000209, 10), New Shape: (836478, 3)
```

The number of reviews also reflects the popularity of a movie. When a movie has few reviews, it might reflect a *cult following* — a group of devotees who don't reflect the opinion of the public at large. You can remove movies with only a few reviews by using the following code:

```
title_total_ratings = (
    reduced_movie_data
```

```
        .groupby('title')['rating']
        .transform('size'))
is_frequently_rated = (
    title_total_ratings > 1000)
reduced_movie_data = reduced_movie_data[
    is_frequently_rated]

print(
    reduced_movie_data
    .groupby('title')['rating']
    .count()
    .sort_values()
    .head(), "\n")

new_shape = reduced_movie_data.shape
print(f"New shape: {new_shape}")
```

The call to transform() selects only movies that have a certain number of reviews, more than 1,000 of them in this case. You can use transform() in a vast number of ways based solely on the function you provide as input, which is the built-in size function in this case. Here is the result of this particular bit of trimming:

```
title
Few Good Men, A (1992)    1003
My Cousin Vinny (1992)    1003
Boogie Nights (1997)      1004
Witness (1985)            1009
Sneakers (1992)           1009
Name: rating, dtype: int64

New shape:  (237212, 3)
```

REMEMBER

The way you shape your data will affect the output of any analysis you perform. You may not get the desired results the first time, so you may end up spending a lot of time trying different shaping methods. The point is to keep trying to shape the data in various ways until you obtain a good result.

Performing collaborative filtering

Making recommendations depends on finding the right kind of information on which to make a comparison. Of course, this is where the art of machine learning comes into play. If making a recommendation only involved performing analysis on data in a particular manner using a specific algorithm, anyone could do it. The art is in choosing the correct data to analyze. In this section, you use a combination of the user ID and the ratings assigned by those users to a particular movie as the means to perform collaborative filtering. In other words, you're assuming that people who have similar tastes in film will rate those movies at a particular level.

After you've shaped your data, you can use it to create a pivot table. (In case you haven't used pivot tables before in products like Excel, you can read about the pandas-specific version used with Python at https://pandas.pydata.org/pandas-docs/stable/reference/api/pandas.DataFrame.pivot.html.) The pivot table will compare user IDs with the reviews that the user has created for particular movies. Here is the code used to make the pivot table:

```
user_rating_pivot = pd.pivot_table(
    reduced_movie_data,
    index='user_id',
    columns='title',
    values='rating',)

print(user_rating_pivot.head())
```

The results might look a little odd because the pivot table will be a sparse matrix, like the sample shown here:

```
title    Untouchables, The  Usual Suspects, The  \
user_id
1                      NaN                  NaN
2                      4.0                  NaN
3                      NaN                  NaN
4                      NaN                  NaN
5                      NaN                  5.0
```

In this case, you see that *The Untouchables* is rated by user 2 and *The Usual Suspects* is rated by user 5. The point is that the rows contain individual user reviews, and the columns are the names of movies they reviewed.

The next step in the process is to obtain a list of reviews for the target movie, *Young Frankenstein.* The following code creates a list of reviewers:

```
target_movie_title = 'Young Frankenstein (1974)'
yf_ratings = user_rating_pivot[target_movie_title]

print(yf_ratings.dropna().head())
```

The output of this part of the code shows that *Young Frankenstein* is popular, so it'll work for the example:

```
user_id
10    5.0
11    3.0
19    5.0
28    5.0
33    3.0
Name: Young Frankenstein (1974), dtype: float64
```

Now that you have sample data to use, you can correlate it with the pivot table as a whole. The following code outputs the movies that most closely match *Young Frankenstein* in appeal by the users who liked *Young Frankenstein*:

```
yf_correlations = user_rating_pivot.corrwith(
    yf_ratings)

print(
    yf_correlations.sort_values(
        ascending=False).head())
```

The output shows that you can derive some interesting results using collaborative filtering techniques:

```
title
Young Frankenstein (1974)                     1.000000
Blazing Saddles (1974)                        0.412395
Alien (1979)                                  0.297567
Willy Wonka and the Chocolate Factory (1971)  0.272574
M*A*S*H (1970)                                0.259304
dtype: float64
```

Even though the correlation results seem a little low (with 1.000000 being the most desirable), the names of most of the movies selected make sense. For example, *Willy Wonka and the Chocolate Factory* (the 1971 version), *Blazing Saddles*, and *Young Frankenstein* all starred Gene Wilder.

Leveraging SVD

A property of SVD is that it compresses the original data to such a level and in such a clever way that, in certain situations, the technique can create new meaningful and useful features, not just compressed variables. The following sections help you understand how SVD works and what role SVD plays in recommender systems.

Explaining the basics of SVD

Factorization is the process of breaking an object apart until you can't break it down further in a mathematical sense. For example, when working with a scalar, such as 18, you can break it down into the product of prime numbers 2 * 3 * 3. You can decompose a matrix as well, breaking it into smaller pieces that describe the matrix using its constituent elements. There are several ways to decompose a matrix, and SVD is one of them. The most significant advantage of using SVD is that every matrix has an SVD, which often makes it more stable than other methods, such as eigendecomposition. Because of this stability, you frequently see it used for the following:

» Compressing

» Denoising

» Data reduction

» Least-squares linear regression

» Image compression

The goal of SVD is to reduce the matrix to its constituent parts so that subsequent matrix calculations are simpler. In viewing SVD, you see the following equation:

$$A = U * \Sigma * VT$$

In this equation:

» A: An m by n matrix that you want to decompose

» U: An m by m matrix

» Σ: An m by n diagonal matrix

» VT: A transpose of an n by n matrix

The diagonal values of Σ are the singular values of the original matrix A. The columns of U are the left-singular values of A, and the rows of VT are the right-singular values of A. Essentially, when you multiply these three matrices together, you end up with the original matrix A. However, you can use the decomposed parts to understand matrix A better. Here's some code that shows how SVD works:

```
import numpy as np
from scipy.linalg import svd

original_matrix = np.array([
```

```
    [1, 2, 3],
    [4, 5, 6],
    [7, 8, 9],
])
print("Original Matrix:")
print(original_matrix)

u_matrix, singular_values, vt_matrix = svd(
    original_matrix)

print("\nU matrix:")
print(u_matrix)
print("\nSingular values (s vector):")
print(singular_values)
print("\nVT matrix (V transposed):")
print(vt_matrix)

sigma_matrix = np.diag(singular_values)
print("\nSigma matrix (for reconstruction):")
print(sigma_matrix)

reconstructed_matrix = (
    u_matrix @ sigma_matrix @ vt_matrix)
print("\nReconstructed matrix:")
print(reconstructed_matrix)
```

This code shows what you need to do to deconstruct the matrix and then reconstruct it when working with a square matrix (3 x 3, in this case). Notice that you
must create a diagonal matrix, Sigma, to obtain the correct dot product multiplication to reconstruct the matrix A later. However, you might not have a square
matrix, which means that you must specify the size of Sigma, like this:

```
sigma_matrix = np.zeros(
    (original_matrix.shape[0],
     original_matrix.shape[1]))

num_columns = original_matrix.shape[1]
singular_values_diag = np.diag(singular_values)

sigma_matrix[:num_columns, :num_columns] = (
    singular_values_diag)

print(sigma_matrix)
```

When you run this code, you see the deconstruction of the matrix A and its recon-
struction as matrix B, as shown in the output:

```
Original Matrix:
[[1 2 3]
 [4 5 6]
 [7 8 9]]

U matrix:
[[-0.21483724  0.88723069  0.40824829]
 [-0.52058739  0.24964395 -0.81649658]
 [-0.82633754 -0.38794278  0.40824829]]

Singular values (s vector):
[1.68481034e+01 1.06836951e+00 1.47280825e-16]

VT matrix (V transposed):
[[-0.47967118 -0.57236779 -0.66506441]
 [-0.77669099 -0.07568647  0.62531805]
 [ 0.40824829 -0.81649658  0.40824829]]

Sigma matrix (for reconstruction):
[[1.68481034e+01 0.00000000e+00 0.00000000e+00]
 [0.00000000e+00 1.06836951e+00 0.00000000e+00]
 [0.00000000e+00 0.00000000e+00 1.47280825e-16]]

Reconstructed matrix:
[[1. 2. 3.]
 [4. 5. 6.]
 [7. 8. 9.]]
```

Ideally, in machine learning, you can get the best results when your features don't
entirely correlate with each other and each one has some predictive power with
respect to the response you're modeling. In reality, your features often do correlate with each other, displaying a high degree of redundancy in the information
available to the dataset.

Having redundant data means that the same information is spread across multiple
features. If it's precisely the same information, it represents a perfect collinearity.
If, instead, it's not exactly the same information but varies in some way, you
have collinearity between two features or multicollinearity between more than
two features.

Redundant data is a problem that statistical theory created solutions to address long ago (because statistical computations can suffer a lot from multicollinearity). This chapter presents the topic from a statistical perspective using the concepts of variance, covariance, and correlation. You can imagine each feature as bearing different informative components, mixed in different proportions:

>> **Unique variance:** The share of information that's unique to a particular feature, and when correlated or associated with the response, it can add a direct contribution to the prediction of the response itself.

>> **Shared variance:** The share of information that is common with other features. Such communality could be because of a causal relationship between them (variance and its applicability are discussed in Chapter 7). In this case, if the shared information is relevant to the response, the learning algorithm will have a difficult time choosing which feature to pick up. And when a feature is picked up for its shared variance, it also brings along its specific random noise.

>> **Random noise component:** Information that is caused by measurement problems or randomness and doesn't help map the response, but that sometimes, by mere chance (yes, luck or misfortune is part of being random), can appear related to the reaction itself.

Unique variance, shared variance, and random noise fuse together and can't be separated easily. Using feature selection, you reduce the impact of noise by selecting the minimum set of features that work best with your machine learning algorithm. Another possible approach is based on the idea that you can fuse that redundant information together using a weighted average, thus creating a new feature whose main component is the shared variance of multiple features, and its noise is an average of the previous noise and unique variance.

For instance, if A, B, and C share the same variance, by employing compression, you can obtain a component (which is viewed as a new feature) made up of the weighted summation of the three features, such as 0.5 * A + 0.3 * B + 0.2 * C. You decide the weights based on a particular technique using SVD, called *principal component analysis* (PCA), which is discussed in Chapter 11.

SVD has various applications, not just in compressing data but also in finding latent factors (hidden features in your data) and in recommender systems, which are systems for discovering what someone might like in terms of products or films based on previous selections.

Understanding the SVD connection

If your data contains hints and clues about a hidden cause or motif, an SVD can put them together and offer you proper answers and insights. That is especially true when your data is made up of interesting pieces of information like the ones in the following list:

>> **Text in documents hints at ideas and meaningful categories:** Just as you can make up your mind about discussion topics by reading blogs and newsgroups, so can SVD help you deduce a meaningful classification of groups of documents or the specific topics being written about in each of them.

>> **Reviews of specific movies or books hint at your personal preferences and larger product categories:** If you say on a rating site that you loved the original *Star Trek* series, the algorithm can easily determine what you like in terms of other films, consumer products, or even personality types.

An example of a method based on SVD is latent semantic indexing (LSI), which has been successfully used to associate documents and words based on the idea that words, though different, tend to have the same meaning when placed in similar contexts. This type of analysis suggests not only synonymous words but also higher grouping concepts. For example, an LSI analysis on some sample sports news may group baseball teams of the Major League based solely on the co-occurrence of team names in similar articles, without any previous knowledge of what a baseball team or the Major League is.

Other interesting applications for data reduction include systems that generate recommendations about things you may like to buy or learn more about. You likely have several opportunities to see recommenders in action. On most e-commerce websites, after logging in, visiting some product pages, and rating or putting a product into your electronic basket, you see other buying opportunities based on different customers' previous experiences. (As mentioned previously, this method is called *collaborative filtering.*) SVD can implement collaborative filtering in a more robust manner, relying not only on information from individual products but also on the broader context of a product within a set. For example, collaborative filtering can determine not only that you liked the film *Raiders of the Lost Ark* but also that you generally like all action and adventure movies.

Seeing SVD in action

The "Performing collaborative filtering" section, earlier in this chapter, shows one technique for making movie recommendations from the MovieLens dataset. This section shows how to use SVD to perform the same task. You can implement collaborative recommendations based on simple means or frequencies calculated from other customers' sets of purchased items, or on ratings using SVD. This approach helps you reliably generate recommendations, even for products the vendor seldom sells or that are relatively new to users. For this example, you use a well-known database created by the MovieLens website, which collects ratings from users of movies they liked or disliked. This example relies on the same MovieLens dataframe you created earlier and begins by building a movie index on it using the following code:

```
ratings_pivot_df = movie_lens.pivot_table(
    values='rating',
    index='user_id',
    columns='title',
    fill_value=0)

movie_titles_index = ratings_pivot_df.columns
```

Pandas will help create a data table crossing information in rows about users and in columns about movie titles. A movie index will keep track of what movie each column represents.

```
from sklearn.decomposition import TruncatedSVD

svd_model = TruncatedSVD(
    n_components=15,
    random_state=101)

ratings_values_transposed = (
    ratings_pivot_df.values.T)
item_latent_features = svd_model.fit_transform(
    ratings_values_transposed)
```

The TruncatedSVD class reduces the data table to fifteen components. This class offers a more scalable algorithm than SciPy's linalg.svd. TruncatedSVD computes result matrices of exactly the shape you decide by the n_components parameter (the full resulting matrices are not calculated), resulting in a faster output and less memory usage.

By calculating the Vh matrix, you can reduce the ratings of different but similar users (each user's scores are expressed by row) into compressed dimensions that reconstruct general tastes and preferences. Please also notice that because you're interested in the Vh matrix (the columns/movies reduction), but the algorithm provides you with only the U matrix (the decomposition based on rows), you need to input the transposition of the data table (by transposition, columns become rows and you obtain `TruncatedSVD` output, which is the Vh matrix). You now look for a specific movie:

```
target_movie_title = (
    'Star Wars: Episode V - '
    'The Empire Strikes Back (1980)'
)

movie_idx = list(movie_titles_index).index(
    target_movie_title)

print(f"Movie index: {movie_idx}")

latent_features_for_movie = item_latent_features[
    movie_idx]
print(latent_features_for_movie)
```

The output points out the index of a *Star Wars* episode and its SVD coordinates:

```
movie index: 3154
[184.72254552 -17.77612872 47.33450866 51.4664494
  47.92058216 17.65033116 14.3574635 -12.82219207
  17.51347857 5.46888807 7.5430805 -0.57117869
 -30.74032355 2.4088565 -22.50368497]
```

Using the movie label, you can find out what column the movie is in (column index 3154 in this case) and print the values of the fifteen components. This sequence provides the movie profile. You now try getting all the movies with scores similar to the target movie and highly correlated with it. A good strategy is to calculate a correlation matrix of all movies, get the slice related to your movie, and find out inside it which movie titles are the most related (characterized by high positive correlation — say, at least 0.985) by using indexing, as shown in the following code:

```
import numpy as np

item_similarity_matrix = np.corrcoef(
    item_latent_features)

target_movie_correlations = item_similarity_matrix[
    movie_idx]

is_highly_correlated = (
    (target_movie_correlations > 0.985) &
```

```
        (target_movie_correlations < 1.0))

similar_movie_titles = list(
    movie_titles_index[is_highly_correlated])
print(similar_movie_titles)
```

The code will return the names of films most similar to your movie; they are intended as suggestions based on a preference for that film. Your output may vary somewhat from the list shown. (Try different values for P, such as 0.9, to see how many movies you get back.)

```
['Star Wars: Episode IV - A New Hope (1977)',
 'Star Wars: Episode VI - Return of the Jedi (1983)']
```

Star Wars fans who enjoyed Episode V would also like to see *Star Wars Episodes IV* and *VI* (of course, as expected).

REMEMBER

SVD will always find the best way to relate a row or column in your data, discovering complex interactions or relations that you didn't imagine before. You don't need to imagine anything in advance; it's entirely a data-driven approach.

6
The Part of Tens

IN THIS CHAPTER

» Figuring out if you need more data

» Validating your model correctly

» Tuning your solutions

» Creating and selecting the features you need

» Combining the best algorithms

Chapter **19**

Ten Ways to Improve Your Machine Learning Models

Now that your algorithm has finished learning from the data, you're pondering the results from your test set and wondering whether you can improve them or have reached the best possible outcome. This chapter introduces several checks and actions that hint at methods you can use to improve machine learning performance and achieve a more generalizable predictor that performs well not only on your test set but also on new, unseen data. This list of ten techniques offers you opportunities to improve the outcome achieved using machine learning algorithms.

REMEMBER

Monitoring performance on the training set shows how well the algorithm fits the data it learned from. Training results are typically overly optimistic because algorithms can overfit the training data, essentially memorizing it to some degree. The following advice helps you achieve a better outcome when using a test set. A k-fold cross-validation estimate or results from a held-out test set provide an estimate of how well your solution might work when using new data.

Studying Learning Curves

As a first step to improving your results, you need to determine the problems with your model. Learning curves involve plotting model performance on the training set and a separate validation set (or using cross-validation scores) against varying amounts of training data. You'll immediately notice whether you find much difference between your training and validation errors. A wide initial difference (low in-sample and high out-of-sample errors) is a sign of high variance (overfitting). Conversely, having high training and high validation errors that are close together is a sign of high bias (underfitting).

You must also understand how the model behaves when the sample size increases. When variance is the problem, the in-sample error should increase as the number of training examples grows because the model will find it harder to memorize all the new instances you are feeding it. On the other hand, the out-of-sample error should decrease as the model learns more rules in light of the increased evidence provided by a larger sample.

When bias is the problem, both training and validation errors tend to be high and plateau quickly as more data is added. Adding more data provides little benefit for improving validation performance beyond a certain point. At a certain point, no matter how much additional data you provide, the model's out-of-sample performance won't improve. The earlier the lack of improvement happens, the more biased your model is. When you notice bias, more data provides little benefit to your results, and you should change models or try to make the present model more complex. For instance, when using a linear model, you can rely on interactions or polynomial expansion to reduce bias.

Variance problems react well when you supply more data. To correct this problem, determine whether the validation and training error curves appear to be converging as the training set size increases, and check whether you can obtain enough data. When getting enough data isn't viable (because, for instance, the curves are too far apart), you have to simplify the model, for example, through feature selection, by regularization like L1 or L2 (you can find the best settings via hyperparameter tuning).

Using Cross-Validation Correctly

A common issue when you build machine learning models is when you observe a significant difference between performance estimates hinted by cross-validation and the actual performance on a held-out test set or new data. This discrepancy often occurs when something went wrong with the setup of cross-validation, because of some data leakage during pre-processing, or because of a significant difference between the data distribution between your train and test sets.

REMEMBER

Cross-validation hints when your steps (data preparation, data and feature selection, hyperparameter fixing, or model selection) are correct. While CV estimates won't perfectly match test set performance, it's crucial that they reliably rank different models or hyperparameter choices. If CV indicates model A is better than model B, we expect model A to also perform better on the test set. Generally, there are two reasons that the cross-validation estimates can vary from the actual error results:

>> **Leakage:** Information flows from the validation or from the test set (or even the training response in some contexts) into the training process. This problem often happens when you apply preprocessing to pooled training and test data. (When pooling, you vertically stack training and test matrices to work on only a single matrix without replicating the same operations twice on the data.)

REMEMBER

You can pool training and test sets together to preprocess them more easily. However, you must remember that you shouldn't use the test data to compute statistics for missing case imputation, scaling (normalization or standardization), or dimensionality reduction. When you use the pooled data for these three purposes, information from the test set easily and unnoticeably leaks into your training process, making your work unreliable.

>> **Snooping:** Also called *adaptive overfitting*, snooping is a problem when you test your model too often on the test set and adapt your model, in a conscious or even unconscious way, to solutions that perform better on the test set.

>> **Incorrect sampling:** When dealing with imbalanced classes, simple random sampling for cross-validation might result in folds with highly skewed or even missing classes. You should test stratified sampling, a statistical sampling method that ensures that for each cross-validation fold, you draw the sample response classes in the same proportion as found in the training set.

Choosing the Right Error or Score Metric

Trying to optimize an error metric based on the median error by using a learning algorithm based on the mean error won't provide you with the best results unless you manage the optimization process in a fashion that works in favor of your chosen metric. When solving a problem using data and machine learning, you need to analyze the situation and determine the ideal metric to optimize. Examples can help a lot. You can get many of them from academic papers and public machine learning contests that carefully define specific problems in terms of data and the most suitable error/score metric to use. Look for a contest whose objective and data are similar to yours, then check the requested metric.

TIP

Contests can provide great inspiration on more than just error metrics. You can easily learn how to manage data applications, use machine learning tricks, and perform brilliant feature creation. For example, look at the knowledge base offered by websites such as Kaggle that provide hundreds of available contests, all with data, best metrics, and plenty of hints from experts to help you optimally learn from data.

Check whether the loss function of the machine learning algorithm you want to use aligns with your chosen metric. If the algorithm uses another metric, try to influence it by searching for the best combination of hyperparameters to maximize your metric. You can achieve that goal by doing a grid search for the best cross-validation result using your metric as a target.

Searching for the Best Hyperparameters

Most algorithms perform well out of the box using the default hyperparameter settings. However, you can consistently achieve better results by testing different hyperparameters. All you have to do is to perform a random search (see Chapter 9, which also compares grid search to random search), thus searching among the number of hyperparameter combinations to test in a smarter way. Finally, you evaluate the results using the correct error or score metric. The search takes time (with random search, you should try at least 30 iterations), but a search can improve your results (perhaps not drastically, but significantly).

TIP

When a search takes too long to complete, you can often achieve the same results by working on a sample of your original data or by using fewer cross-validation folds. Fewer examples chosen at random require fewer computations, but they usually hint at the same solution. Another trick that can save time and effort is to go for fewer folds in cross-validation. Often, using three folds can speed up the process and hint at similar best hyperparameters as those you obtain using more folds.

Testing Multiple Models

The no-free-lunch theorem should always inspire you, reminding you not to fall in love with specific learning approaches just because they brought interesting results in the past. As a good practice, test multiple models, starting with the basic ones — the models that have more bias than variance. You should always favor simple solutions over complex ones. You may discover that a simple solution performs better. For example, you may want to keep things simple and use a linear model instead of a more sophisticated, tree-based ensemble of models.

TIP

Representing the performance of different models using the same chart is helpful before choosing the best one to solve your problem. You can place models used to predict consumer behavior, such as a response to a commercial offer, in special gain charts and lift charts. These charts show how your model performs by partitioning its results into deciles or smaller parts. Because you may be interested only in the consumers who are most likely to respond to your offer, ordering predictions from most to least likely will emphasize how good your models are at predicting the most promising customers.

Testing multiple models and *introspecting* them (understanding which features work better with them) can also provide suggestions as to which features to transform for feature creation or which features to leave out when making feature selections.

Applying Feature Engineering

If bias still affects your model, you have little choice but to create new features that improve the model's performance. Every new feature can make guessing the target response easier. For instance, if classes aren't linearly separable, feature creation is the only way to change a situation that your machine learning algorithm cannot handle correctly.

Automatic feature creation is possible using polynomial expansion or specialized libraries. With a different approach, support vector machines, by means of the kernel trick, can automatically look for nonlinear relationships between features in higher-dimensional feature spaces in a computationally fast and memory-optimal way.

However, nothing can substitute for your expertise and understanding of the method needed to solve the data problem that the algorithm is trying to learn. You can create features based on your knowledge and ideas of how things work in the wild. Humans are still unbeatable in doing so, and machines can't easily replace them. Feature creation is more art than science, and an undoubtedly human art.

Selecting Features

If the estimated variance is high and your algorithm relies on many features (tree-based algorithms choose features they learn from), you must prune some features for better results. In this context, reducing the number of features in your data matrix is advisable by keeping those with the highest predictive value.

Regularization is always an option when working with linear models, linear support vector machines, or neural networks. L1 and L2 can reduce the influence of redundant variables or even remove them from the model (see Chapter 12). Stability selection leverages the L1 ability to exclude less useful variables, and the technique resamples by bootstrapping the training data to confirm the exclusion.

TIP

You can find an implementation of stability selection in this repository: https://github.com/scikit-learn-contrib/stability-selection, complete with installation instructions. In addition, you can practice using the RandomizedLogisticRegression and RandomizedLasso Scikit-learn functions in the linear_model module.

Apart from stability selection, Scikit-learn offers some forward greedy algorithms like Sequential Forward Selection that iteratively add to the model the single feature that provides the best improvement to the score. Recursive feature elimination tests whether it's worth keeping a feature in a model by trying the model with the feature present or absent. In both cases, only features that effectively decrease model errors are kept in the learning process. Always in Scikit-learn, you can also check the feature_selection module and its recursive selector at https://scikit-learn.org/stable/modules/feature_selection.html#recursive-feature-elimination.

Looking for More Data

After trying all the previous suggestions, you may still have a high variance of predictions. In this case, your only option is to increase your training set size. Try expanding your sample by providing new data, which could translate into new cases or features. If you want to add more cases, see whether you have similar data. You can often find more data, but it may lack labeling, that is, the response variable. Spending time labeling new data or asking others to label it for you may prove a significant investment. Complex models can be significantly improved with additional training examples. Adding data makes parameter estimation much more reliable and disambiguates cases where the machine learning algorithm can't determine which rule to extract.

To add new features, locate an open-source data source to match your data with its entries. Another great way to obtain new cases and features is by scraping the data from the web. Often, data is available from different sources or through an application programming interface (API). For instance, Google APIs offer many geographical and business information sources. By scripting a scraping session, you can obtain new data that can provide a different perspective on your learning problem. New features help by offering alternative ways to separate your classes, which you do by making the relationship between the response and the predictors more linear and less ambiguous.

TIP

Another solution, if you have large amounts of unstructured data (such as text or images) that you cannot use, is to create synthetic data using large language models (LLMs) such as OpenAI ChatGPT or Google Gemini. LLMs seem particularly good at creating structured data if given the right instructions (prompts). For instance, you could extract from generic text named entities (like geographical or company names), classify sentiment, summarize topics into classes, and generate many other structured features that would be time-consuming to create manually.

Blending Models

Machine learning involves building many models and creating predictions with different expected error performances. It may surprise you that you can get even better results by averaging the models together. The principle is quite simple: The estimated variance is random; thus, by averaging many different models, you can enhance the *signal* (the correct prediction) and rule out the noise that will often cancel itself (opposite errors sum to zero).

REMEMBER

Sometimes, the results from an algorithm that performs well, mixed with the results from a simpler algorithm that doesn't work as well, can create better predictions than using a single algorithm. Don't underestimate contributions delivered from simpler models, such as linear models, when you average their results with the output from more sophisticated algorithms, such as gradient boosting.

It's the same principle you seek when applying ensembles of learners, such as tree bagging and boosting ensembles. However, this time you use the technique on complete and heterogeneous models that you prepare for evaluation. In this case, if the result needs to guess a complex target function, different models may catch other parts of that function. Only by averaging results output by different simple and complex models can you approximate a model you can't build otherwise.

Stacking Models

Stacking can provide better performance for the same reasons that averaging works. In stacking, you build your machine learning models in two (sometimes even more) stages. This technique initially predicts multiple results using different algorithms, all learning from the features present in your data, using a cross-validation procedure to avoid leakage. During the second phase, instead of providing features that a new model will know, you give the model the predictions of the other, previously trained models.

When guessing complex target functions, a two-stage approach is justified. You can approximate them only by using multiple models together and then combining the predictions smartly. A simple logistic regression or a complex tree ensemble can be used as a second-stage model.

Chapter **20**

Ten Guidelines for Ethical Data Usage

A common misconception is that anything that appears on the Internet is automatically considered public domain, including people's faces and all their personal information. This problem has become even more acute because training modern generative AI, such as large language models (LLMs) and diffusion models for image generation, requires incredible amounts of diverse data. Consequently, many people and creators, from artists and authors to individuals who casually post content on social networks, are discovering that their art and work have been used to train AI models without permission or compensation. This has led to several lawsuits as well as actions taken by authors and publishers against many companies developing large language models such as Meta, OpenAI, Microsoft, and Anthropic.

To safely use data you find on the Internet, it's best practice to assume all data is copyrighted and not in the public domain unless explicitly stated otherwise. Even people who realize that material is copyrighted will often fall back on fair use principles. Fair use can be a very tricky subject. Beyond copyright and fair use, the use of online data for training AI, especially when it involves personal information, is a matter of concern. Regulations such as the European Union's GDPR and AI Act, or California's CCPA (now CPRA), provide frameworks for data protection. At the time of writing, new data governance laws regarding AI are being debated and implemented globally.

No matter where you stand on the free use issue, you still need to consider the ethical use of data that you obtain, no matter what the source might be, which is what this chapter considers.

Obtaining Permission

Some research, such as that in healthcare, requires identifying individuals within a dataset. Sourcing Personally Identifiable Information (PII) without the necessary consent or on a valid legal basis is not advisable, and often it turns out to be illegal. PII collected without the proper procedures and safeguards may be incomplete or even incorrect, rendering any following analysis unreliable and potentially biased. Moreover, you may incur significant legal and financial risks, infringe individual privacy rights, and violate data protection laws when sourcing PII in this way.

LLMs present new challenges for the protection of personal information. LLMs are incredibly good at storing and reproducing verbatim from their training data. If any PII happens to be ingested by an LLM during training, it may emerge later in unexpected situations or under solicitation. Moreover, removing PII from an LLM is not as easy as deleting entries from a database table.

The best way to obtain data with PII is to get consent from the individuals involved or ensure a solid legal basis exists. You can find several resources online for obtaining permission, but keep in mind that requirements may vary depending on the country you are in. As part of the solution, you must also consider the California Consumer Privacy Act (CCPA), as amended by the CPRA, the General Data Protection Regulation (GDPR), and other mandates that require you to obfuscate or delete PII on request.

Using Sanitization Techniques

It's easy to confuse data sanitization (also known as data de-identification or data anonymization) with data cleaning, a typical operation necessary before feeding data to machine learning algorithms. *Data sanitization* involves removing personal information, such as name, address, telephone number, ID, and other similar details, from a dataset so that identifying a particular individual in the dataset becomes very difficult and the risk of personal identification is significantly minimized.

In addition to text and dataset variables, you must consider every kind of data. For instance, if you are working with collections of photos, it is paramount that you take steps to blur faces and remove car plates from images. You can apply a number of techniques to meet this goal:

>> **Remove the feature:** When it comes to names, removing the feature will protect privacy while keeping the data usable in most cases, if the feature is not essential for the analysis or model training. This is the most straightforward and effective method of sanitization.

>> **Replace the feature:** You may need an ID for the cases in a dataset to identify the case, rather than the user. This process is a little touchier because you can use pseudonymization, where a linkage is maintained (even securely and separately) between the original ID and a randomly generated unique ID, or you can remove any correlation between the user's original personal identifier and the new case identifier, which should be a randomized unique value (a procedure called anonymization).

>> **Generalization and aggregation of features:** This involves making data less specific, for instance, by replacing one's birth date with just the year of birth or an age range, or grouping geographical localizations into larger areas. With careful aggregation, you can create a new feature for quantitative data, which is a mathematical aggregation of several personally identifiable features. A problem arises when there is a way to reverse-engineer the aggregation into the original values.

>> **Automated sanitization:** There are tools, often leveraging machine learning, such as Named Entity Recognition (NER) models for text, that can automatically detect and attempt to remove, mask, or replace PII across various data types. Services like Google Cloud Data Loss Prevention (DLP) or AWS Macie, as well as various open-source libraries, offer such capabilities. However, using automation without oversight can lead to unexpected results. Someone might even be able to reverse engineer the process, or the data might become unusable in its new form.

Avoiding Inference Pitfalls

When collecting data, some users will refuse to share personally identifiable information, such as gender and age. A common but ill–advised practice is to infer this information when a user's picture or other information is available. For example, a machine learning application might try to infer gender using the person's name or infer age using facial analysis.

The problem is that inference has many pitfalls. Names that are associated with one gender in a particular culture may be assigned to the other gender in other cultures. People can also choose gender-neutral names, so making an assumption based on a name is a bad idea. Furthermore, inferring gender based on names or appearance fails to account for the diversity of gender identities. A person may also identify as being intersex, rather than male or female, as well as transgender, and so on, which can introduce bias into the dataset and subsequent analyses, because inference attempts to impose a binary classification, thus failing to represent the individual situations accurately.

The problem with age inference is even more profound. For example, a machine learning algorithm may infer the wrong age due to variations in skin tone, lighting, image quality, or other subtle differences in the images. If the data is biased toward any specific demographic group, age estimations could be significantly inaccurate for other subgroups. The same could be said of premature aging and many different situations that cause natural physical changes.

REMEMBER

The bottom line is that inferring sensitive personal attributes, such as gender or age, is a problem from an ethical perspective and prone to significant inaccuracies that may introduce bias into your data. If a particular sensitive attribute is missing for your analysis because the person hasn't supplied it, we suggest, where possible, to design analyses that do not depend on the missing attribute or to exclude the case from specific analyses requiring it.

Using Generalizations Correctly

Applying statistical or machine learning outcomes inappropriately can result in an individual being mistreated in some manner. It's essential to remember that statistics apply to groups, not to individuals (this is referred to as the ecological fallacy). Similarly, you can't make broad generalizations or stereotypes about a group by looking at the group's individuals. Some examples of ecological fallacy happening when using machine learning algorithms or AI systems in practice are:

>> Despite all the other indicators being favorable, being refused a loan because living in an area where defaults have been high in the past.

>> Deciding police allocation based on historical crime statistics may lead to over policing certain areas and reinforcing crime records, thus creating a feedback loop.

Examples regarding wrong generalizations generated from data are:

>> Training an AI for recruitment purposes, and some past successful hires, with similar sociodemographics, for a tech role, are generalized by the AI so that anyone who is demographically similar to those past hires is hired.

>> Image recognition systems trained predominantly on images from a specific sociodemographic group often perform poorly or incorrectly when applied to other groups.

In both cases, the problem is that models are learning from the data they are given. If this data or the assumptions for its use are based on faulty generalizations, the model will reproduce and even amplify these errors.

Shunning Discriminatory Practices

Discriminatory data collection practices can cause machine learning algorithms to produce biased, unfair, or unreliable results, especially when applied to certain demographic groups. Focusing on a particular group can lead to a form of myopia, making the results for a larger, more diverse population less clear, potentially inaccurate, and poorly generalizable.

The use of skewed results becomes a serious problem when dealing with individuals in ways that can have severe, negative consequences. For example, automation is now used in some situations related to the administration of justice, such as for pre-trial detention, sentencing, and parole to provide social benefits or for tax control. When working with people, a human in the loop is crucial, but it is not a panacea that guarantees the algorithms used to offer insights or possible options will remain fair. It is also necessary that we design the interaction between humans and AI correctly and train humans to overcome their own biases, ensuring fairness with these new tools.

Detecting Black Swans in Code

A *black swan*, a term coined by Nassim Nicholas Taleb, is a highly improbable event that is also unpredictable and produces a disproportionate impact. When a black swan happens, after initially being completely baffled, we tend to rationalize the event and reason that we could have avoided it, even if the event was unpredictable. Examples of recent black swans are:

>> The COVID-19 pandemic, which made all our forecasting models fail to predict and unable to cope (because they had nothing historically comparable in their data)

>> The GameStop surge in 2021, driven by social media, caught many hedge funds off guard and defied normal market expectations

>> The rapid emergence of advanced generative AI

In machine learning, we encounter a similar situation when an algorithm attempts to predict outside the patterns it has learned and the previously observed data distributions. Bayesian methods can provide a framework for updating probabilities based on new evidence, which can help assess the likelihood of seemingly rare but not unforeseen events. Hence, they can do little with black swans.

The focus for ML systems should therefore shift from attempting to predict black swans to building systems that are, in the words of Taleb, robust and antifragile. The idea is to create AI systems that can withstand, adapt to, or even benefit from unexpected shocks. This can be done by:

>> Doing stress tests on algorithms, even using extreme synthetic data.

>> Implementing anomaly detection and out-of-distribution systems for early warnings of significant deviations or novel patterns that may signal increased risks of the appearance of black swans.

>> Implementing systems that monitor model drifting (model change due to data) and that can adapt quickly by retraining.

>> Designing a system that can gently degrade if something unexpected happens, not shatter abruptly.

>> Ensuring humans are in the loop, overseeing critical decisions when models suddenly and unexpectedly fail.

Understanding the Process

Government requirements, such as the EU's General Data Protection Regulation (GDPR), specify that when a model automatically produces decisions that have a significant impact on individuals, organizations should be able to explain to the affected individuals the logic behind the decision and how a machine learning algorithm generated a particular output. The point is that organizations using machine learning should guarantee a certain level of transparency and explainability when they delegate decisions to algorithms.

There are techniques, known as Explainable AI (XAI), such as LIME, SHAP, or counterfactual explanations, that can help identify the driving factors behind a prediction, even when a very complex algorithm, like a deep learning model, is involved. If your algorithm is shown to favor one group over another in decision-making, these techniques help you to explain why and describe the process that occurs to come up with that decision.

REMEMBER

For high-stakes decisions with significant impact on individuals, ethically and legally, putting a machine learning algorithm together for use on personal data and treating it as a black box is not possible. This principle is further reinforced by recent regulations, such as the EU AI Act, which states transparency and explainability obligations for AI systems considered high-risk because they impact people's lives and rights.

Considering the Consequences

Anyone who spends enough time working with machine learning applications soon comes to realize that a machine learning algorithm can't think in a human sense, has no moral compass, and definitely can't make ethical decisions based on values or understanding. Consequently, a machine learning algorithm can't grasp the consequences of any particular action initiated as part of the output from the application in which it resides. Fully automating any process, therefore, requires careful consideration, as machine learning systems lack the contextual understanding and ethical judgment of humans.

When considering the ethical treatment of anything using machine learning, it's imperative that humans remain in the loop to make those decisions that the algorithm can't make. Machine learning algorithms, as tools, are unable to take on the responsibility. However, how humans are integrated in the process, what information they have, their own biases, and the pressures they face when judging the output from an algorithm are crucial. Ultimately, humans and institutions that develop, deploy, and manage AI are responsible for both legal and ethical implications.

Balancing Decision-Making

The goals of any machine learning application are based on the decisions made by the humans who created it. Many current application strategies favor maximum speed, efficiency, and profit. However, these goals may conflict with the resource and time requirements required by ethical assessments, fairness audits, and responsible development practices.

When working with certain types of goals, such as determining whether to buy or sell on the stock market in algorithmic trading or how to have a self-driving car avoid hitting a pedestrian on the street, optimizing for speed and accuracy is a clear and acceptable purpose. Instead, optimizing for correct decision-making is challenging because adopting different ethical frameworks (for instance, utilitarian, deontological, or others) can lead to various solutions, all with profound implications.

Hence, when creating a machine learning algorithm for any purpose that affects other human beings, developing such algorithms requires balancing computational goals (such as speed or accuracy on specific metrics) with ethical considerations and potential real-world impacts (such as therapeutic value or fairness), the responsibility for which lies with the human builders and their values. Any algorithm should have safeguards to prevent the wrong outcome when the output can have tangible, hard-to-reverse effects on the human who receives it.

Verifying a Data Source

After reading this chapter, you may decide to use any of the many public domain or paid datasets for your research. Gathering your own data may seem like too much trouble given all of the requirements. The problem is that using a third-party dataset doesn't relieve you of the obligation to act in an ethical manner. When searching for a preexisting dataset online, consider the source and understand how the data was collected. The datasets assembled by government entities or schools often have clearer provenance and usage rights, reducing potential legal or ethical issues.

You also need to abide by any rules set by the creator of a third-party dataset. Typically, you can find notes on the download site, within a readme file, or within the dataset files themselves that tell you about any restrictions and requirements. Paying close attention to such notes is essential to ensuring that you don't end up in a lawsuit over the data use. When working with any dataset, it helps to have written permission to use it unless you know for certain that the dataset is in the public domain. A dataset creator will often post a notice on the dataset download site that the dataset is in the public domain. If you don't see such a notice, assuming that the dataset is copyrighted and you need permission to use it is always safer, especially for public-facing or commercial applications.

Index

decoder models, 354

deduction, 30

deep learning
  cat neuron, 286
  convolutional neural network, 287, 290
  overview, 285
  recurrent neural networks, 293–301
  vanishing gradient, 286

DeepMind, 132

degenerate (singular) matrix, 117

deque, 92–93

Descartes, René, 10

deterministic actions, decision trees, 181

Dick, Philip K., 9

dictionaries
  AFINN-111 dictionary, 368
  creating, 99
  defined, 92, 99

dir() function, 75

Directed Acyclic Graph (DAG), 267

discriminatory practices, data use, 415

distributions, statistics, 126

Domingos, Pedro, 30, 40

dot product, 111

draw with repetition, bootstrapping, 160

dtreeviz library, 180

E

e-commerce, analyzing reviews from, 368–373

editing cells, Google Colab, 66

Editor setting, Google Colab, 63

EfficientNetV2B0 CNN architecture, 347

Einstein, Albert, 155

ElliQ robot, 38

embedding, 366

encoder models, 354

encoding, 27, 268

ensembles
  averaging approach, 323–325
  bagging, 314
  boosting, 315–322
  decision trees, 304–314
  overview, 303

ensembling of predictors, 165–166

environment variables, 91

errata, 4

error (score) metrics, 405–406

error function, 136

ERT (Extremely Randomized Trees), 308

escape character, Python, 98

ethical data use
  black swans, 415–416
  consequences, 417
  data inference, 413–414
  data sanitization, 412
  data sources, 418
  decision-making, 417–418
  discriminatory practices, 415
  generalizations, 414–415
  obtaining permission, 412
  overview, 411
  transparency, 416–417

Euclidean distance, 198

evaluation, learning algorithm, 33

evolutionaries, 30, 31

executable code, 48

Explainable AI (XAI), 29, 416

Extremely Randomized Trees (ERT), 308

F

factorization, 392

fad uses, AI, 14

fantasy uses, AI, 13–16

Fashion-MNIST dataset, 79, 289–291

feature creation
  improving algorithm performance with, 407–408
  pruning, 408

feature engineering, 27

feature map, 288

feature selection, 164–165

features
  cross-validation, 238–240
  solving overfitting, 240–244

feed-forward input, perceptron, 266–269

filter, 288

filters parameter, 342

fine-tuning, 335, 366

fitness function, evolutionary algorithms, 31

forecasting model, 148

form fields, 62

fraud detection, 14

Freund, Yoav, 315

Friedman, Jerome, 318

Fukushima, Kunihiko, 333

functions

    activation functions, 265–266, 269, 270–272, 281–282, 286

    kernel functions, 257–259

    learning, 135–137

    Python, 86–90

G

Galton, Francis, 304

Gated Recurrent Units (GRUs), 296, 353–354, 364

Gaussian clustering, 200

Gaussian Naïve Bayes, 189

GBM (gradient boosting machines) algorithm, 318–319

GDPR (General Data Protection Regulation), 416

General Data Protection Regulation (GDPR), 416

generalizations

    ethical data use, 414–415

    learning algorithms, 33

    sample data, 148–150

generative AI (genAI), 8, 21, 38, 42

geographic information systems (GIS) sources, 26

Gini importance (mean decrease impurity), 312

GitHub, 53

    GitHub Gists, 61

    using for existing notebooks, 57

    using to save notebooks, 60–61

goal seeking (planning), 17

Google

    as data source, 26

    Ngram Viewer, 359

Google Colab

    advantages, 49

    in browser, 50

    characteristics of, 49

    code cells, creating, 62–64

    code execution, 68–69

    Colab Pro, 53

    commands, 52

    creating new notebook, 56

    defining, 48

    displaying the TOC, 67

    downloading notebooks, 62

    editing cells, 66

    features, 52–54, 62

    free computing resources, 49

    getting notebook information, 67–68

    Google account, 55

    GPU on, 339, 340

    hardware options for running code in the cloud, 71–73

    Help menu, 70

    integration with Google ecosystem, 49

    and Jupyter, 50–51

    keyboard shortcuts, 53–54

    magic functions on, 74–76

    moving cells, 66

    opening existing notebooks, 56–58

    performing multimedia integration, 76–78

    rich document support, 49

    saving notebooks, 59–61

    secrets section on, 73–74

    Settings dialog box, 53

    settings tabs, 53

    sharing notebook, 69–70

    special cells, creating, 65–66

    tasks in, 62–66

    text cells, creating, 65

    understanding, 49–50

    uploading notebook, 58–59

    using hardware acceleration, 66–67

    using local runtime support, 51–52

    viewing notebook, 67–68

    working with notebooks, 55–62

    zero setup, 49

Google Docs, 55

Google Drive, and Colab, 56–57

Google Gemini, 20, 28, 38, 50, 264, 364, 409

Gorman, Kristen, 204

GPT (Generative Pre-trained Transformer) series, 354

GPUs (graphical processing units), 11–12, 66

gradient boosting machines (GBM) algorithm, 318–319

numeric data types, 82

open-source community, 16

operator precedence, 86

relational operators, 85

storing data, 92–99

unary operators, 83

Python for Data Science For Dummies, 81

PyTorch, 278

Q

qualitative features

  defined, 108

  learning, 132

  linear regression, 230

quantitative features

  defined, 107–108

  learning, 132

queues, defined, 93

%quickref function, 74

Quinlan, Ross, 108, 178, 179

R

R language, 18, 48

R squared (coefficient of determination), 227–229

Radial Basis Function (RBF), 258

Random Forests ensemble, 306–309

random initialization, 372

random noise component, 395

random sampling, 126, 141, 147

random-search, cross-validation, 163

RAPIDS package, 260

Raschka, Sebastian, 223

rating data

  collaborative filtering, 387–391, 396

  limits of, 386–387

  MovieLens dataset, 382–386

raw text, 362–363

RBF (Radial Basis Function), 258

recommender systems, 32

  Amazon, 381

  Netflix, 381

  overview, 379–380

  rating data, 382–391

reasons for using, 380–381

social networks' use of, 381–382

SVD and, 391–399

Tapestry, 381

Rectified Linear Units (ReLU), 281

recurrent neural networks (RNNs), 264, 267, 293–301, 353, 363–364

Recursive Feature Elimination (RFE) iterative strategy, 165

redundant data, 395

reference layer, neural networks, 269

regression, linear, 151, 220–235

  gradient descent optimization, 223

  one-hot encoding, 230

  ordinary least squares, 223

  outliers, 231

  polynomial expansion, 232

  qualitative feature, 230

  R squared, 227–229

  residuals, 231

regression tasks, supervised learning, 131

reinforcement learning, 11, 131–132

relational operators, Python, 85

ReLU (Rectified Linear Units), 281

representation

  capability, 133

  knowledge representation, 17

  learner algorithms, 33

  and optimization, 136

residuals, linear regression, 231

ResNet CNN architecture, 334

resource scheduling, 15

response vectors, 112

reusable functions, Python, 87–88

reward hacking, 131

RF algorithm, 309–311

RFE (Recursive Feature Elimination) iterative strategy, 165

Ridge (L2) regularization, 242–244

RMSE (root mean squared error), 227–229

RNNs (recurrent neural networks), 264, 267, 293–301, 353, 363–364

Roborock S8 MaxV Ultra, 37

robotics, 17

robots, 37–38

Roosevelt, Franklin D., 148
root mean squared error (RMSE), 227–229
Rosenblatt, Frank, 172, 264
runtime, 51

S

safety systems, 15
sample data, 107
  balancing simplicity with complexity, 153–154
  bias and variance, 150–152
  bootstrapping, 160
  classifier reports, 146
  complex mapping, 153
  cross-validation, 158–159, 161–165
  generalization, 148–150
  in-sample data, 148
  labeling, 146
  leakage traps, 165–167
  learning curves, 155–157
  leave-one-out cross-validation, 160
  no-free-lunch theorem, 154
  Occam's razor, Occam's, 154–155
  out-of-sample data errors, 147
  random sampling, 147
  splitting, 157–158
sampling
  incorrect sampling, 405
  optimizing learning, 140–141
  random sampling, 126, 141, 147
  stratified sampling, 126, 141
  subsampling, 140
saturation, 266
scalars
  defined, 106
  NumPy library, 109
scatterplot, 197, 238
Schapire, Robert, 315
Schmidhuber, Jürgen, 333
Scikit-learn package, 16, 78, 100, 157, 162, 164, 165, 183, 247, 259–260, 262, 299, 307, 312, 370, 373, 408
  AdaBoost function, 317
  blending and stacking, 323–325
  GBM algorithm, 320

KNN algorithm, 214, 217
SVMs, 259–260, 262
tuning K-means algorithm, 203, 205
score (error) metrics, 405–406
scoring function, 136
scoring opinions and sentiments
  analyzing reviews from e-commerce, 368–373
  improving analysis using pre-trained model, 373–377
  input data, 355–357
  natural language processing, 352–353
  overview, 351
  processing and enhancing text, 357–362
  raw text, 362–363
  resorting to neural network technology, 363–364
  self-attention models, 365–367
  using scoring and classification, 368–377
scratch code cell, 62
selection bias, 149
self-attention models, 365–367
semantic similarity, 366
separation problem, SVMs, 252–253
sequences, 92
sets, Python, 98–99
Settings dialog box, Google Colab
  AI Assistance, 53
  Colab Pro setting, 53
  Editor setting, 53
  GitHub, 53
  Miscellaneous setting, 53
  Site setting, 53
SGD (stochastic gradient descent), 142, 223, 245–249
Shakespeare dataset, 79
shared variance, 395
similarity
  clustering, 199–203
  K-means algorithm, 199–212
  KNN algorithm, 212–217
  measuring similarity between vectors, 196–198
  overview, 195–196
  supervised clustering algorithm, 195
  unsupervised clustering algorithm, 196
simple linear regression, 221
singular (degenerate) matrix, 117

tokenization, 365

toy datasets, 146

TPU (tensor processing unit), 11–12, 40, 66

training, 157. *See also* sample data
  data, 32–33, 148
  phase, 132
  supervised learning, 130–131

transfer learning, 335–336

transformer architecture, 367

transformers package, 374–375

transparency, data use, 416–417

transposition, 116

triangle inequality, 197

trigram, 359

tuples
  defined, 92
  Python, 96–97

Turing, Alan, 10, 352

Turing Test, 1

"Two Cultures" paper (Breiman), 29, 164

U

unary operators, Python, 83

underestimation, split data, 158

underfitting, 152

unigrams, 360

unique variance, 395

univariate distributions, 126

univariate statistics, feature selection, 164

universal approximators, neural networks, 273

universal function approximator, 285

Universal Transformation Format 8-bit (UTF-8), 363

unsupervised clustering algorithm, 196. *See also* K-means algorithm

unsupervised learning, 11, 131

userdata, 73

UTF-8 (Universal Transformation Format 8-bit), 363

V

validation, 157

vanishing gradient, deep learning, 286

Vapnik, Vladimir, 251, 253

variance
  of estimates, avoiding, 165–167
  sample data, 150–152
  statistics, 126, 153

Variance Ratio (Calinski and Harabasz score), 210–211

vectors
  defined, 107
  measuring similarity between, 196–198
  vector multiplication, 111

VGGNet CNN architecture, 334

vibe coding, 42–43

W

wait times, predicting, 16

Wald, Abraham, 149

weak learners, 314, 317

weight vector, 173

weights
  backpropagation, 31
  perceptron, 269–272

wget command, 383

Wine dataset, 80

within-cluster dispersion, 210

within-cluster sum of squares (WSS), 202

Wolpert, David, 154

word embedding, 354, 366

World Economic Forum
  Future of Jobs Report 2025, 41

WSS (within-cluster sum of squares), 202

X

XAI (Explainable AI), 29, 416

XGBoost, 320–321

Z

zip() function, Python, 96

About the Authors

Luca Massaron is a data scientist and a marketing research director specialized in AI, machine learning, multivariate statistical analysis, and customer insights, with over a decade of experience in solving real-world problems and generating value for stakeholders by applying reasoning, statistics, data mining, and algorithms. From being a pioneer of web audience analysis in Italy to achieving the rank of Grandmaster and becoming a top ten competitor on Kaggle, he has always been passionate about everything related to data and analysis, as well as demonstrating the potential of data-driven knowledge discovery to both experts and non-experts. Favoring simplicity over unnecessary sophistication, he believes that a great deal can be achieved in data science by understanding and practicing the essentials of it. Luca is also a Google Developer Expert (GDE) in AI, Kaggle, and Cloud.

John Paul Mueller was a freelance author and technical editor. He had writing in his blood, having produced 119 books and more than 600 articles to date. The topics ranged from networking to artificial intelligence and from database management to heads-down programming. Some of his more current books included discussions of data science, machine learning, and algorithms. His technical editing skills helped more than 70 authors refine the content of their manuscripts. John passed away in 2024. He authored or coauthored 60 books for Wiley during his career and will be dearly missed.

Dedication

From Luca: I dedicate this book to my daughter, Amelia, who is part of a generation that will witness the general adoption of artificial intelligence in the world. Growing up, I hope that Amelia will manage to invent her life and her happiness under these surprisingly mutable skies. Nevertheless, Amelia, never forget that "she who knows, owns her own future." Never give up, aspire to fly higher.

Author's Acknowledgments

From Luca: My greatest thanks to my family, Yukiko and Amelia, for their support and loving patience during the writing of this book.

Publisher's Acknowledgments

Executive Editor: Steven Hayes

Project Editor: Katharine Dvorak

Technical Editor: Rod Stephens

Senior Editorial Assistant: Hanna Sytsma

Production Editor: Tamilmani Varadharaj

Cover Image: © sankai/Getty Images